RETIREMENT RIGHTS

THE BENEFITS
OF GROWING OLDER

NANCY LEVITIN

AVON BOOKS  NEW YORK

To my Baba

I would like to thank the following colleagues for their invaluable assistance: Eric Michaels, tax partner at Witman, Stadtmauer and Michaels; Cindy Hounsell, staff attorney at the Pension Rights Center; David Udell, New York State Disability Advocacy Project coordinator at Legal Services for the Elderly; Marilyn Fisher, Certified Financial Planner with John Hancock Financial Services; Kenneth Scholen, director of the National Center for Home Equity Conversion; Marvin Rotenberg, executive vice-president and director of Retirement Advisory Services at Fleet Investment Services; and Paul Miller, insurance representative at Diversified Financial Management.

I would also like to extend my heartfelt appreciation to my husband, Mitch, without whom I would have had neither the time nor the fortitude to complete this project.

This publication is not engaged in rendering legal, accounting or other professional services. If legal advice or other expert assistance is required, the services of a competent professional should be sought.

AVON BOOKS
A division of
The Hearst Corporation
1350 Avenue of the Americas
New York, New York 10019

Copyright © 1994 by Nancy Levitin
Published by arrangement with the author
Library of Congress Catalog Card Number: 93-49888
ISBN: 0-380-76894-1

Library of Congress Cataloging in Publication Data:
Levitin, Nancy.
    Retirement rights / Nancy Levitin.
       p.   cm.
Includes bibliographical references.
1. Retirement—United States.   2. Retirees—United States—Life skill guides.   3. Retirement income—United States—Planning.
I. Title.
HQ1063.2.U6L48   1994
306.3'8—dc20

93-49888
CIP

First Avon Books Trade Printing: September 1994

AVON TRADEMARK REG. U.S. PAT. OFF. AND IN OTHER COUNTRIES, MARCA REGISTRADA, HECHO EN U.S.A.

Printed in the U.S.A.

ARC   10 9 8 7 6 5 4 3 2 1

TABLE OF CONTENTS

INTRODUCTION

For a young person it is almost a sin—and certainly a danger—to be too much occupied with himself; but for the aging person it is a duty and a necessity to give serious attention to himself.

—CARL GUSTAV JUNG (1933)

I have always liked this quote, but never known quite why. What does it mean to give "serious attention" to oneself? And why is it both "a duty and a necessity"?

When I think of giving serious attention to the self, I think of listening to one's inner voice. And when I think of listening to one's inner voice, I think of learning the answers to such questions as: What is making me happy? What is missing from my life? What do I want for the future?

Knowing the answers to these difficult questions is great, but it's not enough. The answers take you only halfway to personal contentment. To go the extra mile, you must know how to transform your hopes, dreams, and aspirations into reality. To do this, you need information. Lots and lots of information.

As an elder law attorney, I dispense information. I educate my clients about housing opportunities, educational programs, and nutritional services. I talk about the rules of benefit programs, private insurance, and financial planning. I discuss legal rights and the tax code. I even give out information about how to get information.

Perhaps that is why I am drawn to Jung's quote. It affirms what I do as an elder law attorney.

Retirement Rights is my attempt to empower you to give special attention to yourself. In these chapters, you will find the information you need to go from *knowing* what you want in life to *getting* it—without hiring a lawyer, financial planner, social worker, or insurance agent.

For example, you may know that you miss working. Going to the office each day provided you with personal satisfaction, and retirement has left a void in your life. What do you do next? For starters, you can turn to Chapter 1 for information about how to take advantage of employment opportunities for older adults. Or you can read about work alternatives: what you can accomplish as a volunteer, the new skills you can learn by going back to school, or the bargains that are available to you as an older traveler.

Do you have concerns completely unrelated to work? Is your health troubling you? Do you feel that nothing will be right as long as you have that pain in your leg or tightness in your chest?

Information is some of the best medicine. Wouldn't you feel better knowing that you can get help paying your medical bills, that you are eligible for a wealth of health-related services in your own home, and that your community offers a range of support services to its older residents? After reading Chapters 2 through 5, 9, and 10, you will know exactly whom to call and where to go for the assistance you require. Chapter 15 will provide you with the information you need to find the most suitable housing arrangement to meet your health care needs.

One of the biggest obstacles to personal happiness for old and young alike is the feeling of impotence. Our system is rife with huge impersonal bureaucracies that seem almost designed to diminish and demoralize the individual. The Social Security Administration, your local department of social services, the Department of Housing and Urban Development, and the Internal Revenue Service are just a few of the monoliths you are bound to encounter as an older American.

Don't let these institutions get the better of you. You have more legal rights than you probably know about. Medicaid may only award you 4 hours of home care services a day instead of the 12 you requested. You will learn in Chapter 5 how to state your best case before an impartial administrative judge. Social Security may determine that you are not entitled to disability benefits, despite the fact that you can't sit for more than 15 minutes, walk more than three blocks, or pick up your 14-pound granddaughter. Chapters 7 and 8 cover all you need to know about each level of appeal available to you. When Medicare refuses to pay your nursing home bill, Chapters 3 through 5 will prepare you to march right into federal court. You will have the information you need to flex your legal muscles.

And last, but certainly not least, you may have financial worries. Do you feel that you could get everything you want—if you could only afford it? You may be surprised to learn about some of the ways you can ease your financial straits that are covered in Chapters 3, 5, 8, 10, and 12. For example, you may learn that you can increase your monthly income by tapping into the equity in your home. Or you may discover that you qualify for a low-interest loan to renovate your house, free medical assistance, and a daily hot meal for only $2. You may also learn that you have not been taking advantage of all the tax benefits available to you.

Are your money concerns of a different nature? Are you more worried about whether your savings are invested wisely and your pension plan is safe? If these questions keep you up at night, take a look at Chapters 11 and 13. You can read about the pros and cons of several different types of investments, with special tips for older investors. And you can learn all you need to know about your retirement savings: When can you withdraw them? Will you be charged a penalty? Is there any way to reduce the taxes you will owe? What will happen to your retirement plan when you stop working? Chapter 14 sheds light on the role life insurance can play in your financial plan, while Chapter 15 provides a discussion of alternative housing arrangements.

By the time you finish reading *Retirement Rights*, when you hear your inner voice saying, "This is what I need," you can confidently respond, "And I know just how to get it."

1.
ENJOYING SOCIAL AND RECREATIONAL BENEFITS

If I had peace to sit and sing,
Then I could make a lovely thing . . .

—ANNA WICKHAM, "THE SINGER"

Leisure time is a gift. While you are raising a family and pursuing a career, your leisure time is at a premium. Only now, when your family is grown and you are retired, might you have some leisure time to fill. What an enviable task.

Your options are almost limitless. You may want to pack a suitcase and do some traveling, pack a briefcase and return to work, or pack a satchel and return to school. Or you may want to start an exercise regimen, get involved in volunteer work, learn a new cooking style, or campaign for your favorite candidate.

Or you may want to do nothing. Just "take a sun bath and listen to the hours, formulating, and disintegrating under the pines."[1] If relaxing in a sunbath sounds too good to pass up, please feel free to skip this chapter.

TRAVEL

You now have the time to visit out-of-state relatives, tour Europe, take a second honeymoon, or drive cross-country. Before you tell the post office to hold your mail, however, make sure you know about all the benefits available to older travelers. Also be aware of some pitfalls to avoid on your journeys.

---

[1] Zelda Fitzgerald, "Journal" (1938).

In this section, we will take a look at travel discounts, tours and charters, elderhostel, volunteer vacations, travel companions, travel insurance, and health care abroad. For general information about foreign travel, consult the free pamphlet "Travel Tips for Senior Citizens," which is available by calling or writing:

> **Bureau of Consular Affairs**
> Department of State
> Washington, DC 20520
> 202-647-1488

TRAVEL DISCOUNTS

Most major bus, train, and air carriers offer travel discounts to older adults. Reduced fares and other promotions make off-season travel especially affordable. Travel agents are a good source of information about discount travel packages.

The Golden Age Passport, available through the U.S. Department of the Interior, gives Americans over age 62 free entry to all national parks and recreation areas, and a 50 percent discount on such facilities as boating and camping. You can apply for the passport at any national park that charges an entrance fee. You will be required to show proof of age (a driver's license will do).

For more information about the Golden Age and Golden Eagle Passports, contact:

> **Consumer Information Center**
> P.O. Box 100
> Pueblo, CO 81002
> Request the free pamphlet "Golden Eagle/Golden Age/Golden Access Passports."
>
> **National Park Service**
> Department of the Interior
> P.O. Box 37127
> Washington, DC 20013
> 202-485-9666
> Request information describing the parks and government vacation areas.

Senior discounts are also available at many museums, parks, and restaurants. A number of hotels offer discounts for seniors in the middle of the week and in off-peak periods.

TOURS AND CHARTERS

A well-run tour or charter can take many of the worries out of travel. Lodging, meals, and sightseeing are all arranged for you, and the pesky problems that arise during even the best-planned trip are taken care of, almost mysteriously.

Unfortunately, every tour and charter is not worry-free. Sometimes signing up for a trip means signing up for trouble. What can you do to protect yourself?

➤ **TIP #1** *Ask a lot of questions.*

- What is included in the price?
- What is the company's refund policy?
- Are the scheduled hotels reputable and well-located?
- How long has the company been in business?

➤ **TIP #2** *Check with the Better Business Bureau.*

Before you commit yourself to a tour or charter company, find out if any complaints have been filed against the company with the Better Business Bureau. If complaints have been filed, find out how they were resolved.

➤ **TIP #3** *Read the fine print.*

Make sure there are no hidden costs. What restrictions, if any, apply to the advertised rate? Are you protected if the scheduled trip does not take place? For a free pamphlet entitled, "How to Read a Tour Brochure," write to:

> **United States Tour Operators Association**
> 211 East 51st Street
> New York, NY 10022

➤ **TIP #4** *Do not pay for the trip with cash.*

If you pay with a charge card, you may be protected if the tour is canceled or something goes wrong. Likewise, if you pay with a check, you may be able to stop payment if a problem arises.

ℹ️ For more information

Cruise Lines International Association
500 Fifth Avenue, Suite 1407
New York, NY 10110
Request the free booklet "Cruising: Answers to Your Questions."

Consumer Information Center
P.O. Box 100
Pueblo, CO 81002

Request the free publication "Access Travel: Airports," which has information about the accessibility of 553 airport terminals worldwide to assist travelers with mobility limitations.

ELDERHOSTEL

Elderhostel travel offers you the double benefit of a reasonably priced vacation and an education. Elderhostel trips are available in many geographic locations, and classes are offered in a range of subject matters. Participants usually stay in college dormitories and eat in campus dining facilities, unless they travel overseas. The cost of an elderhostel vacation includes room, meals, classes, entertainment, and field trips at an educational institution for 5 or 6 days. Transportation is extra.

To find out about domestic and international elderhostel travel, group rates, and discounts, write or call:

Elderhostel
75 Federal Street
Boston, MA 02110
617-426-8056

VOLUNTEER VACATIONS

Volunteer vacations are often called the Peace Corps for older Americans. Participants can experience such diverse adventures as teaching English to students in Poland, advising Russian entrepreneurs, organizing a school library in Jamaica, helping a Guatemalan community recover from an earthquake, and teaching crafts to poor children in the Mississippi Delta. Volunteers must pay for their own air transportation, plus fees (ranging from $300 to $2,500) to cover food and shelter expenses, as well as some of the cost of supplies, if needed.

The following organizations sponsor volunteer vacations:

Global Volunteers
375 East Little Canada Road
St. Paul, MN 55117-1628
800-487-1074

Request a free catalog of volunteer opportunities in the United States, Central America, Russia, Poland, Tanzania, Indonesia, Tonga, and other locations.

Habitat for Humanity International
121 Habitat Street
Americus, GA 31709
800-HABITAT (422-4828)

Request free information on how you can help build affordable housing.

American Association for International Aging
1133 20th Street, N.W.
Washington, DC 20036
202-833-8893

Send a check for $12.95 to receive "65 Ways To Be Involved in International Development: A Retired American's Guide to Participation in Local, National and International Activities."

TRAVEL COMPANIONS

If you are uncomfortable traveling alone, but do not like group tours, you may want to consider hiring a private travel companion. You can hire a travel companion from an agency that screens and trains its employees to handle the needs of older travelers. A travel companion will assist you with accommodations, baggage, medical needs, and transportation.

TRAVEL INSURANCE

Travel insurance is available to cover trip cancellations, lost or stolen baggage, airline strikes, and bad weather.

Before you purchase travel insurance, make sure your existing insurance does not provide the coverage you need. Homeowners' and renters' policies sometimes cover the loss of baggage or valuables, and even may cover you for risks encountered on a tour. Credit card companies have also started providing travel benefits to their card-carrying vacationers.

HEALTH CARE ABROAD

Obtaining medical care in a foreign country can be difficult, frightening, and costly. With limited exceptions, Medicare does not pay for care received outside the United States. (For exceptions, see page 34.) Also, most foreign hospitals do not accept American health insurance. If you are admitted to a hospital abroad, you will probably have to pay your bill in full before you will be discharged. When you get home, your insurance company may reimburse you for some of the costs of your care, depending on your coverage.

Several insurers now provide medical coverage overseas. Some companies offer assistance finding a doctor, an interpreter, and legal assistance in a foreign country. You can contact the following organizations for additional information about medical insurance and assistance abroad:

NEAR, Inc.
450 Prairie Avenue
Calumet City, IL 60409
800-654-6700

Wallach and Company
107 West Federal Street
P.O. Box 480
Middleburg, VA 22117-0480
800-237-6615

International Association for Medical Assistance to Travelers (IAMAT)
417 Center Street
Lewiston, NY 14092
716-754-4883

IAMAT is a nonprofit organization that anyone can join for no charge, although donations are requested. Members receive a worldwide directory of participating physicians who accept a reduced payment schedule for IAMAT members. Members also receive a clinical record for their doctor to complete before their departure, immunization information, and some additional services and benefits.

International SOS Assistance, Inc.
P.O. Box 11568
Philadelphia, PA 19116
800-523-8930

International SOS Assistance, Inc., does not sell medical insurance. Rather, it provides members with medical information about foreign countries, the names of English-speaking doctors abroad, medical monitoring of foreign hospitalizations, and ready access to medical specialists. The cost is $40 for a 14-day membership, and $3 for each additional day.

Most foreign embassies and consulates are also available to assist Americans who need emergency medical services abroad. U.S. consular officers will arrange for a friend or family member in the United States to wire you funds.

If you are on a tour, your guide should be able to help you find medical care and an English-speaking doctor.

TIPSHEET FOR MEDICAL NEEDS ABROAD

To prepare for your medical needs abroad, follow these guidelines.

- Keep your medications in their original containers, and pack a copy of the written prescription with the generic drug name.
- Pack an extra pair of eyeglasses (or contact lenses) and your prescription.
- Wear a Medic Alert bracelet or neck tag listing your allergies, health problems, and other important medical information. For more information, contact:

Medic Alert Foundation International
2323 Colorado
Turlock, CA 95380
209-668-3333

- Pack a medical kit that includes:

  Small flashlight.
  Scissors.
  Bandages.
  First aid cream.
  Aspirin.
  Your doctor's address and telephone number.

- Do not travel to high altitudes if you have heart disease.
- When traveling abroad, drink bottled water.

HEALTH CARE IN THE AIR

If you are getting to your travel destination by air, you should also know what you can do to minimize flight-related health problems. Ailments ranging from headaches, nausea, and backaches to pneumonia, blood clots, and bronchitis have been associated with air travel.

Here's what you can do to protect your health in the sky.

- Make yourself comfortable. The seats in an airplane are almost designed to cause health problems. They limit your ability to move and put pressure on the back of your thighs. The combined effect is to restrict the circulation in your legs. While this causes no problems in the majority of travelers, you may experience some swelling in your ankles and feet.

The best remedy is to take frequent walks in the aisle (at least one an hour). If you can get a seat on the aisle, all the better. You should travel in loose clothing, avoid crossing your legs, wear support stockings, take off your shoes, and elevate your feet.

• Keep up your fluids. When it comes to air quality, an airplane is like a desert on wings. Your eyes, nose, and throat dry out, increasing the risk of infection. Dehydration can cause digestive problems, discomfort, and fatigue.

To reverse the effects of dehydration, drink plenty of water (at least 8 ounces an hour) and moisten your eyes with saline drops and your skin with a moisturizer. Stay away from caffeinated drinks, alcoholic beverages, and salty foods, which speed up dehydration.

• Keep your ears open. Air travel poses special risks to the ears of young and old alike. A plane's descent puts pressure on the middle ear. This can cause the Eustachian tube to collapse, or even rupture, filling the middle ear with fluid.

To protect your ears, take a decongestant before you take off and an hour before you land. For flights of more than 4 hours, use a nasal spray within the hour before you land, and again when you are in descent. Chewing gum also helps. If your ears remain blocked, close your mouth, pinch your nose, and force air up from your lungs into your ears. Repeat this several times during the descent.

• Bon appetit. You do not have to eat the high-fat, high-salt fare that airlines try to pass off as food. If you call at least 24 hours before your flight, you may be able to select a low-fat, low-salt, low-calorie, vegetarian, or kosher meal, or a meal for diabetics. You can also bring along your own healthy snacks and sandwiches, in case your flight is delayed or your specially ordered meal is not available.

Jet Smart by Diana Fairechild, published by Flyana Rhyme, provides air travelers with two hundred tips for a safer and healthier trip. You can purchase the book for $12.95 from a bookstore, or for $14.95 by calling 800-524-8477 and placing an order.

EXERCISE

The benefits of regular exercise have been drilled into us: longer life expectancy, higher energy level, reduced stress, improved sleep, enhanced self-confidence and self-esteem, and a generally cheerier outlook on life. Exercise appears to strengthen heart and lungs, lower blood pressure, maintain body weight, guard against the onset of osteoporosis and diabetes, and maximize strength and flexibility.

But is there anything special you should know about exercising in the second half of your life? Is exercise still a good idea, even if you have an illness or disability?

The answer to both questions is yes.

After you have spoken with your doctor about your exercise plans, keep these tips in mind as you swing into action:

• Start slow and easy. A 5- or 10-minute workout twice a week is a good beginning. If you're feeling up to it, add on a few more minutes of exercise each week. When you are up to about 15 to 30 minutes of exercise three or four times a week, you should feel proud of achieving an ideal exercise regimen.

• Warm up before each workout session. As the body ages, warm-ups become increasingly important. Your muscles, tendons, and ligaments lose some elasticity with age. This leaves them more susceptible to such injuries as strains and tears. Five to 15 minutes of pre-exercise stretching is great.

• Slow down after each workout session. Letting your body cool down after exercising is as important as warming up. A good way to wind down is to slow the pace of your ordinary exercise activities. Stretching is another way to slow down after exercising.

• Stick with your exercise routine. You will benefit the most from exercising if you keep up regular workouts. To help yourself stay motivated:

  • Enter into a pact with a friend. Agree to motivate each other to exercise.
  • Choose activities that you enjoy. Decide whether you prefer exercising alone, with one friend, or in a group. Do you prefer exercising outdoors or indoors?
  • If possible, exercise first thing in the morning. Distractions tend to increase as the day progresses.

• If you exercise alone, make sure someone knows your exercise schedule. This is a good precaution in case something happens to you while exercising.

• Listen to your body. Forget the expression "No pain, no gain." Do not bravely continue exercising through shortness of breath, muscle cramps, or chest pain. Instead, give your doctor a call. You may be advised to take a short break from exercise, or to change or reduce your activities.

Even if you are recovering from an illness or injury, exercise may be just what the doctor ordered. Regular exercise has been shown to have a remarkable effect in helping the human body repair itself. Of course, be sure to consult your doctor before starting any new fitness program.

For more information about exercise and age, request a list of publications and information sources from:

National Institute on Aging/Exercise
Building 31, Room 5C35
Bethesda, MD 20892

WALKING

Walking is one of the best exercises for people in every generation. Lower-intensity exercises that last longer periods of time have been found to offer some of the best cardiovascular benefits. Walking gives your heart the aerobic benefit of sustained activity, and your mind the serenity of undisturbed time.

SEX

Although hardly an Olympic event, sex is one of the most fun ways to give your body (and another body) a good aerobic workout.

Recent studies have shown that older adults are experiencing a heightened level of sexual activity. According to the 1993 Janus Report on Sexual Behavior, about half of the men and women age 65 or older surveyed reported having a "reasonably active" sex life. In interviews, the subjects of the study listed a number of advantages to sex late in life: more time to enjoy lovemaking, no worry about pregnancy, and greater intimacy with a long-term partner.

Nothing prevents older people from continuing to enjoy an active sex life. Most sex-related problems that do arise are attributable to illness, medication, or depression, and most are now treatable.

MEN

Older men retain the capacity for erection and ejaculation well into their later years. They may, however, experience a longer response time with age. More direct stimulation may be required. Some medications can also affect an older man's ability to attain an erection, including drugs to treat high blood pressure or depression. Doctors can often resolve these problems by lowering dosages or changing prescriptions.

WOMEN

Almost every change in a woman's sexual functioning is related to the female hormone estrogen. Estrogen levels drop between ages 48 and 53, when most women reach menopause. Lowered levels of estrogen have been tied to changes in the shape, flexibility, and lubrication of the vagina. Other problems commonly associated with menopause are diminished interest in sex, vaginal dryness or shrinkage, and pain during intercourse. Millions of women worldwide start hormone replacement therapy after menopause to reverse these symptoms, as well as to prevent heart disease and osteoporosis. There are risks and benefits associated with taking hormones. The benefits may include clearer arteries and lower cholesterol levels.

The risks may include heightened incidence of breast and uterine cancer. Homeopathic remedies, such as acupuncture and herbs, have also been found to relieve post-menopausal difficulties.

PSYCHOLOGICAL PROBLEMS

Emotional factors, such as poor body image and fear of impotence, can depress an older adult's sex drive. Although these mental blocks can often be dealt with through therapy, many older people are not comfortable talking about sex with a stranger.

The best way to deal with these problems is to understand and reject the myths surrounding age and sex. A man who has trouble sustaining an erection on one occasion may conclude that he has become impotent with age. The link between age and impotency is a myth, but it may be so powerful that it leaves the man psychologically unable to overcome the problem. Temporarily shifting the focus away from intercourse and to other expressions of sexuality, such as hugging, kissing, and caressing, can help.

Women who believe the myth that a mature body is not sexually attractive may likewise suppress their sexual feelings. Two ways to overcome these fears are to start exercising and to focus on attractive body parts and ignore the rest.

ILLNESS, DISEASE, AND SEX

Very few medical conditions require complete abstinence from sex. Here is a list of a few common illnesses and diseases and their impact on sexual functioning.

- Heart attack. Most doctors give a green light to sexual intercourse 12 to 16 weeks after a heart attack.
- Stroke. Sexual functioning is rarely affected by stroke. Medical devices are available to compensate for weak and paralyzed body parts.
- Hysterectomy (removal of the womb) and mastectomy (removal of the breast). Sexual functioning is not affected if the surgery is performed correctly. Most post-operative problems are psychological.
- Prostatectomy (removal of the prostate gland). This operation rarely affects sexual functioning, unless the "perineal" approach (through the perineum) is used for biopsy when early cancer is suspected.

RECREATIONAL PROGRAMS

Chances are, your community offers a number of exercise programs that are especially designed for older adults. To find out about fitness programs and exercise classes in your area, contact:

- YMCA, YWCA, YMHA, or YWHA.
- Colleges and universities.
- Churches and synagogues.
- Park district.
- Senior citizens' center.
- Community or civic centers.
- Agency on aging; call 800-677-1116 for local number.

COOKING

Food has probably served a significant and meaningful role in your life. Your spouse might have wooed you over a candlelight dinner. When your children were babies, they may have splattered mushed peas and bananas all over your kitchen walls. Most of us have nurtured friendships over home-cooked meals and bottles of wine.

The value and importance of food does not diminish over time. Your physical and mental health are as dependent on good food now as ever.

But you may have found that your attitude toward food has changed over the years. You may have lost interest in cooking because cooking for one is not as much fun as cooking for two or more. Or perhaps you can no longer afford to buy the foods you like. Or maybe you find that you lack the energy to prepare three full meals a day. Or you no longer know what to eat because you hear so much contradictory information about nutrition.

Statistics show that at least 25 percent of the elderly are malnourished. If you have neglected your nutritional needs, and would like to revive your interest in food, this section is for you.

COOKING FOR ONE

Get your creative juices flowing. Here are some hints for cooking for one:

- Share large packages of food with a friend.
- Buy your frozen vegetables in a bag rather than a box so you can refreeze the unused portion.
- Ask the person who works in the meat, poultry, or produce department of your local supermarket to repackage a smaller quantity of a product for you.
- Freeze part of each meal you prepare for another day.

- Plan meals that you can prepare in appropriate quantities, such as pasta and stir-fry meat, chicken, and vegetables.
- Invite a friend over for a meal.
- Organize a pot-luck dinner with your friends or neighbors. Assign a dish to each participant so you do not end up with three desserts and no entree.
- Look for single-serving frozen and canned foods.
- Purchase single-serving portions at the supermarket delicatessen, appetizer counter, meat department, and bakery.

AFFORDING MEALTIME

Too many older Americans are unable to afford to eat properly. If money is tight, these hints might help:

- Keep purchases of prepackaged foods to a minimum. Ounce for ounce, they consume more of your food dollars.
- Clip coupons and check newspaper ads and flyers for bargains. Plan your menu around items on sale, but don't waste your money on high-priced foods with low nutritional value just because you have a coupon for them.
- Use unit pricing. Unit pricing lets you compare the same quantity of different brands to see which costs the least. Generic (or "no-name") brands and store brands are almost always less expensive than name brands.
- Stock up on sale items. Check expiration dates to make sure the item will not go bad before you have had an opportunity to use it.
- Beware of foods that are advertised as "natural" or "organic." They usually cost more, and rarely offer significant nutritional advantages.
- Avoid waste by dividing leftovers into individual servings and freezing for a later meal.
- Keep your eye on the supermarket scanner. Make sure that the price that comes up when your item is scanned by the cashier conforms with the price marked on the item or advertised in the circular. If there is a mistake, insist on being charged the lower price, even if it means holding up the line.
- Find out if you are eligible for inexpensive or free meals. Call the Elder Care Locator (800-677-1116), your local department of social services, or a senior center for the information you need.
- Find out if you are eligible for food stamps. Food stamps are coupons issued by the federal government that you can use instead of cash to purchase food.

If you are over age 60 or disabled, your food stamp eligibility will depend on a formula that takes into account your income and expenses, and your resources (which cannot exceed $2,000 for an individual or $3,000 for a couple). The 1994 flat gross monthly income limits of $756 for an individual and $1,022 for a couple don't apply to households with an elderly or disabled person.

For a guide on shopping for and preparing healthy economical meals, write to:

> **Consumer Information Center**
> P.O. Box 100
> Pueblo, CO 81002
> Send $2.50 for the publication "Thrifty Meals for Two."

Too Tired to Cook

There is no question that it is easier to warm up a can of beans than to prepare, cook, and serve a complete meal. But rallying the energy you need to prepare a good meal will pay off in the long run because eating well will boost your energy. Here are some motivational tips for reluctant cooks everywhere:

- Plan your meals in advance. If you wait until your stomach is growling, you can be sure that your energy level will be at its all-time low.
- When you are cooking, prepare larger amounts than you immediately need. Freeze the extra portions for another day when you *really* don't feel like cooking.
- Try new recipes. You can get exciting cooking ideas from magazines, newspapers, and television.
- Develop recipes for quick meals. Broiling, stir-frying, and microwaving are great time savers.
- Invite a friend over for lunch or dinner. Cooking for someone else is usually more fun than cooking for yourself. And you may even get a free meal out of it, if the invitation is returned!

Nutrition Confusion

Nutrition information can make anyone's head spin.

We've all experienced this: On the morning news you hear that a particular vitamin has been found to reduce your risk of a heart attack. You rush off to the store (practically giving yourself a heart attack in the process) to stock up on foods rich in that vitamin. While unpacking your grocery bags, you put on the evening news just in time to learn about a new report linking high doses of the vitamin-of-the-moment to different health problems. You decide right then and there to swear off food forever.

Instead of following the latest nutritional fad, let the following time-tested principles of nutrition guide your eating habits.

- Eat a varied diet including fresh fruits and vegetables, whole grain and enriched breads, cereals, rice, pasta, fish, poultry, lean meats, beans, nuts, milk, cheese, and low-fat dairy products.
- Stay away from foods that are high in salt, sugar, and fat.
- Only consume egg yolks two to three times a week, unless your doctor has recommended otherwise.
- Choose monounsaturated fats such as olive and canola oil over butter, lard, palm oil, and coconut oil.
- Try to eat foods as close to their natural form as possible. Highly processed foods have lower nutritional value.
- Read labels. Make special note of the item that appears first on the list of ingredients because that item is present in the largest quantity. If you are buying beef stew, for example, you want meat, not gravy, to be the first item. Also, review the amount of calories, protein, carbohydrates, fat, and sodium per serving. Don't forget to look at what constitutes a serving. Is a "serving" only enough to feed a mouse?
- Check the freshness date on perishables.
- To avoid fat, trim meat before cooking; broil, bake, or boil instead of frying in fat; drain off cooked fat and remove hardened fat before reheating.
- Preserve vitamins by eating vegetables raw or lightly steamed or stir-fried.
- If you are on medication, ask your doctor if you should change your diet either to avoid adverse interactions or to compensate for a nutritional deficit.
- Drink six to eight glasses of water a day. As you age, changes in your digestive system increase the danger of dehydration.
- Fiber, which is found in whole-grain bread and cereals, raw or slightly cooked vegetables, fruits, and dried peas and beans, is important to maintaining regular waste elimination and controlling cholesterol.
- High-calorie foods become increasingly dangerous as you age. Metabolism slows down later in life, so pastries, cakes, candy, and alcohol are more likely to put on extra pounds. Also, your body's ability to process blood sugar decreases over time. Pass over white and brown sugar, honey, and syrups in favor of fresh fruits and canned fruit packed in water and juice concentrate.

For more information on healthy eating, write to:

National Institute on Aging/Food
Building 31, Room 5C35
Bethesda, MD 20892
Request the free publications "Nutrition: A Lifelong Concern," "Dietary Supplements: More Is Not Always Better," and "Be Sensible About Salt."

AARP Fulfillment
601 E Street, N.W.
Washington, DC 20049
202-434-2277
Request the free publications "Eating for Your Health" and "How Does *Your* Nutrition Measure Up?"

Consumer Information Center
P.O. Box 100
Pueblo, CO 81002
Request the free publication "Nutrition and the Elderly."

For information on food safety, call the U.S. Food and Drug Administration. The number appears in the blue pages of your telephone directory.

EDUCATION

Learning is a lifelong undertaking. If you have always wanted to study Russian, master Greek mythology, or learn to write poetry, now may be the time to take that class. This section discusses four popular educational programs for older adults.

INSTITUTES OF LIFETIME LEARNING

The concept behind Institutes of Lifetime Learning is to have retired individuals design a curriculum to teach other older adults. Each Institute of Lifetime Learning is sponsored by a local college. To receive the "Directory of Centers for Older Learners" and "Community College Programs for Older Adults," contact:

AARP Fulfillment
601 E Street, N.W.
Washington, DC 20049
202-434-2277

DISCOVER THROUGH THE HUMANITIES

Discover Through the Humanities is a discussion program that meets in communities throughout the country in sites frequented by older adults, such as adult day care centers, senior centers, nursing homes, and nutrition centers. The program offers seventeen discussion topics on aspects of aging. Examples of topics include work, memories, and making peace with the past. For information about starting a discussion program in your neighborhood, including assistance in finding materials, fundraising, publicity, and program selection, write to:

National Council on Aging
409 Third Street, S.W., Suite 200
Washington, DC 20024
202-479-1200

SENIORNET

SeniorNet teaches people age 55 and over about computers. The average age of SeniorNet members is 67.

The organization offers computer classes to older adults in senior centers, schools, medical clinics, and nursing homes across the country. To find out about a training site near you, or to become a member of SeniorNet, write to:

SeniorNet
399 Arguello Boulevard
San Francisco, CA 94118
415-750-5030

An annual membership costs $25. Benefits of membership include a quarterly newsletter and various discounts. The booklet *Computers for Kids Over 60* is free with membership or can be purchased for $14.95. Access to a national on-line electronic network costs members an additional $9.95 a month. The national on-line network enables members to communicate with each other by using a personal computer and modem. On the network, members can participate in discussion groups on such diverse topics as current events, travel, and gardening, and access information about a variety of subjects, ranging from bridge to financial planning. Letters on the network fall into such thought-provoking categories as generation-to-generation advice, longevity, and the meaning of life. On-line counseling for beginner and advanced computer users is also available.

ADULT EDUCATION

Many communities offer adult education classes on a wide variety of subjects. Classes are usually held in a local school or community center. You can find out about adult education programs in your area by contacting a local senior center, community center, or the Chamber of Commerce. You can also write to:

U.S. Department of Education
Division of Vocational and Technical Education
400 Maryland Avenue, S.W.
Washington, DC 20202-7100
202-205-9872

VOLUNTEERISM

As a volunteer, you can use your lifetime of experience to help others and, in the process, have some fun yourself. A number of different volunteer programs are specifically designed for older adults. Some of these programs are summarized below.

FOSTER GRANDPARENT PROGRAM

The Foster Grandparent Program (FGP) provides physically, mentally, and emotionally disturbed children with adult companions and teachers on a one-to-one basis. Children who have been abused and juvenile delinquents can also participate in the program. Foster grandparents receive 40 hours of training before they begin service, and 4 hours of additional training each month they participate in the program. Volunteers in the FGP must be over 60 years of age and low-income. Volunteers who work at least 20 hours a week receive a small stipend, accident and liability insurance, a meal on the days they work, transportation, and an annual physical exam. For information about the FGP, contact the ACTION office in your state or the national ACTION office:

ACTION
1100 Vermont Avenue, N.W., 6th Floor
Washington, DC 20525
202-606-4855

RETIRED SENIOR VOLUNTEER PROGRAM

The Retired Senior Volunteer Program (RSVP) is also sponsored by the federal ACTION agency. RSVP volunteers provide a variety of services, including health care, companionship, security, education, and financial and social services to old and young alike at day care centers, nursing homes, schools, libraries, courts, crisis centers, and other locations in the community. In some communities, RSVP volunteers operate runaway shelters, organize widows' support groups, and offer occupational counseling to first-time offenders. RSVP volunteers are paid for the costs they incur while volunteering, such as transportation and other out-of-pocket expenses. They also receive accident and liability insurance while on service. RSVP volunteers must be at least 60 years of age. To find out more about RSVP, contact the ACTION office in your state or the national ACTION office:

ACTION
1100 Vermont Avenue, N.W., 6th Floor
Washington, DC 20525
202-606-4855

SENIOR COMPANIONS

The federal ACTION agency also sponsors the Senior Companions Program (SCP). SCP volunteers assist mentally, emotionally, and physically impaired elderly individuals who live in the community by providing companionship, help with errands, financial counseling, health care, and nutritional assistance. The goal of Senior Companions is to help the elderly live independently at home for as long as possible. Senior Companions must be age 60 or older and low-income. In return for 20 hours of service each week, SCP volunteers receive a small tax-free allowance, a meal on the days they work, transportation, insurance, and an annual physical examination. More information about SCP is available from the ACTION office in your state or the national ACTION office:

ACTION
1100 Vermont Avenue, N.W., 6th Floor
Washington, DC 20525
202-606-4855

VOLUNTEER TUTORS

School volunteers help educate the children of America in a number of important ways. They tutor students for whom English is a second language. They help students pursue such extracurricular interests as art, music, and drama. They educate students about career choices.

If you are interested in offering your services as a volunteer in a local school, contact your local school superintendent's office, or call or write:

National Association of Partners in Education
209 Madison Street
Alexandria, VA 22314
703-836-4880

For a $10 membership fee, the National Association of Partners in Education will put you in touch with local volunteer programs and provide you with liability insurance, a newsletter, and discounts on publications and the annual conference.

AARP Fulfillment
601 E Street, N.W.
Washington, D.C. 20049
202-434-2277

Request the free booklet "Becoming a School Partner."

SERVICE CORPS OF RETIRED EXECUTIVES

The Service Corps of Retired Executives (SCORE) uses retired businesspeople volunteers to assist owners and managers of struggling small businesses. SCORE volunteers draw on their business experience to provide counseling and training in the areas of management, expansion, marketing, and distribution. More than four hundred local SCORE chapters are located throughout the country. For information about SCORE, contact the regional Small Business Administration office, look for the SCORE listing in your local telephone directory, or write:

National SCORE Office
409 Third Street, S.W., Suite 5900
Washington, DC 20024
202-205-6762

ENVIRONMENTAL ADVOCATE

If you enjoy working with animals, or like to work outdoors, you may want to consider volunteering with the U.S. Fish and Wildlife Service, the National Forest Service, or the National Park Service.

As a U.S. Fish and Wildlife Service volunteer, you can commute to work in a wildlife refuge or fish hatchery. To find out about volunteer programs with the Fish and Wildlife Service, call or write:

U.S. Fish and Wildlife Service
4401 North Fairfax Drive
Arlington, VA 22203
703-358-2043; 703-358-1786

As a volunteer with the National Forest Service, you will help maintain and improve the nation's forests and grasslands by doing light construction work, yard work, or clerical work. Depending on the job, you may reside on-site in a trailer, barracks, government housing, or rental housing, or commute to the job site each day. To offer your services as a volunteer, call or write:

USDA Forest Service
Human Resources Program
14th Street and Independence Avenue, S.W.
P.O. Box 96090
Washington, DC 20090-6090
703-235-8834

To find out about volunteer opportunities with the National Park Service, request an application from whichever national park that interests you most. Soon after you submit your application, you will be notified about available volunteer positions that match your skills, abilities, and preferences.

NURSING HOME ADVOCATE (OMBUDSMAN)

Volunteer ombudsmen protect the rights and interests of the institutionalized elderly. Ombudsmen investigate and resolve complaints made by nursing home residents, relatives of residents, and professionals who work with the elderly (such as health care and social services workers) regarding quality of care and financial issues. Ombudsmen are given the training and legal authority to work with nursing home personnel and public agencies to improve nursing home conditions. Most ombudsmen volunteer 3 to 4 hours each week. To find out about becoming an ombudsman in your community, contact your state unit on aging (see Appendix 1).

HOSPITAL VOLUNTEERS

Volunteers in hospitals do everything from helping patients write and mail letters, to directing out-of-town visitors around the area, to tutoring ill children and cuddling newborns in the nursery. To get more information about becoming a hospital volunteer, contact a local medical facility.

AMERICAN CANCER SOCIETY

The American Cancer Society has a volunteer program that looks for individuals to provide companionship to cancer patients, drive patients to their doctors, run errands for homebound patients, and relieve full-time caregivers. If interested, contact the local chapter of the American Cancer Society to offer your services as a volunteer.

AARP VOLUNTEER PROGRAMS

The American Association of Retired Persons (AARP) sponsors a number of volunteer programs in a wide variety of areas. As an AARP volunteer you can:

- Teach driver education classes to older drivers.
- Educate older voters about political issues that affect them.
- Lobby state legislators to enact laws that benefit the elderly.
- Help older people get their insurance companies, Medicare, and Medicaid to cover their medical bills.
- Provide retirement counseling to workers and employers.
- Assist older taxpayers with their tax returns.
- Teach mature women about financial matters.
- Temporarily relieve people who are providing care to seriously ill friends or family members.
- Offer career counseling to individuals interested in obtaining employment.

If you are interested in becoming a volunteer, you must register with the AARP Volunteer Talent Bank. As part of the registration process, you will be asked a number of questions about your experience and interests. Based on your answers, you will be matched with volunteer programs in your geographic area.

Of course, volunteering is just that: voluntary. You are under no obligation to accept the volunteer positions offered to you. The AARP Volunteer Talent Bank matches volunteers with AARP's own volunteer programs as well as with such organizations as the March of Dimes, the Red Cross, the Peace Corps, other federal volunteer programs, and local organizations in your community. To become an AARP volunteer, contact:

AARP Volunteer Talent Bank
601 E Street, N.W.
Washington, DC 20049
202-434-2277

EMPLOYMENT

Statistics show that about 27 percent of the estimated 52.4 million Americans age 55 or older have paying jobs. Their reasons for staying in, or returning to, the work force are usually financial and/or personal: They need the extra cash, or they enjoy the fulfillment of putting in a day of work.

Older workers offer employers a number of proven benefits. According to studies performed by The Commonwealth Fund, a New York City-based nonprofit group, productivity and profits increase, and employee turnover decreases, with the hiring of older workers. The more mature workforce also takes fewer sick days than its younger counterpart.

If you are interested in seeking employment, you may want to look to the following groups for assistance.

AMERICAN ASSOCIATION OF RETIRED PERSONS

The American Association of Retired Persons (AARP) offers a number of programs to help older workers obtain and hold employment. Some of these programs include:

- Career counseling.
- Advocacy assistance under the Age Discrimination Act.
- Publications.
- Workers' Equity Initiative (a computerized data base of employers who have special programs for older workers).

For help finding work, contact:

AARP Fulfillment
601 E Street, N.W.
Washington, DC 20049
202-434-2277

Request the free publications "Working Options—How to Plan Your Job Search, Your Work Life" and "How to Stay Employable: A Guide for the

Mid-life and Older Worker." Learn the location and date of the next AARP WORKS, a series of eight workshops that covers a number of aspects of finding employment. The workshops are offered twice a year at about eighty locations in thirty states. They cost $35. More than half of the workshop participants find new jobs.

ELDER CRAFTERS

If you are a craftsperson age 55 or older, you may be interested in selling your work through an Elder Crafters or Elder Craftsman consignment shop. About seventy-five independent retail stores throughout the country feature the work of older craftspeople. Each submission is reviewed by a selection committee before it is placed in the store. Most stores accept out-of-state submissions. Here are the addresses of two Elder Crafts stores:

Elder Crafters
405 Cameron Street
Alexandria, VA 22314
703-683-4338

Elder Craftsman
135 East 65th Street
New York, NY 10021
212-861-3294

NATIONAL CENTER/CAUCUS ON BLACK AGED SENIOR EMPLOYMENT PROGRAM

The National Center/Caucus on Black Aged (NCCBA) Senior Employment Program operates a placement program for adults age 55 and over who are seeking employment in the private sector, nonprofit organizations, and public agencies. NCCBA also offers minority training and development programs in nursing home administration. For more information about these programs, contact:

National Center/Caucus on Black Aged
1424 K Street, N.W., Suite 500
Washington, DC 20005
202-637-8400

AREA AGENCY ON AGING PROGRAMS

Your local area agency on aging can provide you with information about the following programs that assist older employees:

- The Senior Community Service Employment Program helps low-income persons age 55 or older obtain part-time work in community service.
- The Job Training Partnership Act provides training to individuals age 55 or older who are interested in working in the private sector.

To find out the address and telephone number of your local area agency on aging, call the Elder Care Locator at 800-677-1116. You can also contact your state unit on aging for information (see Appendix 1).

ADDITIONAL SOURCES OF INFORMATION AND ASSISTANCE

Forty Plus is a self-help organization for professional and managerial employees age 40 and older that offers training sessions on how to conduct an effective job search. The cost of club membership varies from city to city, but is about $300 plus a $30 monthly fee. Forty Plus also offers office space, computers, phones, and a fax machine for member job-seekers. Look in your telephone directory for the chapter nearest you. There are chapters in more than fifteen cities nationwide.

The National Council on Aging and the National Council of Senior Citizens provide part-time employment opportunities for older workers in public agencies, community service agencies, libraries, hospitals, and schools. Applicants must be age 55 or older and low-income. Participants in the program work 20 hours a week, usually for minimum wage. For information, contact:

National Council on Aging
409 Third Street, S.W., Suite 200
Washington, DC 20024
202-479-1200

National Council of Senior Citizens
1331 F Street, N.W.
Washington, DC 20004
202-347-8800

Your state employment development department, listed in the state listings in the blue pages of your telephone book, provides information about resources for finding retraining programs, older worker networks, and direct service employment agencies.

Employment agencies are also sources of permanent or temporary, full-time or part-time employment. They are listed in the yellow pages of your telephone book. Some employment agencies advertise special services for older workers.

ℹ️ *For more information*

Older Women's League
666 11th Street, N.W., Suite 700
Washington, DC 20001
202-783-6686

Send $7 for the primer "Older Women and Job Discrimination" or $12 for the handbook "Building Public/Private Coalitions for Older Women's Employment." Add $2.50 for shipping and handling.

U.S. Equal Employment Opportunity Commission (EEOC)
1801 L Street, N.W.
Washington, DC 20507
202-663-4900

You can get the number of the EEOC field office nearest you by calling the national office or looking in the blue pages of your telephone book under the U.S. Government listings. Employees age 40 and older should report age-related discrimination in the workplace to their local EEOC office.

POLITICAL ACTION

If you are tired of wishing "they" would do something about a problem, you may want to consider becoming more involved in politics. By joining forces with other older adults, you can often effect change through the political system. A number of organizations coordinate political action on behalf of the elderly.

AMERICAN ASSOCIATION OF RETIRED PERSONS

As an AARP member, you support the largest lobbying organization for older people. AARP advocates legislative change on the national and state levels in the areas of Social Security, Medicare, health care, age discrimination, abuse of the elderly, housing, and consumer issues. AARP membership entitles you to a monthly news bulletin; a bimonthly magazine; numerous free booklets on an array of subjects including finance, health, housing, long-term care, caregiving, consumer rights, and retirement; discounts for auto rentals, hotels, prescription drugs, and insurance; investment programs; travel tours; and an auto club. To find out about AARP's activities, contact:

American Association of Retired Persons
601 E Street, N.W.
Washington, DC 20049
202-434-2277

OLDER WOMEN'S LEAGUE

The Older Women's League (OWL) uses canvassing and lobbying to protect and enhance the interests of older widowed and divorced women. Some of the issues on OWL's agenda include Social Security reform, pension equity, availability of health care, insurance, employment opportunities, and the needs of caregivers. As a member of OWL you will receive a newsletter, updates on national legislative developments, discounts on insurance plans and OWL publications, and an opportunity to participate in local and state activities. For information on becoming a member, contact the national OWL office:

Older Women's League
666 11th Street, N.W., Suite 300
Washington, DC 20001
202-783-6686

GRAY PANTHERS

The Gray Panthers has worked since 1970 to bring national attention to the problems of the elderly. Currently, the Gray Panthers is working to achieve a national system of health care, add more units of affordable housing, secure the future of the Social Security trust fund, protect elderly renters, and promote age equality. Members of the Gray Panthers receive a quarterly newsletter, a bimonthly update on health issues, and a bimonthly review of legislative developments. Members can also work with their local Gray Panthers chapter on issues of special concern within their community. To find out more about the Gray Panthers, write to the national office:

Gray Panthers
2025 Pennsylvania Avenue, N.W., Suite 821
Washington, DC 20006
202-466-3132

NATIONAL COUNCIL OF SENIOR CITIZENS

The National Council of Senior Citizens (NCSC) is most famous for successfully advocating the establishment of the Medicare program in 1961. Since then, NCSC has worked to protect the interests of older people in the areas of Social Security, housing, Medicare, Medicaid, employment opportunities, and community-based social and nutritional services. Right now, NCSC is lobbying for national health care. NCSC members receive a monthly newsletter that summarizes legislative developments affecting the elderly, in addition to other benefits. For information, contact:

National Council of Senior Citizens
1331 F Street, N.W.
Washington, DC 20004
202-347-8800

NATIONAL ALLIANCE OF SENIOR CITIZENS, INC.

The National Alliance of Senior Citizens, Inc. (NASC), is a nonprofit membership organization that offers older adults a range of benefits, services, and policy research. NASC championed the repeal of the Medicare Catastrophic Coverage Act, opposes mandatory retirement age statutes, and promotes Social Security and health care reform. NASC members receive a newsletter, a variety of discounts, and travel services. The annual membership fee is $10 for an individual and $15 for a couple. For more information, contact:

National Alliance of Senior Citizens
1700 18th Street, N.W., Suite 401
Washington, DC 20009
202-986-0117

INDIVIDUAL ADVOCACY

If you would like to voice your opinion about national issues of special interest to older adults, you can write to your local representatives or send a letter to:

Administration on Aging
U.S. Department of Health and Human Services
330 Independence Avenue, S.W.
Washington, DC 20201

or:

Chairman
Select Committee on Aging
712 House Office Building, Annex 1
Washington, DC 20515

2.

UNDERSTANDING MEDICARE BENEFITS

Selma was a "shoebox" client. That is, she came to my office with a shoebox full of papers that included letters from Medicare, claim forms, hospital bills, bills from a home care agency, collection notices, receipts, canceled checks, notes scribbled on small pieces of paper, and a recipe for tuna surprise.

About a year before contacting me, Selma had broken her hip. She was treated at a hospital and, when she was discharged, received some help at home. At the time of her accident, Selma was on Medicare. Because she did not fully understand the Medicare system, Selma was having trouble obtaining coverage for her medical bills.

Selma needed to know: Which of her many papers were important? What medical bills were covered? How much would she have to pay out-of-pocket?

Without a doubt, one of the most important benefits you are entitled to receive as an older American is public health insurance. In 1965 the U.S. Congress established Medicare, the federal health insurance program for the elderly and disabled. Medicare was one of the Great Society programs signed into law by President Lyndon Johnson. Medicare now finances health care for about 36 million elderly and disabled Americans.

Some of President Clinton's health care advisers have recommended eliminating Medicare and incorporating the program in a national system of managed competition. Under such a proposal, Medicare beneficiaries would become members of health care plans, such as health maintenance organizations (HMOs), and would receive their medical services from providers that participate in the plan.

This proposal is unlikely to be implemented for several years, if at all. What is more likely to happen is that the federal government will give states incentives to encourage their Medicare beneficiaries to join health care plans voluntarily. The concern of many older Americans is that these incentives may make health care outside a plan so expensive that Medicare beneficiaries will effectively be forced to join a plan. Joining a plan would be voluntary in name only.

In any event, under the current system, Medicare beneficiaries are covered for basic hospital and medical services they receive from any health care provider. The provider need not belong to any health care network.

Medicare pays for about 65 to 70 percent of the health care costs of covered older adults. Why not more?

There are several reasons. Some medical expenses fall outside the scope of Medicare coverage. For example, Medicare does not cover prescription drugs and many of the costs associated with long-term chronic or disabling illnesses. Medicare beneficiaries also have to pay part of the cost of their covered medical services in the form of deductibles and co-payments. Finally, some medical expenses go uncovered because Medicare beneficiaries do not know how to get the most out of the Medicare system.

Medicare is an extremely complicated program governed by detailed regulations set out in volumes of very small print. Even the supposed experts who work within the Medicare system have large gaps in their knowledge of the rules, as you will undoubtedly discover.

As a beneficiary, you do not need to know every detail about the Medicare program. You only need to know the rules that will help you collect the maximum amount of benefits you are entitled to receive.

This chapter gives you an overview of the Medicare system by covering the following topics, each in a separate section:

- Administration of Medicare.
- Eligibility rules for Medicare coverage.
- Medicare-covered services.
- Costs of Medicare.
- Questions, explanations, and examples.

Introductory guidelines for some sections will point you in the direction of the information that most directly pertains to your situation.

Chapter 3 will complete your understanding of Medicare by personalizing the discussion. You will learn how to apply for coverage, how to get Medicare to pay your bills, and what to do if Medicare denies coverage. Finally, in Chapter 4 you will learn what you can do to fill in the gaps in your Medicare coverage.

ADMINISTRATION OF MEDICARE

Several players work together to run the Medicare system.

The U.S. Department of Health and Human Services (DHHS), a federal agency, administers the Medicare program nationwide.

The Health Care Financing Administration (HCFA), a division of DHHS, sets Medicare policy.

The Social Security Administration (SSA), through its local offices across the country, processes Medicare applications.

Private insurance companies, such as Blue Cross/Blue Shield, Group Health Insurance (GHI), and Travelers, have contracts with the HCFA to process Medicare claims. Insurance companies that handle Part A claims (hospital, nursing home, home care, and hospice claims) are called intermediaries. Insurance companies that handle Part B claims (doctors and outpatient service claims) are called carriers.

Peer review organizations (PROs) are groups of doctors, nurses, and therapists the federal government pays to determine whether hospital services provided to Medicare beneficiaries are medically necessary and appropriate.

Utilization review committees (URCs) are groups of health care professionals that hospitals and skilled nursing facilities employ to determine whether services provided to institutionalized and hospitalized beneficiaries are covered by Medicare. Decisions made by URCs can be appealed to PROs (for hospital claims) and Medicare intermediaries (for nursing facility claims).

ELIGIBILITY FOR MEDICARE

WHERE TO FIND WHAT YOU NEED

- If you are interested in learning about the general eligibility rules that apply to coverage of hospital, nursing home, home care, and hospice bills, see page 33.
- If you need information about special eligibility rules that apply to particular types of benefits, see the following pages:

Hospital coverage	Page 34
Nursing home coverage	Page 34
Home care coverage	Page 39
Hospice coverage	Page 41

- If you are interested in learning about the general eligibility rules that apply to coverage of doctors' bills and other outpatient services, see page 42.

Medicare is divided into two parts: Part A, which is called hospital insurance, and Part B, which is called medical insurance.

Part A benefits actually include more than hospital coverage. Also covered under Part A are:

- Skilled nursing facility services.
- Home health care services.
- Hospice care.

Likewise, "medical insurance" does not adequately describe the coverage that is available under Medicare Part B. Part B covers:

- Doctors' bills.
- Diagnostic tests.
- Certain other outpatient services.

Eligibility for each part of the Medicare program is governed by a general set of rules. In addition, a special set of rules governs eligibility for specific Part A benefits.

PART A GENERAL ELIGIBILITY RULES

You can qualify for Part A coverage either automatically or through enrollment.

AUTOMATIC ELIGIBILITY

You are automatically eligible for Part A Medicare benefits if you are age 65 or older and receiving Social Security retirement benefits, Railroad Retirement benefits, or benefits as the family member or survivor of a worker covered by Social Security.

You are also automatically eligible if you are under age 65 and eligible for Social Security disability benefits for 24 months. (Note: The 24-month eligibility period required for Medicare coverage starts to run as of the date you are found disabled, not the date you receive your first benefit check.)

If you fit into one of these automatic eligibility categories, you will be enrolled in the Part A Medicare program without filing an application and without paying a premium.

ELIGIBILITY THROUGH ENROLLMENT

If you are not automatically eligible for Part A coverage, you can voluntarily enroll by filing an application with Social Security as long as you are age 65 or older and eligible for (but not receiving) Social Security retirement benefits or Railroad Retirement benefits.

You can also enroll in Part A if you, your spouse, or any of your dependents has permanent kidney failure, or if you are age 65 or older and pay an annual premium for Part A Medicare coverage ($245 a month in 1994). Voluntary enrollees who have to pay a Part A premium should think twice before jumping on the Medicare bandwagon. They may be better off purchasing private insurance coverage, depending on the relative costs and coverage.

If you have to file a Part A application, call Social Security's toll-free number (800-772-1213) to set up an appointment at your local Social Security office. A Social Security representative will be able to give you the forms you need.

SPECIAL PART A ELIGIBILITY RULES

HOSPITAL BENEFITS

You may have Medicare Part A coverage, and you may be in the hospital, but you will not have Medicare coverage of your hospital bills unless you meet two additional eligibility requirements.

First, the hospital must "participate" in Medicare. Participating hospitals are under contract with Medicare to accept Medicare reimbursement. You will find that most hospitals participate in Medicare. Personnel in the hospital admissions or administrative office can confirm whether you are in a participating facility.

There are two important exceptions to the participation requirement:

1. Emergency care. If you have to receive immediate medical attention at a hospital or risk death or serious bodily harm, Medicare will pay your bills at a nonparticipating facility, but only until the emergency passes. Once you are well enough to be transferred or discharged, your coverage will stop.

2. Foreign hospitals. You are not covered for hospital care abroad, with the limited exception of care you receive in a Canadian or Mexican hospital if you live closer to one of these hospitals than to a participating American hospital, or if you require emergency care in Canada while traveling to or from Alaska.

The second prerequisite to getting Medicare to pay your hospital bills is that your doctor must certify your need for inpatient hospital care. Unless your doctor states in writing that you could not have been treated on an outpatient basis, or received care at home, you can kiss Medicare coverage of your hospital bills goodbye.

To find out what hospital services Medicare covers, see page 43 below. For information about how much of your hospital bills Medicare will pay, go to page 51.

SKILLED NURSING FACILITY BENEFITS

To say that Medicare coverage of nursing home care is limited is an understatement. To say that Medicare coverage of nursing home care is very *very* limited is more like it. In fact, Medicare only covers about 2 percent of all nursing home costs in the United States. It is not surprising, therefore, that many Medicare beneficiaries do not know Medicare covers nursing home bills at all.

Medicare Part A coverage is only available to residents of a special category of nursing homes called participating skilled nursing facilities (SNFs). A "participating" facility has been approved by Medicare to accept Medicare reimbursement. You can ask someone in the administrative office of a nursing facility whether the home participates in Medicare.

Medicare's official definition of the "skilled nursing facility" part of the requirement is remarkably unhelpful: "A [skilled nursing facility is a] specially qualified facility with the staff and equipment to provide skilled nursing care or rehabilitation services."[1] Suffice it to say that anyone in the admissions office of a nursing home will be able to tell you that the entire home qualifies as a SNF, one wing of the home qualifies, or none of the home qualifies (see page 44 for an additional discussion of SNFs). To find the locations of skilled nursing facilities in your area, contact your local Medicare intermediary (see Appendix 2).

Not every resident of a participating SNF is covered under Medicare. To be covered, a resident must meet the following additional eligibility requirements:

- Enter the SNF after having been hospitalized for at least 3 days in a row, not counting the day of discharge.
- Enter the SNF within 30 days of being discharged from the hospital.
- Have written medical certification of the need for institutionalization in the SNF.
- Have written medical certification that admission to the SNF is necessary for the continued treatment of the conditions for which the patient was treated in the hospital.
- Have written medical certification that skilled nursing or rehabilitation services are required at least 5 days a week.

Let's look at each of these requirements in turn.

3-Day Prior Hospitalization

This requirement is deceptively straightforward. Here are some points you should know about the need for a 3-day prior hospitalization:

- When figuring the 3-day period, include the day of admission but not the day of discharge. For example, if you enter the hospital on March 1 and are discharged to a SNF on March 3, your SNF institutionalization will not be covered.
- You can extend your hospital stay to meet the 3-day requirement by appeal-

---

[1] The Medicare Handbook is published annually by the U.S. Department of Health and Human Services, Health Care Financing Administration, and is available in every Social Security Office.

ing a hospital's determination that you are ready for discharge. If the hospital URC notifies you that you no longer require hospital care, request PRO review. You will not have to pay for your hospital care while the PRO is reviewing your case, even if you eventually lose. While the appeal is pending, you should meet the 3-day requirement. (If you receive notice of your intended discharge from the PRO instead of the URC, file an appeal. If you eventually lose, you will have to pay a few hundred dollars for your uncovered days of hospital care, but this is small potatoes compared to the thousands of dollars you stand to collect in Medicare coverage of your nursing home bills.)

- If you leave the SNF, and are readmitted within 30 days, you do not need another 3-day prior hospitalization to qualify for Medicare coverage in the SNF.

Institutionalization Within 30 Days of Discharge

This is the second part of the timing requirement for SNF coverage. Once again, you should know the ins and outs of this requirement:

- The 30 days start to run the day following the date of your discharge. For example, if you leave the hospital on October 1, your 30 days start to run on October 2. This means that you must start receiving skilled care in a SNF by October 31.
- You may be able to get an extension of the 30-day period. The extension is only available if receiving continued treatment in the SNF within 30 days of your hospital discharge is not "medically appropriate," and your doctor can predict precisely when institutionalization will be appropriate. Say, for example, you were hospitalized for treatment of a heart attack. You must undergo physical therapy to regain your mobility, but starting to exercise right away could be dangerous. Your doctor states in writing that you should enter the SNF to undergo rehabilitation 6 weeks after you are discharged from the hospital.
- If you do not need to enter the SNF within 30 days of your hospital discharge, and you cannot get an extension, try to stay out of the hospital for at least 60 days. After 60 days, you start a new benefit period (see page 44 for the definition of benefit period). Once you have started a new hospital benefit period, you qualify for a new period of SNF coverage. This means that if you are in the hospital for 3 consecutive days, and enter a SNF within 30 days of your discharge, you will be eligible for Medicare in the SNF.

Medical Certification of Need for Institutionalization

A few things in life are absolutely certain: The sun always rises in the east. Moss grows on the north side of the tree. And Medicare will try to save money whenever and wherever possible. The less Medicare *has* to pay to treat you, the less Medicare *will* pay.

What this means in practice is that Medicare will not pay for you to receive costly treatment as a resident of a skilled nursing facility if you can be adequately (and less expensively) treated at home or on an outpatient basis. Due to the high cost of inpatient care, Medicare requires your doctor to certify your need for resident care in a SNF as a prerequisite of coverage.

Continuity of Care

Medicare also does not want to pay for any care in the SNF that is not related to an acute medical condition. To prove to Medicare that your SNF admission is essential to your recovery from an illness or injury, your doctor must explain in writing how your need for institutionalization is related to your hospitalization. The purpose of your admission to the nursing facility must be to receive care for the same medical condition that landed you in the hospital.

For example, you entered the hospital following a stroke. Your doctor states in writing that the stroke left you partially paralyzed, and you need the services of physical and occupational therapists. Voilà. You should meet the continuity of care requirement.

Medical Certification of Need for Daily Skilled Nursing or Rehabilitation Services

This is the last part of the medical certification requirement, but certainly not the least important part.

Medicare pays primarily for skilled medical services. These include such skilled nursing services as the management of catheters, tube feedings, and ostomies, the maintenance of sterile bandages and serious skin disorders, and the administration of intravenous and intramuscular injections, as well as the skilled rehabilitation services of qualified physical, speech, and occupational therapists.

Medicare does not cover unskilled custodial care, which includes help with such daily activities as walking, dressing, eating, and bathing, and such simple health-related tasks as changing nonsterile dressings, giving oral medications, and assisting with an exercise regimen.

You probably see the problem already. Many nursing home residents do not require skilled medical services. They only require unskilled help with their personal needs.

To establish your need for skilled care in a nursing facility, see if you fit into one of the following patient profiles. The patients described below require skilled nursing or rehabilitation services:

- Patient had a hip replacement and needs physical therapy to learn how to stand and walk.

- Patient had a stroke and needs occupational therapy to learn new ways to take care of personal needs, and speech therapy to improve communication skills.
- Patient has Parkinson's disease and needs therapy services to prevent further deterioration in level of functioning.
- Patient has an ulcerous skin condition and needs a nurse to clean and anoint the skin.
- Patient has lost bowel and bladder control and needs a nurse to manage retraining in bowel and bladder control.
- Patient is an insulin-dependent diabetic and needs a nurse to teach self-administration of intravenous injections.
- Patient had a tracheostomy and needs a nurse to insert, clean, and replace the tracheostomy.
- Patient has an infected wound and needs a nurse to apply medicated dressings and monitor progress.
- Patient recently had a limb amputated and needs to be taught how to attach, maintain, and use a prosthesis.

If your situation resembles any of these examples, tell your doctor to emphasize the similarity in a written certification of your need for skilled care. Otherwise, share the following points with your doctor:

1. You need skilled care if your doctor orders a nurse or therapist to visit you frequently to assess your progress and determine whether changes in your plan of care are indicated. For example, you need skilled care if your doctor wants a physical therapist to check on a daily basis that you are performing your exercises correctly and deriving the intended benefits.

2. You need skilled care if you have more than one medical condition, and the treatment of one condition may impact the other condition. For example, if you have a blood disorder and are also taking oral medications for a heart condition, you must be monitored by a skilled nurse for adverse interactions between the heart medications and the blood condition.

3. You need skilled care if you receive several unskilled services that must be coordinated by a skilled nurse. For example, you have high blood pressure, arthritis, and a tendency to develop skin sores. You take oral medications for high blood pressure, exercise to improve flexibility, and apply skin ointment. Although you do not require any skilled medical care, skilled personnel must oversee your treatment plan.

Establishing a need for skilled care is only half the battle. Your doctor must also certify that you need these skilled services at least 5 days a week.

Now that you know whether you are eligible for Medicare coverage in a SNF, go to page 44 to learn what services Medicare covers within a SNF, and page 52 for information about the extent of Medicare coverage.

HOME HEALTH CARE BENEFITS

Given your druthers, you would probably prefer to recuperate from an illness or injury at home rather than in an institution. No institution is furnished with well-worn furniture that has finally started to fit the contours of your body, or is equipped with a kitchen stocked with your favorite foods.

But, as you have probably come to expect by now, Medicare does not jump at the opportunity to pay your home care bills. To get Medicare to cover your care at home, you must meet each of the following requirements:

- You must receive services from a Medicare certified home health agency (CHHA).
- You must be confined to your home.
- Your doctor must have prescribed a plan of home care treatment for you.
- You must require skilled nursing care, physical therapy, or speech therapy on a part-time or intermittent basis.

Once again, let's look at each requirement more closely.

Medicare Certified Home Health Agency

Medicare certified agencies have signed a contract with Medicare, agreeing to accept Medicare reimbursement as payment in full for covered services they provide to Medicare beneficiaries. To find a CHHA (pronounced "cha"), you can look in the yellow pages of your telephone book under Home Health Service (keeping your eyes open for agencies that advertise Medicare certification), ask your doctor, or get a referral from the discharge planners in the hospital. Personnel in the admissions office of any home care agency will be able to tell you whether the agency is Medicare certified.

Confinement to Home

No, you do not have to be under house arrest to qualify for Medicare home care coverage. You only have to be unable to leave your home without some assistance, either from another person or from a device (such as a cane, walker, or wheelchair). You also must only leave your home for short periods of time. Brief outings to the doctor or the corner grocery store should not disqualify you for Medicare coverage at home.

Doctor-Prescribed Home Care Plan

Medicare will not pay for home health care unless your doctor has indicated that your medical needs can be met at home. And even then, the CHHA will still have to visit your home to determine whether you are an appropriate candidate for home care services. The agency will evaluate your candidacy based on your medical needs, living arrangement, and availability of informal caregivers (such as family members).

Part-Time or Intermittent Skilled Care

Since skilled care is discussed in depth in connection with SNF coverage (see page 34), we will move directly to the "part-time or intermittent" portion of this requirement. If you think you know the meaning of the words "part-time" and "intermittent," think again. These words are terms of art under the Medicare program:

- Part-time means less than 8 hours a day, and no more than 35 hours a week.
- Intermittent means less than 7 days a week, and no more than 35 hours a week.

These two time limits, taken together, proscribe the amount of care you must receive to qualify for Medicare home care coverage. For example, you can receive skilled care a few hours a day, every day of the week (say 4 hours a day, Monday through Sunday), or more hours a day, fewer days of the week (say 7 hours a day, Monday through Friday).

Two more points you should know about the required frequency of skilled home care services: What is the minimum amount of care you must receive to qualify for coverage, and is there any way to raise the cap on the maximum amount of care you can receive?

Good questions.

Let's look at the minimum amount of required care first. You must receive skilled care at least once every 60 days to qualify for Medicare coverage. If you need skilled care at home less frequently than once every 60 days, you will only qualify if your less frequent need for care is "medically predictable." For example, if you are on a medication regimen, and must be seen by a skilled nurse once every 3 months to make sure you are continuing to respond to treatment, you should still qualify for coverage.

Now the maximum. Medicare will cover as many as 8 hours a day, 7 days a week, of home care services, but only for a finite and predictable period of time. Specifically, Medicare will pay for up to 56 hours a week of home care services for up to 21 days. After that, Medicare coverage is limited to part-time or intermittent care.

If you receive part-time or intermittent skilled care, and otherwise qualify for coverage, Medicare should pay your home care bills *indefinitely*. No, this is not a typographical error. Medicare home care coverage can continue for an unlimited period of time, as long as the care is medically necessary.

There is a lot of confusion about this point, both within the Medicare system and among health care providers. Medicare has been known to deny home care claims based on a fictitious and arbitrary "limit on duration," and more than one hospital discharge planner has spread the rumor about a 3-, 4-, or 6-week cap on Medicare home care coverage. Don't buy it. (For information about appealing a claim denied for exceeding a limit on duration, see page 74.) Your potential Medicare home care coverage is unlimited.

Once you know you qualify for Medicare at home, see page 45 to find out what home care services Medicare will cover. Information about how much Medicare will pay toward your home care expenses can be found on page 255.

HOSPICE BENEFITS

Hospice care is provided to terminally ill patients and their families. The philosophy behind hospice care is that some terminally ill patients need relief from their pain, control of their symptoms, and emotional support, more than aggressive treatment of their medical condition.

A patient who elects to receive hospice care instead of regular Medicare benefits will be covered for the hospice services if three conditions are met:

- A doctor has certified that the patient is terminally ill.
- The hospice services are provided by a Medicare-certified hospice program.
- The patient is treated under a plan of care.

Each of these requirements is examined in turn.

Terminally Ill

A patient is terminally ill if a medical condition is expected to cause death within 6 months.

Medicare Certification

The administrator of the hospice program will be able to tell you whether the program has been approved to accept Medicare reimbursement.

Plan of Care

Within 2 days of the patient's entry into a hospice program, a team of doctors, nurses, social workers, and psychologists must develop an oral plan of care for the patient. Within 8 days of entry, a written plan of care based on the oral care plan must be signed.

To learn more about covered hospice services, see page 47. To learn about the extent of Medicare reimbursement of hospice care services, see page 52.

PART B GENERAL ELIGIBILITY RULES

Unlike Part A eligibility, eligibility for Part B is never automatic. Also, unlike Part A, there are no special eligibility requirements for particular Part B services.

If you meet the two qualifying criteria set out below, you must still pay a monthly premium to get Part B coverage (unlike Part A, where only a minority of beneficiaries pay a premium).

QUALIFYING CRITERIA

You qualify for Part B coverage if you are age 65 or over or you are disabled for 24 months, and you are a citizen of the United States or a lawful resident of the United States for at least 5 years before applying for coverage.

MONTHLY PREMIUM

If you meet the qualifying criteria, you can receive Part B coverage if you pay a monthly premium. In 1994 the premium is $41.10 a month. The amount of the premium increases each year. For the cost, you probably cannot find comparable coverage.

MEDICARE BENEFITS

WHERE TO FIND WHAT YOU NEED

- For information about hospitalization benefits covered by Medicare, see page 43.
- For information about skilled nursing facility benefits covered by Medicare, see page 44.
- For information about home health care benefits covered by Medicare, see page 45.
- For information about hospice benefits covered by Medicare, see page 47.
- For information about other medical benefits covered by Medicare, see page 48.

COVERED HOSPITALIZATION BENEFITS

To get a sense of the breadth of Medicare coverage of hospital services, let's first look at what hospital services Medicare does *not* cover:

- Private duty nurses.
- Personal luxury items (such as a television or telephone in your room).
- Private room (unless medically necessary).

Three items. That should give you some idea of what's to come. Here's the list of hospital services that *are* covered under Medicare Part A:

- A semiprivate room (two to four beds).
- Meals, including special diets.
- Routine nursing services.
- Services of staff residents, interns, and specialists (and nonstaff workers, such as psychologists and therapists, who are under contract with the hospital).
- Intensive care unit, coronary care unit, and other special care units.
- Drugs administered at the hospital (and drugs that are used on an outpatient basis if outpatient use enables the patient to be discharged earlier).
- Blood transfusions (after the first 3 pints).
- Laboratory tests and diagnostic services performed at the hospital (but if the hospital is not properly equipped, off-site testing facilities are covered).
- X-rays, radiation therapy, and other radiology services that are billed by the hospital.
- Medical supplies (such as casts, surgical dressings, and catheters).
- Use of medical equipment, such as a wheelchair (but the purchase of medical equipment is covered under Part B).
- Costs of operations (including anesthesia services) and post-operative recovery rooms.
- Rehabilitation services, including physical, speech, and occupational therapy services (that your doctor should certify in writing must be performed by qualified therapists to "maintain or restore" your functional well-being).
- Medical social services, which include social and psychological counseling and discharge planning.
- Necessary hospitalizations for dental treatment (either due to severity of the dental procedure or underlying physical condition, such as heart disease).

- Necessary hospitalizations for treatment of alcoholism and detoxification (if medical complications are likely).
- Psychiatric hospitalizations (lifetime total of 190 days of coverage).

Note: Doctors' fees incurred during a hospitalization, including the fees of surgeons and anesthesiologists that are not employed by the hospital, are covered under Medicare Part B (see page 48).

As you can see, Medicare coverage of hospital services is quite comprehensive. However, this coverage does not continue forever. There is a limit to how long you are covered for care in a hospital. The extent of your Part A hospital coverage is defined in terms of benefit periods and a lifetime reserve.

A benefit period starts the first day you enter a hospital, and ends when you are out of the hospital for 60 days in a row. During each benefit period you are entitled to 90 days of coverage in the hospital. There is no limit to the number of benefit periods you may have.

To illustrate, Jane is hospitalized from March 1 to April 15. During the hospitalization, she uses 46 of her 90 days of coverage. She is discharged, but then reenters the hospital more than 60 days after her discharge. Jane starts a new benefit period when she reenters the hospital, and gets another 90 days of coverage. If she had reentered the hospital within 60 days of her discharge, she would only have had 44 (90 minus 46) days of coverage left.

But what happens if Jane remains in the hospital for more than 90 days? Is she eligible for any additional coverage?

Yes, by dipping into her lifetime reserve. Every Medicare beneficiary is entitled to 60 reserve days of hospitalization coverage in addition to the 90 days obtained during each benefit period. These 60 additional days of coverage can be used any time during the beneficiary's lifetime, but once they are used they are not renewed.

Continuing the example, when Jane reenters the hospital after having been out for more than 60 days, she is admitted for 100 days. She uses up her 90 days of coverage and 10 days of her lifetime reserve. The next time Jane enters the hospital she may get another 90 days of coverage (if she is out of the hospital for at least 60 days), but only has 50 days of her lifetime reserve left.

SKILLED NURSING FACILITY BENEFITS

Once you are found to qualify for Medicare coverage in a skilled nursing facility (see page 34), Medicare will cover the following services:

- A semiprivate room (two to four beds in a room).
- Meals.
- Regular nursing services.

- Rehabilitation services (such as physical, speech, and occupational therapy).
- Drugs administered by the nursing home.
- Blood transfusions (after the first 3 pints).
- Medical supplies (such as casts, surgical dressings, and catheters).
- Use of appliances (such as a wheelchair).

Medicare will not cover the following SNF services, even if you otherwise qualify for coverage:

- Private duty nurses.
- Personal luxury items (such as a television, telephone, or radio in your room).
- Private room (unless medically necessary).
- Custodial care services (assistance with personal care activities, such as eating, walking, grooming, bathing, and toileting).

(Note: Doctors' fees incurred by SNF residents are covered under Part B (see page 48).

You are entitled to 100 days of coverage in a skilled nursing facility if you enter the nursing home within 30 days after being discharged from the hospital, and your hospitalization lasted at least 3 days. Once your 100 days of coverage are exhausted, you are only eligible for an additional 100 days of coverage if you reenter the hospital after you have been out of the hospital for at least 60 days, remain hospitalized for at least 3 days, and then enter the nursing home within 30 days of your hospital discharge. (See page 36 for additional information about qualifying for Medicare coverage.)

HOME HEALTH CARE BENEFITS

In the discussion about qualifying for Medicare home care coverage, you learned that you are only eligible for Medicare home care coverage if you require part-time or intermittent skilled care (see page 40). But that is not the full extent of Medicare benefits available to you at home.

As long as you receive the part-time or intermittent services of a skilled nurse, physical therapist, or speech therapist, Medicare will also cover the following services:

- Part-time home health aides.
- Occupational therapists.

- Medical social services.
- Medical supplies and equipment (80 percent of Medicare's approved charge).

Let's look briefly at each of these covered services.

HOME HEALTH AIDES (HHA)

As long as you are receiving skilled care from a nurse or therapist (physical or speech), Medicare will also cover the "reasonable and necessary" unskilled services a home health aide (HHA) provides. At most, Medicare will cover a total of 35 hours of combined nursing, therapy, and HHA services. Medicare will not pay for the services of an HHA unless you also require some type of skilled care.

Medicare will only cover HHA services that aid your recovery, recuperation, or treatment. If the services of an HHA are not related to a medical illness or injury, they will probably not be covered. For example, an HHA who helps you with a prescribed exercise routine or assists you with your medication regimen should be covered. Similarly, an HHA who does light housework around your home while your surgical wound heals should be covered. However, an HHA who performs general household chores or personal care services for you will rarely be covered, even if you require assistance getting dressed in the morning, carrying bundles home from the market, or sweeping your floor. Medicare will pay for an HHA only when your need for an HHA is medically indicated.

OCCUPATIONAL THERAPISTS

The goal of occupational therapy is to help patients regain their independence following an illness or injury. If you have lost the ability to care for your personal needs, an occupational therapist will teach you new ways to perform your daily activities. For example, if your right side is paralyzed by a stroke, an occupational therapist can teach you how to dress yourself using only your left arm.

MEDICAL SOCIAL SERVICES

Medical social services help patients overcome emotional and financial problems that stand in the way of their recovery. For example, a patient who has been neglecting personal hygiene and is becoming increasingly withdrawn can often benefit from the intervention of a medical social service worker. The worker would assess the patient's needs and make appropriate referrals to resources in the community. The patient in the example might be referred to an affordable counseling center and an adult day care program.

MEDICAL SUPPLIES AND EQUIPMENT

Medicare covers part of the cost of "durable" medical equipment. Durable medical equipment is nondisposable. A wheelchair is durable medical equipment; a bandage is not.

The two most important prerequisites to getting Medicare to pay for your medical equipment are (1) the equipment must have a medical purpose, and (2) the equipment must substantially improve your medical condition. An example shows how these requirements are applied in practice.

Imagine an asthmatic patient who breathes easier in air-conditioned rooms. Medicare will not pay for the air conditioner because the main purpose of an air conditioner is not medical. If that same asthmatic patient put in a claim for coverage of a home sauna, Medicare would probably deny the claim for coverage as well, on the grounds that the patient could derive comparable health benefits by taking a hot steamy shower. Medicare would, however, cover an oxygen tank.

Medicare never covers the following home care services:

- Round-the-clock nursing care at home.
- Homemaker and housekeeping services not connected to medical treatment.
- Prescription drugs administered at home (but drugs your doctor must administer may be covered under Part B).
- Home-delivered meals.
- Blood transfusions.
- Nutritional services.
- Transportation services.

(Note: The same home health care benefits are provided under both parts of the Medicare program. If you are covered under Part A and Part B, your home health care coverage will fall under Part A. Part B home health care coverage is only available if you are not enrolled in Part A.)

HOSPICE CARE BENEFITS

A hospice is a public agency or private organization that provides pain relief and support services to a terminally ill patient and the patient's family, either in the patient's home or at an outside facility. A hospice team usually includes doctors, nurses, homemakers, and social workers.

The hospice benefits that are covered under Part A of the Medicare program include:

- Doctors' services.
- Nursing services.
- Pain relief and symptom management drugs.
- Therapy (physical, speech, and occupational therapy).
- Home health aide and homemaker services.
- Medical social services.
- Medical supplies and equipment.
- Counseling.
- Short-term inpatient hospital care of up to 5 days.

Beneficiaries who elect hospice coverage are not covered for the general medical treatment of their terminal illness (except to the extent necessary to control pain and symptoms). For example, Medicare would not cover the chemotherapy treatments of a terminally ill cancer patient who opted to collect Medicare-covered hospice benefits. Standard Medicare benefits are only available in connection with the treatment of conditions unrelated to the terminal illness. If the terminally ill cancer patient developed pneumonia, for example, Medicare would cover the costs of treating that condition. At any time a patient can elect out of hospice care and start receiving standard Medicare coverage.

Hospice benefits can continue indefinitely, as long as the patient's doctor continues to certify that the patient is terminally ill.

OTHER MEDICAL BENEFITS

Take a seat. The list of benefits covered under Part B of the Medicare program is extensive:

- Doctors' services.
- Surgical services, including anesthesiologists, radiologists, and pathologists.
- Emergency room care.
- Laboratory work performed by a Medicare-approved laboratory.
- Diagnostic tests and procedures.
- X-rays and injections you receive in a doctor's office or as an outpatient at a hospital.
- Services of your doctor's nurses.
- Drugs administered at the hospital on an outpatient basis or at a doctor's office.

- Blood transfusions.
- Ambulatory surgical services at Medicare-approved centers.
- Outpatient physical, speech, and occupational therapy.
- Outpatient hospital care.
- Home health services (see page 39).
- Ambulance transportation services, if medically necessary.
- Medical equipment and supplies, such as body braces, pacemakers, intraocular lenses and eyeglasses after cataract surgery, casts, oxygen equipment, wheelchairs, and hospital beds.
- Prosthetic devices, such as artificial limbs and braces.
- Pneumococcal and hepatitis B vaccinations, and immunizations to prevent immediate risk of infection.
- Kidney dialysis and transplants.
- Screening PAP smear.
- Screening mammography.
- Second opinion before surgery.
- Clinical psychologist.
- Clinical social worker, in certain settings.
- Nonroutine foot care by a licensed podiatrist, such as treatment of ingrown toenails, bunion deformities, and heel spurs.
- Foot care for patients who are being treated by a medical doctor for a related condition, such as vascular disease or diabetes.

The list of noncovered medical services is also lengthy:

- Routine physical examinations.
- Routine foot care, such as the removal of corns and calluses.
- Routine dental care, such as root canal therapy, treatment of impacted teeth, and filling, removing, or replacing teeth. (With certain medical conditions, some work on the teeth and gums is covered.)
- Eye examinations for prescribing eyeglasses or contact lenses.
- Eyeglasses or contact lenses, in most cases.
- Hearing examinations for fitting hearing aids.
- Hearing aids.
- Immunizations (except if required due to injury or immediate risk of infection, and pneumococcal and hepatitis B vaccines).

- Cosmetic surgery (except if required due to injury or to improve functioning of malformed body part).
- Services received outside the United States.
- Acupuncture.
- Chiropractic services (except for manual manipulation to correct a misaligned vertebrae of the spine).
- Christian Science practitioners' services.
- Prescription drugs that need not be administered by a physician.
- Over-the-counter drugs and medicines.
- Injections that you can administer yourself (such as insulin).
- Orthopedic shoes.

Now that you know what is and is not covered under Medicare, you probably want to know: How much will all this coverage cost?

COSTS OF MEDICARE

WHERE TO FIND WHAT YOU NEED

- If you want information about Medicare premiums, see this page, below.
- If you want information about Medicare co-insurance, see page 51.
- If you want information about Medicare deductibles, see page 55.

There is truly no such thing as a free lunch. At least not when it comes to having Medicare pay your medical bills.

The amount of money you must pay for your Medicare coverage will depend on the specific coverage you receive. Your obligations to pay premiums, co-insurance, and deductibles for Medicare Parts A and B are examined below.

PREMIUM

The premium is the monthly cost of your Medicare coverage.

PART A PREMIUM

You do not have to pay any premium for Part A benefits if you are at least 65 years old and eligible for Social Security.

If you are 65, but ineligible for Social Security, you can enroll in Medicare Part A by paying a monthly premium. The 1994 premium for Part A voluntary enrollees is $245 a month.

PART B PREMIUM

In 1994 every beneficiary must pay a premium of $41.10 a month for Part B coverage.

You can pay the Part B premium directly to the Health Care Financing Administration in Washington, D.C., or have it deducted from your monthly Social Security check. It is best to have the premium deducted from your benefit check so you don't have to worry about missing a payment and losing coverage. If your coverage lapses for nonpayment, you will have to wait to reapply for coverage and may lose valuable benefits. (See page 65 for more on applying for Medicare.)

CO-INSURANCE (CO-PAYMENT)

Co-insurance is the amount of each medical bill Medicare does not cover. You must pay the co-insurance portion of each covered bill you submit to Medicare.

For example, if the co-insurance amount is $75 and the amount of your medical bill is $300, you must pay $75 of the bill before your Medicare coverage will kick in.

PART A CO-INSURANCE

The amount of the Part A co-insurance depends on the specific benefit being paid.

Hospital Bills

You do not have to pay any co-insurance for the first 60 days of each covered hospitalization. After the 60th day, however, you are responsible for paying a co-insurance. The 1994 co-insurance rates are:

Day 1–60 of hospitalization $0

Day 61–90 of hospitalization $174/day

Day 91–150 of hospitalization $348/day

If you are hospitalized for 70 days, for example, your total co-insurance obligation will be $1,740 ($174 per day for the 10 days between days 61 and 70), assuming the daily hospital rate exceeds $174.

Skilled Nursing Facility Bills

You do not have to pay any co-insurance for the first 20 days of care you receive in a skilled nursing facility. After the 20th day, however, there is a co-insurance. The amounts of the co-insurance in 1994 are:

Day 1–20 of nursing facility stay $0
Day 21–100 of nursing facility stay $87/day

Home Health Care Bills

There is never any co-insurance.

Hospice

Two co-insurance obligations are associated with hospice benefits.

1. The beneficiary must pay 5 percent of the cost of drugs for the terminal illness, or $5 for each prescription, whichever is less.
2. The beneficiary must pay up to 5 percent of the cost of each day of inpatient respite care. Inpatient respite care pays for up to 5 days of inpatient hospital care for the terminally ill patient to provide temporary relief to the full-time caregiver.

PART B CO-INSURANCE

In all cases, you must pay a co-insurance equal to 20 percent of Medicare's "approved charge." Medicare's approved charge is the fee that Medicare assigns to each type of medical service. The approved charge is supposed to reflect the average cost of the medical service in different geographic regions of the country.

Unfortunately, Medicare's approved charges rarely reflect the actual cost of receiving medical care; they are almost always lower than the actual charges. This means that Medicare beneficiaries usually end up paying their doctor some amount in addition to the 20 percent co-insurance, unless the doctor agrees to accept Medicare's approved charge as the entire fee. Such a doctor is said to take assignment. Doctors who always take assignment are called participating providers.

A doctor who "takes Medicare" does not necessarily take Medicare assignment. The only way to know whether or not a doctor will accept Medicare's approved fee as payment in full is to ask.

Patients of providers that take assignment only have to pay the 20 percent co-insurance (plus the annual Part B deductible). They do not have to pay the difference between Medicare's approved charge and the doctor's actual charge. A doctor who does not take assignment, and who bills Medicare patients an amount in excess of the Medicare-approved amount, engages in a practice called balance billing.

Assume, for example, your doctor charges $300 for a procedure. The Medicare-approved charge is $100. If the doctor takes assignment, you only have to pay 20 percent of the approved charge, or $20. A doctor who does not take assignment will balance bill you for $200, the difference between the approved charge and the actual charge, in addition to the $20 co-insurance payment.

Before January 1, 1991, there were no limits on balance billing. Physicians who did not take assignment could charge their Medicare patients whatever they wanted. This changed with the passage of a federal law that caps the fees these doctors can charge their Medicare patients. The cap has dropped every year since passage of the legislation. In 1991, doctors could not charge their Medicare patients more than 25 percent over the Medicare-approved rate for most services. This percentage went down to 20 percent on January 1, 1992, and bottomed out at 15 percent on January 1, 1993.

Unfortunately, despite the law, many doctors continue to charge their Medicare patients in excess of the legal limits. Sometimes the doctor's ignorance is to blame, other times a malfunctioning computer chip is at fault. Your doctor is bound by the legal limits on balance billing, even if you agree in writing to pay some additional fee for your doctor's services.

The federal Health Care Financing Administration (HCFA), which oversees Medicare, has historically been lax in enforcing the law limiting balance billing. As a result, thousands of Medicare beneficiaries have been overcharged for medical care.

To determine the maximum fee your doctor is permitted to charge, multiply the Medicare approved fee by 1.15 (115 percent). For example, if the Medicare-approved charge for a procedure is $100, a non-assignment doctor cannot charge a Medicare patient more than $115. This means that the beneficiary's out-of-pocket cost is limited to $35 (the 20 percent co-insurance—$20, plus the difference between the approved charge and the doctor's actual fee—$15).

You can learn the maximum fees doctors in your area are permitted to charge Medicare beneficiaries by calling the private insurance company that administers Part B Medicare claims in your area (the Medicare carrier; see Appendix 3). To find out the maximum permitted charge for a particular medical service, give the person who answers the phone the following information:

- Your doctor's name.
- The procedure code for the specific medical service in question (which you can usually get from your doctor).

If your doctor does not know the procedure code, you will have to wait until you receive your Explanation of Medicare Benefits (EOMB) from Medicare to see if you have been overcharged by your doctor.

The EOMB tells you how your claims for Medicare coverage have been resolved. Most carriers now include on the EOMB an indication of the maximum fee allowed under federal law. Does your doctor's fee exceed that limit? If it does, you may have an overcharge on your hands.

The first thing you should do upon learning that you have been overcharged is contact your doctor. If your doctor refuses to refund your money promptly, notify the Medicare carrier in your area (see Appendix 3). The carrier will give your doctor 30 days either to refund your money or to appeal the carrier's decision. The carrier will also start monitoring your doctor's billing practices to check for additional overcharges, and to see that timely refunds are made.

Some states have gone further than the federal law in limiting charges to Medicare beneficiaries. For example, non-participating doctors in Maine, Massachusetts, Pennsylvania, and Rhode Island are not permitted to charge their Medicare beneficiaries any amount in excess of the 20 percent co-insurance payment. New York's limit on balance billing is 10 percent of the Medicare-approved fee. Connecticut, Vermont, and Ohio ban any balance billing for low-income Medicare beneficiaries. The EOMB will not reflect the state's restriction on balance billing.

The effectiveness of state caps on balance billing is often compromised by the absence of any enforcement mechanism. In many states, the only way to know if your doctor's bill exceeds the applicable limit in your state is to wait for your EOMB, and then calculate the maximum charge on your own. There will be no other indication of overcharges on the EOMB.

When you use only participating providers, or providers that take assignment, you eliminate the risk of an overcharge. You also save money on your medical bills. Since participating and assignment doctors cannot charge even a penny above Medicare's approved rate, you never have to pay more than 20 percent of Medicare's approved charge (your co-insurance).

Another bonus of using participating and assignment doctors is convenience. You can leave your wallet at home because these doctors don't require payment at the time of treatment. They submit a claim for payment directly to Medicare, and then you receive notice from Medicare telling you how much you owe your doctor (for your deductible and co-insurance). Even though the law also requires nonparticipating and nonassignment doctors to submit a claim to Medicare on your behalf, these doctors are permitted to request immediate payment from you—and they usually do. You must then await reimbursement from Medicare.

The primary disadvantage of seeing only participating and assignment doctors is that your freedom to choose your health care providers is limited. Not every doctor accepts Medicare's approved rates. There are, however, large numbers of qualified physicians who do accept Medicare's approved charges as payment in full. You can find participating providers in your area by referring to the "Medicare-

Participating Physician/Supplier Directory," which is available from any of the following sources:

- Your local Medicare carrier (see Appendix 3).
- A local Social Security office (call 800-772-1213 for the telephone number of the office nearest you).
- State unit on aging (see Appendix 1).
- Senior citizens' organizations.

If you have a longstanding relationship with a nonparticipating doctor, or are eager to get the opinion of a nonparticipating doctor who is highly recommended, ask the doctor to accept Medicare (take assignment) in your case. You have absolutely nothing to lose by asking and, who knows, you may get lucky! Many doctors who do not always participate in Medicare will accept assignment in certain cases.

DEDUCTIBLE

The deductible is the amount you must spend on your bills before Medicare coverage begins. For example, if the deductible is $500, and you have hospital bills totaling $1,500, you must pay the first $500 before you can look to Medicare for coverage.

The deductible is not a one-shot deal. For Part A hospital coverage, you have to pay a new deductible each benefit period. (Benefit periods are explained on page 44.) For Part B coverage, you have to pay a new deductible each year.

PART A DEDUCTIBLE

The amount of the Part A deductible depends on the specific benefit being paid.

- Hospital bills: $696 per benefit period in 1994.
- Skilled nursing facility bills: no deductible.
- Home health care bills: no deductible.
- Hospice bills: no deductible.

PART B DEDUCTIBLE

You must pay an annual deductible for Part B coverage. In 1994 the deductible is $100 a year.

QUESTIONS, EXPLANATIONS, AND EXAMPLES

As an older American, you may have a number of questions concerning your Medicare coverage. Are you entitled to benefits? If so, which medical services will Medicare pay for? Will your Medicare coverage cost you anything? What medical expenses are your responsibility?

The scenarios that follow will help you use the information in this chapter to analyze Medicare coverage and compute out-of-pocket costs.

HOSPITALIZATION SCENARIO

When you turned 62, you started collecting Social Security retirement benefits. At age 65, you received a Medicare card in the mail.

On an icy day in December you take a nasty fall and break your hip. You are hospitalized for 2 weeks in a semiprivate room. The only luxuries you allow yourself are a telephone and a private duty nurse for the first 2 days.

Soon after your discharge, you develop an infection in your surgical site. You ignore the pain for a couple of months, hoping it will go away. Unfortunately, it only gets worse. Finally, after 3 months, you make an appointment with your doctor. Your doctor scolds you for waiting so long, and immediately admits you to the hospital. The infection has spread, and you must remain hospitalized for 150 days.

ARE YOU COVERED UNDER MEDICARE?

Yes. When you turned 65 you automatically qualified for Medicare Part A coverage. You did not even have to file an application because you were already receiving Social Security retirement benefits. If you also started paying a monthly premium, you qualified for Part B coverage as well.

WHAT WILL MEDICARE PAY FOR?

Medicare will pay for every day of both hospital stays. Your first stay was well within the 90 days of coverage you are entitled to receive during each benefit period. Your second stay was covered because you were out of the hospital for more than 60 days after your first discharge. This means that you qualified for another 90 days of coverage upon readmission. The full 150 days of your second stay were covered because, after you exhausted your 90 days of coverage, you used your 60-day lifetime reserve. For all future hospitalizations, however, you will only be covered for up to 90 days. Your lifetime reserve will not be renewed.

Most of the major expenses you incurred during your hospital stays will be covered by Medicare Part A. These include your semiprivate room, meals, regular nursing services, drugs provided by the hospital, lab tests, X-rays, casts, use of a wheelchair, operating room costs, and physical therapy. Your doctor's fees will be covered under Medicare Part B.

WHAT ARE YOUR OUT-OF-POCKET EXPENSES?

You must pay for the telephone and private nurse with your own money. You are also obligated to pay two Part A inpatient hospital deductibles of $696 each. You owe two deductibles because you had two benefit periods (since you were out of the hospital for more than 60 days between hospitalizations). Finally, you are responsible for some co-insurance payments during your second hospitalization. For the 61st through 90th day of the hospitalization, you owe $174 per day. And for days 91 to 150 (your lifetime reserve), you owe $348 per day.

SKILLED NURSING FACILITY SCENARIO

At age 72, while still working as a lawyer, you have a stroke. You are admitted to a hospital, where you remain for several weeks. The severity of the stroke has left you unable to walk, dress yourself, or feed yourself. You, your family, and the hospital staff agree that you cannot return home until you complete several months of intensive physical therapy. The hospital discharges you to a nursing home.

You are in the nursing home for 3 months, with a telephone and a television in your room. During those 3 months you see a physical therapist twice a day. In addition, an aide helps you get in and out of bed, get dressed in the morning, and eat your meals.

After 3 months you are well enough to return home.

ARE YOU COVERED UNDER MEDICARE?

Yes, as long as you filed a Medicare application with Social Security. Since you did not start collecting Social Security retirement benefits at age 65, you were not automatically enrolled in Medicare Part A. Skilled nursing facility benefits are provided under Part A of the Medicare program.

WHAT WILL MEDICARE PAY FOR?

Every day of your stay in the skilled nursing facility will be covered by Medicare. You are entitled to up to 100 days of care in a skilled nursing facility as long as you entered the nursing facility within 30 days of a covered hospital stay of more than 3 days in duration, and you required skilled rehabilitation services in the nursing facility on a daily basis.

Your semiprivate room, meals, regular nursing services, rehabilitation services, drugs administered by the nursing home, and walker will all be covered by Medicare.

WHAT ARE YOUR OUT-OF-POCKET EXPENSES?

You must pay for the television, the telephone, and the aide who provided you with custodial care services.

During days 21 through 100 of your institutionalization you must also pay a daily co-insurance of $87.

HOME HEALTH CARE SCENARIO

You are 75 years old and you find yourself increasingly short of breath. Your doctor says you require immediate heart surgery.

After a normal post-operative recovery, you are discharged home. Your physician instructs the hospital social worker to arrange for a nurse to come to your house one hour a week for 3 weeks to check your surgical scar, a rehabilitation therapist to come in daily to teach you some exercises, and a home health aide for 3 hours a day for 3 weeks to monitor your vital signs and assist you with your exercises. You are also set up with a hospital bed (to keep your head elevated) and an oxygen tank at home. The doctor advises you to use a walker, and not to leave the house by yourself.

ARE YOU COVERED UNDER MEDICARE?

Yes. Even if you kept working past normal retirement age and never applied for Medicare, you would have started collecting Social Security retirement benefits at age 70. This would have automatically qualified you for Medicare Part A coverage.

WHAT WILL MEDICARE PAY FOR?

Medicare will pay some of your home care expenses because you qualify for coverage. You are confined to your home (since you are unable to leave the home without assistance), your physician set up a home health plan for you, and you require part-time skilled nursing or therapy services.

The Medicare-covered services include the skilled nursing and therapy services, as well as the part-time unskilled services of a home health aide. Part of the costs of the hospital bed, oxygen tank, and walker is also covered.

WHAT ARE YOUR OUT-OF-POCKET EXPENSES?

The only expense you have is a 20 percent co-insurance for the medical equipment.

OUTPATIENT CARE SCENARIOS

SCENARIO #1

You have had a headache for 3 days, and decide to get it checked out by your doctor. Your physician charges $55 for an office visit. The Medicare approved fee for an office visit in your area is $50 (within the cap on balance billing). Your doctor does not participate in Medicare, and will not take assignment in your case. You have already paid your Part B annual deductible of $100. Medicare will pay your physician $32 (80 percent of $50). You will be billed $23 (the 20 percent co-insurance—$18, plus the difference between Medicare's approved fee and your physician's actual fee—$5).

SCENARIO #2

Your spouse has been after you to see your internist for a general check-up. You finally give in. While you're at it, you decide to make an appointment with your dentist to look at a tooth that's been bugging you, and your ophthalmologist to see if you need a new prescription for your glasses. Medicare Part B does not pay for any of these services.

SCENARIO #3

While in line at the supermarket, you suddenly experience an excruciating stabbing pain in your lower abdomen. You cry out. Someone calls an ambulance, and you are rushed to the nearest emergency room. Luckily, you are paid up on your Part B coverage since the premium has been automatically deducted from your Social Security check. Medicare pays 80 percent of the approved emergency room bill. You pay the remaining 20 percent, plus your $100 annual deductible.

SUPPLEMENTAL (MEDIGAP) INSURANCE

Private insurance is available to pay the co-insurance, deductible, and premiums Medicare beneficiaries would otherwise have to pay for with their own money. These policies that fill in the gaps in Medicare's coverage are appropriately called Medigap policies.

Federal law requires every state to offer ten standard Medigap policies. Each of the ten policies must provide certain basic benefits; beyond that, the states are free to offer different combinations of benefits. The basic benefits include coverage of the Part A deductible, the Part A co-insurance, and the Part B co-insurance. Other coverage options include payment of the Part B deductible, emergency care abroad, doctors' fees in excess of Medicare-approved charges, preventive care, and prescription drugs.

Some states offer a special type of Medigap insurance called Medicare SELECT.[2] Beneficiaries insured under a Medicare SELECT policy pay 15 percent to 20 percent less than the cost of traditional Medigap policies, but must agree to see only specified doctors called preferred providers. A directory of preferred providers is given to the insured beneficiaries. A beneficiary who sees a doctor outside the network of preferred providers is still covered by Medicare, but is not entitled to coverage under the Medicare SELECT policy.

For more on Medicare Supplemental Insurance, see Chapter 4.

COMMON MEDICARE QUESTIONS AND ANSWERS

WHAT IS THE DIFFERENCE BETWEEN MEDICARE AND MEDICAID?

Medicare is a federal health insurance program that covers almost everybody age 65 or older, regardless of income. Medicaid is a joint federal-state medical assistance program that provides health benefits to certain groups of financially needy people.

WHAT IS THE DIFFERENCE BETWEEN MEDICARE PART A AND PART B?

Medicare Part A, the hospital insurance program, covers inpatient hospital care, skilled nursing facility care, home health care, and hospice care. Medicare Part B, the medical insurance program, pays for doctors' services, outpatient hospital services, therapy services, home health care services, and medical supplies.

HOW MUCH DOES MEDICARE COST?

In 1994 every Medicare beneficiary must pay $41.10 a year to enroll in Part B. A small number of beneficiaries pay a $245 premium for Medicare Part A.

---

[2] Medicare SELECT is, or soon should be, available in Alabama, Arizona, California, Florida, Indiana, Kentucky, Michigan, Minnesota, Missouri, North Dakota, Ohio, Oregon, Texas, and Wisconsin.

Medicare beneficiaries must also pay some deductibles and co-insurance payments. In 1994 these amounted to $696 inpatient hospital deductible, $174 co-insurance payment for days 61 through 90 of an inpatient hospitalization, $87 co-insurance payment for days 21 through 100 in a skilled nursing facility, $100 a year deductible for Part B benefits, and 20 percent of Medicare's approved charge for Part B services.

IF YOU ARE IN AND OUT OF THE HOSPITAL SEVERAL TIMES A YEAR, WILL MEDICARE PAY ALL YOUR HOSPITAL BILLS?

Medicare pays for 90 days of inpatient hospital care during each benefit period. You start a new benefit period every time you enter the hospital after having been out of the hospital for at least 60 days. If you reenter the hospital within 60 days of a prior hospitalization discharge, your 90 days of coverage are reduced by the duration of the prior hospitalization. You also get a one-time use of 60 additional days of hospital coverage (a lifetime reserve). Once you use these 60 days, they are not renewed.

ARE THERE ANY RESTRICTIONS ON WHICH DOCTORS YOU SEE?

No, but a doctor who takes assignment will accept Medicare's approved charge as full payment of the fee. You will only be responsible for 20 percent of Medicare's approved charge (the Part B co-insurance). If your doctor does not take assignment, you will have to pay the difference between Medicare's approved charge and your doctor's fee, plus the 20 percent Part B co-insurance. However, there are limits to what doctors who do not take assignment can charge Medicare beneficiaries.

HOW DO YOU GET MEDICARE TO PAY YOUR MEDICAL BILLS?

When you first enter a hospital or skilled nursing facility, or sign up with a home health care agency, present your Medicare card. If your care is covered, the hospital, nursing facility, or home care agency will bill Medicare directly for your services. You will only have to pay your deductible, co-insurance, and fees for any services not covered by Medicare. When you see a doctor, you will have to pay your 20 percent co-insurance if your doctor takes assignment; otherwise, you will probably have to pay the doctor's entire bill and wait for reimbursement from Medicare. Your doctor is supposed to file a Medicare claim for you, whether or not the doctor takes assignment. (Getting Medicare to pay your bills is covered in greater detail in Chapter 3.)

HOW CAN YOU KEEP TRACK OF WHICH MEDICAL BILLS HAVE ALREADY BEEN PAID BY MEDICARE, WHICH BILLS YOU HAVE TO PAY, AND WHICH BILLS YOU HAVE TO SUBMIT TO YOUR PRIVATE INSURANCE CARRIER?

If you would like to hire someone to help organize, file, and track your health insurance claims, you need a claims assistance professional. For information about this new service, you can request the free publication "What is a Claims Assistance Professional" from:

National Association of Claims Assistance Professionals, Inc.
4724 Florence Avenue
Downers Grove, IL 60515

WHOM DO YOU CONTACT FOR INFORMATION ABOUT MEDICARE?

If you have general questions about Medicare Part A, you can call the Beneficiary Services Bureau at 315-448-7500. If you would like to receive a record of Medicare Part A payments made on your behalf, call 315-474-7100.

If you have a question about whether a particular service is covered under Part B, or the extent of coverage, or when you can expect to be reimbursed on a Part B claim, you need to call the Medicare carrier that serves your area. The names and addresses of Medicare carriers and the areas they serve are listed in Appendix 3.

ℹ️ *For more information*

U.S. Department of Health and Human Services
Health Care Financing Administration
6325 Security Boulevard
Baltimore, MD 21207

For the general rules that govern the Medicare program, request "The Medicare Handbook," Publication Number HCFA 10050.

HCFA Medicare Information Hotline
800-638-6833

Call for information about general Medicare issues, Medigap insurance, second opinions for surgery, and to report Medicare fraud.

AARP/MMAP
601 E Street, N.W.
Washington, DC 20049
202-434-2277

Call or write for information on the nearest Medicare/Medicaid Assistance Program.

United Seniors Health Cooperative
1331 H Street, N.W., 5th Floor
Washington, DC 20005
202-393-6222

For a $10 annual membership fee, you receive a newsletter and free counseling on Medicare and Medigap insurance.

BACK TO SELMA

We started by dividing all of Selma's papers into two piles. The pile on the right involved Medicare Part A, the pile to the left, Part B. Within each pile we separated claim forms, bills, Medicare correspondence, and miscellaneous notes.

We tackled the hospital bills first. Since the hospital submitted bills for Selma's care directly to Medicare for payment, Selma only had to pay the hospital her Part A deductible, co-insurance for part of her stay, and fees for her uncovered services.

Notices from the home care agency were easy. The agency had submitted claims for payment directly to Medicare. Since Selma did not owe any balance on her Part A deductible (which she paid in full to the hospital), and did not have to pay any co-insurance, she only had to pay for the homemaker who had helped her with some household chores and 20 percent of the cost of a wheelchair.

By the time Selma left my office, she had a neat manila folder tucked under her arm with the bills that remained to be paid paper-clipped together.

3.
MAXIMIZING MEDICARE BENEFITS

At age 68, Jack was still working as a computer technician. He didn't know how much longer he could continue to work, however, because his Parkinson's disease was worsening.

Jack had started receiving Medicare Part A coverage when he turned 65, but had declined Part B coverage because he was still covered under his employer's group health plan.

When Jack came to see me, his medical expenses had started to mount. He had bills from his doctor, a hospital, and a nursing home, and wanted to make sure that he was not losing out on any Medicare benefits.

Maximizing your Medicare benefits often means compensating for flaws in the Medicare system. You don't want to be the victim of:

- An erroneous denial of coverage made by an overworked Medicare employee.
- A miscalculation of benefits made by a Medicare worker who does not fully understand the relevant regulations.
- An unduly restrictive interpretation of a rule made by Medicare officials who have been repeatedly reprimanded by the federal judiciary.

You will not fall victim to the Medicare system if you understand your rights as a Medicare beneficiary. To get the most out of the Medicare insurance program, you must know:

- How to apply for coverage.
- How to collect your benefits.
- How to appeal a denial of Medicare coverage.

By providing you with answers to these important questions, this chapter will help you get every last red cent of Medicare coverage coming to you.

HOW DO YOU APPLY FOR MEDICARE?

As discussed in Chapter 2, there are two parts to the Medicare program: Part A, which includes coverage of inpatient hospital care, skilled nursing facility care, home health care, and hospice care, and Part B, which includes coverage of doctors' bills and other outpatient services. The eligibility rules for each part of the Medicare program are also explained in Chapter 2. Assuming you are eligible for coverage, this section goes over the rules on how to apply for coverage.

Part A rules about filing applications are different than the rules that apply to Part B. The rules for both parts of the Medicare program are covered in this section.

APPLYING FOR PART A MEDICARE BENEFITS

WHO MUST FILE AN APPLICATION?

Whether you have to file an application for Part A Medicare benefits depends on your status.

You do *not* have to file an application for Part A Medicare benefits if:

- You are a "normal" retiree who retires at age 65 and starts collecting Social Security or Railroad Retirement benefits. Your application for retirement benefits will serve as an application for Medicare coverage. You will automatically be enrolled in Medicare Part A as of the month of your 65th birthday.
- You are an early retiree who retires before age 65. Your Medicare benefits will automatically start when you reach age 65.
- You are a disability retiree who cannot work due to a disability and collects Social Security disability benefits. Your Medicare benefits will automatically start after you have been eligible for disability benefits for 24 months.

You must file an application for Part A Medicare benefits at your local Social Security office if:

- You are a late retiree who continues to work after age 65.
- You are a government retiree who has left government service.
- You are a voluntary enrollee who is paying a premium for Part A coverage (see page 33 for the definition of voluntary enrollee).
- You, your spouse, or your dependent child has permanent kidney failure.

HOW DO YOU APPLY FOR PART A COVERAGE?

Before you do anything, call or visit your local Social Security office (the address and number will be listed in the blue pages of your telephone book in the U.S. Government section), or call Social Security's toll-free number (800-772-1213) to schedule an appointment at your local office. You will need to complete Form SSA-18F5 to start your Part A application rolling. You will also eventually need to submit proof of your age, Social Security number, and statement of the previous year's income. (See page 33 for a more detailed discussion of the application documentation requirements.)

WHEN SHOULD YOU FILE AN APPLICATION FOR PART A BENEFITS?

When an elephant sits on it. Oops. That's when it's time to buy a new fence.

But seriously, keep one eye on the calendar when you approach your 65th birthday. If you will not automatically qualify for Medicare when you turn 65 (based on your receipt of Social Security or Railroad Retirement benefits), you should file your Medicare Part A application 3 months before you blow out the candles on your 65th birthday. (Penalties for late enrollment are covered in the section on Part B applications.)

Why the rush? Because you never know when illness may strike. If you find yourself laid up in the hospital with a broken hip before you get around to filing your Medicare Part A application, you'll also need treatment of the multiple contusions you get from kicking yourself for being a procrastinator.

If you are only a moderate procrastinator, as opposed to a pathological procrastinator, you may be in luck. Retroactive Medicare coverage is available for up to 6 months before the month you file your Medicare application (assuming you are otherwise eligible during those months). This means that you will be covered for the hospital care you receive at age 65½, even if you don't apply for Part A until just before your 66th birthday. If you delay applying for more than 6 months, however, your luck will run out.

WHEN DOES YOUR MEDICARE ELIGIBILITY BEGIN?

A few pages ago you learned that you become eligible for Part A coverage at age 65. Not exactly.

You actually become eligible for Part A coverage on the first day of the month you turn 65. That's even better. If your day of nativity is June 30, you can get Medicare coverage as of June 1 (assuming you qualify automatically or file a timely application).

APPLYING FOR PART B MEDICARE BENEFITS

WHO MUST FILE AN APPLICATION?

Whether you have to apply for Part B Medicare benefits also depends on your status. You do not have to file an application for Medicare Part B benefits if you are 65 or older and automatically eligible for Part A Medicare benefits (see page 33). Your application for Social Security or Railroad Retirement benefits will be treated as an application for Medicare Part B coverage. The monthly Part B premium will start to be deducted from your Social Security or Railroad Retirement check. If you decline Part B coverage at age 65, either because you have other insurance or because you do not want to pay the Part B premium, you can enroll in Part B at a later time by filing an application. (But you really should purchase Part B coverage at age 65 unless you're already covered through your employer. Dollar for dollar, you probably won't find cheaper coverage.)

You must file an application for Part B Medicare benefits at your local Social Security office if you are 65 or older and not automatically eligible for Part A Medicare benefits.

HOW DO YOU APPLY FOR PART B COVERAGE?

You apply for Part B the same way you apply for Part A (see page 66). The only difference is that you need to complete Form SSA-4040.

WHEN SHOULD YOU FILE AN APPLICATION FOR PART B BENEFITS?

Proper timing of your application for Medicare Part B is crucial. A poorly timed application can mean the unnecessary loss of medical coverage. What are the best and worst times to file your Part B application?

The best time to file your application is during the period that starts 3 months before your 65th birthday, and ends with the month of your 65th birthday. For example, if your birthday is September 25 (like mine), you should file your application anytime between June 1 and August 31. If you file within this period, your Medicare coverage will begin on the first day of your birthday month (September 1, for me).

Your second best option is to file your application in the month of your 65th birthday. Since Medicare needs some time to process your application, coverage will probably not start for at least a month. (Continuing the example, a September application would get me coverage in October.)

Your third best option is to file your application within 3 months after the end of the month in which you turn 65. If you file at that time, the earliest your Medicare coverage will begin is 2 months after the month of your application. (Beating the example to death, if I apply in October, my coverage should begin in December. A November application will get me covered as of February, and a December application means my coverage will start in March.)

Your worst option is to file your application during the "general enrollment period." If you do not file your Part A or B application during the 3-month period before or after your birthday month, you must wait for a general enrollment period to apply. The general enrollment period runs from January 1 through March 31 each year. Whenever you apply during the general enrollment period, you are covered as of July 1 of the year you apply. (Returning to the example one last time: December comes and goes, and I do not file my Part B application. When the general enrollment period begins on January 1, I apply for Part B. I must wait until July 1 for my coverage to start.)

If you use this worst option and apply during the general enrollment period, waiting until July 1 for your Part A or B coverage to begin may not even be the worst of your problems. You may also be penalized for delaying your application by being charged a higher monthly premium.

The amount of the penalty will be a 10 percent higher monthly premium for each full year (starting to run from the first day of your birthday month) you could have applied for Part A or B but didn't. For example, if you turned 65 on June 15, 1992, but did not apply for Part B until January 1994, you will be penalized for a one-year delay (from June 1992 to June 1993). Your monthly Part B premium will equal the 1994 premium ($41.10) plus 10 percent of the premium ($4.10), or $45.20.

There are only two circumstances under which you can avoid this penalty. First, if you delay applying for Part A because you are covered under a prepaid health plan (such as a health maintenance organization or competitive medical plan), you can sign up for premium Part A up to 8 months after your plan coverage has ended.

Second, if you delay applying for Part B benefits because you are covered under a group health insurance plan through your employer, you can put off filing your Part B application up to 7 months after the termination of your employment or group coverage, whichever happens first. This is called the Special Enrollment Period.

HOW DO YOU COLLECT BENEFITS?

WHERE TO FIND WHAT YOU NEED

- The procedures you must follow to collect your Medicare benefits will depend on the coverage you are seeking. Here is where to find the claims procedures that apply to specific types of medical bills:

HOSPITAL BILLS

There are four steps to obtaining Medicare coverage of your hospital bills:

1. Presenting your Medicare card.
2. Undergoing review.
3. Receiving your coverage determination.
4. Appealing your coverage determination.

PRESENTING YOUR MEDICARE CARD

When you enter a hospital, show your Medicare card to the admissions personnel. This will trigger a review of your Medicare eligibility.

UNDERGOING REVIEW

An initial determination of whether your hospital services are covered by Medicare will be made by the hospital's utilization review committee (URC) and/or the federal government's peer review organization (PRO).

RECEIVING YOUR COVERAGE DETERMINATION

Usually within 2 or 3 days of your admission, the URC or PRO will notify you of its coverage determination. Insist on getting this decision in writing.

If you are *not* notified in writing that Medicare will not cover your care, don't do anything. The hospital will submit your bills directly to the local Medicare intermediary (the insurance company under contract to pay the covered bills of Medicare beneficiaries). If the intermediary approves the claim, you will only have to pay the Medicare deductible, co-insurance, and fees for any hospital services Medicare does not cover (see page 34.)

If the intermediary does not approve the claim on the grounds that the care you received was not "medically necessary and appropriate," you still may not have to pay your outstanding hospital bills under something called the waiver of liability.

The waiver of liability applies only if you do not receive written notice of noncoverage from the URC or PRO. With the waiver of liability, you are not required to pay any medical bills you had no reason to know Medicare would not cover. Only if the URC or PRO alerted you in writing that Medicare coverage would probably *not* be available do you have to dip into your own pockets to pay your uncovered medical bills.

To take advantage of the waiver of liability, you must steadfastly refuse to pay the hospital bills, no matter how much pressure you get from the hospital. Don't just ignore the hospital bills. Write the hospital a letter that makes the following points:

- "I am refusing to pay the enclosed bills under the waiver of liability provision that is described in the Medicare Handbook." (Include a copy of the relevant text if possible. See page 62 for information on obtaining the handbook.)
- "I never received written notice from the hospital or my doctor that my care would not be covered by Medicare."
- "I had every reason to believe that the services I received in the hospital were appropriate and necessary for the treatment of my medical condition."
- "Since I could not reasonably have been expected to know that Medicare would not cover my hospital care, I am not responsible for paying these bills."

Make sure you include your Medicare number (from your Medicare card) and your account number (from the hospital bills) at the top of the letter.

If the bills keep coming, as they probably will, continue returning them, unpaid, with a copy of your letter. After you have received about three past due notices from the hospital, call the hospital billing office. If the bills don't stop, call the Medicare intermediary (Appendix 2), or seek out professional assistance (see page 482).

If you receive written notice from the hospital that Medicare coverage probably will *not* be available, everything changes. Then your priority is to get an official Medicare determination. How do you get an official Medicare determination?

1. Look at the written notice of noncoverage. Who issued it? If it comes from the hospital URC, proceed to Step #2. If it comes from the Medicare PRO, proceed to Step #3.

2. A decision from the hospital URC is not an official Medicare determination. You have the right to get an official Medicare determination by having your claim submitted to the Medicare PRO. The exact procedure you must follow depends on which of the following two URC notices of noncoverage you receive:

    - A notice of noncoverage that states that your physician agrees with the hospital's determination. You must request

PRO review by noon of the first workday after you receive this type of notice, or you become responsible for your hospital bills. If you lose the appeal, you must start paying for your hospital care as of noon on the day after the PRO has completed its review. With this type of notice, it is imperative that you enlist your doctor's cooperation. Unless you can convince your doctor that you need more time in the hospital, your chances of prevailing are slim.

• A notice of noncoverage that states that your physician disagrees with the hospital's determination. Immediately request PRO review through the hospital's patient advocacy office. The hospital must request PRO review on your behalf, and then so notify you in writing. The PRO will then have 3 working days to make a decision on your claim. During these 3 days you cannot be discharged from the hospital or billed for your hospital care. If your claim is denied, you will become liable for your hospital bills as of the third day after you receive notice of the PRO's decision.

(Note: If you decide not to appeal either of these URC notices of noncoverage, you can still remain in the hospital for 2 "grace" days at no cost to you.)

3. If the initial notice of noncoverage comes from the PRO, not the URC, you already have an official Medicare determination. You will become personally responsible for your hospital bills as of the third day after the date you receive the notice of noncoverage (Friday, if you receive the notice on Tuesday).

You receive a notice of noncoverage on Wednesday. Wait until sometime before noon on Thursday to request PRO review. If you request PRO review on Wednesday, you can lose out on a day of hospital coverage.

APPEALING YOUR COVERAGE DETERMINATION

You are ready to start your appeal when you have an official Medicare determination from the PRO (either an initial decision or a URC decision that the PRO has reviewed). For information about reconsideration, the first level of appeal, see page 82.

SKILLED NURSING FACILITY BILLS

There are four steps to obtaining Medicare coverage of your skilled nursing facility bills:

1. Presenting your Medicare card.
2. Undergoing review.
3. Receiving your coverage determination.
4. Appealing your coverage determination.

PRESENTING YOUR MEDICARE CARD

When you are admitted to a skilled nursing facility, present your Medicare card at the admissions office. Admissions personnel will arrange for a review of your Medicare eligibility.

If you apply for Medicare coverage of your stay in a skilled nursing facility, the law prevents the nursing home from charging you any money unless and until Medicare denies your claim for coverage. Unfortunately, this law is repeatedly and blatantly violated by the nursing home industry. In many areas of the country, the demand for nursing home beds so far exceeds the supply that consumers are reluctant to make waves by asserting this right. If you want to file a complaint against a nursing home that is charging you cash up front, despite your pending Medicare claim, contact your local long-term care ombudsman. This number should be available from your local department of aging.

UNDERGOING REVIEW

The SNF conducts the initial review of your eligibility for Medicare coverage in the facility.

RECEIVING YOUR COVERAGE DETERMINATION

Usually you will receive a decision about your coverage from the facility within 2 days of your admission.

If you receive a written notice of noncoverage, you have the right to ask the facility to submit your claim to the Medicare intermediary by checking off the appropriate box on the notice of noncoverage. This is called a demand bill. If the intermediary denies your claim in an "official initial determination," you must start paying your bills or agree in writing to pay your bills if Medicare denies coverage.

If you *don't* receive a written notice of noncoverage, the nursing home will start submitting bills for your care directly to the Medicare intermediary for payment.

If the intermediary pays, great. If the Medicare intermediary refuses to cover your bills, you still may not be responsible for your outstanding nursing home bills since you never received a written notice of noncoverage. For more on the waiver of liability, see page 69.

APPEALING YOUR COVERAGE DETERMINATION

When you have an official written denial notice from the Medicare intermediary, you are ready to proceed to reconsideration, the first level of appeal (see page 82).

HOME HEALTH CARE BILLS

There are four steps to obtaining Medicare coverage of your home health care bills:

1. Presenting your Medicare card.
2. Undergoing review.
3. Receiving your coverage determination.
4. Appealing your coverage determination.

PRESENTING YOUR MEDICARE CARD

Start your quest for Medicare-covered home health benefits by locating a Medicare Certified Home Health Agency (CHHA or "cha"). A neighborhood hospital or your local Medicare intermediary (listed in Appendix 2) should be able to provide you with the names and addresses of nearby CHHAs. Present your Medicare card at the CHHA, and request an assessment of your home care needs.

The CHHA will send someone to assess your need for home health benefits. This assessment can sometimes take place in the hospital if you are awaiting discharge, or in your home after discharge.

It's always a good idea to speak to your doctor before you undergo a CHHA assessment. Your doctor's opinion about your need for home health benefits will often mean the difference between Medicare coverage and noncoverage.

UNDERGOING REVIEW

Based on its assessment of your home care needs, the CHHA may or may not agree to accept you as a patient. Regardless of whether Medicare coverage is available, the CHHA is free to reject your application for care. If your application at one CHHA is denied, don't despair. You can always reapply to a different CHHA.

A CHHA that approves your application for treatment will draw up a plan of care for you. Your doctor will have to sign the care plan to indicate his approval.

RECEIVING YOUR COVERAGE DETERMINATION

The CHHA's preparation of a care plan is not an official determination that Medicare coverage is available. However, if the CHHA doesn't notify you in writing that your home health benefits will not be covered by Medicare, you're virtually home free. Even if Medicare ultimately denies coverage of the home care services in an official determination, you will not be responsible for the cost of the care. The CHHA will have to absorb the cost of treating you because the CHHA erroneously believed your care would be covered by Medicare.

The situation is entirely different if the CHHA provides you with written notice that Medicare coverage will not be available (a notice of noncoverage), or that you are only covered for fewer hours of care than you requested. If you receive such a notice you can agree in writing to pay for the uncovered services privately and insist that the CHHA submit a claim to the Medicare intermediary on your behalf (a no-payment claim).

Remember, the CHHA's determination that full Medicare coverage is not available is not an official Medicare determination. If your no-payment claim is ultimately approved by Medicare, you will be reimbursed by Medicare for the out-of-pocket payments you made to the CHHA.

If you don't actually start to receive home care services, Medicare will not review your claim for coverage. As already mentioned, some agencies will only start your benefits after issuing a notice of noncoverage if you agree to pay for the care up front. Other agencies will start to provide care if you sign a statement promising to pay privately if your claim for Medicare coverage is denied on appeal (rather than insisting on payment up front). If an attorney is handling your Medicare appeal, your attorney may be able to convince the agency to "carry" your case (and not require immediate payment) by proving that Medicare eventually covered other similar claims.

The CHHA may express some reluctance when asked to submit a no-payment claim to Medicare on your behalf. If Medicare approves the no-payment claim, the agency may be hit with a penalty. Medicare penalizes providers that wrongfully deny Medicare coverage to their patients.

Don't let stonewalling by the agency weaken your resolve. Stick to your guns and insist that the agency submit a no-payment claim to Medicare on your behalf. If the agency doesn't submit the claim, you lose your right to pursue a Medicare appeal.

APPEALING YOUR COVERAGE DETERMINATION

The Medicare intermediary that reviews your no-payment claim for coverage will be very interested in what your doctor has to say about your need for home health care benefits. In fact, the law requires Medicare to give deference to the opinions of your treating physicians.

Say, for example, the CHHA only authorized 15 or 20 hours of weekly services, instead of the 35 hours of care that you sought under Medicare. You stand the best chance of getting the intermediary to approve additional hours of care if your doctor prepares a statement explaining why the additional care is medically reasonable and necessary.

If, despite the best efforts of you and your doctor, the intermediary denies coverage in an official Medicare determination, you are ready to pursue further avenues of appeal, starting with reconsideration (see page 82.)

DOCTORS' BILLS

The procedures you must follow to get Medicare to cover your doctors' bills depend on whether your doctor gets paid on assignment or by direct payment.

ASSIGNMENT METHOD OF PAYMENT

Doctors who take assignment agree to accept Medicare's approved charges as full payment of their bills. Approved charges are fees that Medicare determines to be reasonable for different medical services in different areas of the country. The names of doctors who take assignment are listed in a directory that is available for free from most Social Security or Railroad Retirement Board offices, hospitals, state units on aging (see Appendix 1), senior citizens' organizations, and local Medicare carriers (see Appendix 3).

For example Dr. Jones, a New York City internist, charges $150 for a rectal exam. Medicare's approved charge for a rectal examination by a New York City internist is $100. If Dr. Jones takes assignment, he will accept $100 as full payment of his fee when treating Medicare patients.

How Bills Are Paid

When you are treated by a doctor who takes assignment, you must sign an assignment form. The doctor then submits a bill for payment directly to the local Medicare carrier, which is the insurance company that processes Part B Medicare claims.

If the carrier approves the claim, your doctor will receive a check for 80 percent of Medicare's approved charge. You will then receive a bill from your doctor for the remaining 20 percent of Medicare's approved charge, plus any balance on your deductible.

When Medicare covers care you receive from a provider who takes assignment, you will receive an Explanation of Medicare Benefits (EOMB) form in the mail. This form provides you with the following information:

- What medical bills Medicare covered.
- The amount of Medicare's approved charges.
- The balance of your deductible, if any.
- The amount Medicare paid to your doctors.

You should receive an EOMB within 45 days of the date your provider submits a Part B claim to Medicare. If you have not heard from Medicare within that time, call the Medicare carrier that serves your area (see Appendix 3).

If the Medicare carrier denies the claim, and your doctor never notified you that Medicare coverage would not be available, don't pay your doctor's bill. You are not financially responsible for medical services that you reasonably believed Medicare would cover under the waiver of liability (see page 69). Your doctor was legally obligated to notify you in writing that Medicare coverage would probably not be available. In the absence of notice, he must absorb the cost of your care.

If and when the doctor asks you for payment (and the doctor will ask you for payment), refer the doctor to the section of the Medicare Handbook that explains the waiver of liability. (You can get a free copy of the handbook by calling Social Security's toll-free number, 800-772-1213, or your local Medicare carrier, whose number is listed in Appendix 3, or by stopping at your local Social Security office.)

Your doctor has the right to appeal the carrier's denial of coverage. But whether or not your doctor exercises this right, you are off the hook. Stick to your guns, and keep your checkbook in your pocket. If the doctor continues to pursue you for payment, you may have to look to the carrier (Appendix 3) or a Medicare expert for help (see page 482).

Appealing Carrier Determinations

If you do not qualify for a waiver of liability, and you disagree with any part of the carrier's decision, you can request review. (Review and other levels of appeal are discussed later in this chapter at page 79.)

DIRECT PAYMENT METHOD

Doctors who do not take assignment reserve the right to charge their patients fees that are higher than Medicare's approved charges. But the sky is not the limit. Fees that doctors who do not accept assignment can charge Medicare beneficiaries are capped under federal law and some state laws. Nonassignment doctors can charge their Medicare patients no more than 115 percent of the Medicare-approved fee (see page 53).

Many doctors who do not take assignment require their patients to pay their entire bill before they leave the doctor's office; some are willing to wait until the patient receives a reimbursement check from Medicare.

How to File Claims If Your Doctor Does Not Take Assignment

The law requires every doctor (whether on assignment or not) who treats Medicare beneficiaries to submit Medicare claims on behalf of Medicare patients, at no extra cost to the patient. The claim must be submitted within one year of the date of treatment. If your doctor fails to submit a claim for you, you can submit a claim for yourself as long as you do so before the end of the year *after* the year in which you were treated by the doctor.

When seeing a doctor who does not take assignment, be sure to:

1. Bring your Medicare card and other insurance information to the doctor's office.
2. Ask your physician to submit your claim as quickly as possible.
3. Request a copy of the completed claim form.
4. Follow up with your doctor's office to make sure the claim was submitted as promised.

If your doctor submits your Medicare claim late, or not at all, here's how to submit the Medicare claim yourself:

1. Get a bill from your doctor.
2. Complete a Patient's Request for Medicare Payment (Form 1490S). You can usually get a copy of Form 1490S from your doctor's office, the local Medicare carrier (see Appendix 3), or your local Social Security office (call 800-772-1213). Attach your doctors' bills to the completed form. You can attach more than one bill to each form. Write your name and Medicare number on each bill. Keep copies of everything you send to Medicare.
3. Send the completed Patient's Request for Medicare Payment to your local Medicare carrier within 15 months from the date you were treated by your doctor. (A listing of carriers appears in Appendix 3.) Note the date you mailed the claim to the carrier.
4. Wait for a decision.

Most carriers make a decision within 45 days of receiving a Medicare claim. The carrier will advise you of its decision by written notice in an EOMB. If you have not heard from the carrier within 45 days, call the carrier.

Claim Determinations

If Medicare covers your claim, a check payable to you for 80 percent of the Medicare-approved charge will be attached to the EOMB. You will be responsible for paying your physician:

- The remaining 20 percent of Medicare's approved charges, which you may have already paid at the doctor's office.
- The difference between Medicare's approved charges and the actual amount of your doctor's bill.
- Any outstanding balance on your deductible.

If Medicare does not cover all or part of your claim, you may not be responsible for the uncovered portion of your medical bills. Your liability will depend on whether your doctor notified you in writing, before beginning treatment, that your treatment would not be covered by Medicare and the basis of the denial.

If your doctor did notify you in writing that your treatment would not be covered by Medicare, and you agree in writing to pay the doctor, you will be responsible for the uncovered bills. However, with your doctor's help you may be able to convince Medicare to change its mind and cover the bills. Ask your doctor to prepare a letter explaining why your medical condition necessitated the treatment provided. Attach this letter to the EOMB with a signed note to "please review." Send all three sheets to Medicare, and keep your fingers crossed. Your claim just might be paid on review.

If your doctor failed to give you notice that the service would not be covered by Medicare, and Medicare denies coverage on the grounds that the treatment you received was not medically reasonable or necessary, you may not be responsible for paying the uncovered doctor's bills under the waiver of liability. A denial based on no medical necessity, in Medicare lingo, usually reads like this: "The information we have in your case does not support the need for this treatment." If you get such a notice on your EOMB, think waiver of liability (see page 69).

If you already paid your doctor for the uncovered service, and the waiver of liability applies, you are entitled to a prompt refund from the doctor. If your doctor appeals Medicare's determination of noncoverage, the doctor has up to 15 days after the appeal is denied to refund your money.

If you did not already pay your doctor, you may have to explain the concept of the waiver of liability to your doctor in a letter to stop the barrage of past due notices. The letter should state that:

- Medicare denied coverage of the doctor's services on the ground that the services were "not reasonable and necessary."
- You reasonably believed that the services were medically reasonable and necessary because your doctor prescribed them for you.

- Your doctor was obligated to notify you in writing that the services being provided would probably not be covered by Medicare, and to have you acknowledge this fact in writing.

- Medicare beneficiaries are not responsible for paying medical bills they reasonably believed would be covered by Medicare, as stated in the Medicare Handbook (see page 62). Enclose a copy of the relevant text, if possible.

Send this letter to your doctor, with a copy to the local Medicare carrier (see Appendix 3 for address).

If the delinquent notices keep coming, return each overdue notice with a copy of the letter attached to the bill. If you get nowhere on your own, ask your local Medicare carrier for assistance (listed in Appendix 3). At some point you may need to bring in the hired guns (see page 89 for information about finding legal assistance).

You also should refuse to pay your doctor's bill if Medicare denies coverage on the ground that the service was "part of another service that was performed at the same time." When you receive this message on your EOMB, you know that your doctor erred in billing you separately for each procedure.

Appealing Claim Determinations

If you are not eligible for a waiver of liability, and you disagree with any part of the carrier's decision, your only recourse is to request review. A discussion of Part B appeals follows.

HOW DO YOU FILE AN APPEAL?

There are several stages, or levels, to each Medicare appeal. Part A appeals involve four levels, and Part B appeals involve five levels. Each level of appeal must be pursued in the order stated, but the appeal process stops as soon as you win.

This section first covers Part A appeals, and then moves on to Part B appeals. The procedures that apply to Part A and Part B appeals are very similar.

> **R**emember, Part A provides hospital, skilled nursing facility, home health care, and hospice benefits. Part B provides other types of medical and outpatient services.

Part A Levels of Appeal	Part B Levels of Appeal

Reconsideration
    (conducted by the intermediary)
	Review
	    (conducted by the
	    carrier)
	Carrier hearing
	    (conducted by the
	    carrier)

Administrative hearing
        (conducted by an administrative law
        judge appointed by the Social Security
        Administration)
	Administrative hearing

Appeals Council
        (conducted by employees of the Social
        Security Administration)
	Appeals Council

Federal court (conducted by federal court judges)	Federal court

Before you get started on a formal appeal, you should try to resolve your problem informally. This will save you a lot of time, energy, and possibly money.

The best way to start your informal appeal is with a personal contact. If you find the idea of a person-to-person (or person-to-bureaucrat) confrontation on the telephone unnerving, write a letter instead.

Contact the Medicare intermediary or carrier that denied your claim by phone or mail. The number and address will be printed on the denial notice or the EOMB form (and appear in Appendices 2 and 3). Give the Medicare representative who answers the phone your Medicare claim number and your Claim Control Number. (These numbers are on the denial notice or the EOMB.) Then ask for the following information:

- What is the name of the person you are speaking to?
- What medical services were the subject of the denied claim?
- Why exactly was coverage denied?

Don't forget to make notes:

- What number did you call, and to whom did you speak?
- What day and time did you call?
- What information did you get?

Your next course of action depends on what you learned from Medicare.

Did you learn that your doctor filed a claim for coverage of the wrong medical service? Medicare assigns a three-, four-, or five-digit procedure code to every medical service. If your doctor entered the wrong procedure code by mistake, Medicare will deny coverage on the ground that the selected treatment was not appropriate for your medical condition. You must ask your doctor to resubmit the claim with the correct procedure code.

Did you learn that the claim was denied because the care you received was characterized as "routine"? Routine medical care is not covered by Medicare. Your doctor can resubmit the claim, with an explanation of why the care was necessary to treat your specific medical condition and was not merely routine.

Did you learn that Medicare determined the care you received was not medically reasonable and necessary? To rebut this finding, you will need a letter from your doctor explaining why the care you received was indicated by your specific medical needs, and that the prescribed course of treatment is considered acceptable by the medical community.

Only if you get nowhere with your informal appeal efforts should you embark on the formal appeals process.

For all formal appeals, make sure you:

- Keep copies of everything you submit to Medicare.
- Write down the name of every person you speak to about your case.
- Keep notes on all your related conversations, making sure to record the date and substance of each discussion.
- Whenever possible, send correspondence to Medicare using certified mail with return receipt requested.

If and when you encounter obstacles in the course of your appeal, do not curse the darkness. Light one of the following candles:

- Call your congressional representative. Explain the problem and ask for assistance. After all, your vote put that representative into office.
- Contact a Medicare advocacy group, such as Legal Assistance to Medicare Patients in Connecticut and New Jersey, or the Medicare Beneficiaries Defense Fund in New York City (see page 98).
- Call the local Medicare assistance office of the American Association of Retired Persons. To locate the office nearest you, contact:

AARP/MMAP
601 E Street, N.W.
Washington, DC 20049
202-434-2277

- Call the local bar association to inquire about the availability of attorneys who are willing to handle your Medicare claim for free (pro bono) or on a contingency basis.
- If you think fraud is involved, call the Medicare Fraud Hotline (800-368-5779).

PART A APPEALS

The four levels of appeal for a denied Part A claim are reconsideration, the administrative hearing, Appeals Council review, and federal court litigation. For each level, the discussion that follows addresses the whys, whens, and hows of the appeal.

RECONSIDERATION

The first level of appeal for Part A claims is called reconsideration. The Medicare PRO (the team of health care professionals who review hospital claims for medical necessity) or the Medicare intermediary (the insurance company that decides Part A claims) will make the decision on reconsideration.

Timing of Reconsideration

The time to request reconsideration is after you have an official Medicare determination from the PRO (for hospital care) or the intermediary (for skilled nursing, home health, or hospice care). The timing of your request for reconsideration will depend on the type of coverage you are seeking.

> **D**o not wait 2 days before requesting expedited review. If you do, and the PRO takes 3 days to issue a decision, you may have to pay for one day of hospital care because you will become financially liable on the third day following the date of your initial notice of noncoverage. Of course, if you eventually win your appeal, you will be reimbursed by Medicare.

If you are hospitalized, and disagree with the PRO's determination that you are no longer covered for inpatient care, you should request expedited PRO reconsideration. To request expedited reconsideration, you must call the PRO (see Appendix 4) within 3 days of the date you received the initial notice of noncoverage. (For example, you must call the PRO by Friday if you receive the notice of noncoverage on Tuesday.) The PRO then has only 3 working days to make a decision on your claim.

For all other types of hospital claims (such as billing problems), and skilled nursing, home health, and hospice care claims, you have 60 days to request reconsideration. The PRO or intermediary will then have 30 days to make a decision on your claim.

Requesting Reconsideration

Send a written request for reconsideration to the entity that issued the initial denial of coverage on your claim: the PRO for hospital claims; the intermediary for skilled nursing, home health, and hospice claims.

There are two ways to request reconsideration.

1. Complete a Request for Reconsideration of Part A Health Insurance Benefits (Form HCFA-2649). You can obtain the form by calling the intermediary at the number printed on the initial noncoverage notice, by going to your local Social Security office or by copying the form reprinted in Appendix 5.
2. Prepare a brief letter that includes your Medicare number, the dates you received the disputed services, and a request to "please reconsider" the determination of noncoverage. Attach a copy of the written denial. Keep the originals of all Medicare papers.

For hospital appeals, submit the preprinted form or your letter to the Medicare PRO (see Appendix 4) or your local Social Security office. For skilled nursing facility and home health care appeals, send your request to the Medicare intermediary (see Appendix 2) or your local Social Security office (call 800-772-1213 for the address).

Reconsideration Process

On reconsideration, the Medicare PRO or intermediary will take a new look at your claim. You can submit additional evidence at this stage of review. The best evidence you can submit is:

1. A statement from your doctor explaining why your treatment was medically necessary and should be covered.
2. Hospital records, include laboratory reports and nurses' notes, that were not available to Medicare at the time the initial determination was made. (The administration office of the hospital or nursing home that treated you is required to send Medicare this information upon your request.)

3. Progress and treatment notes prepared by your nurses or therapists, if you are seeking coverage of home care services. (The home health care agency is required to send these records to Medicare upon your request.)

If you are not awarded coverage on reconsideration, do not be discouraged. Very few cases are won on reconsideration. Continue on to the next level of appeal for your Part A claim, the administrative hearing.

ADMINISTRATIVE HEARING

You stand the best chance of getting your Medicare denial reversed at this level of appeal.

Entitlement to an Administrative Hearing

You are only entitled to an administrative hearing if your Medicare claim involves a minimum amount of money.

Type of Appeal	Amount of Claim
Part A hospital appeals of PRO decisions ....$200 or more
Other Part A appeals ....$100 or more

To compute the amount at issue in your Medicare appeal, you must reduce the amount of your reimbursement claim by your outstanding deductible and coinsurance. Imagine, for example, you are appealing to get Medicare to cover a $300 hospital bill. You still owe $200 on your hospital deductible. The value of your claim is only $100, so you are not entitled to an administrative hearing (or any further rights of appeal).

The good news is that you are permitted to accumulate a number of bills incurred during the past 6 months to meet the minimum amount in dispute. For example, if you have three hospital bills totaling $600, you can proceed to an administrative hearing, even if you still owe $200 on your deductible.

Requesting an Administrative Hearing

You must request a hearing within 60 days of the date you receive the reconsidered decision denying your Part A claim.

Medicare assumes that you receive the denial notice 5 days after the notice is sent. When you receive the denial notice in the mail, look at the date of the notice. If it is more than 5 days old, save the envelope and write down the date you actually received the letter. This will come in handy if you miss the deadline for requesting a hearing.

The hearing request can be made by completing Social Security Form HCFA-5011 (which you can get from your local Social Security office or by calling Social Security at 800-772-1213), or by letter. Here is a sample letter requesting an administrative hearing:

Sample Letter Requesting Administrative Hearing

Date

Social Security Administration
Address
City, State, Zip

Re: Your complete name
Your Social Security number

Dear Sir/Madam:

On [insert date you received the reconsideration decision] I received notice that my claim for Medicare benefits had been denied on reconsideration. A copy of that notice is enclosed.

This letter shall serve as my written request for a hearing to be held before an administrative law judge.

Thank you for your prompt attention to this matter.

Sincerely,

Your signature
Your printed name

For hospital appeals, send the completed form or letter to the PRO (see Appendix 4) or your local Social Security office. For skilled nursing facility and home health care appeals, send your request to the Medicare intermediary (see Appendix 2) or your local Social Security office (call also 800-772-1213 for the address). The number of the Medicare intermediary will appear on the notice you receive from Medicare.

After you file your request for a hearing, relax. A hearing may not be scheduled for several months.

Administrative Hearing Process

Administrative hearings are conducted by administrative law judges (commonly called ALJs), who are employees of the Social Security Administration.

What Can You Expect at Your Administrative Hearing?
• The hearing is semiformal. In most cases, the only people in the hearing room will be you, your representative (if any), the ALJ, and the ALJ's assistant.

• The hearing is taped. The ALJ's assistant will turn on a tape recorder when the hearing starts. Occasionally the ALJ may ask the assistant to turn off the tape player in the middle of the hearing. Comments that are made when the tape is not running are off the record. You want to be sure that the tape recorder is on when you testify. If you are not sure whether the tape is on or off, ask the judge if you are on the record. The tape will be very important if you have to appeal your case further. At later stages of appeal, the tape will be used to determine whether the ALJ made any mistakes in reviewing your claim.

• The ALJ will ask you a series of questions. If you do not understand a question, ask the ALJ for an explanation. If you are not sure how to answer a question, tell the ALJ you do not know the answer. Try to keep your answers short and to the point.
• Your representative, if you have one, will have an opportunity to question you after the ALJ has finished questioning you. Your representative's questions should bring out all of the facts that help your case, and clarify your responses to the ALJ's questions.

See page 92 for more on administrative hearings.

What Are Your Rights at the Administrative Hearing?
As a party to an administrative hearing, you have several important rights.

• You have the right to review your Social Security file before your hearing. There are two important reasons you should review your file before the hearing: First, to learn what information Social Security will rely on in deciding your case. If any of the documents in your file is inaccurate, or requires explanation, you can raise these matters at the hearing. Second, to discover whether any evidence is missing from your file. You can submit any missing documents to the ALJ at the hearing. You can even ask the judge to keep the record open so that you can submit documents by mail after the hearing.

If you would like to see your file several days before your scheduled hearing, call the hearing office to find out when the file will be available for review. Your file will always be available for review at the hearing office on the day of your hearing.

• You have the right to present your case in person. The administrative hearing is your best opportunity to present your side of the story. The ALJ is supposed to help you present your case by asking you questions about your claim. If the ALJ does not ask you for information that helps your case, tell the judge you would like to make a statement on the record. A statement that is made on the record is recorded on tape.

• You have the right to appear with a representative. The representative can be any person who is familiar with the facts of your case. You may feel most comfortable hiring a professional advocate, such as a lawyer, paralegal, social worker, or caseworker, or you may prefer appearing with a friend or relative.

Your advocate's job is to make sure the ALJ sees and hears all the evidence that supports your claim for coverage. To build the strongest possible case, your advocate should review your file before the hearing to see that it contains all the necessary documents and ask you questions at the hearing to bring out all the favorable facts of your case.

Administrative Decision

Several weeks after the administrative hearing, you will receive a written decision from the ALJ in the mail. If the ALJ does not award you Medicare coverage, you can proceed with the next level of appeal: Appeals Council review.

APPEALS COUNCIL

The third level of appeal for Part A claims is a review of your claim by the Appeals Council. The Appeals Council is an arm of the Social Security Administration.

Entitlement to Appeals Council Review

The Appeals Council does not accept every case for review. If your case is not accepted for review, your only option is to proceed to the next level of appeal, which is federal court.

If your case is accepted for review, you will probably not have an opportunity to make a personal appearance before the Appeals Council.

Requesting Appeals Council Review

Within 60 days of receiving notice of the ALJ's decision, you may request Appeals Council review by filing a Request for Review of Hearing Decision/Order (Form HA-520), which is available from Social Security, or sending a letter requesting review to the Appeals Council at the address printed in the ALJ's decision.

If possible, you or your representative should submit to the Appeals Council a written statement summarizing the facts that support your claim for coverage. Send the statement by certified mail, return receipt requested. The rest of your file will be forwarded to the Appeals Council by your local Social Security office.

Appeals Council Review Process

The Appeals Council reaches a decision on your claim based on your written statement and the documents in your file.

After reviewing your case, the Appeals Council can take one of three possible actions on your claim:

1. It can affirm the ALJ's denial of benefits, turning down your claim for coverage. You must then decide whether to proceed to the fourth and final level of appeal.

2. It can reverse the ALJ's denial of benefits. You will then be awarded Medicare coverage.

3. It can send the case back for a new administrative hearing. If the Appeals Council finds that the ALJ made a mistake in conducting the hearing or analyzing your claim, a new hearing will be scheduled.

Try not to worry if you do not win your case before the Appeals Council. Not many cases are won at this level of appeal. You must, however, go through Appeals Council review in order to continue on to the last level of appeal, federal court.

FEDERAL COURT

The ultimate level of the Part A appeals process is a lawsuit in federal court.

Entitlement to Federal Court Appeal

You cannot file a federal court appeal unless your claim involves a minimum amount of money:

Type of Appeal	Amount of Claim
Part A hospital appeals of PRO decisions	$2,000 or more
Other Part A appeals	$1,000 or more

If your claim does not involve at least these sums of money, you have no further rights of appeal.

Starting a Federal Court Appeal

A federal lawsuit must be started by filing a complaint within 60 days of the date you receive the Appeals Council's adverse decision.

Assistance With Federal Court Appeal

If and when you reach this stage of appeal, you are probably well-advised to follow the advice of "Dear Abby" and seek professional help. Although you are not required to be represented by a lawyer in federal court, most claimants find representation beneficial. Federal court litigants are expected to know the appropriate standard of proof, submit written arguments in support of their legal position, and sometimes present an oral argument to the judge.

There is no shortage of lawyers who specialize in Medicare and Social Security appeals. You can usually get the names of specialists from your local or state bar association. If you cannot afford a private attorney, you may find a lawyer who is willing to handle the matter on a contingency basis, or you may qualify for the free or low-cost services of a legal aid or legal services attorney. You can find these offices listed under Legal Aid in the telephone book. Unfortunately, due to budget cutbacks, these services are often difficult to obtain.

If you cannot find a lawyer to handle your case, you have some additional options.

- You can file the lawsuit yourself. Most federal courts have a *pro se* office. Personnel in the *pro se* office are trained to help litigants get through the court system without a lawyer.
- You can contact a local community organization. Senior centers, religious groups, social clubs, and unions often have the names of advocates who specialize in problems involving the elderly. One of these organizations may be able to help you or refer you to a Social Security advocate.
- You can call the Elder Care Locator at 800-677-1116 for a referral to free legal assistance.

Standard of Proof

The law requires federal court judges to affirm Medicare determinations that are supported by "substantial evidence." One court has defined substantial evidence as "more than a mere scintilla of evidence." This means that federal court judges should let Medicare denials stand if they are supported by a reasonable amount of evidence.

As a plaintiff bringing a Medicare appeal, this is a very difficult standard of proof for you to meet. Nevertheless, Medicare beneficiaries have traditionally enjoyed a tremendously high success rate in federal court. In 1983, the last full year for which statistics are available, federal court judges determined that 63.7 percent of all Medicare and Social Security denials were unjustified. These denials were either sent back for a new administrative hearing or reversed outright with benefits awarded.

One explanation for the high success rate in federal court is that the Medicare agency stubbornly refuses to follow directives issued by federal court judges. In open violation of prior court decisions, Medicare will continue to deny a claim based on a restrictive interpretation of a regulation that a federal court judge has already found to be illegal. These denials are ultimately reversed when they are appealed in federal court.

Federal Court Procedures

Although you are unlikely ever to need to know the nuts and bolts of a federal court appeal, a few points about federal court procedure may interest you. To start a federal court appeal you must file a complaint. The body of the complaint should set out the facts of the case and your claims for relief. You must pay the court a fee to file a complaint. If you cannot afford the fee, you can request a waiver in an *in forma pauperis* petition. The complaint must be delivered to the defendant, an agency of the U.S. government.

After the defendant answers the complaint, both parties meet at pretrial conferences to attempt to settle the dispute. If the conferences are not fruitful, both parties are given an opportunity to submit legal briefs. After all briefs have been submitted, and both sides have made oral presentations to the judge (if required), the waiting period begins. When the judge finally makes a determination, all parties receive a copy of the written decision in the mail.

PART B APPEALS

You have five levels of appeal to pursue if you disagree with the position Medicare has taken on your Part B claim: review, Part B carrier hearing, administrative hearing, Appeals Council review, and federal court litigation. This section covers each level of appeal, from A to Z; from whether to appeal, through when to appeal and how to appeal. For levels of appeal that are the same for Part A and Part B claims, you will be referred back to the detailed discussions above.

REVIEW

The first formal level of appeal for a Part B decision is called review. You are ready to request review when you have received an EOMB denial notice.

If you are thinking of forgoing a Part B appeal, wait till you hear this: You stand a better than even chance of getting more money from Medicare on appeal. In fact, nearly two-thirds of the claims Medicare denies for lack of medical necessity are eventually reversed. A likely explanation for this high rate of reversal is that every 72 seconds a harried insurance-company employee with a high school degree and no medical training reviews a Medicare claim for medical necessity. The decisions are not reviewed for consistency, and often appear to be completely arbitrary. Your only investment is a minimal amount of time (maybe ten minutes) and money (the cost of a postage stamp). You don't have to be a gambler to appreciate the odds.

Reasons and Timing of Review

You should request Part B review whenever your claim for coverage is denied on the ground that the medical service you received was medically unreasonable or unnecessary, routine, or experimental. A rebuttal letter from your doctor will usually support a reversal of these types of denials.

You should also request Part B review whenever Medicare pays less than 80 percent of your doctor's bill. Although Medicare's partial payment may be correct, more than 50 percent of Part B payments are incorrect due to simple employee error. Once again, you have absolutely nothing to lose by appealing.

You must request review within 6 months of receiving an EOMB on your claim.

Requesting Review

Directions for requesting review are printed on the EOMB. The simplest way to request review is to staple a signed note to the EOMB saying, "Please review," and send it to the Medicare carrier or your local Social Security office (see Appendix 3 for nationwide listing of carriers). In the alternative, you can send the carrier a completed Request for Review (Form HCFA-1964) which is reprinted in Appendix 6. Be sure to keep a copy of everything you send to Medicare.

The carrier's telephone number will be printed on the EOMB. You can call this toll-free number to discuss your case with a claims representative. The representative may tell you that all you need to obtain coverage is some additional documentation. Initial determinations are frequently reversed at this stage of appeal when the beneficiary only needs to supply some missing information.

Review Process

The Part B review is conducted by the Medicare carrier, which is the insurance company that processes Part B Medicare claims. You cannot make a personal appearance before the carrier at the review stage of appeal.

Review usually takes 2 or 3 months. After that time, you will receive a review determination notice in the mail. If the decision is favorable, a check will be attached to the determination notice. If the decision is not favorable, you can continue at the second level of appeal. If you don't hear anything after 3 months, you are well within your rights to call the carrier.

CARRIER HEARING

The second level of a Part B appeal is a hearing before the insurance carrier that denied your claim.

Entitlement to Carrier Hearing

If you are appealing a Part B decision, and your claim (or the total value of several separate claims) involves at least $100, you are entitled to a hearing before the insurance carrier that denied your claim. You can accumulate a number of small claims to reach the $100 minimum.

Requesting Carrier Hearing

You must request a carrier hearing within 6 months of receiving the carrier's determination on review. You can make the request on Medicare's Form HCFA-1965, or by attaching a brief note requesting a hearing to the carrier's prior determination. Submit the hearing request to the carrier (see Appendix 3) or to your local Social Security office (call 800-772-1213).

Carrier Hearing Process

The carrier hearing is a very informal procedure, held either at the insurance carrier's office or at a Social Security office. A hearing officer who has been appointed by the Medicare carrier conducts the hearing.

At the hearing you will have an opportunity to state your case in person. You will also be permitted to present additional evidence and witnesses. As always, the most important evidence you can submit is a statement from your doctor explaining why Medicare should cover the services you received, or why you are entitled to a higher approved charge from Medicare.

If the hearing officer denies your claim, continue on to the next level of appeal, the administrative hearing.

ADMINISTRATIVE HEARING

The third level of appeal for Part B claims is a hearing before an administrative law judge (ALJ). The administrative hearing is exactly the same for Part B claims as for Part A claims, with the exception that Part B appeals must involve a minimum amount in dispute of $500, unless you are appealing your entitlement to Part B coverage (not of a specific claim denial) in which case no minimum amount is required. If your claim does not involve $500 or more, you are not entitled to an administrative hearing and you have no further rights of appeal. If your claim does involve $500 or more, see page 84 for a complete discussion of the administrative hearing.

File your request for an administrative hearing at your local Social Security office.

APPEALS COUNCIL

Appeals Council review is your next step if the ALJ did not rule favorably on your Medicare claim.

To request Appeals Council review, within 60 days of the date of the ALJ's decision, send a completed Form HA-520 to:

> **Social Security Administration**
> Office of Hearings and Appeals
> 5107 Leesburg Pike
> Falls Church, VA 22041-3200

Appeals Council proceedings are exactly the same for Part B claims as for Part A claims. For a complete overview of Appeals Council review, see page 87.

FEDERAL COURT

The ultimate level of appeal for a Part B claim is a lawsuit in federal court. You are not permitted to file a federal court appeal unless your Part B claim involves, at a minimum, $1,000.

In all other respects, Part B federal court appeals are exactly the same as Part A appeals. For an in-depth look at the federal court stage of appeal, see page 88.

SPECIFIC TIPS FOR WINNING YOUR MEDICARE APPEAL

Although the legal bar would like you to think otherwise, you do not necessarily need a lawyer to win your Medicare appeal (although representation will help you negotiate in federal court). Here are some tips that will help tilt the scales of justice in your favor.

REVERSING DENIAL OF ELIGIBILITY FOR PART A MEDICARE

If you have been denied Part A coverage, start by meeting with a representative at your local Social Security office. To prepare for your meeting, pull together all the notices you received from Medicare. Gather the documents you will need to prove your claim.

If the basis of your denial is:	Bring:
Age	Birth certificate Baptismal certificate Hospital records Adoption records Naturalization papers Driver's license
Citizenship	Birth certificate Baptismal certificate U.S. passport Military service records Naturalization certificate INS documentation Evidence of continuous U.S. residence since before January 1, 1972
Disability	Social Security award Social Security check Social Security letter

REVERSING DENIAL OF COVERAGE OF PART A CLAIM

The most common reasons Part A claims are denied are:

- The services were not "medically reasonable and necessary."
- The care was "unskilled."
- The services could have been provided on an outpatient basis.

Each type of denial demands a different appeal strategy.

Medically Reasonable and Necessary

Medicare only covers medical services that are reasonable and necessary. If your claim has been denied as not "medically reasonable and necessary," this is a determination for your doctor to rebut.

Specifically, your doctor should prepare a report stating:

• That the services you received were appropriate for the treatment of your illness or injury. Medicare will not pay for services that are not generally accepted as the standard treatment for your condition, or that are found to be excessive. Your doctor must explain why the care you received was neither unusual nor excessive in light of the complexity or severity of your condition.

• That institutionalization in a hospital or nursing home was necessary for the treatment of your medical condition. Medicare will not pay for inpatient hospital care or institutionalization if it finds you could have been treated less expensively at your doctor's office or at home. Your doctor must explain why you needed to be admitted to the hospital or skilled nursing facility to receive treatment of your condition.

• That an operation ordinarily classified as elective or cosmetic was medically necessary in your case. Medicare will not pay for elective or cosmetic surgery. Your doctor must explain the medical justification for the procedure in your case. For example, reconstructive surgery, which is often elective, may be medically justified following a severe accident.

• That rehabilitative therapy was necessary to improve or maintain your level of functioning. Medicare often denies coverage of therapy services on the grounds that the beneficiary's condition is stable, or is unlikely to improve despite ongoing rehabilitation therapy. This is a particular problem for patients who suffer from degenerative diseases such as Parkinson's disease, or who are slowly recovering from a disabling condition such as a stroke.

Denials based on findings that you have no "restorative potential," or that you have a "stable" or "not improving" medical condition, are often illegal. You do not have to show a potential for improvement to qualify for Medicare-covered services. As long as your doctor states that you require the care to prevent further deterioration in your functioning, the services should be covered.

If the basis of the denial is that the services are "no longer considered necessary" because your condition has improved, or that additional treatment offers no further "therapeutic value," have your doctor, nurse, or therapist prepare a report explaining why you require ongoing care to maintain the benefits of treatment.

Custodial, Not Skilled

As already discussed, the Medicare program was designed to cover skilled care, which is medical care that must be provided by specially trained professional health care workers. As a general matter, unskilled or "custodial care" is not covered by Medicare (see page 46).

The line that distinguishes skilled care from custodial care is blurry, to say the least. Many Medicare beneficiaries have successfully reversed denials based on a finding of unskilled care by using some of the arguments that are summarized on the following page.

Do any of these arguments fit your case?

• A medical condition that ordinarily only requires unskilled care requires skilled care in your case. The law requires Medicare to look at the specific facts of each case when making coverage determinations. Medicare cannot deny a claim simply because *most* people with your condition only require unskilled care. Medicare must consider whether there are medical complications (which must be documented by a physician) that make your situation different.

For example, a person who breaks an arm would not ordinarily require skilled treatment. However, skilled services may be required if that person also has a skin condition that must be closely monitored by a skilled nurse.

• You receive a number of unskilled services that require skilled management and oversight. If you have more than one chronic illness, you may require several different types of care. Even if all the care you require is unskilled, you may need skilled health care workers to coordinate the multiple unskilled services.

For example, a person who is on a special diet, oral medications, and an exercise program for the treatment of diabetes and a heart condition may need skilled management of these three unskilled services.

• You have an unstable medical condition that must be monitored by skilled medical personnel. Even if you only need unskilled care, you may require skilled monitoring if your condition could quickly take a turn for the worse.

For example, a person with congestive heart failure may have to be closely watched for drug reactions and changes in fluid balances and vital signs.

Adequacy of Outpatient Treatment

Medicare will not pay for your inpatient care in a hospital or nursing facility if you could receive comparable treatment on an outpatient basis.

To refute such a determination, you need a detailed statement from your doctor describing the medical services you required and explaining why these services could not be provided without hospitalization or institutionalization.

REVERSING DENIAL OF PART B BENEFITS

Most Part B denials are based on one of these findings:

• The treatment was not "medically reasonable and necessary."
• The treatment was "routine."
• The treatment was "experimental."

Medically Reasonable and Necessary

Medicare only pays for services that are appropriate for the treatment of your illness or injury, not excessive, and not experimental.

You can only prove the medical reasonableness and necessity of the care you receive by submitting supportive statements from your doctor (see page 94).

Routine

Medicare does not cover annual physical check-ups, dental or eye examinations, or any other type of routine preventive care. Your doctor's cooperation is key to refuting a finding that a particular service was routine.

Specifically, your doctor must prepare a statement that makes the following points:

- You were seen for treatment of particular symptoms.
- The examination was appropriate in relation to your complaints.
- Laboratory work and diagnostic testing were necessary to evaluate your condition.

Experimental

Medicare maintains a list of what procedures are appropriate for the treatment of different medical conditions. You can challenge the contents of this list, with your doctor's help.

To prove that a procedure Medicare labels as experimental is, in fact, accepted by the medical community as an appropriate mode of treatment for your medical condition, try to gather the following types of evidence (once again, with your doctor's assistance):

- Medical texts that approve of the treatment method in question.
- A letter from an organization whose members specialize in the treatment of your medical condition (for example, the American Cancer Institute) in defense of the disputed mode of treatment.
- A statement from your doctor explaining why the disputed treatment is appropriate in light of your particular medical needs.

ℹ️ For more information

If you have any questions about Medicare, or need help with your Medicare claim or appeal, contact:

Medicare Beneficiaries Defense Fund
130 West 42nd Street, 17th Floor
New York, NY 10036-7803
212-869-3850

AARP/MMAP
601 E Street, N.W.
Washington, DC 20049
202-434–2277

Elder Care Locator
800-677-1116

BACK TO JACK

Jack and I first discussed the importance of filing a timely application for Medicare Part B benefits. Since Jack was thinking of retiring, which would mean losing his group health insurance, he had to file his application within 7 months of retiring or losing his health coverage, whichever happened first. (To be safe, I recommended applying at least 3 months before he wanted his Medicare coverage to start.)

With that out of the way, we turned our attention to the notices Jack had received from the hospital and nursing home. Jack took some comfort in learning that the denial notices he had received were not official Medicare determinations. He notified the hospital and the nursing home that he wanted his claims submitted directly to the local Medicare intermediary.

In anticipation of a possible Medicare appeal, Jack contacted his doctor and requested a medical report explaining why the care he received was medically reasonable and appropriate, and why it had to be provided on an inpatient basis by skilled health care workers.

By the time Jack left my office, he had fire in his belly . . . and was ready to take on Medicare for all it was worth.

4.
SUPPLEMENTING MEDICARE BENEFITS

A year before coming to see me, Harriet had a stroke. She was admitted to the hospital for a week, and then returned home. A rehabilitation therapist and home attendant came to her house several hours a week to assist her. After 6 weeks, Harriet no longer needed therapy, but she still required help around the house. She also had to be examined once a month to minimize the risk of a second stroke.

Harriet was quite distressed. To her dismay, she had to pay hundreds of dollars toward her medical expenses. She had expected Medicare to pick up the entire tab. She needed to know: How could she ensure more complete health coverage in the future?

How is the Medicare program like a slice of Swiss cheese? They are both full of holes.

To the surprise of many older Americans, routine medical treatment, eyeglasses, prescription drugs, hearing aids, and most custodial care at home and in a nursing home are not covered by Medicare. In addition, Medicare beneficiaries must pay for much of their coverage in the form of premiums, deductibles, and co-insurance payments (see Chapter 2).

You have basically six options for filling the gaps in your Medicare coverage, each of which is discussed in a separate section of this chapter:

- Join a prepayment health care plan.
- Purchase private insurance (Medicare supplemental insurance, long-term care insurance, specific disease insurance).

- Participate in an employer group health plan.
- Look to Workers' Compensation or no-fault insurance.
- Apply for veterans' benefits.
- Apply for Medicaid.

A key at the beginning of each section will help you decide which of these options is best for you.

PREPAYMENT HEALTH CARE PLAN

IS IT FOR YOU?

A prepayment health care plan could be for you if:

- There is a health maintenance organization (HMO) or competitive medical plan (CMP) that serves the area where you live.
- You do not mind receiving your medical care from physicians employed by the HMO or CMP.

Health maintenance organizations and competitive medical plans are two of the most popular types of prepayment health care plans. HMOs and CMPs are called prepayment plans because their members purchase health care in advance by paying a monthly premium. (Some plans also require members to pay a small co-insurance when they receive certain services.) Prepayment plans are unlike the traditional fee-for-service method of paying for health care, where the patient only pays when medical services are actually received.

TYPES OF PLANS

Not every prepayment plan accepts Medicare beneficiaries as members. Prepayment plans that are not under contract with Medicare terminate the memberships of enrollees once they become eligible for Medicare.

Most prepayment plans under contract with Medicare fall into one of two categories: risk contracts and cost contracts. Almost every prepayment plan you will encounter as a Medicare beneficiary will be a risk contract plan.

- Risk contracts. Medicare beneficiaries who enroll in risk contract plans pay a monthly premium, which covers the cost of Medicare deductibles and co-insurance payments. Enrolled beneficiaries must then receive all their care from health care providers who are part of the plan (except for out-of-town emergency care). This is commonly referred to as the lock-in feature of the risk contract. Medical services received outside the plan are not covered by the plan or by Medicare.

• Cost contracts. A small minority of prepayment plans are cost contract plans. As with risk contracts, Medicare beneficiaries who enroll in cost contract plans pay a monthly premium to cover their Medicare deductibles and co-insurance payments. However, enrollees in cost contract plans are permitted to receive medical services from providers outside the plan. These services are covered by Medicare, as long as the beneficiary pays the usual Medicare deductibles, co-payments, and excess physicians' charges (in addition to the monthly charge for plan membership).

There are advantages and disadvantages to each type of prepayment plan. The primary benefit of risk contract plans is lower cost; the downside is that enrollees are not covered for any medical services they receive outside the plan. The primary benefit of cost contract plans is the flexibility to obtain medical care outside the plan; the downside is that enrollees who go outside the plan may end up spending a lot of their own money on Medicare deductibles and co-payments.

SERVICES

Prepayment plans under contract with Medicare are required, at a minimum, to offer all Medicare-covered services. If your plan refuses to cover a particular medical service, you have the same rights of appeal as any other Medicare beneficiary (see Chapter 3).

PREREQUISITES FOR JOINING PREPAYMENT PLAN

If you are a Medicare beneficiary, and are interested in joining a prepayment plan under contract with Medicare, you must:

- Maintain your Part B Medicare coverage (unless you are over age 65 and a member of an HMO or CMP through your employer).
- Live in the area served by the HMO or CMP.

PROS AND CONS OF PREPAYMENT PLAN MEMBERSHIP

Medicare beneficiaries who join either type of prepayment plan give up some degree of freedom in the selection of their doctor. If you have a longstanding relationship with a particular physician, you may not want to join a prepayment plan. However, there are benefits to joining a prepayment plan:

• Medicare beneficiaries on a plan generally pay less for their health care coverage than their non-enrolled counterparts.

• Monthly medical bills are more predictable. Medicare's deductibles and co-insurance payments can add up quickly. With an HMO or CMP, you can estimate how much you will spend on your health care each month. Co-insurance obligations in a prepayment plan are nominal.

• All medical services are provided at one location. You will no longer have to go to different locations to see your doctor, have a blood test, and get an X-ray.

• Prepayment health care plans usually offer broader coverage than Medicare. Most HMOs and CMPs provide their members with preventive care, dental care, eye care, and hearing aids for the same monthly premium. None of these services is covered by Medicare. Some prepayment plans offer additional services, such as screening for illnesses, monitoring drugs for possible interactions, and providing access to ombudsmen to coordinate care and answer questions.

• You do not have to file claims for coverage or bother with any paperwork. With Medicare, you must keep track of your claims and reimbursement. You eliminate this headache by joining a prepayment plan.

• You do not have to pay each time you receive medical care. As a member of a prepayment plan, you only have to write out a premium check once a month (and possibly pay a small co-insurance fee for certain services).

Cautionary Words to Prospective Prepayment Plan Applicants

A lot of abuse occurs in the promotion of prepayment plans to individuals over age 65. Many HMOs and CMPs actively solicit Medicare beneficiaries to join their plans. HMOs in Southern California and South Florida have earned an especially well-deserved reputation for their aggressive sales efforts.

HMO sales representatives have been known to leave out certain important information, or out-and-out lie, when wooing Medicare beneficiaries. If you find yourself being pitched by an HMO salesperson, keep in mind the following warnings:

• Remember that you may be required to get all of your medical care from providers within the plan. One feature of prepayment plans that is most often deemphasized by HMO sales representatives is the lock-in feature. Even if you are not required to receive all your care from providers within the plan, going outside the plan will cost you extra money.

• Find out all you can about the qualifications of the physicians who participate in the plan. Most sales representatives know surprisingly little about the health care providers who participate in their network. Do not let yourself get hooked up with a plan physician unless you know something about the doctor's training and experience.

• Beware of salespeople who hold themselves out as "Medicare consultants" or "Medicare marketing representatives." These titles are absolutely meaningless. Medicare does not have an authorized salesforce.

• Resist high-pressure tactics. If any salesperson warns you that "You will regret not making a decision to join right away," a red light should go on. In all likelihood, the exact opposite is true.

• Make sure the prepayment plan complies with all federal requirements. Compliance information is available from the Health Care Financing Administration (HCFA). HCFA also has data on the number of complaints filed by Medicare recipients against certain HMOs and CMPs.

LEAVING YOUR PLAN

If you are a Medicare beneficiary, and you want to leave your HMO or CMP, simply send a written notice of termination to the plan or your local Social Security office. You will be restored to regular Medicare coverage as of the first day of the following month.

ℹ️ *For more information*

Consumer Information Center
P.O. Box 100
Pueblo, CO 81002
Request a free copy of the booklet "Medicare and Coordinated Care Plans."

Social Security Administration
800-772-1213
Request a free copy of the booklet "Medicare and Prepayment Plans," Publication Number HCFA 02143.

PRIVATE INSURANCE

Three types of insurance policies are of special interest to Medicare beneficiaries:

- Medicare supplemental insurance (Medigap insurance).
- Long-term care insurance.
- Specific disease insurance.

All these policies are sold by private insurance companies. None is sold by the federal government. You should make your decision about purchasing private insurance coverage before you reach age 65.

MEDICARE SUPPLEMENTAL INSURANCE (MEDIGAP INSURANCE)

IS IT FOR YOU?

Medicare supplemental insurance could be for you if:

- You do not belong to a prepaid health plan, such as an HMO or CMP.
- You do not maintain any health insurance coverage purchased before age 65.
- You cannot convert coverage you had under a group plan with your employer to individual coverage when you retire.
- Your income and resources are not close to the limits necessary to qualify for Medicaid (see page 130).

Medicare supplemental insurance, commonly called Medigap insurance, is designed to cover some of the gaps in Medicare's coverage (ergo, its name). About two out of three Medicare beneficiaries over age 65 carry Medicare supplemental insurance.

Medigap insurance is tied in closely with Medicare coverage. It is generally only available to individuals age 65 and over who have Medicare coverage, and covers some or all of the premium, deductible, and co-insurance requirements of Medicare. Medigap insurance generally excludes from coverage many of the same services that Medicare does not cover. For example, most Medigap policies do not pay for custodial nursing home care because this type of care is not covered by Medicare.

Within the last few years, Congress has passed legislation to protect consumers of Medigap insurance. Before the legislation was implemented, there was a lot of abuse among insurance agents who were selling Medicare beneficiaries more Medigap policies than they needed, and a lot of confusion among Medicare beneficiaries who did not know how to select among the array of coverage options. All this changed with the new law.

Insurance companies are now only permitted to sell ten standard Medigap policies.[1] One of the ten standard policies must provide a minimum package of basic benefits. These basic benefits include coverage of:

- The beneficiary's 20 percent Part B co-insurance payment (see page 52).
- The beneficiary's Part A hospital co-insurance payment for days 61 to 90 of hospitalization and the 60 lifetime reserve days (see page 51).
- 365 days of hospitalization at 100 percent coverage.
- The beneficiary's share of blood charges.

The other nine policies must provide this package of basic benefits, in addition to other benefits.

The ten varieties of Medigap policies are listed in the chart that follows. Each policy is known by a policy letter.

The cost of Medigap coverage varies widely from state to state. Policies that include only the basic benefits package are always the least expensive. Here are examples of annual premiums for three of the ten standard Medigap policies[2]:

Policy Letter	Annual Premiums (range)
Policy A	$240 (Hawaii)—$624 (Florida)
Policy E	$498 (Vermont)—$1,059 (Florida)
Policy J	$1,047 (Maine)—$1,977 (Florida)

Some insurance companies set their rates according to the age of the applicant. The older you are, the more your Medigap coverage may cost. AARP and Blue Cross/ Blue Shield, however, usually charge the same premium regardless of the insured's age.

As a general matter, the gaps in your Medicare coverage that are likely to cost the most to fill with Medigap insurance are inpatient hospitalizations exceeding 60 days, and the 20 percent co-insurance for doctors' bills. Policy A, the least expensive policy with its package of basic benefits, covers both of these gaps.

---

[1] Three states—Minnesota, Massachusetts, and Wisconsin—are exempt from the new federal law. These states offer one model Medicare supplement insurance policy with different riders.
[2] The sample premiums are based on estimates provided by the American Association of Retired Persons (AARP). These prices are not intended as quotes. AARP is a nonprofit retirement group that sells all ten standard Medigap policies nationwide. For more information on AARP Medigap policies, call 800-523-5800.

Ten Medicare Supplement Standard Packages
Adopted by NAIC, July 30, 1991

Benefit Options	Packages									
	A	B	C	D	E	F	G	H	I	J
Basic benefits*	✔	✔	✔	✔	✔	✔	✔	✔	✔	✔
SNF co-insurance			✔	✔	✔	✔	✔	✔	✔	✔
Part A deductible			✔	✔	✔	✔	✔	✔	✔	✔
Part B deductible			✔			✔				✔
Part B excess charges—100 percent						✔			✔	✔
Part B excess charges—80 percent							✔			
Foreign travel			✔	✔	✔	✔	✔	✔	✔	✔
At-home recovery				✔			✔		✔	✔
Basic drugs ($1,250 limit)									✔	✔
Extended drugs ($3,000 limit)										✔
Preventive care					✔					✔

* Basic benefits (included in all packages): Hospitalization: Part A co-insurance plus coverage for 365 additional days after Medicare benefits end. Medical expenses: Part B co-insurance (20 percent of Medicare-approved expenses). Blood: first 3 pints of blood each year.

SELECTING A MEDIGAP POLICY

If:	Then Look Into Policy Letter:
You are primarily interested in covering the cost of catastrophic illness.	A or B (B, for a higher premium of about $200 to $300 a year, covers the Part A hospital deductible of $696 in 1994).
You want to cover the cost of treating a long-term chronic illness.	D, G, or I (Policy J offers the same long-term care coverage as D, G, and I, but is not recommended because the additional coverage of the Part B deductible—a $100 value—usually costs at least $100).

You use doctors who do not take assignment (see page 52).

G or I (Policies F and J also cover the excessive doctors' charges, but are not recommended because the additional coverage usually costs at least $100 more. Also, coverage of the full fees charged by doctors who do not take assignment is less important as of January 1, 1992, when a law limiting the fees that doctors can charge their Medicare eligible patients went into effect. Doctors not accepting assignment can only charge 15 percent above the Medicare-approved rate (see page 53). Since the excess charges are so limited, the extra coverage may not be worth the additional premium.

You want the least expensive policy that covers prescription drugs.

H

You want the only policy that covers preventive care.

E (since preventive care coverage is limited to $120 a year, you should not pay more than $120 in additional premiums and administrative costs for this benefit).

You want coverage abroad at minimal extra cost.

C, D, E, F, G, H, I, J

Every insurance company in every state does not offer each of the ten standard policies. States can limit the number of model policies insurance carriers doing business in-state can offer, or can require every in-state insurer to offer certain standard policies.

ADDITIONAL PROTECTIONS FOR CONSUMERS

The new Medigap legislation does more than mandate the ten standard policies discussed above. It also protects purchasers of Medigap insurance by requiring each policy to include the following provisions:

• Guaranteed renewability. An insurer cannot cancel or refuse to renew a Medigap policy based on the insured's health. The only two reasons an insurer can cancel a Medigap policy are: (1) the insured fails to pay premiums; or (2) the insured lied on the application for coverage. With a guaranteed renewable policy the insurance company can, however, increase premiums periodically. Also, if the insured changes policies, coverage can be denied for health reasons.

• Preexisting condition limitations. Insurance companies can only limit or exclude coverage of health conditions for which the insured sought treatment within the 6-month period before the effective date of the Medigap policy. After the policy has been in effect for 6 months, all preexisting conditions must be covered. Don't be fooled by policies that advertise "no medical examination required." Even these policies may have preexisting condition limitations.

• Replacement policies. Certain protections apply to insureds who replace an existing Medigap policy with a new policy. If the old policy was in effect for at least 6 months, the new policy must cover all preexisting conditions. If the old policy was in effect for less than 6 months, the amount of time the old policy was in effect must be applied to the preexisting limitation period of the new policy.

TIPS FOR CONSUMERS OF MEDIGAP INSURANCE

Although shopping for Medicare supplemental insurance has become a lot easier since July 30, 1992, when the new federal legislation went into effect, you can still benefit from the following tips:

► TIP #1 *Comparison shop.*

The cost of Medigap insurance is not regulated by the government. Prices vary widely among insurers. Call a number of different companies to find out what benefits are offered at what prices. Many insurance companies charge different premiums depending on your age and where you live.

► TIP #2 *Select a reputable insurance company.*

Do not buy Medicare supplemental insurance from a little-known company. Your state department of insurance may be able to provide you with information about a company's claims history. You can also learn about an insurance company by reading *Best's Insurance Reports,* which you can find in your public library or writing to:

A. M. Best Company
Oldwick, NJ 08858

► TIP #3 *Do not buy more than one Medigap policy.*

Anyone who tries to sell you more than one Medigap policy is breaking the law. You do not need duplicating coverage, and additional policies are a waste of money.

➤ **TIP #4** *Only deal with a licensed insurance agent.*

States license insurance agents for your protection. Do not purchase insurance from anyone who cannot show you an agent's license. A business card is not a license. A representative from a particular insurance company is not necessarily a licensed agent. You can find out the names of licensed agents in your state by calling your state department of insurance.

➤ **TIP #5** *Do not rush to replace a policy you already own.*

If you are happy with your current Medicare supplemental policy, keep it. You may be entitled to benefits under your existing policy that are not offered by any of the new standardized policies. If you purchase a new policy, you are entitled to credit for the waiting period and preexisting conditions you have met under your old policy.

➤ **TIP #6** *Resist pressure to buy.*

Do not make a hasty decision, even if your insurance agent tells you that the premium will increase soon or that you only have a limited time to enroll. Shop around, ask questions, and speak to friends, relatives, and your doctor about the policy before you sign your first premium check.

➤ **TIP #7** *Do not pay your insurance premiums in cash.*

Use a personal check, money order, or bank check payable to the insurance company to purchase the insurance. Do not give any money to the insurance agent.

➤ **TIP #8** *Do not purchase a policy through the mail.*

If you receive an attractive solicitation in the mail, and would like to find out more about the offering company, call your state department of insurance or state consumer protection agency.

➤ **TIP #9** *Know about your right to a refund.*

By law, you are entitled to take 30 days to look over your Medigap policy. If you decide you do not want the policy within the 30 days, send it back to the insurance company or your agent. The company must give you a full refund of all the money you paid up to that point, no questions asked. Contact your State Department of Insurance if your money is not refunded promptly.

ℹ️ *For more information*

Consumer Information Center
P.O. Box 100
Pueblo, CO 81002

Request a free copy of "Guide to Health Insurance for People with Medicare."

AARP Fulfillment
601 E Street, N.W.
Washington, DC 20049
202-434-2277

Request a free copy of "Medigap: Medicare Supplement Insurance, A Consumer's Guide."

LONG-TERM CARE INSURANCE

IS IT FOR YOU?

Long-term care insurance could be for you if:

- You are between ages 50 and 84 and in decent health (although some insurers do not offer policies to people over age 79).
- You can afford the following sample premiums:

    For a 65-year-old, about $2,000 a year.
    For a 75-year-old, $4,000 or more a year.

- Using the guidelines below, you will *not* qualify for public medical assistance (e.g., Medicaid or Medi-Cal) soon after starting to receive long-term care.

    You are single with assets (excluding your home, car, and personal belongings) of between $40,000 and $100,000 (depending on your area).
    You are married with joint assets (same exclusions as single) of between $100,000 and $200,000 (depending on your area).

- You are concerned about preserving your estate for your heirs.

Medicare and Medicare supplemental insurance cover only a small percentage of the costs of long-term care. Long-term care is the type of care you require if you have a chronic illness or disability that impairs your ability to perform the activities of daily living, which include bathing, dressing, toileting, walking, and feeding. Long-term care includes:

- Nursing care.
- Assistance with personal care needs, such as dressing, eating, walking, and toileting.
- Assistance with household chores.

The most common conditions that necessitate long-term care are Alzheimer's disease and other types of dementia, strokes, and heart attacks. Your chances of needing long-term care are one in three after you reach age 65. For women, this percentage increases to one in two.

Long-term care is very costly. Nursing home fees in some areas top $80,000 a year, and the cost of daily home care is not far behind. Understandably, paying for long-term care is a primary concern of older adults.

To help you research your long-term care insurance options, this section deals with the following topics:

- Guidelines: what daily benefit do you need?
- How long should your benefits last?
- What protections should you look for in a policy?
- Tips for shopping for long-term care insurance.
- Checklist: does your policy protect you?

The section concludes with a discussion of state partnerships on long-term care and a list of resources where you can obtain additional information about long-term care insurance.

GUIDELINES: WHAT DAILY BENEFIT DO YOU NEED?

After you figure out how much you can spend each month on long-term care insurance, you must decide how much coverage you need.

Most long-term care policies pay a specific dollar amount each day you receive covered care. This is called the indemnity model of insurance. As the insured person, you are indemnified, or reimbursed, the amount of money your covered care costs you. The daily benefit amount varies tremendously from policy to policy.

Experts recommend purchasing a daily benefit amount sufficient to cover between 75 and 100 percent of the average nursing home costs in your area. The nursing home benefit can range from $40 to $250 a day.

If you also want home care coverage under your long-term care policy, you should try to purchase a policy that pays a daily home care benefit of at least 50 percent of the daily nursing home benefit. The average home care benefit is between $40 and $250 a day.

The other type of long-term care insurance policy is called the disability model. With this type of coverage, the insurance company pays a benefit to any insured person who becomes disabled and needs care. The amount of the benefit is not tied to the cost of services provided to the disabled person (as with an indemnity policy). Rather, the person insured under a disability policy can spend the monetary benefit in any way.

The primary advantage of a disability-type policy is flexibility. About 70 percent of long-term care is provided by relatives, spouses, children, and neighbors. These informal caregivers can be compensated with the benefits that are paid out under a disability policy. The downside of this flexibility is the risk of abuse. Unscrupulous family members or friends may bilk a disabled individual of insurance benefits that are payable under a disability-type policy.

Indemnity insurance coverage is generally less expensive than disability coverage. The following chart compares average annual premiums in 1993 for comparable coverage under a disability and an indemnity policy:

	Disability Model	**Indemnity Model**
Coverage	Nursing home care; any type of at-home care (even by family member); $100/day	Nursing home care; at-home care by professional skilled or unskilled personnel; $100/day
Waiting period	90 days	100 days
Maximum benefit period	6 years	5 years for each benefit (total of 10 years)
Age/premium	45/$351 50/$473 55/$651 60/$976 65/$1,516 70/$2,307	45/$371 50/$381 55/$530 60/$736 65/$1,097 70/$1,714

HOW LONG SHOULD YOUR BENEFITS LAST?

When selecting a policy, you must also decide on how long you want your coverage to last. You may be able to benefit from the following guidelines.

Nursing Home Coverage

There are three approaches to selecting the length of nursing home coverage under a long-term care policy:

• Coordinate your nursing home benefits with your future Medicaid eligibility. Time your nursing home benefits to last until you become eligible for Medicaid. To figure out approximately how many months of nursing home coverage you need, follow these steps:

Step 1	Enter the approximate value of your assets	$_____
LESS	Medicaid assets limit in your state	– $_____
EQUALS	Subtotal A	= $_____
Step 2	Subtotal A	$_____
LESS	Total deductible you must pay under the long-term care policy	– $_____
EQUALS	Subtotal B	= $_____
Step 3	Subtotal B	$_____
DIVIDED BY	Monthly co-insurance you must pay under the long-term care policy	÷ $_____
EQUALS	Subtotal C	= $_____
Step 4	Deductible period under the policy (in months)	$_____
PLUS	Subtotal C	+ $_____
EQUALS	Grand total	= $_____

The grand total represents the approximate number of months you will require long-term care insurance coverage after you enter a nursing home. At the end of this period, you will be eligible for Medicaid. Once eligible for Medicaid, you will no longer need private nursing home insurance benefits.

If you are likely to qualify for Medicaid benefits within 6 months of needing long-term care, you should not purchase a long-term care insurance policy at all. You may find yourself eligible for Medicaid before you even start collecting your insurance benefits.

• Purchase as much nursing home coverage as you can afford. Some of the more desirable nursing homes favor applicants who can pay for their care with private funds or insurance for the longest period of time. For example, a nursing home may admit an applicant with 5 years of private insurance coverage over an applicant who has only 3 years of coverage and then plans to switch over to Medicaid.

These discriminatory admission practices may or may not be a problem in your community. An elder law attorney or geriatric care social worker should be able to advise you about the situation that prevails in your area. Once an individual is in a nursing home, discrimination is not usually a problem. The law prohibits nursing homes from treating Medicaid and non-Medicaid residents differently.

• Purchase a minimum of 3 years of nursing home coverage. Coverage of less than 3 years will rarely be worth the cost of the insurance.

Home Care Coverage

With home care benefits, you should purchase the longest period of coverage you can afford, with a minimum of 2 years of coverage.

Medicaid programs in many states do not provide extensive home care benefits. Even where Medicaid does cover home care expenses, the quality of home care under Medicaid may be inferior to the quality of care you can purchase with private funds or insurance. For these reasons, many patients do not want to rely on Medicaid to pay their home care bills unless and until it is absolutely necessary.

WHAT PROTECTIONS SHOULD YOU LOOK FOR IN A POLICY?

Imagine paying premiums on a long-term care policy for 30 years, and then finding out that coverage is not available when you finally need it.

To avoid such an unpleasant surprise, make sure your policy contains the following important protections.

• Guaranteed renewability. The policy you purchase should include a written guarantee that the insurance company cannot cancel the policy unless you fail to pay your premiums or are found to have lied on your application. You should have the right to maintain your policy indefinitely. The insurance company should not reserve the right to cancel the policy if your health deteriorates or as you grow older. Beware of policies that are issued by insurance companies that reserve the right to cancel all of their long-term care policies. This could leave you without coverage, and without a right to a refund of the premiums you already paid.

Even if your policy is guaranteed renewable, your premiums may increase periodically. Some agents advertise policies that have level premiums. This means that all policyholders of a given age who purchase the policy at a given time pay the same premium. It does not mean that the insurer does not have the right to increase the premiums for an entire class of policyholders.

• Inflation protection. Health care costs are rising at an average rate of 12 percent a year. Since you may not collect benefits under your long-term care insurance policy for many years, you want your daily benefit amount to increase over time to keep up with inflation. Without inflation protection, the benefit that is adequate today may become worthless over time.

Many insurers offer an inflation protection rider to their long-term care policies. These riders increase the cost of the insurance considerably, usually 30 to 40 percent. The best riders provide 5 percent compound interest for a long period of time, such as 20 years or until a certain age. To keep your insurance premium down, you can select a simple inflation rider. Then you have the option of investing the money you save in reduced premiums to help supplement the cost of your care.

Three types of inflation protection options are:

1. Benefit amounts automatically increase each year (either compounded or simple interest).

2. You have the right to increase periodically your benefit amounts without submitting medical evidence of your insurability.

3. Inflation protection is available, but you must reapply when you opt to increase your benefit.

Beware of the third option!

Only under two circumstances can you afford to forgo inflation protection: if you are of advanced age (75 or older), or if your policy does not pay a fixed daily benefit amount, but rather bases its payments on "reasonable and customary charges."

• Elimination (or waiting) periods. Most policies require you to pay for your own long-term care expenses for a period of time before your coverage will begin. This type of provision is called the elimination or waiting period. Given the high cost of nursing home care, and the fact that about half of all nursing home residents return home within 3 months, you will want to avoid elimination periods of more than a few weeks. Your decision about the length of an elimination period must be based on your financial situation: How long can you afford to pay for your care privately during a waiting period? Can you afford the increased cost of a shorter waiting period? The industry standard for a waiting period is between 20 and 100 days.

• Preexisting condition periods. During the preexisting condition period, the insurance company will not cover expenses related to medical problems you had before your long-term care policy became effective. Many policies have a 6-month preexisting condition period. This means that the insurer is not required to cover your preexisting conditions until 6 months after the effective date of coverage. After 6 months, all prior conditions are covered. Shorter preexisting periods are, of course, more desirable than longer periods. If you are insurable, you should look for coverage of preexisting conditions that are fully disclosed on your application.

• Waiver of premiums. Under most long-term care policies, you can stop paying your premiums at some point after you begin to collect benefits. That point varies from policy to policy. Most policies do not waive premiums for 2 to 3 months after you enter a nursing home, and some do not waive the premiums at all when you are receiving home care coverage. Continuing to pay your premiums while you are receiving long-term care can be a hardship. Shop around for a policy that provides the most favorable waiver of premiums provision. The industry standard is a waiver of premiums 90 days after benefits (at home or in a nursing home) have started.

• Lifetime maximum. Some policies set a limit on the total amount of benefits you can collect under the policy. If the policy includes a maximum coverage provision, the limit should be in terms of a dollar amount, not a number of days. When the limit is set in days, a brief nurse's visit can use up a full day of coverage. Once the benefit limit is reached, no additional coverage is available.

• Broad coverage without undue restrictions. The policy should cover all levels of nursing home care, not just medical care. Most nursing home residents require a combination of medical care, nursing care, and custodial care.

Nursing Home Protections

Avoid policies that limit their nursing home coverage in one or more of the following ways:

• Custodial care is only covered if it is provided in a skilled nursing facility or other high-level facility.

• Nursing home care is only covered if it is "medically necessary." This requirement may be difficult to meet when a nursing home resident only requires custodial care.

• Nursing home care is only covered if it follows a hospitalization. Only about 27 percent of nursing home residents are admitted following a hospitalization.

• Lower levels of care are only covered if the insured first received skilled nursing care. The entry level of care should not determine coverage.

• Custodial care is only provided to individuals who cannot perform two or three "activities of daily living" (ADLs). The five most common ADLs are eating, dressing, toileting, bathing, and getting in and out of beds and chairs. The better long-term care policies do not require the insured to be completely unable to perform the ADLs (or be "totally dependent"). Rather, they provide benefits if the insured requires assistance with the ADLs (or is only "dependent"). Also, look for policies that cover residents who need assistance with two, not three, ADLs.

Home Care Protections

If you are also purchasing home care coverage, your insurance should cover skilled, semiskilled, and unskilled home care services. The services of visiting nurses and therapists, home health aides, homemakers, personal care attendants, adult day care centers, and respite care (which pays for someone to relieve a caregiving family member) should all be covered.

Do *not* purchase a policy that has the following limitations on home care coverage:

- Services are covered only if they are required after a period of hospitalization or nursing home institutionalization.
- Only "medically necessary" services are covered.
- Services are covered only if they are necessary to avoid placing the insured in a nursing home.
- Services are covered only if the insured requires assistance with three ADLs. The better policies require assistance with fewer ADLs.

Coverage of Alzheimer's disease and senile dementia should be explicitly stated.

TIPS FOR SHOPPING FOR LONG-TERM CARE INSURANCE

Long-term care insurance is still a relatively new product. You may not know anyone who has already purchased it, and you may be overwhelmed by your options. The tips in this section will prepare you for your foray into the world of long-term care insurance agents.

➤ TIP #1 *Fill out the application form yourself, or review the form for accuracy after your agent has completed it.*

Some agents minimize their client's medical problems so the application is approved and the agent collects a commission. This can result in problems later. When the insured files a claim for benefits down the road, the insurer can cancel the policy for failure to report accurately the medical history on the application.

➤ TIP #2 *Only buy long-term care insurance from financially sound insurance companies.*

Since you might not start collecting benefits for many years, you want to be sure the insurance company is not in any danger of going bankrupt. Insurance companies are rated on their financial health in *Best's Insurance Reports*. This publication is available in most public libraries. Do not buy long-term care insurance from a company that does not have at least an A+ or A rating from *Best's*. You can also check insurance company ratings from other independent rating agencies, such as Standard and Poor's, Moody's, and Duff and Phelps.

➤ **TIP #3** *Do not purchase a policy that only covers illness and injury.*

Physical frailty, Alzheimer's disease, Parkinson's disease, senility, and dementia should be specifically covered. Policies that exclude coverage of mental illness except for "geriatric disorders" and illnesses with "demonstrable organic disease" generally cover Alzheimer's disease, senility, and dementia. However, to be safe, request specific written assurances from the insurance company.

➤ **TIP #4** *Ask your insurance agent to make sure your medical records are reviewed by the insurer when you apply for a long-term care policy, <u>not</u> when you file a claim for coverage.*

With "preclaim underwriting," the company decides your insurability before you file a claim for benefits. This gives you the security of knowing that the insurance company determined your medical history to be accurate and complete before it approved your application.

Insurance companies that do not do preclaim underwriting do not check into your medical history until you file a claim for coverage. Then the company can look for reasons to deny your claim and rescind your policy. Although you will probably get a refund of your premiums, your long-term care expenses will be left uncovered. If the insurance company agrees to preclaim underwriting, send your medical records directly to the insurer, not your agent.

➤ **TIP #5** *Only purchase long-term care insurance from a company that has a favorable claims-paying history of over 96 percent.*

Your agent should be able to tell you the company's claims-paying history.

➤ **TIP #6** *Read the policy carefully.*

Do not take your agent's word about what the policy says. If you do not understand any part of the policy, ask a friend, relative, or lawyer for assistance. Sometimes you can speak to an insurance expert at your local senior citizens center. You can also get information from your state insurance department or state unit on Aging (see Appendix 1).

➤ **TIP #7** *After you buy a policy, you have 30 days to return the policy and get a full refund of your money.*

You do not have to give the insurance company or your agent any explanation for returning the policy.

CHECKLIST: DOES YOUR POLICY PROTECT YOU?

Check that your policy includes the following features:

1. Written guarantee of renewability.
2. Coverage of all levels of nursing home care.
3. Entry level of care does not determine extent of nursing home coverage.
4. Coverage of all levels of home health care.
5. No requirement of "medical necessity" for nursing home or home care coverage.
6. No requirement of prior hospitalization for nursing home or home care coverage.
7. An inflation rider with increases of at least 5 percent annually (simple or compound, depending on what you can afford) if under age 75 at time of purchase, or payments based on a percentage of reasonable charges.
8. Waiting period that matches the amount of time you are able to cover your long-term care expenses with your private funds (preferably no more than a few weeks).
9. Preexisting condition period of 6 months or less.
10. Waiver of premiums within 90 days of nursing home admission.
11. Lifetime maximum in dollar amounts.
12. Explicit coverage of Alzheimer's disease and physical frailty.
13. Daily benefit amount:
    a. Daily benefit amount for nursing home coverage equal to 75 to 100 percent of average cost in the area.
    b. Daily benefit amount for home care coverage equal to at least 50 percent of the daily nursing home benefit amount.
14. Duration of benefits:
    a. Nursing home benefits last until anticipated Medicaid eligibility, or as long as affordable, but at least 3 years.
    b. Home health care benefits last for as long as you can afford, but at least 2 years.
15. Benefits are paid in addition to other insurance, including Medicare.
16. Insurance company has A+ rating by A. M. Best Company.
17. Benefits are available even if insured is living out of state.

STATE PARTNERSHIPS ON LONG-TERM CARE

State partnerships on long-term care allow people to qualify for public medical assistance (Medicaid) without impoverishing themselves if they buy a state-approved long-term care insurance policy that provides certain minimum benefits. State partnerships on long-term care have recently been restricted by federal legislation.

For more information

National Association of Insurance Commissioners
120 West 12th Street, Suite 1100
Kansas City, MO 64105
816-842-3600

Request a copy of the free booklet "A Shopper's Guide to Long-Term Care Insurance."

AARP Fulfillment
601 E Street, N.W.
Washington, DC 20049
202-434-2277

Request a copy of the free booklet "Before You Buy: A Guide to Long Term Care Insurance."

Health Insurance Association of America
1025 Connecticut Avenue, N.W.
Washington, DC 20036
202-223-7780

Request a copy of the free booklet "The Consumer's Guide to Long Term Care" and a list of companies offering long-term care policies.

United Seniors Health Cooperative
1331 H Street, N.W., 5th Floor
Washington, DC 20005
202-393-6222

For a $10 annual membership fee, you can call for answers to your questions about private insurance.

SPECIFIC DISEASE INSURANCE

IS IT FOR YOU?

Specific disease insurance could be for you if:

- You are *not* a Medicare beneficiary.
- You do not have other major medical insurance.

Specific disease insurance only covers expenses related to the treatment of a single disease, such as cancer, or a group of specified diseases. Coverage under these types of policies is usually limited to the payment of a fixed benefit for specified types of treatment. The benefits are not coordinated with Medicare coverage. If you have Medicare and specific disease insurance, you probably have excessive, and costly, duplication of coverage. You do not need the specific disease insurance.

Some states prohibit the sale of specific disease insurance.

EMPLOYER GROUP HEALTH INSURANCE

IS IT FOR YOU?

Employer group health insurance could be for you if:

- You are employed.
- Your employer offers group health insurance.

Employer group health insurance is available to many working Medicare beneficiaries. Employers often offer their workers insurance coverage under a group health plan. The law requires employers with twenty or more employees to make available to workers age 65 or over the same health insurance coverage offered to younger workers.

If you are eligible for employer-based insurance and Medicare, you must decide whether to accept your employer's coverage.

IF YOU ACCEPT COVERAGE FROM YOUR EMPLOYER

What should you know about agreeing to participate in your employer's group health plan, even after you become eligible for Medicare coverage?

- Take your Part A Medicare coverage. Medicare Part A coverage is free for most beneficiaries, and can supplement the benefits you receive under your group health plan.

- Consider enrolling in Medicare Part B. If the coverage you get of doctors' bills and other outpatient expenses under the group plan is limited, the additional coverage you receive under Part B may be worth the relatively inexpensive premium.

- You must first look to your group health plan to pay your medical expenses. Medicare will only pay for covered expenses that are not reimbursed under the group policy. To maximize your total reimbursement, first file your claims with your employer's insurer. Then, if you do not get full reimbursement of services that are covered by Medicare, send a copy of the benefit statement issued by your employer's insurer to Medicare along with a Medicare claim form.

IF YOU REJECT COVERAGE FROM YOUR EMPLOYER

If you decline coverage under your employer's group health plan, Medicare will be your primary insurer. You may not look to your employer's insurer to pay for services that are covered by Medicare. Some group plans will, however, cover services that are not covered by Medicare, such as routine physical examinations, dental care, and prescription drugs.

ℹ **For more information**

Consumer Information Center
P. O. Box 100
Pueblo, CO 81002
Order a free copy of the booklet "Medicare and Employer Health Plans."

WORKERS' COMPENSATION OR NO-FAULT INSURANCE

IS IT FOR YOU?

Workers' Compensation or no-fault insurance could be for you if:

- You have a work-related illness or injury.
- You were in an accident and receive coverage under a no-fault insurance policy.

Worker's Compensation covers expenses arising from the treatment of work-related illnesses and injuries. No-fault insurance covers expenses related to automobile accidents. Medicare only pays for covered expenses that are not paid for by Workers' Compensation or no-fault insurance.

VETERANS' BENEFITS

Is It for You?

Veterans' benefits could be for you if:

- You served in the military.
- You are eligible for veterans' benefits.

If you are eligible for both Medicare and veterans' benefits, you may look to either program for payment of your medical expenses. Medicare will not, however, pay for:

- Services provided in a Veterans Administration (VA) hospital or other VA facility, except for certain emergency services.
- Services provided in a non-VA hospital, or by a non-VA physician, that have been authorized and paid for by the VA.

Medicare may reimburse veterans for some VA co-insurance payments.

PUBLIC MEDICAL ASSISTANCE (MEDICAID OR MEDI-CAL)

Is It for You?

Public medical assistance could be for you if:
- You are financially needy.
- You are not low-income, but you have high medical expenses and live in a state with a medically-needy program (see page 130).

Although Medicare and Medicaid (Medi-Cal in California) sound alike, they are very different programs. Medicaid is a program of medical assistance for low-income people. Like other welfare programs, Medicaid is paid for with tax dollars. Medicare is a medical insurance program for workers and their families. Like other insurance programs, Medicare is funded largely by its beneficiaries.

The chart that follows summarizes some of the important differences between the two programs.

Medicare	Medicaid
Eligibility does not depend on financial need.	Eligibility depends on financial need.
Medicare is a federal program. The same rules apply across the country.	Medicaid is run by the federal and state governments. Each state has its own Medicaid rules.
You can get information about Medicare from your local Social Security office.	You can get information about Medicaid from your local department of social services or welfare.
Medicare only pays for the treatment of acute medical needs.	Medicaid pays for acute medical treatment as well as long-term chronic care.
Medicare beneficiaries pay for part of their medical expenses in co-insurance and deductibles.	Medicaid recipients do not pay any part of their medical expenses.

You can be eligible for both Medicare and Medicaid. In most states, if you qualify for both programs, Medicaid will pay some or all of the following expenses:

• Your Medicare co-insurance. Medicaid will pay 20 percent of the approved charge not covered by Medicare Part B, in addition to any other co-insurance payments.

• Your Medicare deductible. Medicaid will pay the yearly deductible for Medicare Part A hospital insurance coverage.

• Your Medicare premium. Medicaid will pay the monthly premium for Part B Medicare coverage.

• Medical expenses not covered by Medicare. Every state's Medicaid program is different. In some states, Medicaid pays for many of the services that are not covered by Medicare, such as prescription drugs, dental care, routine medical examinations, and eyeglasses.

Medicaid is covered in depth in Chapter 5.

ℹ️ *For more information*

Consumer Information Center
P. O. Box 100
Pueblo, CO 81002

Order the free booklet "Guide to Health Insurance for People with Medicare."

BACK TO HARRIET

Harriet could supplement her Medicare coverage in a number of ways, starting with the purchase of a Medigap policy. Harriet ended up with an A Medigap policy. The package of basic benefits made the most sense for Harriet because she only used doctors that accept assignment, never traveled abroad, did not anticipate needing $250 worth of prescription drugs, and wanted to save some money for a quality long-term care insurance policy.

When we started looking at long-term care insurance, we focused on policies that provided generous home care benefits. Harriet told me that she never wanted to go to a nursing home. We settled on a policy that guaranteed Harriet a $100 daily home care benefit, and $120 daily nursing home benefit, indexed for inflation for 3 years. The cost of the policy: about $105 a month.

By the time Harriet left my office, she felt more confident about facing an admittedly uncertain future.

5.
QUALIFYING FOR MEDICAID BENEFITS

Larry came to see me about his wife, Louise, who had been suffering from Alzheimer's disease for several years. Recently she had become so confused and disoriented that Larry did not feel that he could continue to care for her at home.

Larry had made the painful decision to place Louise in a nursing home.

On top of his anxiety about being separated from his wife of 53 years, Larry feared for his own financial security. He had heard terrible stories about people being impoverished by a spouse's nursing home expenses. Friends and neighbors fed Larry's fears: One advised Larry to quickly divorce Louise; another suggested giving everything he owned to his daughter; a third recommended using up all his savings and then applying for Medicaid; a fourth mentioned something about a trust.

Larry needed to know: What, if anything, could he do to protect his life savings from the high cost of Louise's care?

Medicaid is a public assistance program that provides medical benefits to people who cannot afford to pay for their own health care. Unfortunately, due to deficiencies in our current health care system, Medicaid has become the number one payer of the long-term care expenses of older Americans.

Medicare and private insurance are rarely available to pay for the unskilled services many chronically disabled individuals require (including help walking, eating, bathing, dressing, and toileting). As a result, even upper- and middle-class older adults now need to know about the Medicaid program.

Long-term care can become outrageously expensive. The annual cost of a nursing home ranges from $35,000 to a mind-boggling $80,000. Round-the-clock care at home can also cost tens of thousands of dollars a year. Only the very rich can afford to pay these exorbitant rates for any extended period of time.

Older people understandably fear that their life savings will be drained by the high cost of long-term care. If you share this fear, you will want to know about steps you can take to protect yourself and your savings in the event you or your spouse requires long-term care.

Before you can develop a strategy for sheltering your savings, you must understand the rules of the game. What is the Medicaid program all about? What coverage and eligibility rules apply? What are the advantages and disadvantages of having Medicaid pay your medical bills? How do you apply for assistance?

After you have the answers to these fundamental questions, you are ready to learn what you can do to take full advantage of the Medicaid program. The chapter ends with a discussion of the impact of disability and death on Medicaid planning.

BASICS OF MEDICAID

Medicaid (Medi-Cal in California) is a joint federal-state medical assistance program that pays benefits to people age 65 or over, or disabled, who meet strict financial eligibility requirements.

Unlike Medicare beneficiaries, Medicaid recipients must demonstrate financial need to qualify for assistance. The rules governing financial eligibility for Medicaid vary somewhat from state to state, but all fall within federal elibility guidelines.

Medicaid recipients must go to doctors, hospitals, pharmacies, home care agencies, and nursing homes that participate in the Medicaid program. Participating health care providers do not charge their Medicaid patients any fees. Instead, these providers accept the patient's Medicaid card as payment in full (like a credit card), and then bill the state for reimbursement. Medicaid pays for prescription drugs and unskilled long term care, goods and services largely left uncovered by Medicare.

MEDICAID COVERAGE

Federal regulations set parameters within which each state is free to design its own Medicaid program. The result is a lack of uniformity among the states. What one state's Medicaid program covers is left uncovered in a neighboring state.

At a minimum, federal law requires every state's Medicaid program to cover the following:

- Hospitalizations.
- Outpatient hospital services, such as clinics.

- Physicians' services.
- Lab tests and X-rays.
- Nursing home care. In some states, such as New York, every nursing home accepts Medicaid. This is not true in other states. Even applicants to nursing homes that accept Medicaid should try to pay privately for a period of time (ideally at least 3 months). This period of private pay makes the applicant who is not already on Medicaid a more attractive candidate for admission.
- Home health care (both nursing and housekeeping services). In most states, Medicaid coverage of home care services is virtually nonexistent. Even in states where Medicaid-covered home care is available, patients are often better off paying for their care at home privately for as long as possible. Sometimes the quality of Medicaid-reimbursed home care services is inferior to private care, and Medicaid recipients cannot hire and fire their aides with the same ease as private-pay patients.

The following additional services are covered under *most* state Medicaid programs:

- Therapy and rehabilitation services.
- Dental care.
- Eyeglasses and dentures.
- Diagnostic, screening, and preventive health services.
- Podiatrists and optometrists.
- Prescription drugs.

Some state Medicaid programs also cover:

- Private-duty nursing.
- Hospice care.
- Personal care services at home.
- Adult day care
- Home-delivered meals.

Your local department of social services or public welfare can advise you about the Medicaid-covered services in your state.

MEDICAID ELIGIBILITY RULES

Medicaid eligibility rules vary from state to state. Although every state's rules must comply with certain federal regulations, there is tremendous variety among the states.

This section answers the following questions about Medicaid eligibility:

- Who is eligible for Medicaid?
- What are the Medicaid income limits?
- What are the Medicaid resource limits?

WHO IS ELIGIBLE FOR MEDICAID?

Depending on the state, the following categories of individuals may be eligible for Medicaid:

- Aged, blind, or disabled SSI recipients. In most states, if you are aged, blind, or disabled, and you receive benefits under the federal Supplemental Security Income (SSI) program (see Chapter 8), you automatically qualify for Medicaid assistance. In a minority of states, known as 209(b) states, you must meet more restrictive requirements.[1] Residents of 209(b) states can find out about these eligibility requirements by contacting their local department of social services or public welfare.

- Certain financially needy Medicare recipients. Every state Medicaid program pays the Medicare premiums, deductibles, and co-payments for certain low-income Medicare beneficiaries.

- "Medically needy" aged, blind, or disabled individuals. Medically needy recipients have income in excess of the Medicaid limits ("excess income"), but not enough income to meet their medical expenses. Medically needy recipients must "spend-down" (in other words, use up) their excess income on their medical expenses before they are eligible to receive any Medicaid benefits. Only some states provide Medicaid benefits to medically needy aged, blind, or disabled individuals.[2]

For example, Donald's monthly income is $900. Since the Medicaid income limit in his state is $400, Donald has $500 excess monthly income ($900 minus $400). Donald is recovering from a stroke. His monthly therapy bill is $1,500. Each month, under his state's one-month medically needy spend-down rule, Donald must pay his therapist $500—his excess monthly income. Medicaid pays the remaining $1,000 of Donald's therapy bill each month.

---

[1] These states are Connecticut, Hawaii, Illinois, Indiana, Minnesota, Missouri, Nebraska, New Hampshire, North Carolina, North Dakota, Ohio, Oklahoma, Utah, and Virginia.

[2] The following states do *not* provide Medicaid coverage to medically needy applicants: Alabama, Alaska, Arizona, Arkansas, Colorado, Delaware, Florida, Idaho, Iowa, Kansas, Louisiana, Mississippi, Nevada, New Jersey, New Mexico, Oklahoma, Oregon, South Dakota, Texas, and Wyoming. In these states, an applicant who has as little as $1 above the Medicaid income limit does not qualify for assistance.

WHAT ARE THE MEDICAID INCOME LIMITS?

Income is the money you receive each month. All income is either earned or unearned, depending on whether it comes from employment or self-employment (earned income) or from another source, such as Social Security, a pension, or investments (unearned income).

Every penny of earned and unearned income counts against your eligibility for Medicaid, unless it is specifically identified as exempt on the following list (which applies in most states):

- Half of all earned income, plus $65.
- $20 of unearned income each month (or $20 of earned income if your unearned income is less than $20).
- Infrequent or irregular income.

> **T**he majority of states use the same income rules to determine eligibility for Medicaid and Supplemental Security Income (SSI). SSI eligibility is covered in detail in Chapter 8.

You can only receive a certain amount of income each month and still qualify for Medicaid. Although the Medicaid income limits vary from state to state, they are always around $500 a month for an individual and $750 a month for a couple (when both members of the couple apply for assistance).

If your income exceeds these limits, don't assume you are not eligible for Medicaid. You may be eligible if you live in a "medically-needy" or "spend-down" state, as opposed to an "income-limit" state.[3] Residents of income-limit states are ineligible for Medicaid if their income is as little as 10 cents over the Medicaid income limit. This is not true for residents of medically-needy states.

In a medically-needy state, income in excess of the Medicaid limits does not disqualify the applicant as long as the applicant's medical expenses are high enough to consume the excess income. For example, assume the Medicaid income limit in a medically-needy state is $500. Roger, a resident, has monthly income of $600. Roger will qualify for Medicaid in any month he incurs $100 ($600 minus $500) in medical bills.

One of the biggest areas of confusion concerns the income limits that apply to spouses of Medicaid recipients. How much income are you allowed to have if you

---

[3] See footnote 2 for a list of income-limit states.

are living with someone who needs Medicaid? What if your spouse enters a nursing home and Medicaid starts paying those bills? Then how much income can you keep?

Let's look at each scenario in turn.

INCOME LIMIT FOR SPOUSE LIVING WITH MEDICAID RECIPIENT IN THE COMMUNITY

When your spouse applies for Medicaid, Medicaid will treat you and your spouse as a single household unit. This means that your spouse's income *and* your income will bear on your spouse's Medicaid eligibility, even if you don't need or want Medicaid. Though harsh, this is the law.

For example, Fred and Wilma, both over age 65, live together in the community. Fred's medical expenses have skyrocketed since his stroke, while Wilma continues to enjoy good health. Fred and Wilma fear that, unless something changes, their savings will be consumed by the high cost of Fred's illness. They decide to look into Medicaid. They soon learn that their total income cannot exceed about $750 a month, the Medicaid income limit for a household of two, even if only Fred applies for Medicaid.

If Wilma was under age 65, and not eligible for SSI based on her age, the situation would change somewhat. Depending on Wilma's income, some of her income might be "deemed" to Fred (see page 216 for a discussion of deeming). If deeming occurs, Fred's total income (including the deemed income) could not exceed the Medicaid limit for a couple; if none of Wilma's income was deemed to Fred, Fred's own income could not exceed the Medicaid limit for a household of one.

INCOME LIMIT FOR SPOUSE MARRIED TO INSTITUTIONALIZED MEDICAID RECIPIENT

Current law gives greater financial security to a healthy spouse whose mate is receiving Medicaid in a nursing home than to a healthy spouse who lives with a Medicaid recipient in the community, discussed above. The spouse who cohabits with a Medicaid recipient must meet the restrictive Medicaid income limits that apply to a couple (about $775 a month in 1994), whereas the spouse who is physically separated from his or her better half in the nursing home is entitled to a more generous "income allowance."

The amount of the income allowance depends on the applicant's state of residence. In 1994 the income allowance ranged from $1,148.75 a month to $1,817 a month.

Let's say your wife recently applied for Medicaid in a nursing home. In your state, the income allowance for the spouse in the community is $1,500. Your own income from Social Security and a pension is $1,000 a month. Your wife's Social

Security benefit is $750 a month. You are allowed to keep your $1,000 of income, plus an additional $500 of your wife's Social Security benefit to bring your total income up to the income allowance.

What happens to the remaining $250 of your wife's income? Since Medicaid assumes almost all of your wife's needs will be met by the nursing home, your wife will be permitted to keep only a very small "personal needs allowance" of between $30 to $70 (depending on the state) to pay for toothpaste, shampoo, haircuts, magazines, and the like. She may also be permitted to keep enough to maintain her private insurance, including Medicare, and pay for over-the-counter drugs not covered by Medicaid. The balance of her income will go to the nursing home, with Medicaid picking up the balance of her tab.

What happens if your spouse is in a nursing home, and your *own* income exceeds the income allowance? In some states Medicaid will ask, but not require, you to contribute a portion of your excess income to the cost of your spouse's nursing home care.

Changing the example above somewhat, say your monthly income is $2,000, not $1,000. Since your income exceeds the income allowance of $1,500, the state may ask you to use some of your extra $500 to defray the cost of your spouse's care. Some local Medicaid offices permit the non-institutionalized spouse who makes a voluntary contribution of income to keep assets in excess of the resource limits. Others don't.

WHAT ARE THE MEDICAID RESOURCE LIMITS?

Medicaid recipients are not permitted to own cash and property that exceed the Medicaid limits. These limits vary from state to state, but generally range from $2,000 to just over $3,000 for a single person, and from $3,000 to just over $4,500 for a couple (if both members of the couple apply for Medicaid).

> **T**he majority of states use the same resource rules to determine eligibility for Medicaid and Supplemental Security Income (SSI). SSI eligibility is covered in detail in Chapter 8.

Only these exempt resources do not affect an applicant's Medicaid eligibility (in most states):

- Applicant's home.
- Household goods and personal effects (up to a "reasonable value" for single applicants in some states).

- Automobile (up to a value of $4,500 for single applicants in some states).
- Burial space for the applicant (and spouse, if any).
- Separate $1,500 burial fund (if applicant has no insurance).
- Life insurance with face value of $1,500 or less.
- Income-producing property (such as land the applicant uses to grow food for personal use).

Each of these exempt resources is explored in greater depth in Chapter 8 on Supplemental Security Income. A closer look at the home, however, is provided here.

HOMESTEAD EXEMPTION

The exemption for the home only applies to your primary residence. A second home, such as a vacation home, will almost always disqualify you for Medicaid (unless the property can't be sold).

Your home remains exempt, even if you move out of it, as long as it remains occupied by your spouse or your minor or disabled child.

What happens to your home if you enter a nursing home for an extended stay, and do not leave behind a spouse or minor or disabled child? The answer depends on whom you ask.

The federal government will tell you that your home remains exempt as long as you express an intent to return home.[4] According to the federal Health Care Financing Administration, if you say, "I plan to return home," your home will remain protected, whether or not your doctor believes your plan to return home is realistic.

Many state Medicaid officials will give you a very different answer. According to them, your home is exempt only as long as you *realistically* plan to return to the community. You may even be required to submit a statement from your doctor certifying that there is a reasonable chance you will be able to return home. Without this medical certification, you may be required to sell your home after a number of months, and possibly reimburse Medicaid for benefits you received pending the sale of your house.

So where does all this confusion leave you? Without an answer to your question, that's where. To get the low-down on how your state treats the unoccupied homes of Medicaid recipients, you must call your local Medicaid office or ask a Medicaid specialist. Many legal services offices have staff attorneys who specialize in Medicaid. You can also try calling your local bar association for the names of Medicaid practitioners.

---

[4] Letter of December 26, 1991 to Joseph Gallant, Commissioner, Commonwealth of Massachusetts Department of Public Welfare, from Ronald Preston, Associate Regional Administrator, Health Care Financing Administration, Region I.

In addition to the home, another area of concern is the resource rules that apply to spouses of Medicaid recipients. How much cash and property are you allowed to keep if your spouse starts receiving Medicaid at home or in a nursing home?

RESOURCE LIMIT FOR SPOUSE LIVING WITH MEDICAID RECIPIENT IN THE COMMUNITY

The same analysis that applies to income limits applies to resource limits (see page 131). Medicaid will treat your and your spouse's property as mutually available, and will hold you both to the Medicaid resource limit for a household of two even if only your spouse requires Medicaid.

RESOURCE LIMIT FOR SPOUSE MARRIED TO INSTITUTIONALIZED MEDICAID RECIPIENT

Once your spouse starts to receive Medicaid in a nursing home, you become entitled to a "resource allowance," just as you become entitled to an income allowance (see page 131). The amount of the allowance will depend on your state of residence. States use one of the following two methods to compute the resource allowance.

1. The resource allowance equals half of what you and your spouse's total assets are worth on the day your spouse enters a nursing home (including assets in your sole name, your spouse's sole name, and your joint names, but excluding such exempt assets as your home, car, and personal property). If half your total resources is less than $14,532 (in 1994), your resource allowance will be $14,532.
2. The resource allowance equals the maximum permitted by law ($72,660 in 1994).

You must call your local Medicaid office or ask a Medicaid advocate how your state computes the resource allowance.

Your spouse in the nursing home is also permitted to retain some assets. The value of these assets cannot exceed the Medicaid resource limit that applies to a single individual (which is generally between $2,000 and just over $3,000, depending on your state).

If these stringent financial eligibility rules have not yet dissuaded you from applying for Medicaid, the following section tells you all you need to know about filing a Medicaid application and appealing a denial of medical assistance.

MEDICAID APPLICATIONS AND APPEALS

In most states, you must file an application for Medicaid at the county office of the department of social services. There are, however, two exceptions. Recipients of Supplemental Security Income (SSI) do not have to apply for Medicaid because they automatically qualify for assistance based on their receipt of SSI. Also, hospitalized patients and nursing home residents rarely have to file their own applications. Employees of the hospital or nursing home are usually charged with this responsibility.

If you are filing your own application, don't listen to Medicaid eligibility workers who may try to talk you out of applying by saying that you are probably not eligible for assistance. File your application anyway, and take your chances. You've got nothing to lose. If the worker refuses to accept your application, ask to speak with the eligibility supervisor. You have the right to insist that your application be accepted and processed.

Your Medicaid application must be supported by certain documents. The most common documents required in connection with a Medicaid application are listed here:

- To prove your identity:

  Birth certificate.
  Marriage certificate with date of birth.
  Passport.
  Immigration or naturalization papers.
  Driver's license.
  Medicare card.

- To prove your citizenship status:

  Birth certificate.
  Citizenship papers.
  Baptismal certificate.
  U.S. passport.
  Military discharge papers.

- To prove your residency:

  Rent receipt on landlord's stationery.
  Recent utility bill in your name.
  Hotel rent receipt.
  Real estate tax bill.
  Current lease.

- To prove your living arrangement:

  Rent receipt or canceled rent check.
  Statement from person helping you pay rent.

Statement from person in whose home you live.

Tax, insurance, utility, and mortgage bills.

- To prove your income:

    Pay stubs.

    Federal income tax return.

    Copy of Social Security, pension, and other benefit check.

    Current bankbooks or statements.

    Statements of dividends.

    Statement of annuity income.

- To prove your resources:

    Savings books or statements showing last 12 months of activity (at a minimum).

    Checking account statements showing last 3 months of activity (at a minimum).

    Stock and bond certificates.

    Deeds, mortgages, and property tax statements.

    Life insurance and annuity policies.

Do not wait until you gather all the necessary documents to file your application. The earlier you file your application, the sooner your Medicaid coverage will begin. You can submit your documents after your application is filed. Also, if you are unable to obtain certain documents despite your best efforts, your application should not be denied unless there is a reason to doubt your eligibility for assistance.

Once you have submitted your application and supporting documentation, you must wait to get a decision in the mail. If you don't hear anything within 3 months, call your local department of social services or public welfare. Medicaid is supposed to process your application within 45 days. If you do not get immediate results following your telephone call, file an appeal. (A sample letter requesting an appeal appears on page 137. See Alternate Paragraph #1.)

Medicaid coverage begins up to 3 months before the date of a Medicaid application, if the applicant is eligible during that time. For example, Sharon entered the hospital on June 1. She did not file a Medicaid application until July 1, and it was approved on August 1. Medicaid covered medical services Sharon received on or after April 1 since Sharon was over age 65, and financially eligible for coverage, as of that date.

When trying to determine whether retroactive Medicaid coverage will be available, look at the date you received the medical services, not the date of the doctor's bill.

Sample Letter Requesting Medicaid Appeal

Date

Fair Hearing Section
Department of Social Services
P.O. Box #
City, State, Zip

Re: [Name of Medicaid applicant]
Case Number: [From denial or termination notice]

Dear Sir/Madam:

Alternate Paragraph #1:
On [insert date of application], I filed an application for Medicaid. I have not received a decision on my application to date. I am requesting a fair hearing based on the county's failure to process my application in a timely manner.

Alternate Paragraph #2:
On [insert date of receipt of notice of denial], I received a notice that my Medicaid application had been denied. A copy of that notice is enclosed with this letter. I am requesting a fair hearing to appeal this determination.

Alternate Paragraph #3:
On [insert date of receipt of notice of termination], I received a notice that my Medicaid benefits were being terminated. A copy of that notice is enclosed with this letter. I am requesting a fair hearing to appeal this determination. Please continue my Medicaid benefits pending my appeal.

Thank you for your attention to this matter.

Sincerely,

Your signature
Your printed name

If you receive notice that your Medicaid application has been denied, review the notice to learn the basis of the denial. Most likely, you have been denied Medicaid for financial reasons. If Medicaid has used the wrong numbers to figure your financial eligibility, gather the documentation you need to prove the mistake. Then call your local department of social services to see if you can resolve the problem informally. If unsuccessful, request an appeal. (A sample letter requesting appeal appears on page 137. See Alternate Paragraph #2.)

Even after you start receiving Medicaid, you may need to appeal a notice of termination. (See Alternate Paragraph #3 of the sample letter.) Make every effort to appeal a termination notice before the date your benefits are to terminate, so your benefits will continue while your appeal is pending. If you lose your case on appeal, Medicaid may seek to recover benefits paid to you during the appeal.

The first level of a Medicaid appeal is a Fair Hearing. Depending on your state, you have up to 90 days to request a Fair Hearing, at which you can state your case in person before an administrative judge. You can also submit evidence and present witnesses. You can appear alone or with a representative, such as a lawyer, paralegal, social worker, or friend.

In most states, if you lose the Fair Hearing, you can file a further appeal in state court.

STRATEGIES FOR
PROTECTING YOUR SAVINGS

As already discussed, Medicaid applicants must meet strict financial eligibility requirements to qualify for benefits. When one member of a couple needs long-term care, and looks to Medicaid for assistance, the finances of both husband and wife are scrutinized. Sometimes a couple must deplete a lifetime of savings before the ill spouse can qualify for assistance.

You may be able to minimize the harsh effect of Medicaid's restrictive rules by taking advantage of some of the strategies discussed in this section.

Before you rush to qualify for Medicaid, however, you should be aware of some of Medicaid's limitations and drawbacks.

• Less freedom of choice. As a Medicaid recipient, you must receive treatment from health care providers who have agreed to participate in the Medicaid program. Many doctors do not accept Medicaid payment. They complain that Medicaid pays too little and entails too much paperwork. If your long-time family physician does not accept Medicaid, you may need to switch to a new doctor. You may also have trouble finding specialists who treat Medicaid patients.

• Lower quality of care. Because Medicaid pays health care workers less than the fees paid by private patients, the pool of qualified workers is smaller. This means that, in certain cases, the quality of the Medicaid-reimbursed medical care is inferior.

• Preapproval requirements. Preapproval may be required before Medicaid will pay for certain health care services, such as home nursing care. If Medicaid does not approve all the care you request, you must pay for the additional care with your private funds or file an appeal.

• Nursing home admissions problems. Not all nursing homes accept Medicaid patients. Even applicants with limited assets who are likely to apply for Medicaid in the near future often have trouble finding desirable nursing home placements. When a family member must enter a nursing home, location, cleanliness, quality of care, and services all become extremely important. Unfortunately, in many areas Medicaid recipients and prospective Medicaid recipients have difficulty finding an available bed in a facility that meets their standards and is located near friends and family.

• Budget problems. Federal and state governments are undergoing a financial crunch, and Medicaid is an extremely expensive program that is a popular target of cost-cutting proposals. There are no guarantees about the future of the Medicaid program. Benefits may be limited and eligibility requirements may be restricted. For these reasons, Medicaid may become an unreliable source of payment for long-term care.

• Public policy considerations. Medicaid was established as a program of medical assistance for the poor. There is an ongoing debate over the appropriateness of "sheltering" assets so that middle- and upper-middle-class individuals can qualify for medical assistance. Attorneys who counsel their clients to protect their savings, and look to Medicaid to pay their medical bills, often analogize the work they do to the work of tax specialists, who advise taxpayers how to take advantage of loopholes in the Tax Code to save money.

If, despite these considerations, you are still interested in pursuing Medicaid, eight strategies for protecting your assets are covered below. A key at the beginning of each section will help you decide whether you can benefit from the planning strategy discussed therein.

INVESTING IN EXEMPT ASSETS

Will you derive maximum benefit from this planning strategy?

- Do you own a home?
- Are you married?
- Do your liquid assets exceed the Medicaid resource limit in your state?

If your house is already paid off, things get a bit more complicated. You may want to consider taking out a new mortgage before your spouse enters the nursing home, and paying it off afterwards. (Only married couples really benefit from this planning technique.)

For example, imagine you and your husband have $40,000 in cash and a house without a mortgage. If your husband was to enter the nursing home and apply for Medicaid, you would only be permitted to keep $20,000 (your spousal allowance if you live in a state that computes spousal allowances using Method #1; see page 134). To protect the other $20,000 of your savings, you can take out a $40,000 mortgage on your home *before* your husband is institutionalized (if your children give you the mortgage, you will save loan fees). Then, when your husband enters the nursing home, your spousal allowance will be $40,000 ($40,000 cash plus the $40,000 mortgage, divided in half). You use the other $40,000 (what is left after you deduct your resource allowance) to pay off the mortage. Your husband will then qualify for Medicaid, and you will have succeeded in protecting $40,000 of your cash, not just $20,000.

Important warning: Do not execute this planning technique on your own. Ask an experienced Medicaid attorney how your state Medicaid office will treat this type of transaction.

If you answered yes to these three questions, this section should be of interest to you.

As noted in the discussion of resources (see page 132), some assets are invisible to Medicaid. These are called exempt assets. Exempt assets do not affect an applicant's eligibility for benefits. Examples of exempt assets include a primary residence, an automobile, household goods and furnishings, personal effects, and life insurance with a face value of $1,500 or less.

Cash is never exempt; it always affects an applicant's eligibility for Medicaid benefits. So, if you have too much cash (including savings, certificates of deposit, stocks, and bonds) to qualify for Medicaid, consider converting the bulk of your cash into exempt assets.

Here are some ways you can accomplish this:

- Pay off the mortgage on your house.
- Repair, remodel, or renovate your house.
- Modify your house to accommodate any physical limitations you may have (see page 298).
- Buy a new piece of furniture, jewelry, or appliances.
- Prepay funeral expenses.

By sheltering nonexempt assets in exempt property, you continue to enjoy your savings without losing out on Medicaid. And it's 100 percent legal, to boot!

INCREASING RESOURCE ALLOWANCE

Will you derive maximum benefit from this planning strategy?

- Are you married?
- Is your spouse in a nursing home, or likely to enter a nursing home in the near future?
- Is your income below your income allowance (see page 130)?
- Do you and your spouse have resources in excess of the resource allowance (see page 132)?

If you answered yes to these four questions, this technique may be for you.

You may be able to keep assets in excess of the resource allowance if your monthly income is less than your income allowance. That is, you may be allowed to retain enough income-producing assets to bring your income up to the income allowance.

An example will demonstrate this planning strategy. Imagine that your monthly income is $500 less than your income allowance. Each year you receive $6,000 less income than you are entitled to receive ($500 a month for 12 months). Medicaid law permits you to keep as much income-generating resources as you need to make up for this shortfall. If your savings are growing at a rate of 5 percent a year, $120,000 will generate $6,000 a year in interest ($120,000 times .05). This means that you should be permitted to keep $120,000, even if that amount exceeds your resource allowance.

SPOUSAL REFUSAL

Will you derive maximum benefit from this planning strategy?

- Are you married?
- Is your spouse in a nursing home, or likely to enter a nursing home in the near future?
- Do your resources exceed the permitted limits (see page 132)?

If you answered yes to these three questions, spousal refusal may be for you.

Spousal refusal is what its name implies: the refusal of one spouse to make money available to pay the medical expenses of the other spouse. Spousal refusal comes into play when one member of a couple requires nursing home care and the other member continues to reside in the community. (In some states, spousal refusal is also permitted when both members of a couple live together in the community and only one of them requires medical assistance.)

For example, Carol, who lives at home, has $100,000. Her husband, Sheldon, who lives in a nursing home, has no money in his name. Carol's resource allowance is $70,000. When the nursing home files a Medicaid application on Sheldon's behalf, Carol signs a statement refusing to make her extra $30,000 available to defray the costs of Sheldon's nursing home care. Sheldon will be awarded Medicaid, as long as he otherwise qualifies.

If this sounds too good to be true, wait. There is a downside to spousal refusal, based on the legal obligation of support, which requires one spouse to support the other spouse. In this example, Carol breaches her obligation to support Sheldon when she refuses to make her extra resources available to pay for the cost of his care.

Sheldon, of course, doesn't care. He would just as soon have Medicaid pay his bills. But Medicaid does care, and the law gives Medicaid the right to stand in Sheldon's shoes for purposes of bringing a support action against Carol. Whether Medicaid will actually bring such a suit depends on where you live—support suits are more common in some areas of the country than others. An experienced Medicaid attorney will be able to advise you about the likelihood of being sued for support in your neck of the woods.

Although the prospect of being sued is frightening, and the idea of refusing to make your money available to your spouse disconcerting, spousal refusal makes sense under the following circumstances:

- You are living in the community, and you need the extra money to protect your own financial security. For example, without the extra money you could not afford future rent increases or home repairs. Most judges are sympathetic to the financial concerns of community spouses who are married to nursing home residents, so you are on strong legal ground if you are sued.

- You are living in the community, and your funds are only a few thousand dollars in excess of your resource allowance. The state may be less likely to incur the costs of bringing legal action when it stands to recover only a small sum of money.
- You are estranged from your spouse in the nursing home, or were married only briefly. You may feel no responsibility to contribute financially to the cost of your spouse's care. The court is also more likely to view your refusal favorably.

Before you make up your mind about spousal refusal, consider the following points:

1. The fear and worry associated with a possible suit may not be worth the money you save.
2. If you are sued, you will probably have to pay attorney fees (unless you find an attorney willing to handle the matter on a contingency basis or pro bono). Some states have also proposed legislation assessing punitive damages against refusing spouses.
3. Spousal refusal often slows down the Medicaid approval process. Even though your spouse in the nursing home will eventually get Medicaid, you may need to file an appeal (see page 138).

GIFT-GIVING

Will you derive maximum benefit from this planning strategy?

- Do your resources exceed the Medicaid limits?
- Do you want to make cash gifts to your children, or other friends or family?

If you answered yes to these two questions, gift-giving may make sense for you.

Understandably, Medicaid does not permit applicants to shelter large sums of money by making gifts and immediately qualifying for benefits. If gift-giving were unrestricted, everybody who anticipated needing costly medical care would be tempted to make large gifts to loved ones and look to the government for medical assistance.

> **D**o not confuse gifts with purchases and exchanges. When you make a gift, you give something away without getting back something of equal value. With a purchase or an exchange, you do get back something of equal value. The discussion in this section only applies to gifts.

Before August 10, 1993, rules restricting gift-giving only applied to Medicaid coverage of nursing home care. Now states are permitted to extend their gift-giving rules to Medicaid eligibility for long term care in the community. Depending on your state of residence, gifts may now affect your eligibility for Medicaid-reimbursed home care services.

Gift-giving restrictions, whether at home or in a nursing home, only apply to gifts that are made by an applicant or the applicant's spouse within 36 months[5] of applying for Medicaid (the "look-back period"). A poorly timed gift can make the gift-giver (or spouse) ineligible for Medicaid for a period of time. The period of ineligibility will depend on when the gift was made and its value.

Many people are under the mistaken impression that the period of ineligibility is always 36 months, regardless of the value of the gift. No. The exact ineligibility period is computed by dividing the value of the gift by the average cost of a nursing home in your area. (You can get this number from your local Medicaid office.) This computation gives you the number of months you are ineligible for Medicaid. Start counting off the months from the month you made the gift, not the month you file an application for Medicaid.

For example, in January, 6 months before you enter a nursing home, you give your son $50,000. You learn from a local Medicaid official that the average cost of a nursing home in your area is $5,000. This gift will make you ineligible for nursing home Medicaid for 10 months ($50,000 divided by $5,000). Medicaid will not be available to pay your nursing home bills until November 1.

There are several exceptions to this gift-giving penalty. The following gifts do not result in any period of Medicaid ineligibility.

- Gifts of any type of property (including a home) to:

    A blind or permanently disabled child of any age or another person for the sole benefit of the blind or disabled child.

    A spouse or another person for the sole benefit of the spouse.

---

[5] Transfers to and from certain trusts are subject to a 60-month look-back period.

- Gifts of a home to:

  > A child under 21, blind, or permanently disabled.

  > A sibling with an ownership interest in the house who resided in the home for at least one year immediately before the applicant entered a nursing home.

  > A nondisabled adult child who resided in the home, and provided care to the applicant, for at least 2 years immediately before the applicant entered a nursing home.

- Gifts of exempt assets other than the home (such as an automobile, household goods, and personal effects) to anyone.

If you are considering using gift-giving to shelter your money, keep the following points in mind:

1. If you make a gift, make sure you keep enough money to pay for your long term care in the event the gift results in a period of Medicaid ineligibility.

2. Do not give away all your money because you will probably be admitted to a better nursing home if you have enough money to pay for your care privately for a period of time (at least 3 months).

3. Beware of making gifts with the understanding that the gift will always be available to you if you need it. Even if the recipient of the gift plans to hold the gift for you, circumstances might cause the loss of the gift. For example, the recipient of the gift might be sued, become divorced, predecease you, or go bankrupt—and the gifted funds could be lost.

4. You will not be penalized for making a gift if you can prove that the purpose of the gift had nothing to do with qualifying for Medicaid. This is difficult to prove, because Medicaid will presume that the purpose of the gift was to qualify for Medicaid. The best way to rebut this presumption is to show a pattern of gift-giving (you have given your daughter $5,000 every year for the past 5 years) or an unexpected need for costly medical care (a sudden stroke).

5. If you make a gift that disqualifies you for Medicaid, and you desperately require medical assistance during the resulting period of ineligibility, you may be eligible for Medicaid under the undue hardship exception. However, this is not something you want to count on. Medicaid interprets the undue hardship exception very narrowly to discourage people from relying on it.

6. You will be permitted to recover gifts after Medicaid eligibility is established. Let's say you give your son $200,000 so your husband can qualify for Medicaid in a nursing home. Your son uses some of the $200,000 to pay your husband's nursing home bills during the resulting period of ineligibility. When the ineligibility period is over, your husband applies for Medicaid. Your son can return

to you whatever is left of the $200,000, and your husband's Medicaid benefits will be safe.

PURCHASING AN ANNUITY

Will you derive maximum benefit from this planning strategy?

- Are you married, and do the combined resources of you and your spouse exceed the resource allowance?
- Does your spouse require nursing home care?

If you answered yes to both of these questions, you may be able to save money by purchasing an annuity.

An annuity has the unique feature of turning an asset into a stream of income. When you purchase an annuity, you invest a sum of money with an insurance company in return for guaranteed payments of income for a specified period of time.

To shelter your money in an annuity, invest the cash you have in excess of your resource allowance, say $100,000, in an annuity when your spouse enters a nursing home. Each month you will receive a check in the mail for several hundred dollars from the annuity. Your receipt of this income will not affect your spouse's eligibility for nursing home Medicaid because it is paid to you (see page 134).

As long as the annuity is irrevocable and nonassignable, Medicaid cannot force you to cash it in and use the proceeds to help pay your spouse's nursing home bills. As long as the annuity term does not exceed your life expectancy, its purchase should be permitted.

Under current law, the purchase of a lifetime annuity is not a gift, so it does not trigger the ineligibility period that gifts can trigger (see page 144). However, since rules governing annuities can change at any time, do not purchase an annuity with the intention of qualifying for Medicaid before you ask a Medicaid expert about the status of the law.

DIVORCE

Will you derive maximum benefit from this planning strategy?

- Are you married?
- Can you handle the idea of divorcing your spouse?

If you answered yes to both of these questions, you may want to consider divorce. Often one member of a married couple requires long-term care before the healthier mate does. Divorce, as a strategy to protect the financial security of the healthier spouse, should only be considered under the following limited circumstances.

- One spouse remains in the community when the other spouse enters a nursing home, and the spouse in the community has substantially more than twice the amount of assets permitted by Medicaid. In 1994 the maximum amount of assets the spouse of an institutionalized Medicaid recipient could retain was $72,660. (This limit may be significantly lower in some states.) In states using the maximum resource limit, divorce may be an option when the community spouse has more than $150,000 in his or her own name.

- In a community property state,[6] the spouse who remains in the community when the other spouse enters a nursing home has substantial "separate" property. Separate property is property that the healthier spouse received as a gift or inheritance.

If you are considering divorce as a planning strategy, keep the following points in mind:

1. A legal separation will not protect any assets because you will still be married.
2. You and your spouse should each be represented by an attorney.
3. State law will largely determine how effectively assets can be protected through divorce.
4. Before you proceed with the divorce, both attorneys should have preliminary discussions with the judge. A judge who is not receptive to the plan can leave the healthier spouse in a worse position by requiring the healthier spouse to support the institutionalized spouse or ordering an equal division of all property, including the house.
5. Court records should clearly reflect that the property is being divided unequally between husband and wife.
6. In states where divorces are only granted for "fault," possible grounds for divorce include extreme cruelty and insanity.
7. Where one spouse lacks capacity, the court must appoint a guardian *ad litem* or other surrogate.

Needless to say, divorce is an extreme approach to asset preservation that raises a number of difficult issues:

---

[6] Arizona, California, Idaho, Nevada, New Mexico, Texas, Washington, and Wisconsin are community property states.

- If you divorce your ailing spouse, will you feel as if you are abandoning your mate during a difficult time? The risk of guilty feelings may not be worth the potential savings.
- How does your religion view divorce?
- Are you prepared for expressions of disapproval from friends and family?

TRUSTS

Will you derive maximum benefit from this planning strategy?

- Are you willing to irrevocably give up access to almost all of your savings?
- Do you want to protect the maximum amount of your savings for your heirs?
- Are you reluctant to give your property outright to your children, or anyone else?

If you answered yes to these three questions, you might be interested in learning more about Medicaid trusts.

Medicaid applicants who try to shelter assets in a trust must exercise extreme caution. Trusts have to be carefully drafted to comply with a number of stringent state and federal laws. An attorney who specializes in Medicaid law and trusts should always be consulted.

Traditionally, if you planned to apply for Medicaid you could shelter your money in a trust by irrevocably giving up access to your property, and only receiving the income that the property in the trust generated. This may no longer be permitted under federal law. The Omnibus Budget Reconciliation Act of 1993 (OBRA '93) includes a provision that throws into doubt the continued legality of so-called income-only trusts. Given the uncertainty surrounding these types of trusts, be sure to consult a knowledgeable elder law attorney before attempting to use a trust to shelter your assets from Medicaid.

Here are some additional points to keep in mind about Medicaid-protected trusts:

1. Revocable trusts never shelter assets from Medicaid. Only irrevocable trusts can shelter your property from Medicaid. An irrevocable trust can never be changed or terminated once it is established.

2. You and your spouse are prohibited from serving as trustees of a trust designed to shelter your money from Medicaid.

3. When you fund a Medicaid trust, you will be treated as making a prohibited gift for purposes of the gift-giving restrictions (see page 144).

4. Medicaid-protected trusts that comply with federal law may not be permitted

under state law. A consultation with an experienced elder law attorney is essential.

LIFE ESTATES

A life estate is a form of property ownership. When you have a life estate, you own the property for the duration of your life. Upon your death, the house automatically becomes the property of the person(s) you selected. Life estates offer the advantage over outright gifts of protecting your interest in the property for the rest of your life. This protection is especially important if the property is your home.

A life estate is an effective way of protecting your house in the event you have to enter a nursing home. If you only have a life estate in your house, you should not be forced to sell your home. At worst, if you hang on to your life estate through the application process, your state Medicaid program may treat you as if you are renting out your home. Your monthly income will then be increased to reflect the fair market rental value of your house. If the property is sold, your income for Medicaid purposes may also increase to reflect your lifetime interest in the property.

If you decide to give away your life estate instead, you will be treated as making a prohibited transfer (unless the gift is specifically permitted under Medicaid law; see page 144). The value of the gift will be based on your life expectancy and the value of the home. Let's say your home is worth $150,000. You only have a life estate in the home; your son owns the future interest of the home. Given your advanced age, the value of your life estate is $50,000. When you enter a nursing home, you give your son your life estate. This gift will result in a 10-month period of ineligibility (based on the formula discussed on page 144). If you had given your son the entire home when you entered the nursing home, you would have been ineligible for Medicaid for a longer period of time.

The creation and gifting of life estates have important tax consequences. These are discussed below at page 357.

HOW TO ANTICIPATE YOUR DISABILITY IN YOUR MEDICAID PLANNING

As you can see from the previous section, there are plenty of ways you can protect your savings from the high cost of long-term care. The question that arises, then, is *when* you should start planning for your possible need for long-term care.

You certainly don't want to give up control over your property prematurely. As long as you are healthy enough to enjoy your money, you should do just that. But there is also a risk to adopting a wait-and-see approach to Medicaid planning. You may lose the opportunity to preserve your money for your heirs if you become incapacitated before you have taken steps to shelter your funds. Once you lose legal capacity, no one can touch your money unless you have given that person the legal authority to do so.

The document you use to authorize another person to manage your finances on your behalf is called a power of attorney. In a power of attorney, you can give someone you know and trust access to your money. The power of attorney must be "durable" if it is to remain in effect after you become incompetent.

Most older people appoint a child (or children) as their agent under a durable power of attorney with the intention of empowering the child to perform such financial transactions as paying the parent's bills and endorsing checks payable to the parent. If you want to give your child the authority to give away your property for purposes of establishing Medicaid eligibility, speak to a qualified attorney. A standard general durable power of attorney that you can pick up in a legal station-ery store may not do the trick, depending on the laws that apply in your state.

A power of attorney is a powerful document. Once you sign a general durable power of attorney, you give another person immediate access to all your property. (Some states permit a "springing" durable power of attorney, which does not "spring" into effect unless and until you become unable to manage your own affairs.) Although the person you appoint in the power of attorney (your agent) is under a legal obligation to act in your best interest, who will sue if that person breaches the obligation? Maybe no one. This is why you should only appoint some-one you trust implicitly as your agent.

HOW TO ANTICIPATE DEATH IN YOUR MEDICAID PLANNING

Most couples hold the majority of their property jointly, with rights of survivor-ship. When one member of the couple dies, the jointly held property automatically becomes the sole property of the surviving spouse. This is fine, unless the surviving spouse is a Medicaid recipient in a nursing home. Then that spouse will have to use up the inheritance on nursing home bills until only $2,000 or $3,000 is left, and the surviving spouse requalifies for Medicaid.

The best way to avoid this scenario is to transfer everything out of the ill spouse's name and into the name of the healthy spouse shortly before or after the ill spouse enters a nursing home. Another important step is to review your wills. If you have the typical "loving" wills ("I leave everything to my husband/wife, he/she leaves everything to me"), you will probably want to get new wills. You do not want your spouse in the nursing home to inherit everything, when you know it will all be lost to the nursing home.

When redoing your wills, you have some options.

- Disinherit your spouse. There is a risk to this option. State law protects surviving spouses by giving them a legal entitlement to a portion (usually one-third or one-half) of a deceased spouse's estate. In some states, institutionalized Medicaid recipients (especially if incompetent) are forced to claim this legal entitlement. The two ways you may be able to avoid this danger is to leave your property to your heirs in a revocable living trust instead of a will, or to have your will spouse waive the right to a portion of your estate. An attorney will be able to explain the details of these options to you.

- Leave a testamentary trust. A testamentary trust is a trust that takes effect at death. While you are alive, you will continue to have full control over your property. At your death, however, the trust can provide that your surviving spouse's inheritance will be protected from certain long-term care expenses (say in a nursing home). You will also have to name a trustee (usually a child) to administer the trust.

For example, if your wife has early Alzheimer's disease, you may want to include a testamentary trust in your will that names your daughter as trustee. The trust can give your daughter the discretion to use the trust funds to finance your wife's care at home, but prohibit your daughter from using the trust to pay for any nursing home expenses other than those not covered by Medicaid (such as a private room). Although your wife will still be entitled to receive a portion of your estate outright (the one-third or one-half share discussed above), the testamentary trust can be used to protect the balance of her inheritance.

A testamentary trust will only control property that you hold in your sole name. Anything you hold jointly with your spouse will pass outright to your spouse upon your death; not into the testamentary trust. Once again, be sure to consult a lawyer if you are considering establishing a testamentary trust.

You should know something else about death and Medicaid. In most states, Medicaid has the right to file a reimbursement claim against the estate of a Medicaid recipient who does not leave a surviving spouse. Sometimes Medicaid can also file a claim against the estate of the spouse of a predeceased Medicaid recipient. Medicaid programs are likely to step up their estate recovery efforts in light of recently-passed federal legislation mandating the establishment of an estate recovery program in each state.

BACK TO LARRY AND LOUISE

In Larry's case, none of the options his friends suggested made sense.

After reviewing Larry and Louise's financial situation and their anticipated health care needs, we developed a game plan. Under the plan, Larry and

Louise set aside a sum of money to secure a desirable nursing home placement for Louise. Larry and Louise also made some carefully timed gifts to their daughter. Finally, Larry decided to refuse to make his excess money available to defray the cost of Louise's nursing home care.

By the end of the meeting Larry realized that Medicaid would pay his wife's nursing home bills without putting him and the rest of his family in the poorhouse.

6.

COLLECTING SOCIAL SECURITY RETIREMENT BENEFITS

Jackie had just turned 64 when she started seriously considering retiring from her job as an editor. Although she knew that she was ready to stop working full-time, she was afraid that she would miss the workplace if she stopped working entirely. She decided to continue doing some editorial work on a free-lance basis after she retired. How, she wondered, would her plans affect her entitlement to Social Security retirement benefits?

One of the great rewards of growing older in America is finally starting to collect money you paid into the Social Security system while you were working. Individuals who retired in 1985 paid into the system less than 9 percent of what they will get back in retirement benefits.

If you are like two-thirds of all retirees, you are probably counting on Social Security to provide at least half of your retirement income. To make sure you and your family collect the largest Social Security benefit you are entitled to receive, you must understand a number of details about the Social Security system. Tedious though they may be, these details will help you maximize your Social Security retirement benefit.

This chapter covers seven important ways you can get the most out of Social Security:

1. Make sure you get credit for all the years you worked.
2. Confirm the accuracy of Social Security's records.
3. Think carefully about when you retire.
4. File a timely application for benefits.

5. Check to see that your benefit amount is computed correctly.
6. Make sure your family members get their full benefits.
7. Consider working after retirement.

Each point is covered in a separate section of this chapter. At the end of the chapter, you will find a brief discussion of the mechanics of collecting your Social Security retirement benefit.

For general information about Social Security benefits, call or visit your local Social Security office, or call Social Security's toll-free number (800-772-1213), and request a copy of "Understanding Social Security" (Publication Number 05-10024). For information specifically about Social Security retirement benefits, request the publication entitled "Retirement" (Publication Number 05-10035).

MAKE SURE YOU GET CREDIT FOR YEARS WORKED

Social Security retirement benefits are paid to employees and self-employed workers (who work for themselves) based on their work history. If you have been an employee or self-employed, two aspects of your work history are relevant to your eligibility for Social Security retirement benefits:

- The type of work you did. You must have worked in covered employment.
- The length of time you worked. You must have worked long enough to earn sufficient quarters of coverage.

Performing the right type of work for a long enough period of time makes you fully insured for Social Security retirement benefits.

The terms "covered employment," "quarters of coverage," and "fully insured" are explained in the following three sections.

COVERED EMPLOYMENT

Covered employment is work that participates in the Social Security system. All types of self-employment participate in the Social Security system.

Workers who are employed in covered employment pay Social Security taxes. The only workers who do not work in covered employment, and do not pay Social Security taxes, are the following:

- Railroad employees. These workers are covered by the Railroad Retirement system. (Some railroad employees qualify for both Railroad Retirement benefits and Social Security benefits.)

- Most federal government employees hired before 1984. These workers are covered by Civil Service Retirement or other pension plans.

- About 25 percent of state and local government employees. Since June 1991, all state and local government units with no pension plan are covered by Social Security. State and local government units with a pension plan can elect whether to join Social Security. If you are a government worker, and would like additional information about your eligibility for Social Security benefits, request the following two free fact sheets from any Social Security office: "Government Pension Offset" (Publication Number 05-10007) and "A Pension From Work Not Covered by Social Security" (Publication Number 05-10045).

- Some school employees who participate in a teachers' pension plan.

- Employees working for nonprofit organizations before 1984. Many of these workers are covered by a private pension.

- Clergy (unless they elect to be covered under Social Security).

- Self-employed workers before 1951.

- "Off the books" workers. Housekeepers, gardeners, and babysitters rarely have Social Security taxes deducted from their pay.

QUARTERS OF COVERAGE

You accumulate quarters of coverage, or credits, by working in covered employment and paying Social Security taxes. You need a minimum number of quarters of coverage to qualify for Social Security benefits. The number of quarters of coverage you require depends on your date of birth.

To get a quarter of coverage, you must earn a certain amount of money in covered employment, as outlined in the chart below. At most, you can accumulate four quarters of coverage a year.

Minimum Earnings Required for a Quarter of Coverage

Year of Employment	Required Earnings
1936–1977	One quarter of coverage for every $50 or more you earned during each 3-month period. In other words, if you earned at least $50 during each of the four 3-month periods in a year, you acquired a total of four quarters of coverage for the year. However, if you earned $50 or more in one 3-month period, but less than $50 in the three other 3-month periods of the year, you only acquired one quarter of coverage for the year.

	Per Quarter	Per Year
1978	$250	$1,000 (4 times $250)
1979	$260	$1,040 (4 times $260)
1980	$290	$1,160 (4 times $290)
1981	$310	$1,240 (4 times $310)
1982	$340	$1,360 (4 times $340)
1983	$370	$1,480 (4 times $370)
1984	$390	$1,560 (4 times $390)
1985	$410	$1,640 (4 times $410)
1986	$440	$1,760 (4 times $440)
1987	$460	$1,840 (4 times $460)
1988	$470	$1,880 (4 times $470)
1989	$500	$2,000 (4 times $500)
1990	$520	$2,080 (4 times $520)
1991	$540	$2,160 (4 times $540)
1992	$570	$2,280 (4 times $570)
1993	$590	$2,360 (4 times $590)
1994	$620	$2,480 (4 times $620)

Let's say, for example, you worked 6 months in 1992, and earned $2,000. According to the chart, you needed to earn at least $570 to acquire one quarter of coverage. Your earnings of $2,000 entitle you to three quarters of coverage (3 times $570 equals $1,710), regardless of how many months you actually worked. You would not be entitled to the fourth quarter of coverage because your annual earnings did not exceed $2,280 (4 times $570).

Most people earn more quarters of coverage than they need to qualify for Social Security benefits. Although additional quarters of coverage do not mean additional benefits, higher earnings do translate into a higher retirement benefit, up to a point.

FULLY INSURED

When you earn enough quarters of coverage to qualify for a particular Social Security benefit, you are fully insured for that benefit. If you were born in 1929 or later, you will need forty quarters of coverage to be fully insured for retirement benefits. If you do not have at least forty quarters of coverage, you are not eligible to collect Social Security benefits when you retire. Most workers earn forty quarters of coverage by working for 10 years in covered employment, at four quarters of coverage a year.

Workers born before 1929 need fewer quarters of coverage to qualify for benefits, as shown in the chart below:

Required Quarters of Coverage (QCs)

Year of Birth	Required QCs	Minimum Years of Employment Needed
1921	32	8 years
1922	33	8 years, 3 months
1923	34	8 years, 6 months
1924	35	8 years, 9 months
1925	36	9 years
1926	37	9 years, 3 months
1927	38	9 years, 6 months
1928	39	9 years, 9 months
1929 and after	40	10 years

You can learn how many quarters of coverage you have by requesting a Personal Earnings and Benefit Estimate Statement (PEBE). PEBEs are covered in this chapter on page 158.

What if you do not have forty quarters of coverage? Have you missed the Social Security benefit boat?

Not necessarily. It's probably not too late to make up your missing quarters of coverage (if you requested and reviewed your PEBE early enough). In 1994 you only needed to earn $620 to acquire one more quarter of coverage. If you earned as little as $2,480 a year, you get four more quarters of coverage posted to your Social Security earnings record. These few additional quarters of coverage might be all that is standing between you and a few hundred dollars a month retirement benefit check.

CONFIRM THE ACCURACY
OF SOCIAL SECURITY'S RECORDS

If you look up "huge and unmanageable bureaucracy" in the dictionary, you will probably find the Social Security Administration's logo. The Social Security system is immense, and prone to error.

Although you may be able to sympathize with Social Security's plight (surely it's no easy task providing a range of benefits to millions of Americans), you do not want to be the one whose Social Security record does not accurately reflect your work history. The only way to protect yourself is to make sure that you get full credit for every month you work, and every dollar you earned, in covered employment.

REQUESTING EARNINGS AND
BENEFIT ESTIMATE STATEMENT

It's cheap and easy to find out how many quarters of coverage Social Security has credited to your account. Simply request a Personal Earnings and Benefit Estimate (PEBE) Statement. The PEBE sets out your complete earnings history.

To get your free PEBE, you must submit a Request for Earnings and Benefit Estimate Statement (Form SSA-7004-PC) to the Social Security Administration. A copy of this form is reprinted in Appendix 7.

When filling out the form, keep the following points in mind:

- Your planned retirement age must be 62 or older.
- Anticipate that your future yearly earnings will be the same as your current earnings, unless you have other information.
- Enter your name exactly as it appears on your Social Security card.

Send your completed Request for Earnings and Benefit Estimate to:

Social Security Administration
Albuquerque Data Operations Center
P.O. Box 27477
Albuquerque, NM 87125-7477

You should receive your PEBE in about a month.

Don't forget! Keep a copy of everything you send to the Social Security Administration. If you think *you're* bad about losing things like your keys, just wait until you start dealing with the Social Security Administration. Social Security misplaces files, and then expects you to replace the lost documents.

The PEBE will provide you with a year-by-year record of your employment history and earnings dating back to 1937, and your estimated retirement benefit at ages 62, 65, and 70.

PEBEs have become so popular that Social Security plans to start automatically sending them out to individuals age 60 and over beginning in 1995. By 1999 every worker, regardless of age, should be receiving an annual PEBE in the mail.

Correcting Mistakes in Your Earnings and Benefit Statement

If you discover a mistake in your PEBE, promptly call Social Security's toll-free number (800-772-1213) or visit your local Social Security office. About 2 to 3 percent of people who check their employment records find errors.

The two most important mistakes to look for are:

• Did you contribute too much in Social Security taxes? Social Security taxes your earnings up to a maximum taxable amount. The money you earn in excess of the maximum taxable amount is not supposed to be reduced by Social Security taxes. To make sure your excess earnings were not taxed, look at which of your earnings were subject to the FICA (Social Security) tax. Compare these earnings to the table of maximum taxable earnings (see page 169). Make sure you were not taxed on money you earned over and above the maximum taxable amounts.

• Is your work and earnings history accurate? Make sure every month you worked, and every dollar you earned, is reported on your earnings record.

To prove that you worked more months or years than have been credited to your account, you must submit any or all of the following documents to Social Security:

- W-2 statements. (If you have not kept these forms, you will have a hard time getting them from your former employer, even if it is still in business. The law only requires employers to hold on to these records for 3 years.)
- Pay stubs.
- Federal income tax returns. To request a copy of a return filed within the

last 6 years, you must submit IRS Form 4506, which you can get by calling 800-TAX-FORM (829-3676).

- Other proof (such as a written statement from your employer).

You must also submit a completed form called Request for Correction in Earnings Record, which you can obtain from the Social Security Administration by calling 800-772-1213 (and which is reprinted in Appendix 8).

There is a time limit for correcting errors in your earnings record, but don't let it discourage you from attempting to correct your earnings record at any time. The time limit is 3 years, 3 months, and 15 days from the date of the error. This means that if your earnings for 1985 were posted incorrectly, you technically had until mid-April 1989 to notify Social Security of the error.

But there are several exceptions to this limit:

- The error is obvious, and apparently due to a clerical mistake.

- The error is a result of fraud.

- Your earnings were posted to the wrong person's account, or for the wrong time period.

The bottom line is that, if you have proof positive that there is a mistake (say W-2 forms, or evidence that your former employer failed to report accurately your wages or pay Social Security taxes on your behalf), the time limit should not prevent you from correcting your record, no matter how long you wait.

If you convince Social Security that an error has been made, your record should be corrected in 6 to 9 months. To make sure that all requested changes have been made, request an updated PEBE about a year after you ask for corrections to be made in your earnings record.

THINK CAREFULLY
ABOUT WHEN YOU RETIRE

You may not have a choice about when you retire. Family, finances, health, or your job may determine the date you stop working. But if you can freely pick your date of retirement, give careful thought to retiring at an age that will get you the most from Social Security.

You can start collecting Social Security retirement benefits as early as age 62, or as late as age 70, whichever retirement age leaves you in the best position.

EARLY RETIREMENT

If you retire early, between ages 62 and 64, you will be eligible for between 80 and 93 percent of the full retirement benefit you would be eligible to receive at normal retirement age (currently age 65). The exact percentage of the reduction will be determined by your age at retirement. The reduced retirement benefit will continue for the rest of your life.

The chart that follows shows how much your full retirement benefit will be reduced for early retirement. Note that this chart only applies to retirees who reach age 62 by 1999. Retirees who reach age 62 in years after 1999 will be subject to somewhat larger reductions as the normal retirement age gradually increases from 65 to 67 (see page 163).

Reduced Benefits for Early Retirees Who Reach 62 by 1999

Retirement Age	Percentage of Full Retirement Benefit Paid Upon Early Retirement
62	80 percent
62½	83⅓ percent
63	86⅔ percent
63½	90 percent
64	93⅓ percent
64½	93⅔ percent
65	100 percent

Does the early retiree get the proverbial worm? When does early retirement make financial sense?

Early retirement entails a clear trade-off: You get the advantage of collecting retirement benefits for a longer period of time than normal age retirees, but your benefit amount is reduced for life. Early retirees collect more total Social Security benefits than their normal retirement age counterparts for the first 15 years of retirement. This means an early retiree who elects to receive benefits at age 62 receives a larger total amount of benefits than a normal age retiree, provided the early retiree does not live past age 77. After age 77 the total amount of benefits paid to those retiring at age 65 exceeds the amount paid to those who retire at age 62.

So how do you make the decision whether to go for a smaller benefit check for a longer period of time (by retiring early) or a larger benefit check for a shorter period of time (by delaying retirement)? Consult your crystal ball, of course. If your crystal ball is in the shop, however, you must base your decision on what you know today.

Ask yourself whether you plan to continue working after retirement. If you plan on continuing to work, as many retirees do, early retirement probably doesn't make sense for you. Your post-retirement income may reduce your Social Security benefit (see page 177).

If you don't plan to earn money after retirement, taking benefits at age 62 may be a good idea. The reason that early retirement makes good financial sense for some workers is best demonstrated with an example.

Rob is considering retiring at age 62. He knows that if he waits until age 65 to retire, his Social Security benefit will be $1,000 a month. If he retires at age 62, his benefit will be $800 (20 percent of $1,000).

Rob decides to retire early. Since he is above to live off his investment income, Rob can invest the $800 in a mutual fund that earns an 8 percent rate of return. By age 65, Rob figures his investment will be worth about $30,000, and will yield about $200 a month in interest.

At age 65, Rob will have $1,000 of monthly income ($800 from Social Security and $200 from his investment), which is about the same as what he would get from Social Security as a normal age retiree. But Rob figures he's still ahead of the game by retiring early. For one thing, he didn't work those 3 extra years. Second, he has an additional $30,000 in the bank.

If you have to retire early due to poor health, you should apply for Social Security disability benefits (see Chapter 7). Once you prove that an illness or injury prevents you from performing any type of work for at least a year or is expected to result in your death, your Social Security benefit will equal the full retirement benefit you would be entitled to receive at normal retirement age (see Chapter 7).

Normal Retirement

Historically, workers routinely retired at age 65. Age 65 was soon dubbed normal retirement age. Workers who waited until age 65 to retire received their full Social Security retirement benefit.

But times are a-changing. People are living, and working, longer. Sixty-five will not be normal retirement age for too much longer.

Starting in the year 2000, Social Security will gradually increase the normal retirement age to age 67. This change will affect people born in 1938 and later.

To find your full retirement age, refer to the following chart:

Increase in Normal Retirement Age

Year of 62nd Birthday	Normal Retirement Age
years through 1999	65
years through 2000	65 years, 2 months
years through 2001	65 years, 4 months
years through 2001	65 years, 6 months
years through 2003	65 years, 8 months
years through 2004	65 years, 10 months
years 2005 through 2016	66 years
years through 2017	66 years, 2 months
years through 2018	66 years, 4 months
years through 2019	66 years, 6 months
years through 2020	66 years, 8 months
years through 2021	66 years, 10 months
year 2022 and beyond	67 years

There is a double benefit to continuing to work until at least normal retirement age. Not only do you avoid the reduction of your retirement benefit for early retirement, you also drive up the amount of your lifetime retirement benefit as you add more high-income years of employment to your earnings record (assuming you get paid more as you mature and progress in your career).

Adding high income years of employment to your earnings record is important because Social Security focuses on high-income years when computing benefit amounts. Social Security only looks at a specified number of years of employment in the benefit computation (see page 173), and those years are the ones in which your earnings from employment were highest.

As you continue to work later in life, you generally accumulate more high-earning years of employment. With every high-earning year of employment you add to your work record, a low- or no-earning year drops out of the computation. This results in a larger lifetime retirement benefit for you and your family.

LATE RETIREMENT

Age 65 may be the normal time to retire, but it is not necessarily the optimum age to retire. Workers who hang in there until age 70 (an age Social Security also threatens to increase) get the following benefits:

• A higher benefit amount. Workers who continue working after normal retirement age collect a higher benefit than those who retire at age 65. This higher benefit is paid to the worker and the worker's eligible family for life.

Benefits for Late Retirement

Year of 65th Birthday	Percentage Increase of Full Retirement Benefit
1982–1989	3 percent increase for each year of employment after age 65 until 70
1990–1991	3.5 percent increase for each year of employment after age 65 until 70
1992–1993	4 percent increase for each year of employment after age 65 until 70
1994–1995	4.5 percent increase for each year of employment after age 65 until 70
1996–1997	5.0 percent increase for each year of employment after age 65 until 70
1998–1999	5.5 percent increase for each year of employment after age 65 until 70
2000–2001	6.0 percent increase for each year of employment after age 65 until 70
2002–2003	6.5 percent increase for each year of employment after age 65 until 70
2004–2005	7.0 percent increase for each year of employment after age 65 until 70
2006–2007	7.5 percent increase for each year of employment after age 65 until 70
2008 or later	8.0 percent increase for each year of employment after age 65 until 70

For example, if you were born in 1924, and do not retire until age 70, your permanent retirement benefit will be 15 percent higher than if you retired at age 65 (5 years of additional employment at 3 percent increase per year is a 15 percent total increased retirement benefit).
• You will add additional years of high earnings to your Social Security record. As explained above in the section on normal age retirement, only a certain number

of your highest-income employment years determine your benefit amount. As you earn more money in your career, you add high earning years to your Social Security record. This raises your average lifetime earnings, and translates into an inflated retirement benefit for life.

A special note to late retirees: Even if you plan to retire after age 65, be sure to contact your local Social Security office about 3 months before you turn 65 to apply for Medicare. The Social Security Administration administers Medicare as well as Social Security. At age 65 you will probably want to apply for Medicare coverage, even if you don't apply for retirement benefits until later. A delay in filing a Medicare application can mean additional costs to you down the road. (Medicare is discussed in depth in Chapters 2, 3 and 4).

If you are contemplating the big R (retirement), you may be curious to learn how much you would receive in Social Security benefits if you retire early, late, or at normal retirement age. You can get this information from the Social Security Administration by requesting a PEBE (see page 158). The PEBE shows workers how additional years of employment will affect their ultimate retirement benefit.

FILE A TIMELY APPLICATION FOR BENEFITS

The time to apply for benefits is about 2 or 3 months before you retire. The consequences of leaving your application to the last minute will depend on your age at retirement.

• Retirement before age 65. At the very latest, file your application by the last day of the month in which you want benefits to start. For example, if you want to retire when you turn 62 on November 16, file your application by November 30. A delay in applying can result in a loss of benefits. In this example, if you apply on December 1, you will lose out on your November benefit check.

• Retirement at age 65 or later. You will be eligible for benefits for up to 6 months before the month you file your application. If you turn 65 on November 16, but do not get around to filing an application until the following May, you will still receive benefits back to your birthday month.

Remember, Social Security retirement benefits do not start automatically when you retire. You must file an application.

You can start your application by calling Social Security's toll-free number (800-772-1213) to schedule an appointment at your local Social Security district office, or just stop in at your local office (you can get the address from the blue pages of the telephone book under U.S. Government, Social Security Administration).

In addition to a completed application, you will eventually need to submit the following documents to Social Security:

- Your Social Security card. If you have lost your card, you will need some record of your Social Security number to apply for a new card. If you do not recall your Social Security number, Social Security can help you track down the number. Do not get a new Social Security number. (If you are applying as an eligible family member, submit the Social Security card of the retired worker.)

- Proof of your age. The following documents, listed in order of preference, will prove your age:

    Birth certificate.

    Baptismal certificate recorded before age 5.

    Passport.

    School records.

    Marriage certificate.

    Life insurance policy.

- Your wage and tax statements (W-2 Forms) for the last 2 years. If you are self-employed, you should bring your last two federal income tax returns and proof of filing (such as a canceled check).

- Proof of military service, if any.

- Your marriage certificate, if you are applying as an eligible spouse.

- Your children's birth certificates, if your children are applying as eligible dependents.

You must submit originals of these documents to Social Security. If you do not have the original documents, you will need to obtain certified copies from the agency that issued the original documents. Social Security can help you obtain certified copies of the documents you need.

Even if you do not have one or more of these documents, do not delay filing your application. The date you file your application is important to getting your full retirement benefit. You can submit these documents after the application process has begun.

Retirement benefit applications take between 6 and 10 weeks to be processed. When a decision has been made on your application, you will receive a written notice in the mail. If you think Social Security has made a mistake, either in denying your application or in miscalculating your benefit amount (see below), follow the instructions on the notice for appealing the determination. You have 60 days from the date you receive the notice to file your appeal.

Always, and I mean always, take the following precautions when dealing with Social Security:

- Keep a copy of everything you submit to Social Security.
- Hand-deliver important documents if at all possible.
- Write your Social Security number on every document you submit.
- Make a note of the name of every person you speak to regarding your application.
- Do not let anyone at the Social Security office talk you out of applying for benefits.

DOUBLE-CHECK YOUR BENEFIT AMOUNT

Your retirement benefit is based on your work record. The more you earned as an employee or self-employed worker, the higher your Social Security retirement benefit will be . . . up to a point. Workers with a lifetime of steady high earnings receive the most generous retirement benefit. A work history marked by years of no or low earnings translates into a reduced benefit amount.

For people who retire in January 1994 at age 65, the maximum monthly Social Security benefit is $1,147. The average monthly Social Security benefit amount in 1994 is $674.

You can estimate your retirement benefit in one of three ways:

1. Request an estimate from Social Security.
2. Compute the approximate benefit amount yourself.
3. Refer to a table of average benefit amounts.

Each way is discussed in turn below.

REQUESTING AN ESTIMATE

To get an estimate of your retirement benefit from Social Security, you need to request a PEBE (see page 158). The PEBE will tell you what retirement benefit you can expect to receive if you retire at age 62, 65, or 70.

COMPUTING THE APPROXIMATE BENEFIT

If you plan to compute your approximate retirement benefit yourself (maybe to check up on Social Security), get out the bottle of aspirin. Calculating Social Security benefits is byzantine in its complexity. You can be sure that your head will be spinning by the time you're through.

The steps outlined below guide you through the computation of a retirement benefit.[1] If you are still working, and don't yet know your total lifetime earnings, you must settle for an estimate of your future retirement benefit.

To get started estimating your retirement benefit, you need an accurate PEBE (see page 158) and a calculator.

ESTIMATING YOUR SOCIAL SECURITY RETIREMENT BENEFIT[2]

Your benefit amount has two components: the average indexed monthly earnings (AIME) and the primary insurance amount (PIA). Here are instructions for estimating each number.

AIME: FIGURING YOUR AVERAGE INDEXED MONTHLY EARNINGS IN NINE SIMPLE (?) STEPS

1. Down the left side of a piece of paper, list your total earnings for each year after 1950. Use your PEBE to get your exact earnings.

2. Only some of your earnings are applied to your retirement account. The maximum amount of earnings Social Security applies to your account in a given year is called the maximum taxable amount. The maximum taxable amount for every year since 1951 is listed in the chart below. Compare your earnings to the maximum taxable amount for each year that you worked. For every year your annual earnings exceeded the maximum taxable amount, cross out your actual earnings and replace with that year's maximum taxable amount.

---

[1] Since the Social Security Administration has changed the manner of computing benefits over the years, a different method of computation may apply to people who first became eligible for retirement benefits before 1983.

[2] If you reached age 62 before 1978, this formula does not apply to you. If you reached age 62 between 1979 and 1984, you are permitted to use this formula if it works to your advantage. You may also be entitled to a special computation method if you worked for many years at rather low earnings levels. A Social Security representative should be able to provide you with further information about the alternative formulas.

Maximum Taxable Amounts

Year of Earnings	Maximum Taxable Amount
1951–1954	$3,600
1955–1958	$4,200
1959–1965	$4,800
1966–1967	$6,600
1968–1971	$7,800
1972	$9,000
1973	$10,800
1974	$13,200
1975	$14,100
1976	$15,300
1977	$16,500
1978	$17,700
1979	$22,900
1980	$25,900
1981	$29,700
1982	$32,400
1983	$35,700
1984	$37,800
1985	$39,600
1986	$42,000
1987	$43,800
1988	$45,000
1989	$48,000
1990	$51,300
1991	$53,400
1992	$55,500
1993	$57,600
1994	$60,600

3. Continuing down the left margin of your paper, add on the years you expect to work before retiring. For each additional year until retirement, list your current salary (or the maximum taxable amount) as your earnings.

4. To adjust your earnings for inflation, multiply each year's earnings by the index number for that year in the chart below. Earnings multiplied by an index number are called indexed earnings. Your indexed earnings reflect what your past earnings are worth in today's dollars.

Index Numbers

Year of Earnings	Index Number
1951	8.1936795
1952	7.7137408
1953	7.3055767
1954	7.2680724
1955	6.9470958
1956	6.4929452
1957	6.2979635
1958	6.2429691
1959	5.9482908
1960	5.7236668
1961	5.6121279
1962	5.3445076
1963	5.2165790
1964	5.0117605
1965	4.9231162
1966	4.6443394
1967	4.3992872
1968	4.1163689
1969	3.8914750
1970	3.7074895
1971	3.5301119
1972	3.2150354
1973	3.0257171
1974	2.8559463
1975	2.6573551
1976	2.4858255
1977	2.3452692
1978	2.1727316
1979	1.9979528
1980	1.8328599
1981	1.6652329
1982	1.5783417
1983	1.5050238
1984	1.4214639
1985	1.3633768
1986	1.3240768
1987	1.2446969
1988	1.1862714
1989	1.1410912

Year of Earnings	Index Number
1990	1.0907096
1991	1.0515239
1992	1.0000000
1993	Not Indexed
1994	Not Indexed

5. Social Security does not consider every year you worked in computing your AIME. Your year of birth determines the number of years of work that are included in your benefit computation. Using the chart below, identify your year of birth. Circle the corresponding number of years of employment that count toward your Social Security benefit.

Year of Birth	Number of Years of Employment
1921	27
1922	28
1923	29
1924	30
1925	31
1926	32
1927	33
1928	34
1929 and later	35

6. Go back to your list of indexed earnings (from #4). Check off the highest earnings for the number of years you circled in #5. For example, if you were born in 1926, check off the 26 years in which you had the highest earnings.

7. Add up the earnings you checked off in #6.

8. Now multiply the number of years of earnings that count toward your AIME (from #5) by 12 to convert the years to months.

9. Divide your total earnings (from #7) by the total number of countable months (from #8) to compute your AIME. Round down to the nearest dollar.

PIA: FIGURING YOUR PRIMARY INSURANCE AMOUNT

Your PIA is the amount of the benefit you are eligible to receive at normal retirement age (currently age 65). If you retire early, you will receive less than your PIA. If you retire late, you will receive more.

Use your AIME (page 168) to compute your PIA using the following chart (which applies in 1993):

If your AIME Is:	Your PIA at Age 65 Equals:
$0–$422	90 percent of your AIME
$423–$2,545	$379.80 plus 32 percent of your AIME in excess of $422
$2,546 or higher	$1,059.16 plus 15 percent of your AIME in excess of $2,545.

For example, if your AIME is $1,001, your PIA (or retirement benefit at age 65) is computed as follows:

1. Determine your AIME in excess of $401 ($1,001 minus $401 equals $600)
2. Determine 32 percent of your excess AIME (32 percent of $600 equals $192)
3. Add $360.90 to the number from #2 ($360.90 plus $192 equals $552.90)

Your retirement benefit at the normal retirement age of 65 would be $552.90 a month.

In 1994, the maximum retirement benefit you can collect at age 65 is $1,147. Regardless of the size of your AIME, your monthly retirement benefit cannot exceed $1,147, unless you put off retiring until after age 65 (see page 164).

Social Security benefits increase in January of each year to reflect increases in the cost of living.

REFERRING TO A TABLE OF BENEFITS

As already noted, there is a third way you can estimate your retirement benefit. This method is called the lazyman's special. Simply look at the table below. The numbers are approximations of what your monthly retirement benefit will be based on a steady work history, average pay raises, and retirement at age 65. According to projected benefits, your Social Security check will replace about 56 percent of your pre-retirement income if you were a low-income worker, about 42 percent of pre-retirement income for the average-income worker, and about 28 percent of pre-retirement income for the maximum-income worker.

Approximate Monthly Single Retirement Benefit at Age 65

Your Age in 1994	Your Present Annual Earnings				
	$20,000	$30,000	$40,000	$50,000	$57,600 or more
45	$886	$1,185	$1,329	$1,470	$1,554
55	$803	$1,078	$1,183	$1,270	$1.315
65	$749	$991	$1,064	$1,112	$1,128

If your spouse is about the same age as you and does not qualify for a higher retirement benefit based on his or her own work record, the following chart estimates the joint retirement benefit for you and your spouse.

Approximate Monthly Joint Retirement Benefit at Age 65

Your Age in 1994	Your Present Annual Earnings				
	$20,000	$30,000	$40,000	$50,000	$57,600 or more
45	$1,329	$1,777	$1,993	$2,205	$2,331
55	$1,204	$1,617	$1,774	$1,905	$1,972
65	$1,123	$1,486	$1,596	$1,668	$1,692

MAKE SURE FAMILY MEMBERS GET THEIR FULL BENEFITS

When you retire, you are not the only person who can start to collect Social Security benefits. Other members of your family may also be eligible for benefits based on your work history. Your current spouse, divorced spouse, and children may qualify for benefits if they meet certain criteria.

The benefits that are paid to your eligible family members are in addition to your retirement benefit. Your benefit amount is not reduced by the amount of your family's benefits. There is, however, a limit on the total amount of Social Security benefits your entire family can collect, called the maximum family benefit (MFB). (Benefits paid to a divorced spouse are not applied toward your MFB.)

The exact amount of your family's maximum benefit depends on your AIME and PIA (page 172). Generally, the MFB ranges from 150 to 180 percent of your PIA. Use the following chart to compute your MFB in 1993:

Worker's PIA	MFB
0–$539	150 percent of worker's PIA
$539.01–$779	$808.50 plus 272 percent of the worker's PIA in excess of $539
$779.01–$1,016	$1,461.30 plus 134 percent of the worker's PIA in excess of $779
$1,016.01 or higher	$1,778.88 plus 175 percent of the worker's PIA in excess of $1,016

For example, a worker's PIA is $800. His excess PIA is $287 ($800 minus $513). His MFB in 1993 is 272 percent of $287 ($780.64), plus $742.50, which equals $1,523.14.

If your family's total benefits exceed your MFB, the benefits payable to your spouse and children will be reduced. Your personal retirement benefit will not be affected.

Here are the eligibility requirements for your family members.

SPOUSE

When you retire, your spouse will be eligible for benefits if he or she is:

- Age 62 or older.
- Any age and caring for your child who is under age 16 or has been disabled since before age 22 *if* you have been married to your spouse for at least a year, *and* your spouse is the parent of your child.

Your spouse's benefit amount will be computed as a percentage of your PIA.

Spouse's Benefits

Basis of Eligibility	Percentage of Your PIA Payable as an Additional Benefit
Spouse age 62–64	37½ percent (to be reduced starting in the year 2000)
Spouse age 65 or older (but as normal retirement age increases, this age requirement will also increase)	50 percent

Spouse of any age caring for your minor or ....50 percent
disabled child

Your spouse's Social Security benefit may be reduced if he or she is entitled to
a government pension.

Ex-Spouse

When you retire, your divorced spouse will be eligible for benefits if he or she
meets all of these requirements:

- Age 62 or older.
- Married to you for at least 10 years.
- Not remarried (or has remarried someone who is receiving Social Security
  benefits as a widow, widower, parent, or disabled child).

Even if you do not retire, your ex-spouse (unlike your current spouse) will be
eligible for benefits when you reach age 62 if both of these requirements are fulfilled:

- The spouse meets the three criteria listed above.
- The divorce is at least 2 years old when your ex-spouse files for benefits
  (unless you started collecting benefits before the divorce, in which case
  there is no 2-year waiting period).

The divorced spouse's benefit amount is the same as the current spouse's benefit,
and has no effect on the amount of benefits available to the current spouse.

Child

When you retire, your child will be eligible for benefits if the child is all of the
following:

- Your natural child (born in or out of wedlock), adopted child, stepchild,
  or dependent grandchild (if the child's parents are deceased or disabled).
- Unmarried.
- Under age 18, under age 19 if in high school, or any age if disabled before
  age 22.

Your child's benefit amount will equal 50 percent of your PIA. If your retired spouse has an individual earnings record, your child's benefit will be 50 percent of the PIA of you or your spouse, whichever is larger.

GRANDCHILD

A grandchild will be eligible for benefits when a grandparent retires only if the grandchild

- Lives with the grandparent.
- Is under the grandparent's care and custody.

CONSIDER WORKING AFTER RETIREMENT

You can collect retirement benefits even if you continue earning money. There are many good reasons people keep working after they start receiving Social Security retirement benefits: They need additional income; they want to remain active in the work force; or they simply enjoy their full- or part-time job.

There are important consequences to working after retirement. The specific rules governing post-retirement work vary depending on when the work is performed (in the year you retire or years thereafter), and whether you work for someone else (as an employee) or for yourself (as a self-employed worker). All of these rules are discussed below.

WORK PERFORMED BY EMPLOYEES IN YEAR OF RETIREMENT

A special rule applies in the first year of retirement. Under this rule, you can collect a benefit check in any month that your earnings fall below the *monthly* earnings limitations. In every year after the year of retirement, your benefit amount is reduced if your *annual* earnings exceed a certain limit. The monthly earnings limitations are one-twelfth of the annual earnings limitations.

Assume, for example, you retire in January 1994 at age 65. Your retirement benefit is $600. For the first and last 3 months of 1994 you work part-time, and earn $2,000 a month. You can collect your full $600 retirement benefit the other six months of 1994. (If these had been your earnings in any other year after you retired, your Social Security benefit for 1994 would have been reduced $1 for every $3 you earned in excess of $11,160, or a reduction of $280 for $840 of excess earnings. See page 177).

WORK PERFORMED BY SELF-EMPLOYED WORKERS IN YEAR OF RETIREMENT

If you are self-employed, special rules may apply in your first year of retirement, if application of these special rules results in a higher benefit for you.

In your first year of retirement, you can collect retirement benefits in any month your earnings from self-employment do not exceed the monthly earnings limitation (see page 176) *and* you do not perform "substantial services."

Social Security has defined substantial services as more than 45 hours a month of self-employment. If you performed less than 15 hours of self-employment in a month, you will not be found to have performed substantial services. If you performed between 15 and 45 hours of self-employment in a month, Social Security will examine the exact nature of your work activities to determine whether you provided substantial services. Some of the factors Social Security will consider include the amount of time you worked, the amount of money you have invested in the business, the presence or absence of a qualified paid manager, and the extent of the services rendered.

WORK PERFORMED BY EMPLOYEES EVERY YEAR AFTER THE FIRST YEAR OF RETIREMENT

Although you are allowed to work while collecting Social Security retirement benefits, money you earn after retirement may reduce the amount of your retirement check. (Once you reach age 70, you can earn as much as you want and your retirement benefit will not be reduced.) You must notify Social Security about all of your post-retirement earnings. Failure to do so can result in penalties.

Your retirement benefit will only be reduced if your post-retirement earnings are sufficiently high. If your earnings are not high enough, you can continue to collect your full retirement benefit in addition to your other earnings. The maximum amount you can earn after retirement without losing any retirement benefits is appropriately called the earnings limitation. The earnings limitation changes from year to year and with your age.

1994 Earnings Limitations

Your Age	Earnings Limitation
Under 65	$8,040 ($670/month)
65–69	$11,160 ($930/month)
70 and over	No limit

The earnings limitation only applies to earnings from work, such as gross wages, bonuses, commissions, fees, vacation pay, cash tips of $20 or more a month, severance pay, and noncash compensation, such as meals. Do not count pensions, annuities, investment income, interest, gifts, inheritances, rental income (unless you are a real estate dealer), sick pay after the 6th full month you last worked or were paid after your employment terminated, and Social Security, veterans, and other government benefits when using the earnings limitation.

If your post-retirement earnings exceed the earnings limitation, your retirement benefits will be reduced as follows:

Your Age	Amount of Reduction
Under 65	Benefits are reduced $1 for every $2 you earn in excess of the earnings limitation
65–69	Benefits are reduced $1 for every $3 you earn in excess of the earnings limitation
70 and over	No reduction

For example, let's say you started collecting $600 a month in retirement benefits in 1994 at age 65. At age 67 you return to part-time work at an annual salary of $15,000. Your earnings limitation is $11,160 (see chart on page 177). You have $3,840 ($15,000 minus $11,160) in excess earnings. Your retirement benefit will be reduced by approximately $1,280 ($3,840 divided by $3).

WORK PERFORMED BY SELF-EMPLOYED WORKERS EVERY YEAR AFTER THE FIRST YEAR OF RETIREMENT

If you are self-employed, the same rules that are discussed above apply to you, but your profits are reduced by your losses to compute earnings for purposes of the earnings limitation.

For information specifically geared to the self-employed worker, visit or call any Social Security office and request the free publication "If You're Self-Employed" (Publication Number 05-10022).

TIPS FOR AVOIDING THE REDUCTION FOR EXCESS EARNINGS

➤ **TIP #1** *When planning your retirement, give special thought to your month of retirement.*

Your choice of a retirement month can affect your benefit amount because money you earn in the months before you retire will not be applied to your earnings limitation. Say, for example, you decide to retire in 1994 at age 65. You keep working in January, February, March, and April 1994, and earn a total of $20,000. This exceeds your earnings limitation by several thousand dollars, but will not affect your Social Security benefit. You can start collecting your full retirement benefit in May 1994, and keep all of your wages.

➤ **TIP #2** *If you want to earn some extra money in the year you retire, keep your eye on the monthly earnings limitation.*

In the year you retire, you can collect your full benefit in any month your earnings do not exceed the monthly earnings limitation (see page 176). This means that if you are 67 years old, you can earn over $800 a month and still collect your full retirement benefit in that month. This is a nice bonus for prospective retirees.

➤ **TIP #3** *Don't get penalized for money you earned before retirement, but did not receive until after retirement.*

For example, if you are an author who completed a novel in 1993, but did not start receiving royalties until after you retired in 1994, your royalty income should not reduce your retirement benefit because you performed the work before you retired.

To request the fact sheet entitled "How Work Affects Your Social Security Benefits" (Publication Number 05-10069), visit or call any Social Security office.

MECHANICS OF COLLECTING YOUR SOCIAL SECURITY RETIREMENT CHECK

Every Social Security beneficiary receives a check on or about the 3rd day of each month. If your check is late, promptly call your local Social Security office to report a lost check. Be ready to provide the Social Security representative with the following information:

- Your name as it appears on the check.
- Your Social Security number.
- The amount of the check.
- The type of Social Security benefit you receive.
- The day of the month you usually receive your check.

The process of issuing a replacement check usually takes about a month. If you have not received a new check in a month, follow up with your local Social Security office.

Your Social Security benefit can be paid in one of three ways:

- Personal payment. You can have your checks sent to your home.
- Direct deposit. You can have your checks sent directly to your bank. Most banks offer direct deposit services. Once you fill out the necessary forms, your bank will arrange for Social Security to deposit your benefit check directly into your savings or checking account. You will have to show your checkbook or other proof of your bank account number to Social Security.

There are four advantages to direct deposit: You do not have to rely on the sometimes unreliable postal service. You do not have to worry about a malfeasant prying open your mailbox. You save yourself a monthly trip to the bank. You may get a few extra days of interest.

- Representative payment. Some beneficiaries are not capable of receiving their own Social Security checks. They may, for example, have a physical or mental impairment that makes them unable to manage their own finances. For these beneficiaries, the Social Security Administration will appoint a trusted friend or family member to receive the check on the beneficiary's behalf. The person who receives the check is called a representative payee or substitute payee.

Once a representative payee is appointed, the benefit check will be made payable to that person. Representative payees are required promptly to deposit benefit checks in a separate bank account on behalf of the beneficiary, and spend the money in the beneficiary's best interest. Representative payees typically use the Social Security benefits to purchase food, clothing, and shelter for the beneficiary, and to pay for any other assistance the beneficiary may require.

Payees can face personal liability. The beneficiary can sue the payee for damages. A payee who misuses benefits can also be prosecuted criminally.

Each year the representative payee must submit to Social Security a completed Representative Payee Report (Form SSA-623) explaining how the benefits were spent. Representative payees are legally obligated to diligently record and receipt all expenditures.

The Social Security Administration is careful about who it selects as a payee. Anyone who wants to be appointed a payee must do the following:

- Explain the nature of the relationship to the beneficiary.
- Submit medical proof of the beneficiary's inability to care for himself or herself.
- Sign a sworn statement promising to spend the benefit check in the best interest of the beneficiary.

For more information about representative payees, call or visit any Social Security office and request a copy of the free brochure "A Guide for Representative Payees" (Publication Number 05-10076).

For information about receiving your Social Security checks if you are out of the country, visit or call any Social Security office to request a free copy of "Your Social Security Checks While You Are Outside the United States" (Publication Number 05-10137).

BACK TO JACKIE

In reaching a decision about continuing to work, Jackie had to come to peace with taking a permanently reduced retirement benefit and possibly sacrificing some of her benefits if her post-retirement earnings from freelance work exceeded the earnings limitation.

Despite these consequences, Jackie decided to go ahead with her retirement plans. To make sure she received the maximum monthly benefit check, she confirmed Social Security's records of her work history and filed an application for benefits 3 months before her anticipated retirement date.

Although Jackie's eagerness to retire came at a cost, she decided that the enjoyment she would get from having additional time to travel, read, and relax poolside more than justified the reduction of her post-retirement income.

7.
COLLECTING SOCIAL SECURITY DISABILITY BENEFITS

Larry had worked as an accountant for 22 years. Suddenly, at age 56, he started having back pain. He found that he was having trouble sitting at his desk for more than 15 minutes at a time. When he tried to pick up a box of tax returns, he dropped the box. He stopped working.

Looking for relief from his pain, Larry went to a number of different doctors. He was examined by internists, orthopedists, and neurologists who poked, prodded, and X-rayed his back.

Larry needed to know: Was he eligible for Social Security disability benefits? How should he go about applying? What would happen to his benefits if he tried to return to work part-time as an accountant?

When a breadwinner become disabled, the resulting loss of income can be devastating. Social Security disability benefits are intended to serve as a safety net for incapacitated workers and their families.

The Social Security disability program can be viewed as a glass that is half full of water, or half empty. Looking at the program in its best light, you will see that:

• The Social Security disability benefit is relatively generous. No matter when you become disabled, the amount of your benefit will equal the benefit you would receive if you retired at age 65.

• You can qualify for Social Security disability benefits at any age. Social Security's disability program is an equal opportunity entitlement program; it does not discriminate based on age. Whether you become unable to work due to disability at age 50, 55, or 60, your entitlement to disability benefits is the same.

- Money is no object when it comes to Social Security disability benefits. You can qualify for a disability check regardless of how much other money you have coming in each month (although too much earned income may prove you are not disabled, or are able to work despite your disability.)
- The cause of your disability is irrelevant to your eligibility for Social Security benefits. Your disability can be the result of an accident, a sudden illness, or a degenerative medical condition. Social Security doesn't care, as long as your medical condition prevents you from working for a long enough period of time.

The dark side of the Social Security disability benefit program is that too many disabled people have to fight Social Security tooth and nail to win an award of disability benefits. On average, a disgraceful 60 percent of all denied disability applications are approved on appeal. The message to take from this statistic is that perseverance is rewarded.

If you are thinking about applying for disability benefits, this chapter promises to make your life a whole lot easier by answering the following ten questions about the Social Security disability program:

1. Who is eligible for disability benefits?
2. How do you prove you are disabled?
3. What family members are entitled to benefits if you are disabled?
4. How and when do you apply for benefits?
5. How is your benefit application decided?
6. What if your benefit application is denied?
7. How much will you receive in disability benefits, and when?
8. What happens to your disability benefits if you return to work?
9. When do your disability benefits end?
10. What other benefits can you collect while receiving disability benefits?

The answer to each of these questions appears in a separate section of this chapter. The information in this chapter is your ammunition, should you have to do battle with Social Security.

WHO IS ELIGIBLE FOR DISABILITY BENEFITS?

You are eligible for Social Security disability benefits if you:

- Have worked long enough in covered employment to earn sufficient quarters of coverage, or credits, to be fully insured for disability benefits.
- Are currently insured for disability benefits.

Each of these elements is discussed below, and in detail on pages 154–158.

COVERED EMPLOYMENT

Covered employment is any type of work (either for an employer or self-employment) that is part of the Social Security system. Almost every job participates in the Social Security system. (See page 155 for a list of jobs that do not.)

QUARTERS OF COVERAGE

To qualify for Social Security benefits, you must have enough quarters of coverage. You earn quarters of coverage by working in covered employment (see page 155).

FULLY INSURED

The number of quarters of coverage you need to be fully insured for disability benefits depend on your year of birth and your age when you become disabled.

If you were born before 1930, refer to the first chart to find out how many quarters of coverage you need to qualify for disability benefits. If you were born in 1930 or later, refer to the second chart.

Quarters of Coverage Required for Disability Benefits
(for those born before 1930)

Year You Became Disabled	Required Quarters of Coverage
1980	29
1981	30
1982	31
1983	32
1984	33
1985	34
1986	35
1987	36
1988	37
1989	38
1990	39
1991 or later	40

Quarters of Coverage Required for Disability Benefits
(for those born in or after 1930)

Age You Became Disabled	Required Quarters of Coverage
42 or younger	20
44	22
46	24
48	26
50	28
52	30
54	32
56	34
58	36
60	38
62 or older	40

Special coverage rules (requiring a shorter work history) apply to individuals who become disabled before age 31.

CURRENTLY INSURED

Being fully insured is not enough to qualify for disability benefits. You must also be currently insured. To be currently insured, you must have earned some of your quarters of coverage within a certain period of time before becoming disabled. Specifically, you must have earned at least twenty of your quarters of coverage in the 10-year period immediately before you became disabled.

Most workers earn twenty quarters of coverage in 5 years of employment (at four quarters of coverage a year). This means that most workers are currently insured for disability benefits if they worked for 5 of the 10 years before the onset of their disability. But the 5 years of employment do not have to be consecutive. This means that you will be eligible for disability benefits if you accumulated at least twenty quarters of coverage (the equivalent of 5 years of employment) at any time during the 10-year period before the onset of your disability.

For example, John worked in an auto factory between 1965 and 1989. In 1989, when he was 58 years old, he stopped working. In 1991, John became disabled and filed for Social Security disability benefits.

Was John fully insured? Yes, because he worked at least forty quarters, or 10 years, between 1965 and 1989.

Was John currently insured? Yes, because he worked at least twenty quarters, or 5 years, in the 10-year period immediately before he became disabled. That is,

John worked between 1985 and 1989 (5 years) within the 10-year period before he became disabled (1981 to 1991).

The currently insured requirement can become an obstacle for the older disability claimant. Here's what can happen: George stops working at age 55. At age 62, he has a stroke and is left disabled. Although he already qualifies for early retirement benefits, he would prefer to start collecting disability benefits because the amount of his check would be larger. Unfortunately, George will not be eligible for disability benefits because he did not work 5 out of the 10 years immediately before the onset of his disability. And the fact that he started working as a young lad at age 17 does not make any difference.

Of course, if George had continued working a few hours a week (just enough to earn a couple of thousand dollars a year), he would have been currently insured for Social Security disability benefits. He could have then started collecting his full retirement benefit at age 62 (since the disability benefit equals the age 65 retirement benefit). As it worked out, however, George had to settle for collecting 80 percent of his full retirement benefit, which is the reduction for early retirement. And it got worse. George also had to forgo Medicare for an extra year (see page 161).

HOW DO YOU PROVE YOU ARE DISABLED?

When you think about being disabled, you probably think about being unable to walk, talk, eat, shop, or dress yourself. Social Security defines disability differently, based solely on your ability to work. If you can work, you are not disabled according to Social Security.

There are basically two parts to Social Security's unique definition of disability. You are disabled if (1) you have a severe physical or mental impairment (or combination of impairments); and (2) that impairment (or combination of impairments) prevents you from doing "substantial gainful activity" for a year or more, or is expected to result in your death.

Each part of this definition is examined below.

SEVERE PHYSICAL OR MENTAL IMPAIRMENT . . .

Social Security is only concerned with medical impairments. Medical impairments are physical or mental conditions that can be discovered by medical means. Unless your alleged disability is substantiated with medical evidence, your chances of winning disability benefits drop to somewhere between slim and none.

Social Security is supposed to seek out medical evidence on your behalf to support your claimed disability. The key words here are "supposed to." Don't trust Social Security to prove that you are disabled for you.

Sample Letter Requesting Records From Hospital/Clinic

Date

Hospital/Clinic
Address
City, State, Zip

Attn: *Medical Records Department*

Your name:
Your date of birth:
Your address at time of treatment:
Dates of treatment:
Clinics:

Dear Sir/Madam:

I am writing this letter in connection with my claim for Social Security disability benefits.

Letter to Clinic:
Please forward a copy of my medical records to the following address: [insert your current mailing address.]

Letter to Hospital:
Please forward a copy of my abstract or discharge summary to the following address: [insert your current mailing address.] I do not need any of the nurse's notes, graphics, or temperature charts.

Since I have not been able to work for some time, any courtesy you can extend with regard to the amount of your fee will be greatly appreciated.

Thank you for your cooperation in this matter.

Sincerely,

Your signature
Your printed name

Sample Letter Requesting Records From Doctor

Date

Doctor's Name
Address
City, State, Zip

Re: Your name
Dates of treatment [if not a current patient]:

Dear Dr. [name]:

I am writing this letter in connection with my claim for Social Security disability benefits.

To win benefits, I must prove to the Social Security Administration that I am unable to work at any kind of job for at least a year. Your opinion as to my disability is the single most important piece of evidence in proving my claim.

If possible, please send me a narrative medical report at your earliest convenience. Specifically, I need documentation of my diagnosis, the basis for the diagnosis, treatments you have prescribed, including medications and their side effects, my prognosis, and suggested limitations on my activities.

Since I have not been able to work for some time, any courtesy you can extend with regard to the amount of your fee will be greatly appreciated.

Thank you for your cooperation.

Sincerely,

Your signature
Your printed name

After you file your disability application, the first thing you should do is make a list of every doctor, hospital, and clinic that has treated you in connection with your disability. You will need to contact each and every one of these sources for a medical report or copy of your medical records.

Start by writing a letter to each provider. Two form letters for requesting medical evidence are shown here; one for hospitals and clinics where you have been treated, and one for your past and current doctors. If you do not get a response within a month, follow up your letter with a telephone call.

Some doctors, and most hospitals, charge a fee for preparing reports and photo-copying medical records. If you are short on funds, you are not alone. This is a common problem among disability claimants who have been unable to work for a period of time. Your best bet is to request a waiver or reduction of the fee. If your request is denied, you must determine whether the report or records will be worth the money. As a general rule, you should make every effort to obtain favorable reports from the doctors who are most familiar with your condition.

A favorable report is one that describes your physical or mental medical condition with specificity, and truthfully states that your medical condition prevents you from working for at least a year or is expected to result in your death. Such a report can easily mean the difference between a win and a loss before the Social Security Administration. The opinions of doctors with whom you have the longest-standing relationships carry the most weight before the Social Security Administration.

Be persistent about obtaining the reports and records you need to support your claim. Now is not the time to worry about whether a doctor's receptionist thinks you're a pain in the neck. Remember, to the victor belong the spoils—which in this case are Social Security disability benefits.

. . . That Prevents You from Working . . .

Only medical conditions that prevent you from working are disabling according to Social Security. In the world of Social Security disability benefits, if you can perform "substantial gainful activity" you are not disabled.

DEFINING SUBSTANTIAL GAINFUL ACTIVITY

Social Security defines substantial gainful activity in terms of dollars and cents. Unlike your health, on which you can't put a price tag, substantial gainful activity is work that pays at least $500 a month. A finding that you are capable of earning at least $500 a month is the death knell for your disability application.

The key phrase here is "capable of earning." You will be denied disability benefits if you are physically and mentally capable of working at a job that pays $500 or more a month, even if:

- You are not physically or mentally able to return to your former job.
- You are overqualified for other types of jobs you can perform that pay $500 or more a month.
- You cannot find a job that you can perform that pays $500 or more a month.

If you are already doing some type of paid or volunteer work, Social Security will consider whether your current work activities demonstrate an ability to earn $500 or more a month. Your current work activities should not prove an ability to perform substantial gainful activity, if any of the following situations apply:

- Your gross earnings, when reduced by impairment-related work expenses (IRWEs), do not exceed $500 a month. IRWEs are expenses you must incur in order to work despite your disability. For example, an IRWE for a worker with a physical disability may be the cost of renting or purchasing a wheelchair. An IRWE for a worker with a hearing impairment may be the cost of hiring a sign interpreter. An IRWE for a worker who is unable to handle the stress of commuting alone may be the cost of hiring an attendant. Other common IRWEs are the costs of modifying a car to accommodate a physical impairment, purchasing a Braille typewriter, paying for prescription drugs, and installing ramps and railings.

- Your gross earnings, when reduced by a subsidy from your employer, do not exceed $500 a month. Some employers, especially in vocational rehabilitation programs, pay their workers a salary that does not accurately reflect the value of the employee's work product. For example, a disabled worker may get paid the same hourly rate as nondisabled workers, even if that worker's output is substantially less. These subsidies are intended to motivate disabled employees to keep working.

- If you are a volunteer, your volunteer work should not hurt your case unless someone would pay you $500 or more a month to perform the same work. If you are doing work as a volunteer that people usually get paid for performing, Social Security will use your volunteer work as evidence that you are capable of doing substantial gainful activity. To be safe, hold off on performing volunteer work while you are seeking disability benefits.

PROVING INABILITY TO PERFORM SUBSTANTIAL ACTIVITY

Social Security will automatically find that you are unable to do substantial gainful activity if you are diagnosed with a medical condition that appears on a list of presumptively disabling medical conditions that is published in the Code of Federal Regulations.[1] If your impairment does not appear on the list, it does not mean you

---

[1] The list can be found in volume 20 of the Code of Federal Regulations (CFR), Part 404, Subpart P, Appendix 1. Many public libraries, and all law libraries, carry the CFR.

are not disabled; it only means you must prove that you cannot do substantial work given your medical condition, age, education, and experience (see below).

Listed Medical Conditions

Once you prove you have one of the following medical conditions, Social Security will presume that you qualify for disability benefits. Here is a partial list of presumptively disabling impairments:

- Respiratory conditions. Diseases of the heart or lungs that fail to respond to medical treatment.
- Orthopedic conditions. Diseases of the joints that severely limit mobility, or loss of function of both arms, both legs, or a leg and an arm.
- Psychiatric conditions. Mental illnesses that seriously interfere with daily functioning.
- Digestive conditions. Disorders that result in severe malnutrition, weakness, and anemia.
- Cancers. Progressive cancers that are nonresponsive to medical treatment.
- Sensory conditions. Statutory blindness, severe hearing impairments, and an organic loss of speech.

Even if your precise medical condition does not appear on the list, you may still be able to benefit from it. Social Security will presume that you are disabled even if the severity of your medical impairments only "equals" the severity of the listed impairments.

To meet this standard, you must prove that you are as functionally limited by your physical, sensory, or emotional impairments as someone who is afflicted with a listed impairment. If you find this standard vague and confusing, you are in good company. Social Security doesn't seem to know exactly what it means to "equal" a listing either. In fact, Social Security has never clearly articulated, or consistently applied, the equivalence test.

Nonlisted Medical Conditions

If you are not found to be presumptively disabled under the list of impairments (either by meeting or equaling a listed impairment), Social Security will determine whether you can return to your past work, or perform other work, given your:

- Medical condition.
- Age.

- Education.
- Work experience.

Medical Condition

Social Security focuses on what functional skills you have lost due to your medical condition. Specifically, Social Security will want to know:

- What physical (or "exertional," in Social Security lingo) tasks are you now incapable of performing? For example, how long can you stand? How far can you walk? How much weight can you lift?
- What nonphysical (or "nonexertional") tasks are you now incapable of performing? For example, do you have any trouble seeing, hearing, concentrating, interacting with others, or following instructions?

Age

The older the better when it comes to winning a disability claim. Imagine two warehouse workers who have the same problem: Neither one can lift more than 30 pounds without experiencing a stabbing pain in the lower back. One worker is 33 years old, and the other is 63 years old. Quite reasonably, Social Security will presume that the younger worker can learn the new skills he needs to return to less arduous work. The older worker is much more likely to qualify for disability benefits.

Education

In the world of disability benefits, a higher education works against you. Take, for example, two receptionists. One has a college education, the other never finished high school. Neither one can continue working as a secretary due to carpal tunnel syndrome, a wrist impairment. The college-educated applicant will have a tougher time convincing Social Security that there is no other work she can perform, given her additional years of education.

Work Experience

When evaluating your work experience, Social Security will pay special attention to whether you performed skilled, semiskilled, or unskilled work, and whether you acquired transferable or nontransferable skills (that is, skills you can use in more than one type of work). The more skilled work in your background, and the more transferable skills you have, the harder you will have to fight for disability benefits.

Once you prove that you are unable to return to your past work, the burden shifts to the Social Security Administration to prove that there is other work you can perform. Proving that you cannot return to your former job is, therefore, very important. Just as a statement from your doctor is vital to proving the existence of a medical impairment, a letter from your former employer can help prove your inability to return to your past work. What follows is a sample letter requesting a statement from a former employer:

Sample Letter Requesting Letter From Employer

Date

Employer's Name
Address
City, State, Zip

Re: Your name
Dates of employment:

Dear [name]:

I am writing this letter in connection with my pending application for Social Security disability benefits.

To win benefits, I must prove to the Social Security Administration that I am unable to work due to my disability.

If possible, please send me a letter describing the duties I was required to perform as your employee (both physical and intellectual) and the problems I had performing those duties.

I would appreciate receiving the letter at your earliest possible convenience. I expect a hearing on my case to be scheduled shortly.

Thank you for your cooperation.

Sincerely,

Your signature
Your printed name

If Social Security finds you can return to work (either your old type of work or some other work), and you disagree, you can file an appeal. (Appeals are discussed in depth on page 197.)

. . . For a Year or More, or Is Expected to Result in Death

This part of Social Security's definition of disability is commonly referred to as the duration requirement. A condition that has not already lasted, and is not expected to last, at least a year or result in your death is not disabling according to Social Security. During the 12 months of the duration requirement, your medical condition must prevent you from doing "substantial gainful activity" (which is discussed at length in the preceding section).

If you have been unable to do substantial work for less than 12 months at the time you apply for disability benefits, your condition must be *expected* to last at least a year or result in your death. You will need to substantiate this expectation with medical documentation. Then, if you return to work within the year, you should not have to return any money to Social Security. (This is not to say Social Security will not seek reimbursement from you. Social Security insists on its right to recover incorrectly paid benefits, even though some federal judges have ruled otherwise.)

WHO ELSE IS ENTITLED TO BENEFITS?

If you qualify for disability benefits, certain members of your family can also collect benefits:

- Minor children. Your unmarried child, stepchild, and adopted child will be eligible for benefits if under age 18, or under age 19 and in high school.

- Disabled children of any age. Your unmarried child, stepchild, or adopted child who became disabled prior to age 22 will be eligible for benefits at any age. Your child's benefits will continue as long as your child remains disabled.

- Spouse. Your spouse will be eligible if he or she is caring for your child who is under age 16 or who has been disabled since at least age 22; is age 62 or older; or is disabled.

- Ex-spouse. Your divorced spouse will be eligible if he or she is age 62 or older and was married to you for at least 10 years.

You must notify the Social Security Administration if any of these family members is eligible for benefits based on your entitlement to disability benefits.

HOW AND WHEN DO YOU APPLY FOR DISABILITY BENEFITS?

If there is any chance that a medical condition might prevent you from working for a period of time approaching a year, you should promptly file a disability application. If your condition improves within the year, the worst that can happen is that your claim may be denied. Also, you can always withdraw your claim.

To start your disability application rolling, call Social Security's toll-free number (800-772-1213) or stop in at your local Social Security office (you can get the address from the blue pages of your telephone book, or by calling Social Security's toll-free number).

Social Security will need several documents from you to process your application—the same documents required in connection with an application for Social Security retirement benefits (see page 166). If you have trouble gathering any of the documents, do not put off filing your application. You do not have to submit these documents with your application. However, the sooner you get the documents to Social Security, the faster your claim will be processed.

Disability applications are more complicated than other Social Security applications. Since your eligibility for disability benefits depends on your medical condition and ability to work, you must also supply Social Security with information about your health and work history.

Specifically, you will have to provide Social Security with the following medical and employment-related information:

- Names, addresses, and phone numbers of doctors, hospitals, and clinics that have treated you, with the approximate dates of treatment.

- Names and addresses of places you have worked over the past 15 years, with approximate dates of employment and a brief description of the nature of your work.

Once again, don't put off filing your application while you pull this information together.

If your disability prevents you from making a personal appearance at a Social Security office, you can file your papers through the mail or send a friend or family member to the office on your behalf. Always keep a copy of everything you submit to Social Security. If you use the mail, send everything certified mail and request a return receipt.

HOW IS YOUR
DISABILITY APPLICATION DECIDED?

Once the Social Security Administration determines that you have enough quarters of coverage to be fully and currently insured for disability benefits, your application will be forwarded to a team of doctors and disability evaluators. This team will review your application and make the initial determination of whether you meet Social Security's definition of disability.

These medical specialists are supposed to get information about your medical condition from doctors who have treated you. Unfortunately, all too often they make little or no effort to collect evidence on your behalf. As already mentioned, you should assume full responsibility for gathering medical documentation to support your claim.

The medical team may ask you to be examined by one or more doctors who are paid by the Social Security Administration. These doctors are called consultative examiners. While some consultative examiners are competent and thorough, many consultative examiners are highly biased and quick to conclude that an applicant is not disabled based on a brief 10-minute examination.

This should not be cause for concern, as long as your own doctor is in your corner. What your doctor says about your disability outweighs any contrary opinions stated by a consultative examiner. So if you have an unfavorable consultative examiner's report in your file, you want to move heaven and earth to get a report from your doctor in support of your claim.

You can also blunt the effect of a negative consultative examiner's report with your testimony, if you appeal your case to an administrative hearing. (Appeals are discussed on page 197.) Specifically, you want to state on the record how long the examination lasted (if it was short), what the doctor did (if not much), and the substance of your discussions with the doctor (if superficial or contradictory). Don't trust your memory. Jot down some notes about what happened in the consultative examiner's office as soon as your examination is over.

If Social Security wants you to have a specific test performed, such as a stress test, you can insist on having your own doctor perform it. But if you refuse to be examined by a consultative examiner, you may be denied disability benefits.

From 3 to 6 months after you file your application, you should receive a notice in the mail that your claim has been approved or denied. If your claim is approved, you will soon receive a certificate of award and booklet describing your disability benefits.

If your claim is denied, roll up your sleeves and file an appeal. A denial does not mean that you are not entitled to disability benefits. In fact, you stand a better than fifty-fifty chance of prevailing on appeal. The worst part about having your application denied is that you lose time. Depending on how far you have to take your appeal, you may not see a benefit check for over a year.

If you file your application within 17 months of becoming disabled, you won't lose out on a cent of benefits. Retroactive disability benefits are available for up to 12 months from the date you apply (*not* the date you finally win your case). You also have a 5-month waiting period before your disability benefits start. After your 5-month waiting period is over, your 12 months of retroactive benefits will begin.

WHAT IF YOUR DISABILITY APPLICATION IS DENIED?

There are four stages to appealing a denial of disability benefits (but you won't necessarily have to go through all four):

- Reconsideration.
- Administrative hearing.
- Appeals Council.
- Federal court.

Each stage of appeal is discussed below.

RECONSIDERATION

If your disability application is denied, and you want to appeal, your first step is to request reconsideration.

TIMING

You have 60 days from the date you receive the initial denial to request reconsideration.

PROCEDURE

You can request reconsideration by following the instructions on the denial notice, or by going to your local Social Security office and filling out a Request for Reconsideration (Form SSA-561-U2), which is reprinted in Appendix 9. Remember to keep a copy of everything you submit to Social Security.

METHOD OF REVIEW

At reconsideration, your claim will be reviewed by a different Social Security representative than the one who made the initial decision on your application. If you want, you can submit additional evidence in support of your claim while your case is being reconsidered. If you have not yet submitted a statement from your doctor, try to get it in time for reconsideration. Occasionally, the representative conducting the reconsideration will call to ask you for some specific additional information.

DECISION

Within 2 or 3 months of requesting reconsideration, you should receive a written decision in the mail. Don't be disappointed if your claim is denied on reconsideration. There is a very low reversal rate at this stage of the appeals process. Most appeals must continue through an administrative hearing.

ADMINISTRATIVE HEARING

You stand the best chance of winning a reversal of the denial of benefits at the administrative hearing. The administrative hearing is your first opportunity to present your case in person to an administrative law judge (ALJ).

TIMING

You must request an administrative hearing within 60 days after you receive written notice that your reconsideration has been denied. Hearings usually take several months to be scheduled. Use this time to your best advantage:

- Gather medical and other evidence that supports your claim, including reports and records from the doctors and hospitals that treated you and possibly a letter from your former employer.

- Arrange for witnesses to testify at your hearing, such as friends and family (who can describe the daily problems you encounter), former employers (who can explain why you had to leave your job), doctors (who can describe your medical problems), and vocational experts and counselors (who can testify why you are unemployable).

- Review your file at Social Security. Call your local Social Security office or the Social Security hearing office to find out when and where the file will be available for review.

A review of your file will reveal whether all the evidence you submitted to Social Security actually made it into the file. If evidence is missing from your file, submit copies of the missing documents to the judge at the hearing. A review of the file will also show what evidence, if any, Social Security has that you are not disabled.

For example, you may see a report from a consultative examiner stating that your back pain does not prevent you from returning to work as a secretary. Knowing this, you can contact your doctor for a letter explaining why your pain prevents you from sitting for the hours required in a secretarial job.

Whenever a consultative examiner says that you are not disabled, it is absolutely critical to get a rebuttal statement from your own doctor. The law requires Social Security to give greater weight to the opinion of your doctor than to the opinion of a consultative examiner. The reasoning for this law is clear: Your doctor has known you longer and is far more familiar with your medical condition. Once your doctor says that you are disabled, you can *almost* start counting your disability benefits. Of course, it's not over till it's over, and you have the award notice in hand, but the importance of a supportive letter from your primary doctor cannot be overstated.

If you are unable to attend the hearing on the scheduled date, promptly call your local Social Security office or the hearing office to reschedule. A new hearing should be scheduled in several months.

If you can make the hearing on the scheduled date, but have not yet received medical reports from all your doctors, do not postpone your hearing. You should go ahead with the hearing on the scheduled date for a couple of reasons:

- If you request a postponement, a new hearing may not be scheduled for several months.
- Most judges will permit you to submit additional evidence after the hearing. At the hearing, simply ask the judge to keep the record open for a period of time (usually 2 to 4 weeks). Describe to the judge the evidence you are waiting to receive and the efforts you have made to obtain the evidence. ALJs almost always permit claimants to submit evidence within a few weeks after the hearing. You can also ask the ALJ for assistance obtaining the missing evidence.

PROCEDURE

You can request an administrative hearing by following the instructions on the reconsideration notice or by visiting your local Social Security office and completing Form HA-501-U5 (see Appendix 10).

METHOD OF REVIEW

The entire hearing is taped, so you should be prepared to speak into a microphone. If the administrative judge does not want something on tape, the judge will go off the record. You want to be sure that all your statements are on the record. Ask the administrative judge if you are on the record before you testify.

You also have the right to be represented by an attorney or other advocate (such as a paralegal, social worker, caseworker, or friend) at the hearing. Free legal assistance is available through legal services and legal aid offices (see Appendix 15). You can also get a referral to an attorney specializing in Social Security disability claims by contacting:

> **National Organization of Social Security Claims Representatives (NOSSCR)**
> 6 Prospect Street
> Midland Park, NJ 07432
> 800-431-2804

NOSSCR also publishes a free brochure entitled "Social Security Disability and SSI Claims: Your Need for Representation."

Your Testimony

Most likely, the ALJ will start the hearing by asking you some questions. The ALJ may also invite you to make an opening statement. On a rare occasion, the ALJ will instruct your representative (if you have one) to do the initial questioning.

Your testimony at the hearing should answer the following important questions:

• What are your medical problems?

Testimony tip: Don't mention only your primary medical problem. Tell the ALJ about every medical problem that interferes with your life either at home or at work. Come to the hearing prepared to talk about your physical and emotional problems (pretty personal stuff) with a complete stranger. If it makes you feel any better, the ALJ has probably heard it all before.

• What are you unable to do as a result of your medical problems?

Testimony tip: The focus of the disability evaluation process is functional capacity. Describe in detail everything you *can't* do. Do you now have problems dressing, feeding, or grooming yourself? Can you still shop, cook, and clean your house? Is it difficult for you to drive, walk, or take public transportation?

• Why are you unable to perform requirements of your former jobs?

Testimony tip: Describe for the ALJ the exact duties you were required to perform in each job you held during the last 15 years. As a general rule, try not to glorify your job duties. The more skills you are found to have, the easier it will be for Social Security to determine that you can do other work.

• Why are you unable to perform any other job?

Testimony tip: You want to emphasize limitations that affect your ability to work at all. For example, if you have a problem concentrating or following instructions, or you need to go to the bathroom frequently, you will not be a good candidate for almost any type of work.

Your Advocate's Role

One of your advocate's primary functions will be to ask you questions that bring out the favorable facts of your case. If you omitted any important information in your initial testimony, or if the judge could misinterpret something you said, your representative can use questions to clarify and complete your testimony.

Another important job for your advocate is to question expert witnesses Social Security may present at your hearing. For example, Social Security sometimes schedules a medical expert to testify about the disabling nature of your condition, or a vocational expert to testify about the kinds of work you can perform. Your advocate can use questions to weaken the opposing experts' testimony.

Finally, your advocate can be a great source of moral support. Although an administrative hearing is supposed to be an informal proceeding, testifying before a judge can still be an intimidating experience. You may find that an advocate's friendly face, or supportive touch on the arm, is just what you need to calm your jumpy nerves.

If you want an attorney to represent you at a Social Security hearing, contact your local bar association or ask friends and family for referrals. Most attorneys who handle these types of cases do not charge a fee unless you win your case. Legal services and legal aid attorneys represent low-income claimants for no charge.

DECISION

Within a month or 2 of your hearing, you should receive a written decision in the mail. If the administrative judge denies your claim after the hearing, you can still take your case to the Appeals Council. If your claim is approved, you may be eligible for benefits going back to a year before the date of your original application.

APPEALS COUNCIL

The Appeals Council is a branch of the Social Security Administration that handles appeals of administrative hearings.

TIMING

You must request Appeals Council review within 60 days of receiving a denial from your administrative hearing.

PROCEDURE

You can request Appeals Council review by filling out Form HA-520-U5 (Appendix 11) at your local Social Security office or sending a letter to the Appeals Council at the address indicated on the hearing decision.

METHOD OF REVIEW

Generally claimants do not appear in person before the Appeals Council. You can, however, submit to the Appeals Council a letter or additional evidence in support of your claim for benefits.

DECISION

The Appeals Council will take one of the following actions after reviewing your case:

1. Decline review. If the Appeals Council refuses to review your claim, your only remaining options are to file a federal court appeal or abandon your case.
2. Affirm the denial of your claim. If the denial is affirmed, you can file a federal court appeal or abandon your case.
3. Reverse the denial of your claim. If the denial is reversed, you will be awarded benefits.
4. Send your case back for a new administrative hearing. If the Appeals Council finds that the judge made an error in evaluating your claim, you will be given an opportunity to present your case at a new hearing.

FEDERAL COURT

A federal court lawsuit is the final level of appeal. Although your local courthouse may be an imposing building with marble steps and stately columns, be brave. The courthouse is there for you to use to vindicate your legal rights. If you are truly disabled, getting Social Security disability benefits is your legal right.

TIMING

To start your federal court appeal, you must file a complaint within 60 days of receiving the Appeals Council's decision.

METHOD OF REVIEW

To proceed with a federal court appeal, hire a lawyer if you can (preferably one with an expertise in Social Security disability appeals). Although legal representation is not required in federal court, it certainly helps. Private attorneys and attorneys with legal services and legal aid offices are available to handle Social Security appeals (see Appendix 15).

If you want to represent yourself in court, you may wish to take advantage of legal services offices and federal courts that have lawyers on staff to advise unrepresented (*pro se*) individuals. These lawyers can help you complete the necessary forms to proceed in federal court, and instruct you in court procedure.

HOW MUCH WILL YOU RECEIVE IN DISABILITY BENEFITS, AND WHEN?

Even if you win an award of benefits, you may have a wait before your monthly checks start sailing through your mail slot. There is a 5-month waiting period for disability benefits. As a general rule, benefits start in the 6th full month of your disability. Once benefits start, your check should arrive on the 3rd day of every month you are eligible for benefits.

If you delayed filing an application for benefits, you may be owed some back benefits. Back benefits are paid for up to 12 months before the date of your application. For example, if you became disabled in March 1990, filed an application for disability benefits in December 1990, and received your approval in February 1991, you would not be eligible for benefits during the 5-month waiting period (April 1990 to August 1990). However, your retroactive benefits should be available as of September 1990 (which is within the 12-month period before you filed your application).

The amount of your disability benefit will depend on your earnings history. The same rules for computing the amount of your retirement benefit apply to your disability benefit. Your disability benefit will equal your Primary Insurance Amount (PIA) at the time you become disabled (see page 171).

Monthly benefits paid to members of your family will equal a percentage of your benefit amount, as outlined below.

Family Benefits

Family Member	Percentage of Your Benefit
Spouse, age 62	$37\frac{1}{2}$ percent (to be gradually reduced starting in the year 2000)
Spouse between ages 62 and 65	Between $37\frac{1}{2}$ percent and 50 percent
Spouse, age 65	50 percent (to be gradually reduced starting in the year 2003)
Spouse at any age if caring for minor (under 16) or disabled child	50 percent
Minor (under 18, or 19 if a full-time student) unmarried child	50 percent
Unmarried child of any age who became disabled before age 22	50 percent

As with retirement benefits, the total benefits paid to your family cannot exceed a certain maximum amount. This amount is called the maximum family benefit (MFB). If your family's total benefits exceed the MFB, your spouse's and children's benefits will be reduced. Your benefit will not be affected.

WHAT HAPPENS TO YOUR BENEFITS IF YOU RETURN TO WORK?

Almost everyone would rather work than sit around collecting disability benefits. Not surprisingly, Social Security prefers to see people working as well. To encourage people to try to return to work, Social Security has adopted several work incentive policies. These policies are discussed below.

For more information about returning to work, you can request a free copy of the booklet "Working While Disabled . . . How Social Security Can Help" (Publication Number 05-10095) or the "Red Book on Work Incentives" (Publication Number 64-030) by calling Social Security's toll-free number (800-772-1213) or visiting a Social Security office.

TRIAL WORK PERIOD

The trial work period enables disability beneficiaries to test their ability to work without losing any of their disability benefits. During the trial work period, disability beneficiaries can earn a salary *and* collect a benefit check.

• A trial work period lasts 9 months. During the trial work period, the money you earn does not affect your disability benefits. Since the 9 months do not have to be consecutive, you can start and stop working several times during one trial work period. You use up a month of your trial work period every time your monthly earnings exceed $200.

• When your trial work period is over, your disability benefits may be terminated if you continue working at substantial gainful activity (which, as discussed on page 189, is work that pays $500 or more a month). Even if your monthly earnings after the end of your trial work period exceed $500, your benefits will continue for an additional 3-month "adjustment period" (see page 206).

• As of January 1, 1992, you are entitled to 9 months of trial work within a rolling 60-month (5-year) period. To find out how many months you have left in your trial work period, add up how many trial months you have used during the last 5 years. If you used 3 months of a trial work period in 1993, when you try to return to work in 1994 you have 6 months left of your trial work period.

• Whenever you file a new application for disability benefits, you start a new period of disability and get a new trial work period. Say you have been collecting disability benefits for 5 years. After a 9-month trial work period, your benefits terminate. Ten years later, your disability returns. You have to file a new application for benefits. If your application is approved, you are entitled to a new 9-month trial work period.

• You will get the most out of your trial work period if you start working at the beginning of a month. The reason: You use up a month of trial work when your total monthly earnings exceed $200, even if you only worked for a few days in the month. An example demonstrates how timing your trial work can save you money.

Compare the situations of Bob and Bill:

	Bob	Bill
Monthly disability benefit	$600	$600
Weekly salary	$525	$525
Monthly salary	$2100	$2100
Commencement of employment	Last week of January 1994	First week of February 1994
Monthly earnings between January 1994 and January 1995 (with months of trial work period and grace period noted)		
January 1994	$525 + $600[2]	$600
February 1994	$2100 + $600[2]	$2100 + $600
March 1994	$2100 + $600[2]	$2100 + $600[2]
April 1994	$2100 + $600[2]	$2100 + $600[2]
May 1994	$2100 + $600[2]	$2100 + $600[2]
June 1994	$2100 + $600[2]	$2100 + $600[2]
July 1994	$2100 + $600[2]	$2100 + $600[2]
August 1994	$2100 + $600[2]	$2100 + $600[2]
September 1994	$2100 + $600[2]	$2100 + $600[2]
October 1994	$2100 + $600[3]	$2100 + $600[2]
November 1994	$2100 + $600[3]	$2100 + $600[3]
December 1994	$2100 + $600[3]	$2100 + $600[3]
January 1995	$2100	$2100 + $600[3]
TOTAL	$32,925	$33,000

[2] Trial work period
[3] Adjustment period (see below)

By carefully timing the beginning of his trial work period, Bill was able to work one less week than Bob and earn $75.00 more than Bob.

ADJUSTMENT PERIODS

If you return to substantial gainful employment (earning over $500 a month), you cannot continue to collect disability benefits. However, your first three over-$500-a-month paychecks will not disqualify you for disability benefits. After your 9-month trial work period, you are entitled to a 3-month adjustment period. During this entire 12-month period, you can collect a paycheck as well as a disability benefit check.

EXTENDED PERIOD OF ELIGIBILITY

Despite your best efforts, your attempt to return to work may fail. You may be able to work for a period of time, but then be forced to leave your job because your condition flares up. Or you may be laid off from work. You are entitled to collect a benefit check for any month that you do not perform substantial gainful activity during the 36-month period that follows the end of your trial work period. This period is called the extended period of eligibility.

During the extended period of eligibility, you automatically requalify for disability benefits during your low- or no-income months (when earnings do not exceed $500 a month) without filing a new application, without submitting medical documentation, and without an additional 5-month waiting period.

CONTINUATION OF MEDICARE

If you return to work while still disabled, and lose your disability benefits, you will not immediately lose your health care coverage. Your Medicare coverage (Part A and Part B) will continue for at least 39 months after the end of your trial work period (see page 204).

When your Medicare coverage terminates, you may be allowed to pay for continued benefits if you are still working, still disabled, and under age 65. The cost of continuing your Medicare coverage will be the same as if you were an eligible retiree. If you can show financial need, the state will pay your Part A Medicare premium.

VOCATIONAL REHABILITATION SERVICES

The Social Security Administration refers some disability beneficiaries for vocational rehabilitation services. Younger beneficiaries are more likely to be referred for vocational training than older beneficiaries. Vocational rehabilitation services teach disability beneficiaries skills that will enable them to return to work. Job training, placement, and counseling are some of the more common vocational services. A beneficiary who refuses to accept vocational rehabilitation services without a good reason may lose disability benefits.

WHEN DO YOUR DISABILITY BENEFITS END?

In addition to the bases for termination discussed above in connection with work incentives, Social Security will terminate your disability benefits if your medical condition improves.

Social Security uses the practices outlined below to determine whether you are still entitled to disability benefits.

CONTINUING DISABILITY REVIEWS

Every disability beneficiary must undergo a periodic continuing disability review by the Social Security Administration. The frequency of the review depends on the nature of the disabling condition, and can be anywhere from once every 18 months to once every 7 years.

On review, Social Security usually requests updated medical evidence from your doctors. You may also be asked to take some medical tests, and be examined by one or more doctors paid by Social Security. Your failure to comply with these requests can result in a termination of your benefits.

Unless Social Security finds your medical condition has improved, or is not as serious as previously thought (using new or improved diagnostic techniques), or is no longer disabling (thanks to advances in medical therapy or technology), your benefits will be continued after review. If your benefits are terminated for medical improvement, make sure you get the 3 additional months of benefits and 39 months of Medicare coverage that you are entitled to receive.

If you disagree with the termination decision, promptly file an appeal. Although you have 60 days to appeal, try to file within 15 days of the date of the termination notice so your benefits will not be interrupted, at least through the administrative hearing. Remember to request a continuation of benefits when you request each stage of appeal. If you lose your administrative hearing, Social Security can ask you to repay the benefits you received pending your appeal. The discussion on page 236 tells you how you may be able to avoid repaying Social Security.

NEW PERIODS OF DISABILITY

New periods of disability rules apply to disability beneficiaries who are terminated from the disability rolls and then reapply for disability benefits within 5 years of their termination.

If you are such a beneficiary, your benefit checks will start in the first full month of your new disability. You will not have a new 5-month waiting period (see page 203). Furthermore, if you were entitled to Medicare based on your prior period of disability, your Medicare coverage will resume when your disability benefits start again. You will not have to complete another 24-month waiting period (see page 209).

WHAT OTHER BENEFITS CAN YOU COLLECT WHILE RECEIVING DISABILITY BENEFITS?

What if your disability benefits are not enough to cover your expenses? Are any other benefits available to you?

SOCIAL SECURITY BENEFITS

You are only permitted to collect one type of Social Security benefit at a time. This means that if you are eligible for both Social Security disability and retirement benefits, you can only collect one benefit or the other. You will receive a disability insurance benefit check until the month in which you reach age 65. Your disability benefit will then end, and your retirement benefit will begin.

SUPPLEMENTAL SECURITY INCOME

Supplemental Security Income (SSI) benefits are paid to disabled individuals who can demonstrate financial need. The purpose of the SSI program is to make sure that every disabled person receives a minimum amount of income each month. SSI benefits are administered by the Social Security Administration.

If you are receiving Social Security disability benefits, you may also be eligible for SSI benefits. Your SSI eligibility will depend on the total amount of your monthly income and resources, including your Social Security income.

The SSI program is covered in great detail in Chapter 8.

PRIVATE DISABILITY PAYMENTS

Many disabled people receive private disability payments from an insurance company or their employer. These private payments do not affect the payment of Social Security disability benefits.

VETERANS' BENEFITS

The Veterans Administration provides veterans with disability coverage. Veterans are permitted to receive their full Social Security disability benefits, even if they are also collecting veterans' benefits.

WORKERS' COMPENSATION BENEFITS AND DISABILITY BENEFITS FROM FEDERAL, STATE, AND CIVIL SERVICE PROGRAMS

Unlike private disability benefits and veterans' benefits, which do not affect Social Security, benefits collected under the Workers' Compensation program or a public civil service program may affect the amount of a Social Security check. If you are under age 65, and collect any of these types of disability benefits in addition to your Social Security disability benefits, your Social Security benefits may be reduced.

The total amount of disability benefits you collect under Social Security, Workers' Compensation, and federal, state, and civil service programs cannot exceed 80 percent of your average earnings before you became disabled. When your Workers' Compensation and public civil service benefits end, however, you can start to collect the full amount of your Social Security disability benefits.

MEDICARE

You automatically qualify for Medicare Part A coverage after you have been collecting Social Security disability benefits for 24 months (not necessarily consecutive). You can get Medicare Part B by paying a monthly premium, just like every other Part B beneficiary (see page 42). Social Security benefits are not affected by your receipt of Medicare coverage.

ℹ️ *For more information*

For general information about the Social Security disability benefit program, you can get the free booklet "Disability" (Publication Number 05-10029) by calling or visiting your local Social Security office.

BACK TO LARRY

Soon after Larry filed his application for disability benefits we contacted his treating internists, orthopedists, and neurologists. His doctors were very cooperative. They provided us with medical reports that documented a lumbosacral strain, low back derangement, and range of motion of the spine limited to 40 to 50 degrees. They also stated that, in their professional opinion, Larry could not engage in any type of substantially gainful employment for at least a year. Larry won his disability benefits.

After about 2 years on disability, Larry decided to try to return to work. He gave notice of his intention to Social Security, dusted off his accountant's shingle, and reopened his office. For 5 months Larry collected disability benefits as well as fees from his clients.

Unfortunately, the pain soon became too much for Larry to bear. He notified Social Security that he could no longer work. Since he was still within his trial work period, his work attempt did not cost him any of his disability benefits.

Larry was relieved to learn that he could continue to count on collecting disability benefits until he started to collect his Social Security retirement benefit at age 65.

8.

COLLECTING SUPPLEMENTAL SECURITY INCOME BENEFITS

When I met Randy he was 68 years old and in difficult financial straits. His $350 Social Security check simply did not cover his rent, food, and other living expenses. He was desperate for help.

I told Randy about the Supplemental Security Income (SSI) program. Although Randy was cheered to learn that there was an additional source of financial assistance for older people, he had some concerns: Would his Social Security check make him ineligible for SSI? How would he ever manage to file an application when he was barely able to leave his apartment? What would happen if his application was denied?

The Supplemental Security Income (SSI) program guarantees a minimum level of income to elderly, blind, or disabled individuals who are in financial need. The federal government funds the SSI program with general tax dollars.

The biggest problem with the SSI program is that not enough people know about it. In fact, studies have shown that only about 40 percent of eligible elderly Americans currently receive SSI. This is a double tragedy. Not only are these low-income older adults doing without an available source of income, they may also be losing out on medical, heating, rental, and food benefits that are provided to SSI recipients.

By the time you finish reading this chapter, you will no longer be one of the many who are unfamiliar with the SSI program. In fact, you will probably know more than you ever wanted to know about SSI. But this knowledge may mean an additional source of benefits for you or someone you know.

The chapter is divided into seven sections. Each section covers an important aspect of the SSI program: background information on SSI, SSI eligibility, SSI benefit amounts, applying for SSI, collecting SSI, appealing denials of SSI, and the rights and responsibilities of SSI beneficiaries.

Within each section, questionnaires, worksheets, and charts help you get the most out of the SSI program.

WHAT IS SSI?

SSI is a public assistance program for elderly and disabled people who are in real financial need. The Social Security Administration runs the SSI program, as well as the other Social Security benefit programs (retirement, disability, and survivors).

Unlike Social Security, eligibility for SSI does not depend on how much an individual worked or earned in the past. There are many other differences between SSI and Social Security benefits, the most important of which are listed in the chart below.

Differences Between Social Security and SSI

Social Security	Supplemental Security Income
Social Security is an insurance program. When you retire or become disabled, you collect money you paid into the Social Security system while you were working.	SSI is a public benefits program. You are entitled to SSI benefits if you are elderly, blind, or disabled and financially needy, even if you never worked.
Social Security is funded by employers, employees, and the self-employed through the Social Security trust fund.	SSI is funded with general tax dollars from the U.S. Treasury.
Eligibility for Social Security benefits does not depend on financial need. You can receive Social Security benefits regardless of your income and assets.	Eligibility for SSI is based on financial need. Your income and assets must be within certain limits to qualify for benefits.

SSI ELIGIBILITY

You must meet all three of these requirements to be eligible for SSI:

1. You must be elderly, blind, or disabled.
2. Your monthly income must be below a certain limit.
3. Your resources, such as savings accounts, must be below a certain limit.

ARE YOU ELDERLY, BLIND, OR DISABLED?

AGE REQUIREMENT

If you are age 65 or over, you meet the age requirement for SSI.

BLINDNESS REQUIREMENT

If your corrected vision (with eyeglasses or contact lenses) is limited to 20/200 or worse, or your field of vision is limited to less than 20 degrees, you meet the blindness requirement for SSI.

DISABILITY REQUIREMENT

You meet the disability requirement for SSI if you have a mental or physical impairment that prevents you from working and earning at least $500 a month for at least 12 months, or is expected to result in your death. The rules for establishing disability for SSI benefits are the same as those that apply to Social Security disability benefits (see Chapter 7) with one exception: There is no 5-month waiting period for SSI benefits to begin.

IS YOUR INCOME LOW ENOUGH?

To understand how your income affects you SSI eligibility, you must be familiar with the following terms:

- Income is the money you receive each month.
- Countable income is the income that affects SSI eligibility.
- Exempt income is the income that does not affect SSI eligibility.
- Earned income is the income you get from working, either as an employee or in self-employment. (Infrequent income of less than $10 a month is not included.)
- Unearned income is the income you get other than through employment, such as Social Security benefits, pension benefits, alimony, gifts, rents, stock dividends, annuities, inheritances, and bank interest.

To qualify for SSI, there is a limit on how much countable income you can receive each month. Your countable income is different than your total income. The next section lists sources of income that are relevant to your SSI eligibility. Sources of income that have no bearing on your SSI eligibility are discussed on page 217.

Once you know your countable income, you are ready to analyze your SSI income eligibility. A budget worksheet is included later in this chapter to assist you in this analysis.

WHAT INCOME IS COUNTABLE UNDER SSI?

Your countable income includes the following earned and unearned sources of income added together. If your monthly countable income is too high, you will not be eligible for any SSI benefits.

• Earned income. The Social Security Administration has devised a formula to determine how much of your earned income is countable:

Total monthly earned income		$_____
LESS	$65	– $ __65__
EQUALS	Subtotal	= $_____
DIVIDED BY	2	÷ __2__
EQUALS	Total countable earned income	= $_____

Social Security does not count more of your earned income to encourage you to work.

After you start receiving SSI, your earned income is reduced even further by your impairment-related work expenses or IRWEs (pronounced "er-wees"). This is important because it could mean a larger monthly SSI benefit check.

IRWEs are the costs of items and services that enable you to work despite your impairment. For example, if you must modify your car to accommodate a physical disability, and you use the car to drive to work, the costs of the modification are IRWEs. Similarly, if you use a wheelchair, walker, or cane to get around, or prescription drugs to control your symptoms, or an inhalator to breathe, the costs of all these products can be deducted from your earned income as IRWEs. You can take the deduction in a single month (for a lump-sum purchase) or each month of the year (for monthly expenses, such as a rental, or for one-twelfth of the cost of a lump-sum purchase). Be sure to bring these expenses to Social Security's attention.

• Monthly Social Security check. The total amount is countable.

• Monthly pension check. The total amount is countable.

• Annuity payments. The total amount is countable.

• Gifts. Only gifts that have a value of more than $20 a month, *and* that you receive regularly (such as month after month), are countable.

• Some interest earned on savings accounts and other investments. Interest payments can be made either monthly or quarterly (once every 3 months). Different rules apply depending on how often your interest is paid.

- If you earn interest monthly, your interest is countable regardless of the amount. For example, a $10 interest payment made each month on a certificate of deposit is counted.

- If you earn interest quarterly, your interest is countable only if it exceeds $20 in the month it is paid. For example, $10 interest paid quarterly on a savings account will not be counted since it is less than $20 in the months it is paid.

• In-kind income. Countable income does not only include cash. In-kind income is gifts of food, clothing, or shelter. You receive in-kind income if, for example:

- Someone pays your rent or mortgage for you.
- Someone pays your utility bills for you.
- Someone buys food or clothing for you.

Gifts of items other than food, clothing, and shelter are not in-kind income. For example, you do not receive countable in-kind income when:

- Someone pays your telephone bill for you.
- Someone pays a housekeeper for you.
- Someone pays your medical bills for you.
- Someone buys a television for you.

If you receive food and shelter from someone else, Social Security will presume that the value of this in-kind income is one-third of the federal SSI benefit. In 1994 the federal SSI benefit is $446 a month for an individual. One-third of $446 is $148.66.

For example, you live and eat all of your meals with your daughter. You do not pay any rent or contribute any money to the food budget. Social Security will presume you have additional in-kind income of $148.66.

The value Social Security assigns to gifts of food and shelter is only a presumption. You will be treated as having less than $148.66 in additional countable income if you have the receipts and canceled checks to prove that the actual value of what you receive is worth less than $148.66. Of course, if you can prove that you pay your share of the household's housing and food expenses, you will not be treated as having any in-kind income.

In many families, children give their parents food and shelter with the tacit understanding that the parents will repay the children whenever they can. There is rarely a formal loan agreement, which is unfortunate. If there was a loan contract, the parents would not be treated as receiving any in-kind income. As long as the parents are obligated to repay their children, they do not have in-kind income. A sample loan agreement follows:

Sample Loan Agreement

Paragraph I   Parties to the agreement
This is a loan agreement between [insert child's name] and [insert parent's name].

Paragraph II   The loan
Between [insert date] and [insert date, or "continuing through the present"], Child loaned goods and/or services to Parent. Child provided the Parent with housing at [insert address], food, and clothing, with the expectation of full repayment.

Paragraph III   Repayment terms
Parent agrees to repay Child the full value of the loaned goods and services in monthly installments at the prevailing rate of interest when Parent starts receiving Supplemental Security Income benefit checks.

Both parent and child should sign and date the loan agreement, and submit a copy to Social Security.

• Deemed income. Odd as it sounds, sometimes SSI counts someone else's income as your income. Deemed income is income that is paid to someone else, but is treated as your countable income. You may have deemed income if:

  • You are married.
  • You live with your spouse.
  • Your spouse is not eligible for SSI because he or she is not elderly, blind, or disabled, or has too much income or resources.

If you meet these three requirements, some of your mate's income could affect your SSI eligibility. An SSI representative at your local Social Security office will be able to help you compute the value of the deemed income.

Where both you and your spouse are eligible for SSI, the income limits that apply to couples will determine your SSI eligibility (see page 218). If you and your spouse's combined income falls below the SSI limit for a couple, you will receive a check for the difference between your total income and the SSI limit for two.

WHAT INCOME IS EXEMPT UNDER SSI?

The sources of income listed below are never counted by SSI. They do not affect your eligibility for benefits.

- $20 a month from any source, except public assistance.
- Funds you receive as reimbursement of your medical expenses.
- Money that you borrow from friends, relatives, or a lending institution as long as you promise to repay the loan.
- Payments received by Holocaust survivors on or after November 1, 1984, from the Federal Republic of Germany.
- Payments made to Japanese-Americans and Aleuts who were in concentration camps during World War II.
- Agent Orange settlement payments.
- Victims' compensation payments.
- Interest you earn on burial space agreements or burial funds.

Budget Worksheet: Computing Your Countable Income

Use the following worksheet to compute your countable income.

Unearned income:

Line 1A	Monthly Social Security	$_____
Line 2A	Monthly pension	+ $_____
Line 3A	Monthly rental income	+ $_____
Line 4A	Monthly interest	+ $_____
Line 5A	Quarterly interest (if over $20 in month paid)	+ $_____
Line 6A	Monthly cash gifts (if over $20 a month and received month after month)	+ $_____
Line 7A	Monthly annuity income	+ $_____
Line 8A	Monthly royalty income	+ $_____
Line 9A	In-kind income (unless actual value is less than $148.66)	$148.66

	Subtotal Unearned income	=	$_____
Line 10A	LESS	–	$ 20.00
Line 11A	Countable monthly unearned income		$_____

Earned income:

Line 1B	Total earned income		$_____
Line 2B	Less $65	–	$ 65.00
	($85 if unearned income is less than $20)		
Line 3B	EQUALS Subtotal	=	$_____
Line 4B	DIVIDED BY 2	÷	2
Line 5B	Countable earned income		$_____

After SSI starts:

Line 6B	LESS impairment-related work expenses	–	$_____
Line 7B	Total countable earned income	=	$_____
Line 8B	Countable monthly earned income		$_____
	(Enter from Line 5B or 7B above)		

Countable (earned and unearned) income:

Enter Line 11A		$_____
PLUS Line 8B	+	$_____
Total Monthly Countable Income	=	$

SSI INCOME LIMITS

SSI income limits are the maximum amounts of countable income you can receive each month and still be eligible for SSI.

To determine whether your income is too high to qualify for SSI, you must compare two numbers: your total monthly countable income and the SSI income limits. Only if your monthly countable income is less than the SSI income limits do you qualify for an SSI benefit.

The SSI income limits change each year. The limits in 1994 are $446 for a single applicant and $669 for a couple.

As long as your income is below the income limits, you may be eligible for some SSI money. The amount of your SSI check will be the difference between your monthly income and the SSI income limits.

For example, Steve and Kathleen Clarke are both 68 years old. Steve's monthly countable income is a $300 pension. Kathleen's monthly countable income is a $200 Social Security check. Since the SSI income limit for a couple is $669, Steve and Kathleen will be entitled to a $169 monthly SSI check ($669 minus $500).

Some states supplement the federal SSI benefit with a state payment. In those states that pay a supplement, the SSI income limits are higher.

SAMPLE WORKSHEET:
WHAT IS MRS. LANE'S SSI INCOME ELIGIBILITY?

Mrs. Lane wants to know if she is eligible for SSI. She lives and eats with her daughter rent-free, and receives the following amounts of income each month:

- $200 Social Security.
- $165 from selling cosmetics door-to-door.
- $50 a month from her other daughter who lives on the West Coast.

Mrs. Lane's total monthly countable income is computed as follows:

Unearned income:

Line 1A	Monthly Social Security		$200.00
Line 2A	Monthly pension	+ $	N/A
Line 3A	Monthly rental income	+ $	N/A
Line 4A	Countable monthly interest	+ $	N/A
Line 5A	Countable quarterly interest (since over $20 in month paid)	+ $	N/A
Line 6A	Countable monthly cash gifts (since over $20 a month and received month after month)	+ $	50.00
Line 7A	Monthly annuity income	+ $	N/A
Line 8A	Monthly royalty income	+ $	N/A
Line 9A	In-kind income	+	$148.66
	Subtotal Unearned income	=	$398.66
Line 10A	LESS	− $	20.00
Line 11A	Countable monthly unearned income	=	$378.66

Earned income:

Line 1B	Total earned income		$165.00
Line 2B	LESS $65	− $	65.00
Line 3B	EQUALS Subtotal	=	$100.00
Line 4B	DIVIDED BY 2	÷	2
Line 5B	Countable earned income	= $	50.00
After SSI starts:			
Line 6B	LESS impairment-related work expenses	− $	N/A
Line 7B	Total countable earned income	$	N/A
Line 8B	Countable monthly earned income (Enter total from Line 5B)	$	50.00

Total countable income:

Line 11A	378.66
PLUS Line 8B	+ $ 50.00
Total Monthly Countable Income	= $428.66

Since Mrs. Lane is seeking benefits as an individual, she must compare her total countable income to the monthly SSI benefit for an individual, which is $446 in 1994.

	SSI federal monthly benefit	$446.00
LESS	Total monthly countable income	$428.66
	SSI benefit	$ 17.34

Mrs. Lane's monthly SSI benefit will be $17.34 (plus the state supplement, if any). To receive this benefit, Mrs. Lane's resources cannot exceed the SSI resource limits, which are discussed in the following sections. Although the SSI benefit amount is negligible, it is sufficient to automatically qualify Mrs. Lane for Medicaid.

How Limited Are Your Resources?

To understand how resources affect SSI eligibility, you must become familiar with the following terms:

- Resources are the assets and property you own, such as your house, bank accounts, car, stocks, jewelry, furniture, and life insurance policies.
- Countable resources are the assets and property that affect your eligibility for SSI.
- Exempt resources are the assets and property that do not affect your SSI eligibility.

To qualify for SSI, your countable resources cannot exceed the SSI resource limit. In 1994 those limits are $2,000 for an individual and $3,000 for a couple.

To determine whether your resources are too high to qualify for SSI, you must identify which resources are counted by SSI and which are not. The following two sections will help you with this process.

WHAT RESOURCES ARE COUNTABLE UNDER SSI?

Most people own a mix of property. They have some cash in the bank, some jewelry in their dresser drawer, some stock certificates in their vault, and a life insurance policy they purchased 35 years ago.

Not every piece of property you own affects your eligibility for SSI. Which of the following types of countable property do you own?

- Cash.
- Stocks.
- Bonds.
- Bank accounts. If you have your money in a joint bank account, or an "in trust for" account, Social Security will treat all of the money in the account as belonging to you (unless you can prove the money really belongs to someone else). A certificate of deposit counts, even if you would have to pay a penalty for cashing it in.
- Retirement accounts, such as an IRA. The entire balance in an individual retirement account (IRA) counts, even if you would be penalized for making an early withdrawal.
- Deemed property. Property that is in your spouse's sole name, or in joint name with you and your spouse, will be counted by Social Security as your property, whether or not your spouse even applies for SSI. (The only difference is that if your spouse also applies for SSI, your total resources must be below the SSI resource limit for a couple; see page 220.)

WHAT RESOURCES ARE EXEMPT UNDER SSI?

What about your other resources? What types of property does Social Security ignore when you file your SSI application?

• Your home (including a cooperative, condominium, or two- or three-family home), if you actually live in the home or intend to return to the home, or if a dependent relative lives in the home. A second home is always counted. Here are a couple of tips to help you take full advantage of the home exemption:

➤ TIP #1 *Plan to return home.*

To make sure the house stays protected if you leave it for an extended stay in the hospital or nursing home, sign a brief statement expressing your intent to return home. Ask your doctor to co-sign the statement. A sample statement follows:

I, [insert your name], own the real property located at [insert your address]. The property is my principal residence. I intend to return to my primary residence when I leave [enter name of hospital, nursing home, or wherever you are currently residing]. [Insert if applicable: My doctor has stated that there is a reasonable chance that my health will permit me to return to the community, as indicated by the signature below.]

Your name

Your doctor's name

➤ **TIP #2** *Invest your nonexempt assets in your home.*

As already mentioned, cash, stocks, bonds, CDs, and such other assets in excess of the SSI limits will you make you ineligible for SSI. But you can continue to benefit from your excess assets and still qualify for SSI. Use them to increase the value of your house. Pay off your mortgage. Buy a new boiler. Add a den. Plant some exotic new foliage. Go wild! Once the money is invested in your house, it is protected. If you later need more cash, you can use your home to secure a loan. The loan will not affect your SSI eligibility (see page 183).

➤ **TIP #3** *Use your nonexempt assets to buy all or part of a home or apartment.*

If you are a renter, or live rent-free with friends or family, and have too many resources to qualify for SSI, consider purchasing some property. You will protect your excess resources, save on rent, qualify for SSI, and own a resource that you can eventually sell or leave to your heirs. If you do not want the responsibility of owning a home or apartment, you may want to consider buying part of a home. For example, if you are living with your son, give your son your excess resources and have your name added to his deed. Property that you hold jointly with someone else will not affect your SSI eligibility, even if you do not live in the property.

• Your automobile. If you use your car to travel to doctors or work, or to perform essential daily activities, such as shopping, your car is not counted no matter how much it is worth. Otherwise, the value of your car in excess of $4,500 is counted.

• Household goods and personal effects (including furniture, appliances, art, clothing, and jewelry) up to a maximum value of $2,000. (The value of these belongings is based on what you could sell them for, not what they would cost to buy new.) The value of your wedding and engagement rings, and medical equipment, such as a hospital bed do not count toward the $2,000 limit. As a practical matter, Social Security does not check up on the value of your personal property.

• Life insurance. If the face value of the policy is less than $1,500, the entire policy is not counted. (The face value is the amount the policy pays upon the death of the insured.) If the face value of the policy exceeds $1,500, the cash value of the policy (the amount of money saved in the cash reserve) is counted.

Term life insurance policies are never counted.

• A burial space (including plots, headstones, markers, caskets, mausoleums) that is intended for use by you or an immediate family member.

• A burial fund. You can have up to $1,500 in your burial fund if you do not have any life insurance, or if the face value of your life insurance exceeds $1,500 (with any cash value applied to the $1,500 limit). If you have a life insurance policy with a face value of $1,500 or less, your burial fund cannot exceed the difference between the face value of the policy and $1,500. The burial fund must be in a separate account. Interest your burial fund earns is not counted.

If you withdraw money from the burial fund for any purpose other than burial, the fund is no longer exempt. Unless you immediately establish another burial fund account for the same amount of money, you will lose the benefit of this exemption.

• Property that you use in your trade or business, such as tools and machines.

Budget Worksheet: Computing Your Countable Resources

Use the following worksheet to compute your countable resources.

Cash (including cash at home, checking accounts, and savings accounts, whether joint, "in trust for," or in your sole name)	$_____
Stocks	+ $_____
Bonds	+ $_____
Deemed resources (only if you live with your spouse, and your spouse is not eligible for SSI—your spouse's resources are counted as yours)	+ $_____
Second home (fair market value)	+ $_____
Automobile (unless you need your car for your daily activities or to travel to doctors or work, then insert figure from Line 3 below)	+ $_____

Line 1	Fair market value	$_____
Line 2	LESS	− $4,500
Line 3	Countable value	= $_____

Household goods and personal effects	+ $_____
(Insert countable value from Line 3	
below)	

Line 1	Fair market value	$_____
Line 2	LESS	− $2,000
Line 3	Countable value	= $_____

Cash value of life insurance	+ $_____
(if face value exceeds $1,500)	
Burial space	+ $_____
Burial fund	+ $_____
(Insert from Line 3A or 5B below)	

If the face value of your life insurance is more than $1,500, or you have no life insurance, go to Line 1A.

If the face value of your life insurance is $1,500 or less, go to Line 1B.

Line 1A	Value of burial fund and/or cash reserve	$_____
Line 2A	LESS	− $1,500
Line 3A	Countable burial fund	= $_____
Line 1B	Exempt burial fund	$1,500
Line 2B	LESS face value of life insurance	− $_____
	Subtotal	= $_____
Line 3B	Value of burial fund	$_____
Line 4B	LESS Subtotal	− $_____
Line 5B	Countable burial fund	= $_____

Total Countable Resources	$_____

EXCEEDING THE SSI RESOURCE LIMITS

The SSI resource limits of $2,000 for a single applicant and $3,000 for a couple have remained the same for at least the last five years. Unlike Social Security benefits, which go up each year to reflect increases in the cost of living, the SSI resource limits have remained stagnant.

If your resources exceed the limits by $50 or less, you will be able to collect your SSI benefit for 1 month.

Even if your total countable resources exceed the resource limit by more than $50, you can still start to collect some SSI benefits if you agree to get rid of your excess nonliquid resources within the following time limits:

Excess Resource	Time Limit
A house or land	Within 6 months
Personal property	Within 3 months

You can get rid of your excess resources by giving them away, lending them out, selling them, or spending them. Always keep receipts to document how you disposed of your excess resources. Once you are within the resource limits, you must repay Social Security for the SSI benefits you received while you had the excess resources.

A few notes about getting rid of excess assets to qualify for SSI.

• You can reduce your excess resources by making a loan to a family member. An intrafamily loan offers the additional benefit of a boost to your monthly income.

Let's say you have $52,000 in the bank, which is $50,000 too much to qualify for SSI. You lend your son $50,000, and he signs a written loan agreement promising to pay you $250 a month, including interest. The portion of the monthly payment that represents a return of your principal is not income to you, and does not affect your SSI eligibility. You can collect a monthly SSI benefit in addition to the $250 loan repayment. Even a nominal SSI benefit helps because SSI recipients automatically qualify for medical assistance (Medicaid). Your son won't be out any money as long as he puts the $50,000 in investments that pay a comparable rate of interest.

• Gifts don't affect SSI eligibility. Unlike the Medicaid program, which does penalize gift-giving under certain circumstances (see page 144), gifts are not restricted under the SSI program.

• If you're planning on reducing your excess resources by making gifts of your property, don't worry too much about gift taxes. Every individual is allowed to give away each year up to $10,000 to any number of different people without any gift tax consequences. Even if your gifts exceed this exempt amount, they will not result in any federal gift tax liability as long as they don't exceed $600,000. A state gift tax may be due, however, depending on your state of residence.

SAMPLE WORKSHEET: WHAT IS MRS. LANE'S SSI RESOURCE ELIGIBILITY?

Mrs. Lane's income does not exceed the SSI income limits, but now she needs to determine whether her resources are too high for SSI.

Mrs. Lane owns the following property:

- House worth 100,000.
- Vacation home worth $50,000.
- Car worth $6,000 that Mrs. Lane regularly uses to go to the doctor for arthritis treatments.
- Savings account with a $500 balance.
- Life insurance policy that pays $1,000 upon her death.
- Burial fund of $2,000.
- Furniture that would be worth $300 if she tried to sell it.
- Kitchen appliances that would be worth $250 if she tried to sell them.
- Jewelry (excluding her wedding band and engagement ring) worth $150 if she tried to sell it.

Social Security computes Mrs. Lane's resource eligibility as follows:

Cash		$ 500
Second home		$50,000
Burial fund (Insert from Line 5B below)		$ 1,500
Line 1B	Exempt burial fund	$1,500
Line 2B	LESS face value of life insurance	− $1,000
	Subtotal	$ 500
Line 3B	Value of burial fund	$2,000
Line 4B	LESS Subtotal	− $ 500
Line 5B	Countable burial fund	$1,500
Total Countable Resources		$52,000

The following resources are exempt for the reasons noted:

- House. Exempt because Mrs. Lane resides in it.
- Car. Exempt because Mrs. Lane uses it to travel to and from her doctor's office.
- Household goods and personal effects. Exempt because total value does not exceed $2,000.
- Life insurance policy. Exempt because face value does not exceed $1,500.

Since Mrs. Lane's total countable resources exceed $2,000, the SSI resource limit for an individual, Mrs. Lane is not eligible for SSI. However, if Mrs. Lane still needs additional income, she may decide to collect SSI payments while she tries to sell her vacation home. She must sign an agreement promising to repay Social Security the SSI benefits she receives while she tries to sell her excess assets.

SSI BENEFIT AMOUNTS

Every SSI beneficiary does not receive the same benefit check each month. While your neighbor's SSI check might be as low as $10, your check could be over $400. Two factors determine the amount of each beneficiary's check.

• Monthly countable income. SSI brings the monthly income of each beneficiary up to the SSI income limit. The closer your income is to the SSI income limit, the smaller the amount of your SSI check. The value of your countable resources will not affect the amount of your SSI benefit check, as long as your resources are below the SSI resource limit.

• State of residence. Some states supplement the federal SSI benefit, which is $446 in 1994. If you live in a state that pays a supplemental SSI benefit, your total SSI monthly payment will be increased. The state and federal SSI benefits are paid in a single check. State supplements can increase the federal SSI benefit to over $500 for an individual and to over $700 for a couple. The SSI resource limit is the same nationwide.

Your benefit amount will be reduced or terminated if you find yourself in either of the following situations:

• You enter a public facility, such as a city or county mental hospital, rest home, halfway house, or prison. You will not be entitled to any SSI benefit.

• You enter a hospital or nursing home for a month or more and Medicaid is paying for more than half your care. Your SSI benefit will be reduced to $30 in 1994 (less $20 and your state supplement, if any). If the facility is licensed by the Department of Health, you will receive a small payment in addition to your reduced benefit. You will only collect your full SSI benefit despite your hospitalization or institutionalization if you meet two criteria:

1. Your doctor certifies in writing that your stay in the facility is not likely to last more than 3 months.

2. You sign a statement that you need the money to pay the expenses of maintaining your house or apartment, such as utilities, taxes, mortgage, or rent.

To continue to receive SSI benefits, you must submit both of these documents to your local Social Security office by day 90 of your stay in the hospital or nursing home, or by the date of your discharge, whichever is earlier.

APPLYING FOR SSI

If you think you might be eligible for SSI, you should file an SSI application as soon as possible. You can collect benefits based on the date of your application. The longer you delay filing an application, the more you may lose in monthly benefits. If you start an application and change your mind about filing, the worst that can happen is that your claim is denied. You can always withdraw your application.

If, in addition to SSI, you are also applying for Social Security benefits, such as retirement, disability, or survivor's benefits, you will have to file a separate application for the Social Security benefits. If you also want to apply for food stamps, make sure you ask the Social Security representative handling your claim for the appropriate application form.

WHERE TO APPLY FOR SSI

You can start an SSI application in any of the following ways:

- Pick up an application at your local Social Security office. To get the earliest possible filing date, complete and return the application to the district office within 60 days.

- Call Social Security's toll-free number (800-772-1213) and either schedule an appointment to complete an SSI application at your local Social Security office or complete the application over the phone. If you complete the application over the phone, it will be sent to you for you to sign and submit to Social Security. You will also be notified about the documents you must submit in connection with your application.

- Write a letter to Social Security stating your interest in applying for SSI. You will be eligible for benefits as of the date Social Security receives your letter. You will then get an application in the mail, which you should complete and file at your local Social Security office.

If you are unable to leave your home, call your local Social Security office to schedule a home visit from an SSI representative. To get the telephone number of your local office:

- Look in the blue pages of your telephone book under U.S. government listings.
- Call Social Security's toll-free number (800-772-1213).

Documenting Your SSI Application

As part of your application you must submit a number of documents, which are listed below.

You may have trouble putting your hands on one or more of the required documents. Do not delay filing your application while you try to track down the missing papers. You will have 30 days from the date you apply to submit supporting documentation. If you are charged a fee in connection with obtaining a particular document, and cannot afford to pay it, Social Security should provide you with financial assistance.

DOCUMENTS YOU NEED

• Your Social Security card. If you do not have your card, bring your Social Security number. If you do not know your number, a Social Security representative should be able to help you find it.

• Proof of residency and citizenship. You can prove that you are a resident of the United States and you intend to remain in the States, by submitting any of the following documents:

- Lease or deed to your home.
- Proof of employment.
- Proof of membership in a religious congregation or social organization.

You can prove that you are a United States citizen, or a lawfully admitted alien, by submitting any of the following documents:

- Certified birth or baptism record.
- Certificate of citizenship or naturalization.
- United States passport.
- INS registration card.
- Reentry permit.
- Any proof of immigration status.

• Proof of your financial eligibility. To substantiate your financial status, bring the following documents:

- Latest tax bill or assessment on property you own other than your home.
- Bank books, stock and bond certificates, annuity agreements, and other evidence of your savings.

- Life insurance policies.
- Automobile registration papers.
- Pay stubs, tax records, a letter from your employer stating your current earnings, or your business records if you are working.
- Copies of checks or notices of awards for court-ordered support and pension, unemployment, retirement, and VA benefits.
- Copies of lease or rental checks, and receipts showing expenses of maintaining property that you rent out.
- Rent, mortgage, tax, utility, and food records to show your living arrangements.

- Proof of age, disability, or blindness. You can prove your age by submitting any of the following documents, listed in order of preference:

- Certified birth certificate.
- Religious record of birth or baptism.
- Passport.
- School records.
- Military records.
- Voting records.
- Immigration records.

To prove that you are blind or disabled you must either submit records and reports from your doctors stating the extent of your impairment or provide Social Security with the names and addresses of doctors, hospitals, and clinics that have treated you. (For more information on documenting a disability claim, see page 189.)

Before awarding you benefits, Social Security may require you to be examined by a consultative examiner—a doctor hired by Social Security to examine claimants who allege blindness or disability (see Chapter 7).

COLLECTING SSI

WHEN WILL YOU RECEIVE YOUR FIRST BENEFIT CHECK?

The time it takes Social Security to approve or deny your application for SSI will depend on the type of application you have filed. If you are applying for SSI based on age, you can expect a decision within 2 months. If you are applying based on blindness or disability, you can expect a decision within 4 months, unless you are already receiving Social Security disability benefits, in which case your application will be approved immediately.

If your SSI application is approved, you will be entitled to benefits back to the date of your application. The first check you receive after your application is approved (in about 10 days) is usually a monthly benefit check. A few months after you receive your first monthly benefit check you will receive a larger retroactive check, which covers the period during which your application was being reviewed.

WHAT IF YOU NEED EMERGENCY ASSISTANCE?

If you qualify for emergency assistance, you will not have to wait until your application is processed to receive one or more SSI payments.

There are two types of emergency payments:

• Emergency advance payment. You can receive one month of SSI benefits when you file your application if you meet all eligibility requirements and have a financial emergency, such as being threatened with eviction, or being unable to afford food, clothing, or medical care.

The maximum amount of the emergency payment is the federal SSI benefit ($446 for an individual, $669 for a couple, in 1994) plus the state supplement, if any. The emergency payment is an advance against your first regular monthly SSI check. This means that your first regular monthly SSI check will be reduced by the amount of the emergency payment. If you are not ultimately awarded SSI, you may have to repay the U.S. Treasury.

• Presumptive disability. You can receive up to 3 months of SSI benefits after you file an application for SSI based on disability if Social Security finds that you are both:

  • Financially eligible for benefits.
  • Probably disabled.

The 3 months of benefits are intended to help you pay your expenses while your SSI application is under review. You do not have to repay these benefits, even if your SSI application is eventually denied.

If you do not qualify for either type of advance SSI payment, your best bet is to look to public assistance (welfare) to keep you going until your SSI application is approved.

WHAT IF YOUR CHECK IS LOST OR STOLEN?

You should receive your SSI check on the 1st of each month. If you do not receive your check by the 4th of the month, report the missing check to Social Security.

If your check is lost, and you are facing a financial emergency, you can apply to Social Security for a "critical payment." In 1994, the maximum amount of the critical payment is $400 for an individual, or each member of a couple if each member of the couple has an emergency, as long as the recipient's SSI benefit is at least that high. The amount of a critical payment is recouped from future SSI checks.

If you have not received your SSI check, but cannot establish a financial emergency, you will have to wait 10 to 15 days for Social Security to process your claim for a replacement check.

SSI APPEALS

You may be unhappy with any number of different types of determinations Social Security may make in connection with your SSI application. For example, Social Security may find you ineligible for benefits because you have too much money, or you have not proven that you are disabled. Or you may think that Social Security has incorrectly computed the amount of your SSI benefit. Perhaps you received a notice that your SSI benefits are being reduced or terminated for some reason or another, and the reason is incorrect.

Regardless of the nature of the determination, the appeals process is the same, encompassing four steps. At every stage of the appeals process you have the right to be represented by an attorney, paralegal, social worker, caseworker, friend, relative, or any other individual who is familiar with the facts of your case. Your representative must file an Appointment of Representative (Form SSA 1696-U4) with Social Security to appear on your behalf.

You must file for every level of appeal within a certain time limit. Look at the date on the notice you are appealing. The time limit starts to run 5 days after the date of the notice. If, when you receive the notice, you see that the date is more than 5 days old, save the envelope and note the date you received the notice. This will be important if you miss the time limit for filing your appeal.

If you miss an appeal deadline, your lateness may be excused for one of the following reasons:

1. You were physically or mentally unable to file an appeal.
2. Your address on the notice was incorrect.

3.   You were out of town when you received the notice.

4.   Any other reasonable excuse (a catch-all reason).

The four steps to the SSI appeals process are summarized below.

RECONSIDERATION

The first level of appeal is called reconsideration.

TIMING

You must request reconsideration within 60 days of receiving a notice from SSI. If you are appealing a determination to reduce or terminate your benefits, you should request reconsideration within 10 days. By requesting reconsideration within 10 days, you are entitled to something called "aid continuing." With aid continuing, your benefits continue uninterrupted while your case is being reconsidered. If you lose on reconsideration, you must repay Social Security the benefits you collected under aid continuing (unless you can get out of repaying Social Security, as discussed on page 236).

REQUESTING RECONSIDERATION

To request reconsideration, you can do either of the following:

- Send or hand deliver a letter to your local Social Security office requesting reconsideration. The letter can be only one sentence long: "I am requesting reconsideration of the notice dated [fill in the date]." Enclose a copy of the notice with your letter.

- File SSA Form 561. You can get a copy of this form from your local Social Security office or by calling Social Security's toll-free number (800-772-1213).

Reconsideration Procedures

You have the right to submit additional evidence in support of your claim at reconsideration.

Don't be surprised if you lose on reconsideration. Very few cases are reversed at this level of appeal. Do not despair. The reversal rate increases as you progress to higher levels of appeal.

ADMINISTRATIVE HEARING

TIMING

To have Social Security schedule an administrative hearing in your case, you must file a request within 60 days of receiving the reconsideration decision.

REQUESTING A HEARING

As with reconsideration requests, you can send a letter to Social Security requesting a hearing or file Form HA-501 at your local Social Security office.

HEARING PROCEDURES

Before the hearing you can, and should, review your file at the hearing office. If you find evidence missing from the file, or you have new evidence, submit whatever additional documentation you have before or at the hearing. You can even ask the judge for time to submit the evidence after the hearing.

At the administrative hearing you will have the opportunity to make a personal appearance before an administrative law judge (ALJ). After you are sworn in, the ALJ will question you and any witnesses who appear at the hearing. If you are represented, your representative will be able to ask you and the witnesses questions after the ALJ's questioning. The entire proceeding will be taped. (Your testimony, and hearings in general, are discussed in greater depth on page 85.)

HEARING DECISION

You will receive a copy of the ALJ's decision in the mail. If the decision is not favorable, you may continue on to the third level, Appeals Council.

APPEALS COUNCIL

TIMING

Within 60 days of the date you receive the ALJ's decision, you must request Appeals Council review.

APPEALS COUNCIL PROCEDURES

The Appeals Council does not review every claim. If the Appeals Council refuses to review your claim, don't take it personally. Just proceed to the fourth level of appeal, federal court.

You will probably not have an opportunity to make a personal appearance before the Appeals Council.

APPEALS COUNCIL DECISION

If the Appeals Council agrees to review your claim, you will get one of three decisions:

1. The ALJ's decision will be affirmed. This means you lose. Your only option is to go to federal court.
2. The ALJ's decision will be reversed. This means you win. Just sit back and wait for your benefits.
3. The ALJ will be found to have made a mistake in reviewing your case. This means you are entitled to a new hearing.

FEDERAL COURT

TIMING

To take your appeal into federal court, you must file a complaint within 60 days from the date you received the Appeals Council decision.

Here are some tips on bringing a federal court appeal:

- Do not bring a lawsuit unless you have a very strong case, and you stand to recover a substantial amount of money.
- Hire an attorney, if possible. The attorney should handle the case on a contingency fee arrangement.
- If you cannot afford the court costs, such as the fee for filing a complaint, apply to the court for a waiver of all court fees.

FEDERAL COURT DECISION

If you lose in federal court, you do not have any further rights of appeal. (For a more in-depth examination of federal court appeals, see page 89.)

RIGHTS AND RESPONSIBILITIES OF SSI BENEFICIARY

The Social Security Administration is like an old friend: It wants you to stay in touch. In fact, Social Security is so intent on keeping up with what is going on in your life that it requires you to notify it every time your financial status or living arrangement changes. This obligation is written right into the SSI application. If you fail to tell Social Security about a relevant change in your circumstances, you could lose your SSI benefits.

Examples of changes you must report to Social Security include:

- Changes in your income.
- Changes in your marital status.
- Address changes.
- Hospitalization and nursing home institutionalization.
- Inheritances and gifts.
- Death of a spouse.

You must report such changes within 10 days of the end of the month in which the change occurs.

Sometimes SSI beneficiaries neglect to report changes that would result in a reduction or termination of their SSI benefits. If Social Security continues to pay SSI to a beneficiary who is no longer entitled to a full benefit check, the result is an overpayment. Overpayments are incorrectly paid benefits.

If you have been overpaid benefits, Social Security will send you a bill for the amount of the overpayment. Your failure to pay the bill authorizes Social Security to start recovering the amount of the overpayment from your future benefits. Social Security can withhold up to 10 percent of your future SSI checks until the overpayment is repaid.

But you may be able to avoid repaying on overpayment in one of two ways: successfully challenge Social Security's finding that benefits were incorrectly paid, or request a waiver. You can pursue both of these routes simultaneously.

To successfully challenge the existence or amount of the overpayment, you must prove that you were entitled to the full amount of your benefit check during the disputed period. To mount this defense, start by filing a request for reconsideration.

To request a waiver, you must prove that the overpayment was not your fault, and *either* that you cannot afford to repay the money *or* that forcing you to repay the money would be unfair. Here's a quick look at each of these requirements:

- Fault. You stand the best chance of being found faultless if one of the following applies: Social Security provided you with incorrect information, Social Security failed to follow through on information you correctly provided to a Social Security representative, or you are poorly educated. You will probably be found at fault if you failed to provide Social Security with information you knew (or should have known) would cause a reduction in your benefits, accepted a payment you knew (or should have known) was incorrect, or out-and-out lied to Social Security.

• Cannot repay. If you are found faultless, you will not be required to repay the overpayment if repayment would jeopardize your financial security. To win on this ground, you must show Social Security that you need all your income to cover your expenses. If you are successful, Social Security will find that "repayment would defeat the purpose of the law."

• Should not have to repay. If you cannot prove inability to repay, you can still get a waiver if you are without fault and repayment "would be against equity and good conscience." To prevail on this ground, you must prove that you relied on the overpaid benefits and would be left in a worse position if forced to repay them. For example, if you signed a new release in reliance on your monthly SSI benefit, you should not have to repay the overpaid benefits.

To request a waiver of an overpayment, you must complete an Overpayment Recovery Questionnaire (Form SSA-632 BK). While your waiver request is pending, you will continue to receive the full amount of your SSI benefit. If your waiver request is denied, you can appeal the determination by requesting reconsideration.

If your claim is denied on reconsideration, and you lose your waiver request, you still have the right to pursue your appeal at an administrative hearing, on Appeals Council review, and in federal court.

BACK TO RANDY

I explained to Randy that his Social Security benefit was not high enough to disqualify him from SSI, and that he had sufficiently low assets to show financial need. I also told Randy that he could complete the entire application for SSI without ever leaving his apartment—starting with a telephone call to Social Security's toll-free number.

Randy's application was approved. In addition to his monthly SSI check, Randy started receiving food stamps and medical assistance. The additional cash and noncash assistance made a big difference in the quality of Randy's life.

9.

FINDING HOME CARE BENEFITS

Rita came to see me soon after her husband Mort had a stroke. He was still in the hospital, but was expected to be discharged within days. The nurses in the hospital discharge office had told Rita that Mort would need help eating, dressing, walking, and going to the bathroom for at least several months after discharge.

Rita desperately wanted her husband to return home, but was afraid she could not meet all his needs alone, especially given her worsening arthritis.

She had many questions: Could she get someone to help her care for Mort at home? How much would it cost? How should she go about finding qualified workers?

Most of us want to live in our own homes for as long as possible. If living at home has become difficult for you or a family member due to illness, injury, or physical frailty, help may be available. Most communities offer a wealth of services to older residents who need assistance living at home.

Your home care plan should be custom-made to meet your special needs. The combination of services that is right for you will depend on your medical condition, finances, and family situation. With a little thought, planning, and research, you can put the perfect home care plan into effect. This chapter will help by answering the following important questions:

- Are you a candidate for home care services?
- What types of home care services are available to you?
- How do you find home care services?
- How will you pay for home health care?
- How do you select home care workers?

- How do you deal with problems with home care workers?
- What community-based services are available?

The answer to each question is explored in a separate section of this chapter. Questionnaires at the beginning of some sections will help you clarify your specific needs, and guide you to the appropriate solutions.

ARE YOU A CANDIDATE FOR HOME CARE?

Before you invest any more time learning about home care, you need to answer a threshold question.

IS IT FOR YOU?

1. Are you having difficulties caring for your personal needs?
2. Are you having difficulties caring for your home?
3. Are you confined to your home?
4. Are you fearful or lonely living alone?
5. Do you need help recovering at home after a hospitalization?

If you answered yes to any of these questions, you are probably a candidate for home care services. The only reasons home care may not be for you are either of the following:

1. You require intensive medical treatment that can only be provided by a team of medical specialists.
2. You require the use of medical equipment that cannot be provided in your home. (Only a very few types of medical equipment are not available at home. Thanks to advances in medical technology, such sophisticated equipment as portable ventilators, pacemaker monitors, kidney dialysis machines, and oxygen tanks are available to patients in their homes. Your physician can advise you about whether the medical services and equipment you need can be provided to you at home.)

Assuming you are a candidate for home care services, the next step is to identify your special home care needs.

WHAT TYPES OF HOME CARE SERVICES ARE AVAILABLE?

Right now you may only have a vague sense that you need some help at home. You may not be clear on exactly what services you need.

The term "home care services" includes personal care services and home health care services. Older patients who are unable to walk, bathe, dress, feed, or toilet themselves due to physical frailty or psychological illness usually require personal care services. Patients who need help recovering from an illness or injury generally require home health care services.

The two charts that follow will help you identify your precise home care needs, and the professionals who can meet them. The first chart lists fifteen different health and personal care needs. Check off as many as apply to you. Then, using this information, continue on to the second chart to find out who is available to service those needs.

IDENTIFYING YOUR HOME CARE NEEDS

What kinds of health care do you need?

1. _____ Medical care, which includes:
   a. Doctors' services.
   b. Development of a home care treatment plan.
2. _____ Highly skilled medical assistance, which includes:
   a. Injection of medications.
   b. Assistance with catheters.
   c. Changing of sterile dressings.
   d. Monitoring of unstable medical conditions.
   e. Checking vital signs.
3. _____ Less skilled health-related assistance, which includes:
   a. Help with oral medications.
   b. Temperature-taking.
   c. Changing of nonsterile dressings.
   d. Assistance with exercise regimen.
4. _____ Movement (physical) rehabilitation, including assistance walking, operating a wheelchair, changing bed position, or using a prosthetic.

5. _____ Occupational rehabilitation, including assistance performing everyday activities, such as bathing, dressing, cooking, and eating.

6. _____ Speech rehabilitation, including assistance overcoming difficulties with speech, language, or swallowing.

7. _____ Assistance with breathing problems.

8. _____ Assistance with kidney dialysis.

9. _____ Assistance with ostomy care and advanced skin care.

10. _____ Assistance with intravenous nutrition or medication.

11. _____ Assistance with liquid nutrition.

12. Nutritional services, other than those listed in #10 and #11, which include:

    a. Planning a special diet to meet particular medical needs.

    b. Receiving instruction on meal preparation.

13. _____ Emotional support services to help cope with medical problems and limitations.

What are your nonmedical needs?

14. _____ Help with household chores, such as cooking, cleaning, and shopping.

15. _____ Help with personal chores, such as bathing, grooming, dressing, toileting, and eating.

You have now identified the kinds of help you need at home. Which home care workers can provide you with this help?

The next chart answers this question. (The numbers in the first column refer to your answers to the chart directly above.)

Identifying the Personnel of Your Home Care Team

If You Checked:	You Require the Services of:
1a. Doctor's services.	Physician (M.D.) Duties: M.D.s determine what medical care you require, prescribe a course of treatment, and help you obtain the necessary care at home. Training: At a minimum, M.D.s must complete medical school and be licensed by the state.

If You Checked:	You Require the Services of:
1b. Development of a home care treatment plan.	Registered nurse (R.N.) Duties: R.N.s are trained to design home care treatment plans that provide the services your physician ordered, to monitor your progress, to instruct you in self-care, and to supervise your home care services. Training: At a minimum, R.N.s must complete 2 years of academic training and be licensed by the state board of nursing examiners.
2. Skilled medical assistance.	Licensed practical nurse (LPN) or Licensed vocational nurse (LVN) Duties: LPNs and LVNs work under the supervision of an R.N. They are trained to perform simpler nursing tasks than R.N.s. Training: LPNs and LVNs must complete 1 year of academic study and be licensed by the state board of licensed vocational nurses.
3. Less skilled medical assistance.	Home health aide (HHA) Duties: HHAs perform simple routine medical tasks, such as checking bandages and helping with mobility exercises. They also assist with personal care (such as dressing, shaving, and bathing), and household chores (such as cooking, shopping, and cleaning). They are generally supervised by an R.N., therapist, or social worker. Training: HHAs are not required to have any academic training or to be licensed. If you also checked #14 or #15, a HHA will be able to assist you.
4. Movement rehabilitation.	Physical therapists help overcome problems of movement with exercise, heat, water, and other methods.
5. Occupational rehabilitation.	Occupational therapists help you regain independence by relearning daily living activities.

If You Checked:	You Require the Services of:
6. Speech rehabilitation.	Speech therapists help improve communication skills.
7. Breathing problems.	Respiration therapists help with breathing difficulties.
8. Dialysis.	Dialysis therapists help treat kidney failure.
9. Ostomy and skin care.	Enterostomal therapists help with ostomy care and advanced skin care.
10. Intravenous therapy.	Infusion therapists maintain intravenous tubes.
11. Liquid nutrition.	Enteral nutrition therapists help you if you cannot eat regular food.
12. Other nutritional services.	Nutritionist (or dietician) Duties: Nutritionists design menus and eating plans to speed recovery or manage medical conditions, such as diabetes, heart problems, and high blood pressure. Training: Nutritionists must have a college degree, complete an internship, and pass an examination administered by the American Dietetic Association.
13. Emotional and financial support services.	Social worker Duties: Social workers help patients come to terms with the disabling effects of an illness or injury. They address the patient's emotional and financial concerns and make referrals to community services and other resources. Training: Social workers must have a bachelor's or master's degree in social work.
14. Household assistance.	Homemaker (or housekeeper) Duties: Homemakers only assist with household chores. They do not perform any personal care or medical tasks. Training: Homemakers are not required to undergo any special training.

If You Checked:	You Require the Services of:
15. Personal care assistance.	Personal care attendant (PCA) Duties: PCAs attend to personal care needs, such as dressing and eating, and assist with cleaning and meal preparation. They do not perform any health-related tasks. Training: PCAs do not undergo any special training.

For an overview of the various services that are available at home, write to:

AARP Fulfillment
601 E Street, N.W.
Washington, DC 20049

(Request Publication Number D955, "A Handbook About Care in the Home.")

Now that you know what kinds of care you need, and who can provide you with this care, you need to know where to find the specific services you need.

HOW DO YOU FIND HOME CARE SERVICES?

Home care services are easy to find—if you know where to look. The following questions will direct you to the best sources for the home care services that you need.

1. Do you require home care services following a hospital discharge?
2. Will you be paying for your home care services privately (either with savings or private insurance)?
3. Are you unable to afford private home care services?
4. Are you covered under Medicare Part A or Part B?

FINDING YOUR HOME CARE PROVIDERS

Using your answers to the questions above, the following chart will direct you to sources of nurses, aides, and attendants to help you at home.

1. Hospital-based home care agency.
Many hospitals have their own home care agency, or have a contract with an outside agency to provide services to patients who are discharged from their facility. Even if the hospital you use has its own home care program, you are always free to use an outside agency.

2. Private home care agency.
In almost every community, numerous private home care agencies are operated as profit making businesses. The largest private chain of home care agencies is Olsten Health Care. Other private agencies include UpJohn Healthcare Services, Medical Personnel Pool, Staff Builders, and Kimberly and Beverly. You can find a private agency by looking in the white pages of the telephone book under the name of a chain of home care agencies, or in the yellow pages under Home Health Services, Homemaker Services, Nurses, or Nursing Services.

or

Nonprofit home health agency.
Nonprofit agencies are generally funded by community or religious organizations, private payments, private insurance, government insurance (Medicare), or public medical assistance (Medicaid). The Visiting Nurse Service (VNS) (sometimes called the Visiting Nurse Association or VNA) is probably the best known nonprofit home care agency. Branches of the VNS and VNA are located in communities across the country. You can find a nonprofit agency by looking in the white pages of the telephone book under Visiting Nurse Association, or by calling:

- State unit on Aging (see Appendix 1).
- Local United Way (sometimes called United Fund or Community Chest) or American Red Cross.
- Local health and welfare council.
- Family service agencies
- Catholic Charities, Jewish Family Services, and other religious groups.
- Elder Care Locator (800-677-1116).

You should be aware of a number of obligations and responsibilities you will have as an employer:

- Withholding taxes. If you hire an employee, and pay that employee $50 or more every 3 months (a limit that may soon be raised), you are also supposed to pay some taxes to the government. Specifically, the law requires you to pay a percentage of the worker's wages in Social Security, Medicare and unemployment taxes. The law also requires you to report your employee's pay to the IRS on a W-2 form by January 31 of the year following the year of employment.

  As a practical matter, the IRS rarely enforces these withholding requirements because usually so little money is at stake. However, if a former worker files a claim for Social Security benefits or unemployment insurance, or wants to make trouble for you, there may be a problem if you have not met the withholding requirements (or if you are nominated to serve as a public official). If you are found to owe past due employment taxes, you will be liable for the tax itself plus interest. You probably will also owe a penalty in the amount of 25 percent for negligence, or 50 percent for fraud, depending on the severity of the error.

- State and local employment taxes. Depending on where you live, you may have to pay additional taxes, such as Workers' Compensation.

- Liability insurance. To make sure you are covered in the event your worker is injured on the job, check your homeowners insurance. You should have liability coverage.

- Illegal aliens. The law prohibits you from hiring an illegal alien. To prove that your employee is in this country legally, you are supposed to have the person fill out and sign the Immigration and Naturalization Service (INS) Form I-9.

or

Direct employment.
Many nurses and therapists seeking temporary employment
are listed with employment agencies and nurses' registries.
You can hire these health care workers directly. Sometimes
you must pay an agency fee.

When you use an employment agency, you become an
employer. This means that you are solely responsible for
supervising your employees. The agency or registry will not
oversee workers once they are placed in your employment.
The agency also does not provide replacements in the event
of absences. You can find names of employment agencies
and nurses' registries in the yellow pages of the telephone
book under Employment Agencies, Nurses, Physical
Therapists, or Occupational Therapists.

3.   Nonprofit home health agency.
Many VNS and VNA agencies accept a certain number of patients who cannot afford to pay for home care services privately.

or

Public health care agencies.
Free home care services are available through public (gov-
ernment-funded) agencies. To qualify for free home care services, you must demonstrate financial need. In addition,
you may be required to meet age and health requirements.
You can get information about public nursing services by
calling:

- Elder Care Locator (800-677-1116).

- Local department of social services or public welfare.

- Public health department.

- Local office on aging or senior citizen affairs.

- State unit on aging (see Appendix 1).

**If You
Answered
Yes To: Look for Home Care Services at:**

4.   Medicare-certified home health agency.
          If you are eligible for Medicare, you may be covered for
          some or all of your home care services. However, Medicare
          only pays for home care services that are provided by an
          agency certified to participate in the Medicare program
          (CHHA). Many agencies, including hospital-based, private,
          and nonprofit agencies, are Medicare-certified. A call to a
          particular agency will let you know if that agency is
          approved for Medicare participation.

The cost of purchasing care varies from source to source. As a general matter,
certified home health agencies that accept Medicare reimbursement charge the
highest fees. Depending on your geographic location, these are the fee ranges:

> Personal care attendant ....$11 to $30 an hour
>
> Home health aide ....$15 to $20 an hour
>
> Registered nurse ....about $100 a visit
>
> Therapist ....about $100 a visit

If you hire a caregiver from an employment agency, you can expect to pay the
following rates (plus taxes; see page 246):

> Personal care attendant ....$8 to $10 an hour
>
> Home health aide ....$12 to $16 an hour
>
> Registered nurse ....$22 to $25 an hour
>
> Therapist ....$22 to $25 an hour

GERIATRIC CARE MANAGEMENT

If you have neither the time nor the inclination to look for home care services
on your own, you might want to hire a care manager. Most care managers are social
workers who specialize in working with older adults and disabled individuals in
the community. For a fee, a care manager will assess your needs, finances, and
insurance coverage, determine what home care services you require, locate sources

for the services, put the services in place, and monitor the services on an ongoing basis.

A qualified geriatric care manager should be intimately familiar with resources available in your local community. For example, the manager should know which home care agencies have the best reputations, what organizations provide low-cost transportation, and who you should call to get home-delivered meals.

If you are thinking of hiring a care manager, here are some questions to ask prospective candidates:

• What experience do you have as a geriatric care manager? You want to hire a care manager who has at least 3 years of experience specifically in geriatric care.

• What professional associations do you belong to? The care manager should belong to the National Association of Private Geriatric Care Managers. If the manager also belongs to the National Association of Social Workers, all the better.

• What professional licenses do you have? Social workers and nurses should be licensed.

• Can you provide references from former clients? Be sure you diligently follow up on every reference provided.

• Can you provide references from community organizations? Ideally, the care manager you hire will have an ongoing relationship with local hospitals, senior centers, and religious organizations.

• Who will be providing the services? Make sure the person you are hiring is actually the person who will be providing you with the services, and not delegating your case to a less experienced associate.

• How do you screen your service providers? An important part of the care manager's job is to put home care services in place. Make sure the care manager knows how to check the experience, reputation, insurance coverage, and qualifications of service providers. Also, inquire about any preexisting obligations that may exist between the care manager and a particular service provider. You want to hire a care manager who is free to employ competing providers.

• Do you carry professional liability insurance, and are you bonded? The answer to both of these questions should be yes.

• What sort of ongoing monitoring of services will you do? The frequency of monitoring is almost always linked to cost. Not surprisingly, the more often the care manager checks in on you, the more you will have to pay.

• Will someone cover for you when you are not working? Someone should be available 24 hours a day to handle emergencies.

• What are your fees and what do they include? Get this information in writing. Also, make sure you know what additional expenses you can expect to incur.

You must exercise caution when hiring a geriatric care manager. The potential for abuse is considerable, especially if you give your care manager the authority to pay your bills for you or a set of keys to your house.

If you plan to employ a care manager, keep these tips in mind:

➤ **TIP #1** *Ask around at the local senior center, hospital, and other community organizations to learn about the care manager's reputation.*

➤ **TIP #2** *Keep only small amounts of money in any account that is accessible to the care manager.*

➤ **TIP #3** *Contact the National Association of Private Geriatric Care Managers (see address and number on page 251) to see if your care manager is listed in NAPGCM's directory; listed social workers claim to have professional credentials or licenses and experience, although this information is not independently verified.*

➤ **TIP #4** *Run a credit check on the care manager.*

➤ **TIP #5** *Call the Better Business Bureau to see if any complaints have been filed against the care manager or the person's agency.*

Private geriatric care managers charge between $30 and $150 an hour. You should figure on paying for at least 3 to 4 hours, which is how long most care managers take to assess your situation and locate appropriate services. If you want the care manager to monitor your home care services on an ongoing basis, you will have to pay for additional time.

Most area agencies on aging offer care management services for free or on a sliding fee scale with the cost based on your income. You can get the names of these organizations by calling the Elder Care Locator at 800-677-1116. Care management services provided by nonprofit organizations are usually free.

ℹ️ For more information

If you would like more information about care management, contact any of the following:

National Council on the Aging
409 Third Street, S.W., Suite 200
Washington, DC 20024
202-479-1200

The National Council on the Aging publishes the care management standards, which are available to the public for $10 plus $2 shipping and handling, and offers several other publications on in-home services for a nominal fee.

National Association of Social Workers
750 First Street, N.E.
Silver Spring, MD 20910
202-408-8600

The National Association of Social Workers publishes the professional standards for social work care management, which are available to the public at no charge. If you have a problem with a professional social worker who is a member of the association, your complaint will be addressed in an adjudication process. You can also get referrals to social workers in your area by calling the association.

AARP Fulfillment
601 E Street, N.W.
Washington, DC 20049
202-434-2277

AARP publishes two booklets on care management entitled "Care Management: Arranging for Long Term Care" and "Miles Away and Still Caring: A Guide for Long-Distance Caregivers." Both publications are available free of charge.

National Association of Private Geriatric Care Managers
655 North Alvernon Way, Suite 108
Tucson, AZ 85711
602-881-8008

The National Association of Private Geriatric Care Managers publishes a directory of private care managers, available to the public for $17.50. You can obtain names of local care managers over the telephone. The association also has an ethics committee, which investigates complaints filed by consumers against its members.

Elder Care Locator
800-677-1116

Call the Elder Care Locator for information about public agencies in your area that provide free or low-cost care management services. Be ready to give the operator your zip code.

All this talk about the impressive variety of services that are available to you at home might leave you wondering: How will you ever pay for all this care?

The answer to this important question can be found in the next section.

HOW WILL YOU PAY FOR HOME CARE SERVICES?

Few people can afford to pay for extensive home care services out of their private funds for very long. Some of the other ways you may be able to finance your home care plan include private health insurance, private long-term care insurance, prepaid health coverage, Medicare, Medicaid, and veterans' benefits. Each of these sources of funding is explored in the following sections.

PRIVATE FUNDING

How much you will have to pay for your home care depends on three factors: the level of care you require, the number of hours of care you require, and your geographic location. Doctors are more expensive than nurses, 8 hours of care a day cost more than 2 hours of care a day, and wages are higher in New York City than in Kansas City.

If you can afford to pay for home care out of your income or savings, there are several ways you can secure home care services. You can sign up with a private, nonprofit, or hospital-based agency. Some nonprofit agencies, including some branches of the VNA and VNS, offer sliding fee scales. Your income will determine the amount of your fee. You can also hire health care workers directly from an employment agency or nurses' registry, or you can locate caregivers on your own through community centers or personal referrals (see page 266).

PRIVATE MEDICAL INSURANCE

Some private health insurance and major medical policies provide home care benefits. You can find out if you are covered for home care services by carefully reading your policy. Look for coverage of some or all of the following:

- Skilled nursing (registered nurse or licensed practical nurse).
- Therapists.
- Dieticians.
- Home health aides.
- Homemakers.
- Medical equipment rentals.

If your policy does not include a section called home care benefits, review the major medical provisions and miscellaneous provisions sections of the policy, or call the insurance company claims department or your insurance agent to ask about home care coverage. If your policy was offered through a union, employer, or another organization, call the personnel or membership office to get the name of the insurance representative you should contact for coverage information.

There is tremendous variety among insurance policies that provide home care benefits. Read your policy closely, keeping an eye out for the following restrictions:

- The policy covers up to a specified amount of daily home care charges.
- The policy sets a limit on the number of home health visits covered each year.
- The policy only covers nursing care, occupational therapy, physical therapy, and home health aides.
- The policy requires you to pay a specified sum of money out-of-pocket (a deductible) before home care bills are covered.
- The policy requires you to pay 20 percent of each home care bill.
- The policy only covers home care services that are recommended by your physician.
- The policy only reimburses home care agencies that are licensed by the state (in states that have licensing laws).
- The policy does not provide home care benefits if you only require assistance with household chores (shopping, cooking, cleaning) or personal care (dressing, bathing, eating).

Most insurance companies require proof that you need at least some medical care at home before they will cover any of your home care expenses. In anticipation of this problem, you should submit to the insurance company a letter from your doctor (written before you start receiving home care services) describing the medical services you need at home.

Once you start to receive home care services, periodically send the insurance company a copy of daily notes prepared by your nurses or therapists. These notes are important to document the nature of the services you receive at home. Keep a copy of everything you send to the insurance company.

PRIVATE LONG-TERM CARE INSURANCE

Your private long-term care insurance policy, if you have one, might cover you for home care services. Although some long-term care policies cover only nursing home expenses, many also pay for home care services. Policies that provide home care coverage usually pay for home health visits by nurses, therapists, home health aides, homemakers, and personal care attendants. Many also pay for adult day care. For a detailed discussion of long-term care insurance, see Chapter 4.

PREPAID HEALTH PLAN

If you are a member of a prepaid health plan, such as a health maintenance organization (HMO), your membership fee entitles you to receive a full range of health care services from a designated group of providers at no additional charge. Home care services prescribed by your HMO doctor will generally be covered.

MEDICARE

Medicare pays for some home care services. As a general matter, Medicare coverage is *not* available if:

- You require round-the-clock (24-hour-a-day, 7-day-a-week) nursing care.
- You only require assistance with household chores or personal care.

You must meet three basic requirements to receive Medicare home care benefits:

1. You must be eligible for Medicare Part A or B.
2. You must qualify for home health services.
3. You home care services must be covered.

Do you meet these three requirements? The following three questionnaires will help you determine if you do.

ARE YOU ELIGIBLE FOR MEDICARE PART A OR B?

1. Are you age 65 or older?
2. If under age 65, have you been collecting Social Security or Railroad Retirement disability benefits for more than 24 months?

If you answer yes to either of these questions, you are probably eligible for Medicare. (See page 32 for an in-depth discussion of Medicare eligibility.)

DO YOU QUALIFY FOR MEDICARE HOME CARE COVERAGE?

1. Are you confined to the home?
    You are confined to the home if you are only able to leave the home with

the assistance of another person or equipment (such as a wheelchair, cane, or walker), and you only leave the home for short and infrequent periods of time.

2. Has your doctor prescribed any of the following home care services?

Skilled nursing care to be performed by a registered nurse, licensed practical nurse, or licensed vocational nurse, or skilled physical or speech therapy, anywhere from once a day (for a predictable and limited period of time) to once every 60 days.

The good news is that if you answered yes to both questions, you qualify for Medicare home care coverage. (See page 33 for an in-depth look at the qualification requirements for Medicare coverage.) The bad news is that qualifying for coverage is only half the battle. The home care services you receive must also be covered for Medicare to pay your home care bills.

To learn whether you are receiving covered home care services, continue on to the third questionnaire. You must answer yes to at least one question to get Medicare coverage.

ARE YOU RECEIVING COVERED HOME CARE SERVICES?

1. Do you receive skilled nursing care?

If yes, the following amounts of skilled nursing care (or combined skilled nursing care and home health aide care) are covered:

    a. Up to 8 hours a day for fewer than 7 days a week (for a maximum of 35 covered hours a week).

    b. Fewer than 8 hours a day for up to 7 days a week (for a maximum of 35 covered hours a week).

    c. Up to 8 hours a day for up to 7 days a week (for a maximum of 56 covered hours a week) for a finite and predictable period of time.

2. Do you receive physical therapy?

Any amount of physical therapy services is covered.

3. Do you receive speech therapy?

Any amount of speech therapy services is covered.

As long as you answered yes to one of these questions, Medicare will also pay for any of the following services you receive at home:

- Occupational therapy to help you resume your daily activities. Medicare covers an unlimited number of hours and visits.

- Medical social services to help you deal with emotional problems that interfere with your recovery. Medicare covers an unlimited number of visits.

- Home health aide (HHA) services to help you with your personal needs, medications, exercises, and walking. Medicare covers a total of 35 hours a week of combined nursing and HHA care.

- Medical supplies or equipment, such as a hospital bed or walker. Medicare covers 80 percent of the "approved charge" of the equipment (see page 45 for a discussion of approved charge.)

Homemaker services are not covered by Medicare. Homemaker services include cooking, cleaning, and shopping. Medicare only covers household services that are essential to the patient's health care at home.

MEDICARE IN THE REAL WORLD

To completely understand the Medicare home care system, you must distinguish theory from practice. In theory, if you are confined to the house and require some skilled nursing care or rehabilitation services, Medicare will pay for up to 56 hours a week of nursing, therapy, or home health aide services.

Unfortunately, in the real world, getting this coverage is a different story.

Medicare beneficiaries must usually wage a battle royal to get more than 10 or 15 hours a week of Medicare-reimbursed home care services. The main reason is that the Medicare reimbursement system discourages Medicare-certified home care agencies from authorizing more extensive home care services. Medicare-certified agencies commonly tell applicants that Medicare will not approve additional hours of home care services.

But this determination is not the end of the story. In fact, it's just the beginning.

PURSUING WHAT IS RIGHTFULLY YOURS

If you persevere, you stand a good chance of getting Medicare to pay for daily nursing services (at least for a limited period of time), as well as home health aide services totaling as many as 35 hours per week. Although Medicare is certainly not giving away extensive home care coverage, vigorous advocacy can go a long way toward getting you the benefits you are entitled to receive under the law.

When trying to get Medicare to pay your home care bills, your first step is to contact a Medicare-certified home health agency. The agency will evaluate your needs and give you its opinion on the availability of Medicare coverage. Most agencies err on the side of denying coverage because they stand to lose money if they incorrectly conclude that coverage is available.

(See Chapter 3 for an extensive discussion of the procedures to follow to get

Medicare to cover your medical bills, and how to appeal a denial of Medicare coverage.)

MEDICAID

Medicaid, a program of medical assistance for people in financial need, pays for some home care services. Although Medicaid coverage varies from state to state, in every state the following home health services are covered by Medicaid:

- Nursing services.
- Home health care (including nursing and housekeeping care).
- Medical supplies and equipment for home use.

Some states also cover the following additional services:

- Therapy services (physical, occupational, and speech).
- Personal care services (assistance with grooming, toileting, eating, bathing, and household chores).
- Household services (help with cooking, cleaning, and shopping).

Medicaid only pays for home care services that are prescribed by a physician, authorized by Medicaid, and provided by a home health agency or licensed nurse approved to participate in the Medicaid program (a Medicaid-certified agency). Since Medicaid pays agencies a lower rate of reimbursement for home care services than the private rate, some agencies do not serve Medicaid patients.

If you are eligible for Medicaid, you can apply for home care benefits by taking the following two steps:

First, have your doctor fill out a Medicaid form that requests information about your medical condition and home care needs. Return the completed form to Medicaid. Your doctor should keep the following tips in mind when completing the medical information form.

➤ **TIP #1** *Medicaid may conclude that an applicant described as dangerous or abusive is not an appropriate candidate for home care.*

➤ **TIP #2** *An applicant who requires assistance taking medicine at night is more likely to qualify for daytime and nighttime care (if split-shift care is available in your state).*

➤ TIP #3 *An applicant who suffers from an unusual frequency of elimination and requires assistance in toileting is often awarded more hours of service; this condition should be clearly noted.*

➤ TIP #4 *An applicant who suffers from anxiety, agitation, wandering, or a sleep disorder may be awarded care throughout the night (if available); these conditions should be specifically mentioned.*

➤ TIP #5 *If the applicant must spend many hours in bed, the doctor should indicate the patient's need for frequent turning, which will support a claim for additional hours of home care.*

➤ TIP #6 *The doctor should make a special note if the applicant uses a cane or walker, and also requires the assistance of another person, to minimize the risk of falls.*

Second, after Medicaid receives the completed medical information form, a Medicaid review team will come to your home to assess your medical and social needs. You should keep the following tips in mind when getting ready for the visit from Medicaid.

➤ TIP #1 *Have a family member present, if possible.*

Medicaid looks most favorably on cases in which there is family nearby to fill in for an absent aide until a replacement can be located, and to give caregiving instructions to aides.

➤ TIP #2 *Make sure the house looks well-kept.*

Medicaid will not authorize home care services if there is any question about the patient's ability to live at home. If there is evidence that the applicant is too disabled to maintain minimum standards of personal and household cleanliness and order, even with assistance, the case may be denied.

When Medicaid has made a decision on your home care application, you will receive a written notice in the mail. If your application is denied, or Medicaid fails to approve the kind of services or hours of care you need, you may want to file an appeal. To appeal your claim, you must request a Fair Hearing within 60 days from the date you receive the written denial. There are two ways to request a Fair Hearing: Either call the number that is printed on the denial notice, or send a letter to the address on the notice. A sample letter requesting a Fair Hearing follows.

Sample Letter Requesting Medicaid Fair Hearing

Date

Fair Hearing Section
Address [from determination notice]
City, State, Zip

Re: Your name
Case number: [From top of the determination notice]

Dear Sir/Madam:

I received a notice of decision, dated [insert date of decision], on my application for home care benefits. A copy of that notice is enclosed.

I would like to appeal this determination. Please notify me as soon as you have scheduled a Fair Hearing in this case.

Thank you.

Sincerely,

Your signature
Your printed name

Remember, the availability of Medicaid-covered home care services varies from state to state. You'll be tilting at windmills if you file an appeal to get more hours of care than are available under your state's Medicaid program. You can contact your local department of social services or public welfare to find out about your state's Medicaid benefits, or wait for a decision to be made on your application.

See Chapter 5 for an extensive discussion of all aspects of the Medicaid program.

SPECIAL GOVERNMENT FUNDS

In-home services, including homemaker, home health aide, personal care, chore, escort, and shopping services, may be available at little or no charge to low-income elderly under the Older Americans Act or Title XX of the Social Security Act. To find out more about these services, call the Elder Care Locator (800-677-1116) or contact your local social services department, public welfare department, city or county office on aging, state unit on aging (see Appendix 1), or local Alzheimer's Association chapter. For the phone number of the Alzheimer's Association chapter nearest you, call 800-621-0379. In Illinois, call 708-933-1000.

VETERANS' SERVICES

Some veterans are entitled to packages of medical benefits that include home care services. Unfortunately, many VA plans only offer home care services to veterans with a service-related disability. Additional home care benefits are available to some dependent family members of veterans.

Your local Veterans Administration office can provide you with additional information about home care benefits for veterans. Call 800-827-1000 to be connected with your regional office. If you are not satisfied with the information or services you receive from your local office, contact:

> **Veterans Administration General Information Office**
> 810 Vermont Avenue, N.W.
> Washington, DC 20420
> 202-233-4000

Before you can put your home care plan into effect, you must select your home care workers. What do you need to know to be a smart home care consumer?

HOW DO YOU SELECT SERVICE PROVIDERS?

When it comes to picking the agency and workers that will provide you with home care services, you must be confident that the agency has a well-earned reputation of quality and service, and the health care workers are competent and compassionate. The answers you get to the questions listed here will help you decide whether the agency and workers are right for you.

QUESTIONS FOR HOME CARE AGENCY

STATUS OF AGENCY

• Is the agency licensed? Every state except Alabama, Iowa, Massachusetts, Michigan, Oklahoma, Vermont, West Virginia, and Wyoming requires agencies that provide more than homemaker or personal care services to be licensed. Some agencies are not licensed because they do not meet the state's tax status requirements; others are unlicensed because they only provide one highly specialized service. Do not reject an otherwise perfect agency out of hand just because it is not licensed. Contact the state department of health or consumer affairs for more information about the agency. However, if you find two equally perfect agencies, one licensed and one unlicensed, go with the licensed agency.

• Is the agency certified? If you want Medicare or Medicaid to pay for your home care services, the agency must be Medicare or Medicaid certified.

• Is the agency accredited? An agency that is accredited meets the standards of a national organization. The accreditation process is voluntary. Many agencies choose not to become accredited because accreditation costs the agency money. Three organizations accredit home care agencies:

- Joint Commission on the Accreditation of Healthcare Organizations (JCAHO).

- National League for Nursing (NLN) accredits community nursing services, such as visiting nurse associations and home health agencies.

- Foundation for Hospice and Homecare/The National HomeCaring Council accredits agencies that provide home health services and homemaker services.

A lack of accreditation does not mean that the agency is unsatisfactory. However, you should select an accredited agency if accreditation is required by your private insurance company as a condition of coverage, or if you are deciding between two otherwise equal agencies.

• Is the agency bonded? Bonded agencies have a fund of money set aside to pay you if you sue the agency and win. For example, if you sue an agency because an employee treated you carelessly, and win, money will be available to pay your damages. You do not have this security with a nonbonded agency. Since most agencies are bonded, there is no reason to selected a nonbonded agency. A few agencies also bond their employees, but this is less common. If, for example, you sue a bonded employee for theft, and win, the bond will cover your damages.

DEVELOPMENT AND ADMINISTRATION OF PLAN OF CARE

• Does the agency send out a registered nurse or social worker to evaluate you in your home? You should have a professional evaluation in your home before you contract with a home care agency.

• Does the agency consult with your family and physician when developing your plan of care? Since your family and physician are most familiar with your personal and medical needs, they should have input into your plan of care.

• Does the agency put the plan of care in writing? You should be given a written plan of care that details the duties and schedules of each home care worker.

• Who oversees the administration of your plan of care? Licensed practical and vocational nurses and home health aides performing health-related tasks should be supervised by a registered nurse. The supervisor should come to your home at least every 3 months to observe the workers and address any problems or complaints you may have. A social worker can supervise homemaker and personal care services.

AGENCY AND EMPLOYEE REFERENCES

• Will the agency provide you with references from other professionals who are familiar with the agency, such as hospitals, community organizations, and social workers? It yes, follow up on the references. They may be your best source of information about the agency. If no, try to find an agency that is better known in the community.

• Does each agency employee have two or more written references on file? The answer to this question should be yes. Although you may not be permitted to see the references, you should still ask the question. An agency will get into more trouble for making an affirmative misrepresentation than for not making a representation about references one way or the other.

FINANCIAL MATTERS

• Does the agency spell out its services, costs, and payment procedures in writing? If the agency does not willingly provide you with a free copy of this information, find a different agency.

• Do the agency's quoted fees cover all services? Make sure there are no separate charges for Social Security taxes, travel costs, and other miscellaneous expenses.

SERVICES

• Does the agency provide all the services you require? If the agency does not provide all the services you need, find out who will be providing the additional services. Also, find out how the agency can guarantee the competence of the outside providers.

• Does the agency require you to receive services for a minimum number of hours or days each week? You should only receive the amount of home care you need. Avoid agencies that have minimum service requirements.

• Will a supervisor always be available to you, either through an answering service or a beeper service? Ideally, you will be able to contact the agency 24 hours a day.

• Will a replacement worker be provided within 1 to 3 hours, except in unusual circumstances? The agency should guarantee absent workers will be promptly replaced. Also, if you complain about a worker, a replacement should be promptly assigned to your case.

PERSONNEL

• Are the staff doctors, nurses, and physical therapists licensed? Every state requires these health care workers to be licensed. Do not sign a contract with an agency that does not guarantee that these employees are licensed.

• Are the dieticians, social workers, and therapists certified? These health care workers should be certified by their national professional organizations. They are certified when they pass a test or provide proof of their work experience.

• Some states license social workers, occupational therapists, speech therapists, and respiratory therapists. If you live in such a state, are these health care workers licensed? These workers should be licensed in those states where licensing is available.

• Are staff nurses required to undergo an annual physical examination? Better agencies require proof of physical fitness.

• What training is required of the staff homemakers and home health aides? Ideally, homemakers and HHAs should have at least 60 hours of training, covering basic nursing, personal care, nutrition, home safety, and social skills. Ongoing training should also be required. Some agencies offer special training in working with older adults, which is a bonus.

• Can you hire a worker on a trial basis? This is a nice option to have, but certainly not essential.

• Are any workers specially trained to deal with Alzheimer's disease and related disorders?

Once you find an acceptable agency, you are halfway home—so to speak. You still have to find acceptable health care workers. If possible, interview the workers before they start working for you. You may not have an opportunity to interview your prospective workers if your home care will be financed with public funds.

QUESTIONS FOR CAREGIVERS

The purpose of the personal interview is to make sure that you are compatible with the workers you will be bringing into your home. There are three parts to the interview:

PERSONAL QUESTIONS

- Please tell me a little bit about your background.
- How did you get into the health care field?
- How long have you been in this field?
- What is it that you enjoy or dislike about working with older people?
- What formal education or training have you had?
- What have been some of your previous jobs?
- What are your plans for the future?
- Do you have family in the area?
- What do you like to do in your spare time?

QUESTIONS ABOUT YOUR PLAN OF CARE

- What do you understand to be your primary tasks?
- What are your views on teaching patients to meet as many of their own needs as possible?
- What do you plan to do when I do not require your immediate attention?
- What do you see as my long- and short-term goals?
- Do you have the following skills:

    Cook food a particular way.

    Perform a particular health-related task.

    Understand certain written instructions.

QUESTIONS TO ASSESS GOOD JUDGMENT

- What would you do if I lost consciousness?
- What would you do if something caught fire in the oven?
- What would you do if you heard someone breaking into the house?
- Can you describe a time you were forced to act in an emergency?

Once you have selected your home care providers, and services begin, things may not go as smoothly as you had hoped. What should you do if you run into problems with your home care workers?

HOW DO YOU RESOLVE PROBLEMS WITH HOME CARE WORKERS?

No matter how carefully you select your home care team, you should be prepared to deal with conflicts and dissatisfaction. For example, you should know what to do if:

- The worker routinely fails to put in a full work day, or frequently calls in sick.
- The worker does not treat you with care and respect.
- You suspect the worker is stealing from you.
- The worker does not keep your home clean enough.

These situations, if left unattended, can get out of hand. You can take several steps to nip the problem in the bud.

- Try talking to the worker. If the worker is untrustworthy or hostile, however, go straight to the supervisor.

- If you do not get anywhere talking to the worker, or are uncomfortable approaching the worker, contact the supervisor at the agency. You can call or write a letter, depending on how quickly the problem needs to be addressed. Keep notes about all your phone conversations, and copies of every written communication. If the situation does not improve within a week or so, start looking for a new agency and new workers.

- If the agency does not cooperate, file a formal complaint with the appropriate organization. If the agency is private, write to:

  - City, county, or state office of consumer affairs.
  - State attorney general's office.
  - State department of health.
  - Better Business Bureau.

- If the agency is nonprofit, write to:

  - Agency's board of directors.
  - Community organization that funds the agency.

- If the agency is Medicare or Medicaid certified, write to:

  - Your elected representatives.
  - State or local department of social services or public welfare (Medicaid certified).

　　　　　• Regional office of the Health Care Financing Administration (Medicare certified).

• If you have a problem with a particular worker, write to the organization that licenses or certifies the worker's profession.

• If the problem involves theft or physical or mental abuse, call the police.

WHAT COMMUNITY-BASED SERVICES ARE AVAILABLE?

Many communities offer an array of services to their homebound residents. The list that follows will help you locate the community-based services that are of most interest to you.

• If you would like to have meals delivered to your home, refer to the section on home-delivered meals on page 267.

• If you would like to have somewhere to go to get an inexpensive nutritious meal, refer to the section on nutrition services on page 267.

• If you would like to speak with a social worker about your emotional or financial problems, refer to the section on social services on page 267.

• If you would like someone to visit you at home, assist you with small household chores, or accompany you on errands, refer to the section on home companions on page 268.

• If you are fearful of being home alone in the event of an emergency, refer to the section on emergency services on page 268.

• If you are concerned that something might happen to you at home, and no one would know, refer to the section on telephone reassurance programs on page 268.

• If you need assistance getting around town, refer to the section on transportation and escort services on page 269.

• If you would like somewhere to go during the day for social activities, refer to the sections on adult day care centers and senior centers on pages 269 and 270.

• If you are terminally ill and would like trained personnel to come to your home to make the rest of your life as comfortable and fulfilling as possible, refer to the section on hospice care on page 270.

A number of community-based services are administered by your local area agency on aging. The best way to find out about these services is to call the Elder Care Locator between 9 A.M. and 5 P.M. (Eastern Standard Time) at 800-677-1116.

The Elder Care Locator is jointly sponsored by the United States Administration on Aging and the National Association of Area Agencies on Aging.

Tell the operator who answers the telephone your zip code and give a brief description of the type of service you are looking for. You can get referrals to state and local agencies that offer safety, security, and companionship programs; transportation, nutrition, social, and recreational services; elder abuse assistance; free or low-cost legal help; and a range of other community-based services.

Your state unit on aging is another good source of information about services available to older residents (see Appendix 1).

HOME-DELIVERED MEALS

In most communities, home-delivered meals (commonly called meals on wheels or homebound meals) are available to residents who are over age 60 and home-bound or unable to prepare their own meals. At a minimum, home-delivered meals are available once a day, 5 days a week. A number of programs offer two meals a day, most can accommodate special dietary needs, and some also serve meals on weekends. Recipients of home-delivered meals pay, on average, about $4 per meal. Some programs have no fee or a sliding fee scale so the cost depends on your ability to pay. You can find out about home-delivered meal programs in your community by calling the Elder Care Locator (800-677-1116) or your local senior citizen center or office of aging, or by looking up Meals on Wheels in the white pages of your telephone book.

NUTRITION SERVICES

Malnutrition among older Americans is a serious problem. In most communities, you can get a nutritious meal at the local senior center, church, synagogue, or senior housing complex for a nominal charge (usually $2 to $4 per meal). If you cannot afford the fee, it will be waived. Some programs even provide transportation to and from the site. For more information on nutrition services, contact your local senior center, state unit on aging (see Appendix 1), or Elder Care Locator (800-677-1116).

SOCIAL SERVICES

If you need help coping with emotional or financial problems, you may want to speak with a social worker. Social workers are trained to provide a range of support services to patients and their families. They are usually knowledgeable about resources available in the community, and can discuss sources of funding to help pay your medical expenses. In addition, these professionals can refer you to other experts in the fields of health care, finance, and law. Some social workers also offer psychological counseling.

You can hire a social worker through the Visiting Nurse Service or Visiting Nurse Association or another home care agency, or look in the yellow pages of the telephone book under Social Services or Social Worker. The social services department of a hospital should also be able to provide you with the names of social workers.

HOME COMPANIONS

If you would like someone to visit you at home, assist you with small household tasks, read or write letters for you, run local errands, or accompany you to appointments outside the house, you may want to participate in a home companionship or friendly visitor program. Many communities have organizations of volunteers who visit homebound seniors free of charge. You can find out if such an organization exists in your community by calling the Elder Care Locator (800-677-1116), your local senior citizen center, church or synagogue, Visiting Nurse Association, or high school community service groups.

EMERGENCY SERVICES

If you are fearful of being home alone when an emergency arises, you should look into purchasing an emergency response system (ERS). An ERS enables you to alert a hospital or emergency response unit by pushing a button or speaking into an intercom if you need immediate assistance. The cost of a personal emergency response system can be as high as $2,500 for the equipment, plus a monthly fee of about $30. As an alternative, you can lease a system from a manufacturer or local hospital. Free systems may be available through your local area agency on aging. Call the Elder Care Locator (800-677-1116) for details. You can get information about installing an ERS from a local hospital, fire department, or emergency medical service, or by looking under Paging and Signaling Services in the yellow pages of the telephone book.

TELEPHONE REASSURANCE PROGRAMS

If you are worried that something could happen to you at home and no one would know, you may want to find out if your community has a telephone reassurance program. These programs arrange for volunteers to keep in daily telephone contact with homebound seniors. If you cannot be reached by phone on a given day, someone will check in on you personally, or call your neighbors, family, or emergency personnel. There is no fee for this service. Find out if such a program operates in your community by calling the Elder Care Locator (800-677-1116), a local church, synagogue, or senior citizen center, or the Visiting Nurse Association.

TRANSPORTATION AND ESCORT SERVICES

Most communities offer transportation services at reduced cost to help older residents get around town. Volunteer drivers, or a bus, taxi, or van service, provide the transportation. Escorts help the frail elderly leave their homes by providing physical assistance and protection. You can get information about such services by calling the Elder Care Locator (800-677-1116), your local senior citizen center, or the state department of public health or social services. Volunteer driver programs are also sponsored by churches, synagogues, and high school community service clubs.

ADULT DAY CARE PROGRAMS

There are two types of adult day care programs: multipurpose programs and day hospital programs.

Multipurpose programs emphasize social interaction and activities. Meals and transportation may be provided. These programs provide minimal medical services.

Day hospital programs are usually affiliated with a health care institution. Patients from the institution are referred to the program for health care, rehabilitation, and treatment. Day hospital programs provide some or all of the following services: nursing, physical therapy, occupational therapy, speech therapy, eye examinations, podiatry, social services, personal care, meals, transportation, and recreational activities.

Most adult day care programs are open 5 days a week, 9 A.M. to 5 P.M. Participants pay for adult day care in one of the following ways:

- Some centers charge all participants a flat fee. The average fee is $30 to $50 a day.
- Some centers charge participants a sliding fee. The amount of the fee depends on the participant's income.
- Some centers do not charge any fee.
- Some centers accept Medicaid payments.
- Some adult day care charges may be covered by Medicare.

To find out more about adult day care centers in your community, contact the local department of senior citizen affairs or social services, or call the Elder Care Locator (800-677-1116). Also inquire whether any local hospitals, nursing homes, or religious organizations operate an adult day care center.

SENIOR CENTERS

Senior citizen centers are places where independent and healthy older adults gather. The centers offer a variety of services and programs including meals, recreational activities, social events, health screening, lectures, continuing education classes, and medical information. Some centers provide transportation to participants. There is no charge to attend a senior citizen center. There may, however, be a small fee for some special events, such as a night at the theater. Your local department of senior citizen affairs will be able to provide you with information about senior centers in your neighborhood, or you can call the Elder Care Locator (800-677-1116).

HOSPICE CARE

Hospice care is provided to terminally ill individuals and their families, usually 24 hours a day, 7 days a week. The purpose of hospice care is to provide the patient and the patient's family with emotional, physical, and spiritual support through a difficult time. The services are designed to minimize the patient's pain and discomfort, add meaning to the final days of the patient's life, and enable the patient to remain at home for as long as possible. Aggressive medical treatment is not part of hospice care.

Some home health agencies and hospitals sponsor hospice programs. Medicare pays for hospice care provided to terminally ill beneficiaries by a Medicare-certified hospice program.

The American Association of Retired Persons (AARP) has prepared a free, 47-page booklet entitled "Staying at Home: A Guide to Long Term Care and Housing" to help families find community, housing, and medical services for a frail elderly person in the community. To order the booklet (publication D14986), contact:

AARP Fulfillment
601 E Street NW
Washington, DC 20049
202-434-3910

BACK TO RITA

Our first task was to assess Rita and Mort's home care needs: Mort required rehabilitation therapy and help with his personal needs. Rita had arthritis and needed help with the housekeeping. Since these services could be easily provided at home, Rita and Mort were prime candidates for home care.

We then had to consider how Rita and Mort would pay for their home care services. A review of their health insurance policies revealed that no private coverage was available, and a look at their bank balances established that they were not eligible for Medicaid. We concluded that Medicare was their best bet. Mort, a Medicare beneficiary, qualified for coverage because he could not leave home without assistance and required rehabilitation services. His therapist and home health aide were covered, but Medicare coverage was not available for the housekeeper. Rita and Mort had to cover this expense with their own money.

Hospital social workers arranged for the home care services through an agency affiliated with the hospital.

By the time Mort was ready to be discharged, Rita eagerly awaited his homecoming, confident that she could meet all his needs with the help of her home care team.

10.
BENEFITS THAT SUPPORT INDEPENDENT LIVING

When Ann came to see me, she was very troubled. Living at home alone was becoming increasingly difficult, but she absolutely and positively did not want to move. She liked having all her friends nearby and knowing which stores carried the freshest fish and cheapest lightbulbs.

I asked Ann to describe her problems at home. She told me that she could no longer bend down to clean the floors, could not afford to have her roof repaired, and was afraid she would fall in her house and be unable to summon help.

She needed to know: Was there anything she could do to make living at home alone easier and safer?

Do you sometimes wonder how much longer you can continue to live in your present accommodations?

- Are you having trouble affording your house or apartment?
- Are medical problems starting to interfere with your ability to care for yourself?
- Has your neighborhood changed so that you question your personal safety?
- Are you feeling alone and isolated?
- Are you unable to get around your home due to a physical impairment?

If you answered yes to one or more of these questions, you may be thinking about giving up your independent living arrangement.

Moving is not the only answer to your housing problems. If you are looking for a way to remain in your current living quarters, this chapter is for you. Each section of the chapter suggests alternative ways (other than moving) you can overcome four of the most common concerns of the older home or apartment dweller: finances, safety and security, mobility limitations, and deteriorating health.

If you end up remaining where you are, you will not be alone. A recent Harvard study found that only 20 percent of adults over age 55 had moved, and only 25 percent planned to move within the next 5 years. In the over-65 population, only 1 percent planned to move in the years ahead.

FINANCIAL CONCERNS

Many homeowners are "house rich." They live in an expensive home worth thousands of dollars, but cannot make ends meet each month with their Social Security and pension income. Large numbers of renters have a similar problem. They find their fixed income is insufficient to cover the monthly rent, food, and utility bills, which keep going up and up and up, year after year.

If you are having trouble affording your house or apartment, don't move (no pun intended) until you read this section. Help may be available.

This section will first cover a number of options that are available to financially strapped homeowners, then discuss sources of financial assistance for renters. The section concludes with some suggestions for getting help with your utility bills.

TAPPING INTO HOME EQUITY

Home equity is the money you have invested in your house. If the mortgage on your house is paid off, or almost paid off, you probably have a lot of home equity.

An example will illustrate how your home equity may be the solution to your cash flow problems. Mary and John bought a house for $100,000. They made a $20,000 downpayment and took out an $80,000 mortgage. Their home equity is only $20,000, the amount they have invested in the house. In 10 years Mary and John have paid off their mortgage. Their home has increased in value to $150,000. At this point their home equity is $150,000, the value of their home.

Mary and John can use their $150,000 of home equity to generate a source of income. They can:

- Take out a home equity line of credit.
- Refinance their home.
- Take out a second mortgage on their home.

- Take out a reverse mortgage on their home.
- Enter into a sale leaseback arrangement.

Each of these options is discussed below in a question and answer format.

HOME EQUITY LINE OF CREDIT

• What is a home equity line of credit? With a home equity line of credit, the equity in your home secures a line of credit. You can take out a cash loan against the line of credit at any time, and for any reason. The line of credit is capped at a percentage of the value of your home equity.

• What are your obligations with a home equity line of credit? You must repay money you borrow on an equity line of credit in monthly installments. You must also pay any loan fees or points, and an annual fee for maintaining the equity account.

• How do you arrange a home equity line of credit? Home equity lines of credit are readily available through banks, savings and loans, mortgage companies, and local loan companies.

• What are the advantages of a home equity line of credit? Interest rates charged on home equity lines of credit may be lower than other types of loans. In addition, up to $100,000 (or the value of the home, if less) of interest paid on a home equity line of credit is tax deductible.

• What are the disadvantages of a home equity line of credit? There are often associated costs, including an application fee and maintenance charges. Also, since your home secures the line of credit, you risk losing your home if you fall behind in your monthly payments. Finally, there may be a minimum withdrawal amount, and repayment begins as soon as you take out a loan.

• Is a home equity line of credit for you? You are probably eligible for a home equity line of credit if you own a home without a substantial mortgage and have sufficient income to repay the loan. However, an equity line of credit is probably not for you if you are already having trouble covering your expenses with your monthly income. With a home equity line of credit, your monthly expenses will increase because you will have to make monthly payments on your loan. If you cannot repay the loan each month, you risk losing your home.

REFINANCING YOUR HOME

• What is home refinancing? When you refinance your home, you take out a new mortgage. You can use part of the new mortgage to pay off any remaining balance on your original mortgage, and spend the rest of the new mortgage any way you choose.

• What are your obligations when you refinance your home? You must repay your new mortgage just as you had to pay back your original mortgage. You will also be responsible for any loan fees and points the lender charges.

• How do you arrange a refinancing of your home? You can refinance your home through most banks, savings and loans, mortgage companies, and local loan companies.

• What are the advantages of home refinancing? You get a lump sum of cash to spend as you please.

• What are the disadvantages of home refinancing? Depending on what has happened to interest rates since you took out your original mortgage, you may have to pay a higher rate of interest when you refinance your mortgage. You will also have to pay points and other costs of borrowing money. Finally, refinancing postpones the day you own your home outright.

• Is home refinancing for you? You should only refinance your home if you need a lump sum of money for a specific purpose. Try to avoid refinancing if you are paying a low rate of interest on your original mortgage, or if you have almost paid off your original mortgage.

SECOND MORTGAGES

• What is a second mortgage? A second mortgage is a loan that is secured by the equity in your home. The lender pays you the loaned amount in a single lump sum payment.

• What are your obligations with a second mortgage? You must repay the lender in monthly payments. Usually the term of the loan is between 5 and 15 years. You must also pay the lender loan fees or points.

• How do you arrange for a second mortgage? Second mortgages are available from banks, savings and loans, mortgage companies, and loan companies.

• What are the advantages of a second mortgage? You get a lump sum of money to spend as you please. If you use a second mortgage to pay for medical expenses, the interest on the loan is tax deductible.

• What are the disadvantages of a second mortgage? Since your home secures the second mortgage, you risk losing your home if you fall behind in your monthly payments, which can be quite high. The interest rates on second mortgages can be 2 or 3 percentage points above current mortgage rates.

• Is a second mortgage for you? If you are already having trouble covering your monthly expenses, you should make every effort to avoid taking out a second mortgage on your home. If you need additional money to pay for medical expenses, a second mortgage may make sense because the interest on the second mortgage may be tax deductible.

HOME EQUITY CONVERSION PLANS

As a homeowner, you can get cash out of the equity in your home using several methods that fall under the umbrella category of home equity conversion plans. Every home equity conversion plan offers you the following features:

• You do not have to leave your home. You can receive regular loan payments based on the value of your home equity while you continue to reside in your home.

• You do not have to make regular monthly loan payments. You repay the lender by pledging the equity you own in your home.

• You will have to pay some cash for the loan. You will be responsible for some or all of the following expenses: application fee, interest, sales commissions, and closing costs. These costs can be as high as $8,000.

• You will probably not benefit from any additional appreciation on the value of your home after you enter into a home equity plan.

• The more home equity you have, the more cash you can collect under a home equity plan.

• If you still have a large mortgage on your home, you will probably not qualify for a home equity plan.

This section will discuss two types of home equity conversion plans: The reverse mortgage and the sale leaseback.

For more information about home equity conversion plans, write or call:

Federal National Mortgage Association (Fannie Mae)
8007-FANNIE (800-732-6643)

Request the free pamphlet on FHA-insured reverse mortgages and a list of FHA-insured lenders.

AARP Fulfillment
601 E Street, N.W.
Washington, DC 20049
202-434-6030

Request the free booklet "Home-Made Money—A Consumer's Guide to Home Equity Conversion," a list of FHA- and privately-insured lenders, and a list of agencies that provide counseling service to prospective borrowers.

National Center for Home Equity Conversion (NCHEC)
7373 147th Street
Apple Valley, MN 55124
612-953-4474

NCHEC publishes an easy-to-read guide to reverse mortgages entitled *Retirement Income on the House,* which you can purchase for $24.95, plus $4.50 shipping and handling, by calling 800-247-6553. Send a self-addressed stamped envelope to NCHEC to receive an updated list of lenders.

Home Equity Conversion Plan: Reverse Mortgages

• What is a reverse mortgage? A reverse mortgage is appropriately named because it is the opposite of a typical mortgage.

With a typical mortgage, you borrow money from a bank and, during the term of the mortgage, you make monthly payments to the bank to repay the principal and interest of the loan. With a reverse mortgage, the bank sends you monthly payments of income based on the value of your home. You do not have to repay the loan until you move or sell your home, or your estate must repay the loan after your death. You can continue to reside in your home during the term of the loan. Two common varieties of reverse mortgages are described below.

Short-Term Reverse Mortgage

• What is the duration of a short-term mortgage? Short-term reverse mortgages can last up to 12 years. The average short-term reverse mortgage is for 7 years. Payments under a short-term reverse mortgage stop if you move or die during the term of the mortgage.

• How do you repay a short-term mortgage? In one of the following ways:

1. Sell the house and repay the lender out of the proceeds of the sale. If the house has increased in value over the term of the mortgage, you will be left with some money after you repay the lender, which you can use to purchase new living quarters.

2. Take out a new loan. This option will only be available to you if your home has increased in value over the term of the mortgage.

• Is a short-term reverse mortgage for you? Depending on the value of your house, you may be able to obtain a short-term reverse mortgage that provides you with the added monthly income you need for the rest of the time you intend to live in your house. If your life expectancy, or the time you intend to remain in your home, is less than 10 years, you may want to consider a short-term reverse mortgage. For example, if you plan to move to a retirement community within 5 or 6 years, an 8- or 10-year reverse mortgage makes sense. Likewise, if your life expectancy is 3 years, and you need additional funds to pay for home care services, a 5-year mortgage would be appropriate.

A short-term mortgage is not for you if you want to leave the family home to your children or other beneficiaries upon your death, or if you are under 70, healthy, and plan to live in your home for the rest of your life.

Long-Term Reverse Mortgage

•   What is the duration of a long-term reverse mortgage? You do not have to repay a long-term reverse mortgage until you move, sell your house, or die (and then your estate is responsible for repaying the lender).

•   How do you repay a long-term mortgage? When your home is sold, either during your life or by your estate after your death, the lender must be repaid out of the proceeds of the sale. You do not have to sell your home during your lifetime to repay the mortgage.

•   Is a long-term reverse mortgage for you? Yes, if you intend to live in your house for the rest of your life and are not planning on leaving your house to your heirs.

•   How much money can you borrow with a reverse mortgage? The amount of money you can borrow depends on four factors:

1.   Value of your home equity.
2.   Your age.
3.   Current market value of your home.
4.   Prevailing interest rates.

If you are getting an FHA-insured loan, there is a cap on the amount of home equity you can use to secure the loan. The amount of equity backing the loan cannot exceed the limits of the FHA insurance, which vary from region to region. In most rural areas the maximum amount of insured equity is $67,500; the maximum increases to about $152,000 in the nation's highest-cost housing markets.

The effect of these insurance caps is to limit the amount of money you can borrow against your home, even if the value of your home equity far exceeds the FHA-insured limits. For example, a 65-year-old homeowner with $225,000 home equity who takes out an FHA-insured reverse mortgage would only receive a maximum monthly payment of about $400 for as long as he stays in the house. A 75-year-old would collect more, about $585 a month, because he has a shorter life expectancy.

These limits don't apply to privately-insured mortgages. Under a privately-insured mortgage, a 74-year-old wife and 85-year-old husband with $225,000 in home equity could receive $927 a month as long as either of them resided in the home.

•   What are your payment options with a reverse mortgage? Under many reverse mortgages you are given a choice of three methods of payment: (1) monthly payments for a term of years or as long as you occupy the home, which may enable you to more comfortably cover your monthly expenses; (2) a single lump-sum payment, which is a good idea if your income is generally sufficient to cover your expenses, but you need a chunk of cash to repair or improve your house, or pay off some old bills; or (3) a line of credit, which is a nice way to secure a ready source of cash should the need arise. A line of credit is probably the most popular, and surely the simplest, payment option. Some lenders even offer a payment schedule that keeps up with inflation. Payments start low and increase year after year.

• What are the benefits of a reverse mortgage? There are a number of important advantages to a reverse mortgage:

1. You get an additional source of monthly income, which you are free to use to pay utility, food, or medical bills, to make home repairs, or to take a vacation.

2. You can continue to own, and reside in, your home during the term of the mortgage.

3. You only pay interest as you receive the monthly checks from the lender. That is, you do not pay interest on the full amount of the loan for the entire term of the mortgage. This is unlike a standard mortgage, where you pay interest on the large loan balance from the day you take out the mortgage.

4. The income you receive from a reverse mortgage does not affect eligibility for such public benefits as Supplemental Security Income (SSI) or Medicaid as long as you spend the income in the month you receive it. Payments from a reverse mortgage that you hold into a subsequent month may adversely affect your SSI and Medicaid eligibility. Knowing this, you should collect your mortgage payments as early in the month as possible, so you have the maximum amount of time to spend the money.

5. Income from a reverse mortgage is not taxed.

6. With most reverse mortgages, you can repay the loan at any time without penalty.

7. The lender can only look to your house for repayment. Your bank accounts and other investments are fully protected. In addition, the lender can never pursue your heirs or the other assets in your estate for repayment.

8. Unlike home equity plans, second mortgages, and home refinancing, reverse mortgages do not increase your monthly expenses. You do not have to repay the lender each month. Rather, the entire amount of the reverse mortgage comes due at the end of the term of the loan, when you move, sell your house, or die, depending on the type of reverse mortgage you select.

• What are the disadvantages of a reverse mortgage? Don't make the mistake of viewing reverse mortgages as a cure-all. Keep your eyes open to their drawbacks:

1. Once your home equity is gone, it's gone for good. After you move or die,

and the accumulated debt comes due, the equity in your home will not be available to pay for you or your spouse's nursing home care, or your grand-child's college education. If the debt comes due on account of death, your estate will have to sell the house and repay the lender. Your heirs will only receive whatever is left after the debt is repaid.

2. Under most reverse mortgages, you are charged a compound interest rate. (Compound interest means that you pay interest on accumulated unpaid interest.) The interest rate on a reverse mortgage is normally comparable to the rate on a conventional self-liquidating mortgage.

3. You will probably have to pay a loan application fee, closing costs, and the costs of an appraisal, title insurance, and escrow fees to take out a reverse mortgage.

4. The interest you pay on a reverse mortgage will not be tax deductible until you pay off the entire loan, which will not happen until you sell your home, move out of your home, or die.

• How do you qualify for a reverse mortgage? You qualify for a reverse mortgage based on the value of your home, not your income. To get a reverse mortgage, you must own your home without a mortgage or with a small mortgage. You must also meet a minimum age requirement, which is often 62 years old.

The federal government now offers FHA insurance for reverse mortgages made to homeowners age 62 or older. The FHA insurance protects lenders against home-owners who do not repay their mortgage. The availability of FHA insurance has encouraged more lenders to make these types of loans to older homeowners. If you are over age 62, you can qualify for an FHA-insured reverse mortgage if you also meet these four criteria:

1. You occupy your home as your principal residence.

2. You have little or no balance due on your mortgage.

3. Your home meets housing code standards.

4. You agree to accept mortgage counseling from a federally approved counselor, which is usually a local nonprofit social service agency.

Owners of FHA-approved condominiums can qualify for an FHA-insured reverse, unlike owners of cooperatives.

To find a federal counseling center near you, call the U.S. Department of Housing and Urban Development hotline (800-733-3238). Residents of Pennsylvania should call 800-822-1174.

• How do you apply for a reverse mortgage? Many banks, savings and loans, mortgage brokers, and other finance companies offer FHA-insured reverse mortgages. Some mortgage brokers now offer reverse mortgages in several states. These brokers include Directors Mortgage (Riverside, California), ARCS Mortgage (Calabasas, California), Amerifirst Mortgage (Hempstead, New York), and International Mortgage (Owings Mills, Maryland). Two of the larger companies offering privately-insured mortgages in several states are Transamerica Homefirst (San Francisco, California) and Freedom Home Equity Partners (Irvine, California).

Home Equity Conversion Plan: Sale Leaseback

• What is a sale leaseback? With a sale leaseback, you transfer title of your home to a buyer. In return, the buyer promises to make monthly payments to you, and to permit you to remain in your home for a specified period of time—usually the rest of your life. Finally, you agree to pay the buyer rent while you remain in the home.

For example, imagine your home is worth $100,000. You sell your home to Bob, who agrees to let you continue to occupy the house for as long as you want. According to the terms of the sale, Bob does the following:

- Agrees to pay you a 10 percent down payment.
- Agrees to make monthly payments for a term of years.
- Agrees to pay all taxes, insurance, and maintenance expenses.
- Takes title to the property.

The terms of the sale require you to:

- Agree to pay Bob $600 a month, a reasonable rent for the home.
- Purchase a deferred annuity out of the down payment to provide you with monthly income when Bob has paid off his mortgage after the specified term of years.
- Transfer title to the home to Bob.

Bob benefits from this arrangement in four ways:

1. He gets a regular monthly rental income from you.
2. He will probably make a profit on the sale of your home after your death, or if you decide to move.
3. He should be able to deduct interest, expenses, and depreciation, as long as he paid fair market value for the property and charges a fair market rent.
4. He gets a stepped-up basis, so he will pay little or no capital gains taxes if he sells the property before it appreciates significantly more in value (see page 352).

• What are the advantages to you of a sale leaseback? When you enter into a sale leaseback arrangement, you benefit in five ways:

1. You collect a downpayment from the purchaser.
2. You are guaranteed a monthly income for life.
3. You can continue to live in your home for the rest of your life, or move at any time you choose.
4. Your rent increases can be limited to increases in the cost of living.
5. You should be able to avoid paying tax on $125,000 of the profit you realize on the sale of your house by using the one-time exclusion (see page 354).

Even if the investor sells your house to another purchaser, your right to remain in the house is protected.

The primary benefit of a sale leaseback arrangement over a reverse mortgage is lower cost. Since no bank or mortgage company is involved, you do not pay any loan fees or interest on the money you receive.

• What are the disadvantages of a sale leaseback? There are several:

1. You may have trouble tracking down a buyer who is willing to defer taking possession of your home for an indefinite period of time. Most sale leaseback arrangements are made between parent and child.
2. You will have to hire an attorney (and probably spend at least $500) to negotiate and prepare the sale leaseback contract. The National Center for Home Equity Conversion sells model sale leaseback contracts with accompanying forms and detailed explanatory notes. These materials are a good resource for attorneys who lack experience in arranging sale leasebacks. To purchase the model forms, send a check for $29 to:

   National Center for Home Equity Conversion (NCHEC)
   7373 147th Street
   Apple Valley, MN 55124

3. You will not benefit from future increases in the value of your home.
4. You will lose your eligibility for federal and state property tax benefits.
5. You will become a tenant. If your landlord is not responsive to your needs and complaints, you may find yourself in landlord-tenant court.
6. Interest that you earn on the buyer's installment note may affect your SSI and Medicaid eligibility.

7. You will not be able to leave your home to your heirs when you die.

8. The additional income you receive may increase your income tax liability.

• What should you know about entering into a sale leaseback arrangement? To avoid future problems, make sure your contract includes the following protections:

- A lifetime lease, reserving the right to share the house with someone else (say an aide, boarder, or a paramour).
- A rent control clause limiting increases to a cost of living index, or setting fixed rent increases that correspond to increased mortgage payments by the buyer.
- A requirement that all subsequent buyers honor your lifetime lease.
- A provision explicitly assigning responsibility for taxes, insurance, repairs, and maintenance to the buyer.
- A reservation of the right to cancel the sale leaseback arrangement if the buyer transfers ownership of the property.
- A paragraph spelling out your rights in the event the buyer misses a mortgage payment.

The note or mortgage that is executed in conjunction with the sale leaseback contract should include a restriction so that it cannot be converted to cash. Without such a restriction, the note or mortgage could affect your eligibility for public benefits, such as Supplemental Security Income and Medicaid. With the restriction, the payments you receive under a sale leaseback will not affect your benefit eligibility as long as you spend the income in the month you receive it. If you retain an income payment into a subsequent month, part of the payment will be counted as a resource (the difference between what the buyer pays you on the note and the amount you pay the buyer for rent). This could affect your eligibility for SSI and Medicaid.

• What are your obligations under a sale leaseback? You must make monthly rental payments to the purchaser of your home.

• Is a sale leaseback for you? If you are 65, in good health, and plan to remain in your home for the rest of your life, a sale leaseback might make sense.

• How do you arrange a sale leaseback? Usually participants in sale leasebacks either are related to the homeowner or are real estate syndicates. A lawyer, certified public accountant, or real estate firm that has developed an expertise in sale leaseback arrangements may be able to help you locate a buyer. Your local bar association, realtors association, and professional associations for accountants may also be good sources of assistance.

Once you have located an investor, you should consult an attorney. The terms of the sale leaseback agreement must be carefully drafted for tax purposes and to protect your lifetime lease and your entitlement to public benefits.

RENTAL ASSISTANCE

The Federal Department of Housing and Urban Development (HUD) also administers a number of rental assistance programs. Three of these programs are discussed below.

SECTION 8 HOUSING

One of the largest rental assistance programs ever established by Congress is commonly called the Section 8 housing program because it was created under Section 8 of the Community Development Act. If you are eligible for Section 8 housing, the federal government will pay part of your rent directly to your landlord.

To qualify for Section 8 assistance:

- You or your spouse must be at least 62 years of age or disabled.
- Your income and assets must be within the limits set by the federal government.
- You must find a landlord who participates in the Section 8 program.
- You must find an apartment where the rent falls within the limits set by the federal government.

Many communities have a waiting list for Section 8 housing. Preference is sometimes given to residents of the community in which the Section 8 housing is located.

The exact amount of rental assistance you receive will depend on your income and your health. Participants in the Section 8 program never pay more than 30 percent of their income for rent.

The Section 8 program is administered by your local housing authority, which can provide you with additional information and application forms.

HOUSING VOUCHERS

Under the housing voucher program, a low-income elderly tenant receives a coupon that is worth the difference between 30 percent of the tenant's income and the market rental value of the apartment. This coupon helps the tenant pay the rent. Unlike the Section 8 program, landlords do not have to agree to participate in the voucher program. The voucher program is administered by the local housing authority, which can provide you with additional information.

PUBLIC HOUSING

Public housing enables low-income elderly individuals to continue to live independently in the community. Rents in public housing are set by the government below market value.

The exact eligibility requirements for public housing vary from community to community. As a general matter, applicants must meet strict income, asset, and residency requirements to qualify for public housing. Applicants who have been evicted, are living in substandard housing, or pay more than 50 percent of their income for rent usually get preference. In most areas there is a waiting list for public housing.

Unfortunately, some public housing programs discriminate against frail or disabled applicants. This discrimination violates a federal law called the Fair Housing Amendments Act of 1988 (FHAA). The FHAA protects the housing rights of the elderly and disabled. The courts have ruled that the FHAA prohibits public housing authorities from inquiring about your ability to live independently, or requiring you to provide medical records, when you apply for public housing. As long as you can pay the rent on time, maintain your apartment (even if you require the assistance of others), and avoid disruptive behavior, you are "suitable for tenancy."

To obtain additional information about applying for public housing, contact your local housing authority.

UTILITY ASSISTANCE

One of your highest housing expenses is probably heat. If you are having trouble affording the cost of heating your home, you may be interested in the following sources of assistance.

HOME ENERGY ASSISTANCE PROGRAM

The Home Energy Assistance Program (HEAP) is a federal program that helps low-income homeowners and renters pay the high cost of purchasing energy. In some states, HEAP assistance is limited to heating expenses; other states also help pay lighting and cooking costs. Some states also make HEAP funds available to pay for the repair or maintenance of heating equipment and weatherization. HEAP assistance is available to homeowners and renters who pay for heat in their rent.

To qualify for HEAP benefits, you must show that your income falls below a certain limit. You will automatically qualify for HEAP benefits if you fit into one of the following categories:

- You receive Supplemental Security Income (SSI).
- You receive food stamps.
- You receive public assistance or welfare.

To apply for HEAP you must file an application with the local department of social services or public welfare. You should file your application as early in the year as possible. Once the federal funds allocated to HEAP for the year are exhausted, no additional funds are made available.

When your application has been reviewed, you will receive a written decision in the mail. If you are denied HEAP assistance, you can request an administrative hearing. The written decision will explain how to appeal the denial of HEAP benefits.

If you are approved for HEAP, the type of assistance you receive will vary, depending on your state of residence.

To find out more about HEAP, contact your local department of social services or public welfare.

HOME ENERGY AUDIT AND LOAN PROGRAM

Most states offer some type of energy audit and loan program. Although the specific eligibility rules for the program differ from state to state, in most states residents who own or rent a one- to four-family home built before a certain year qualify for assistance. Eligibility for the program does not depend on income.

Audit and loan programs have two parts:

- Part 1. Experts in energy efficiency conduct a free survey of your home to see how you can save money on your energy bills.
- Part 2. Interest-free or low-interest loans may be available if you can achieve sufficient energy savings by making home modifications. The amount of the loan will depend on the size of the living quarters and the required modifications.

Common home modifications include:

- Insulating the home.
- Weatherizing exterior doors and windows.
- Installing storm windows.

To find out more about the energy audit and loan program in your state, call your state public service commission.

WEATHERIZATION ASSISTANCE PROGRAM

Many counties and states, and some nonprofit organizations, have weatherization assistance programs that make funds available to home and apartment owners for purposes of improving energy efficiency. The funds can be used to repair a furnace, insulate windows, and undertake similar measures to improve energy efficiency.

To get a referral to a weatherization assistance program in your area, contact:

Department of Energy
Division of Weatherization Assistance
1000 Independence Avenue, S.W.
Washington, DC 20585
202-586-2207

DISCOUNTED UTILITY FEES

Some energy and utility companies offer reduced rates to older residents. Call your local energy or utility company to find out about senior citizen discounts.

Oil Buyers' Cooperatives

In neighborhoods throughout the country, homeowners are joining oil buyers' cooperatives to save money on their oil bills. By joining forces in a cooperative, individual homeowners get the purchasing power they need to negotiate with local fuel oil companies for lower prices. Many cooperatives also offer their members information on energy conservation, and free or low-cost energy audits. The annual fee for joining an oil buyers' cooperative can range from $10 to $30, depending on your area of the country.

For information on joining an oil buyers' cooperative in the Washington, D.C.–Baltimore area, contact:

Buyers Up
P.O. Box 18795
Washington, DC 20036
202-659-2500

If you live outside the Washington, D.C.–Baltimore area, Buyers Up may be able to refer you to a cooperative in your area.

SAFETY AND SECURITY CONCERNS

A number of frightening things can happen to you at home: You might lose consciousness and nobody would know. You could slip while getting out of the bathtub. Your oven mitt might catch fire. A robber could break into your house. These events, though terrifying, should not drive you out of your house or apartment. You can take a number of precautionary steps to prevent them from ever occurring.

SAFETY CHECK PROGRAMS

If you are concerned that something bad could happen to you in your home, and no one would know, you may want to join a safety check program; such programs are available in many communities to secure the well-being of older residents.

Four of the most popular safety check programs are described below.

TELEPHONE REASSURANCE PROGRAM

A volunteer calls you each day at a certain time. If you do not answer the phone on a given day, the volunteer will call the friend, neighbor, or relative you designated in advance. That individual will either come to your house or contact emergency personnel to make sure you are all right. You can find out if your community has such a program by calling your local department of senior citizen affairs. If you are interested in starting a telephone reassurance program in your neighborhood, you should contact a volunteer community organization, senior center, or service club.

POSTAL ALERT PROGRAM

Under the postal alert program, your mail carrier is responsible for notifying the authorities if your mail starts to accumulate. Most postal alert programs are sponsored by local community organizations, such as the United Way or Red Cross. When you register for the program, you will receive a sticker to put inside your mailbox. You can find out if your community has a postal alert program, or receive information about starting a program, by calling your local post office and asking to speak to the postmaster.

NEIGHBORHOOD WATCH

Neighborhood watch programs organize and train residents to police their own community. Participants in neighborhood watch programs are assigned times to patrol the local streets and report any suspicious activity to the police. Neighborhood watch workers also work with the local police precinct to educate the public about crime prevention. For information about setting up a neighborhood watch program in your community, contact:

National Sheriffs' Association
1450 Duke Street
Alexandria, VA 22314
800-659-2500

National Crime Prevention Council
1700 K Street, N.W.
Washington, DC 20006
202-466-6272

For information on what you can do to heighten crime and drug awareness in your community, contact:

National Association of Town Watch
P.O. Box 303
Wynnewood, PA 19096
215-649-7055

EMERGENCY RESPONSE SYSTEMS

An emergency response system (ERS) enables you to call immediately for help by pressing a button in a convenient location in your house or around your neck. When you push the button, personnel in a private emergency response center, hospital, or 800 number are alerted. You can rent a PERS from one of the fifteen or so manufacturers in the United States or from a hospital for between $15 and $30 a month. The cost of purchasing a PERS can be as low as $200 or as high as $2,500 for the equipment, plus a monthly operating fee of about $30. If you cannot afford to purchase or lease a PERS, contact your local area agency on aging. You may be able to get a PERS at no cost to you. For more information on acquiring a PERS, contact:

AARP Fulfillment
601 E Street, N.W.
Washington, DC 20049
202-434-2277

(Request the free booklet "Meeting the Need for Security and Independence," which answers a number of questions about personal response systems and reviews several popular models.)

ACCIDENT-PROOFING YOUR HOME

Your home is a dangerous place. Most accidents, falls, and fractures occur at home. But the good news is that most at-home accidents are preventable. If you are afraid that you may fall or otherwise injure yourself at home, you may want to look into accident-proofing your home. A number of simple and inexpensive precautions can make each room of your home a safer place to live:

BATHROOM

- Install sturdy grab bars near the toilet seat, shower, and bathtub. Make sure the grab bars are securely attached to the wall, not just the tiles, and that they support your weight. Do not use towel racks or soap holders as grab bars.
- Put a skidproof rubber mat, nonskid treads, or rubber decals on the bottom of your bathtub or shower.
- Use a bench with rubber-tipped legs when showering or bathing.
- Make sure your bathroom mat has a skidproof rubber back.
- Use unbreakable plastic cups and soap dishes instead of glass.
- Shower and bathtub doors should be made of plastic or safety glass.
- When you are not using your electrical appliances, unplug them from the wall.
- Do not touch any electrical appliance if any part of your body is wet.
- Do not lock your bathroom door.
- Throw away old medications.

KITCHEN

- Store heavy cans and jars at waist height.
- If you must use high shelves or cabinets, keep a steady nonslip low stepstool handy.
- Keep your sharp knives separate from your other utensils.
- Be sure to close cupboard doors and drawers immediately after use.
- Keep your towels and oven mitts away from the burners.
- Buy cookware with heat-proof handles and pots with handles on both sides.
- Periodically clean your oven fan exhaust filters.
- Make sure your sleeves do not hang away from your body when you are cooking.
- Keep pot handles away from the edge of the stove and other burners.
- Unplug small appliances when not in use.

- Do not try to repair appliances yourself.
- Do not turn on your microwave oven unless there is food inside.

BEDROOM

- Do not clutter the area around your bed with electrical cords, shoes, or clothing.
- Keep a lamp, flashlight, and telephone within easy reach of your bed.
- Install a nightlight near your bed.
- Make sure the bulbs in your overhead fixture and other lamps are the correct wattage or do not exceed 60 watts.
- Do not fall asleep with a heating pad on.
- Leave your electric blanket uncovered while in use.

LIVING ROOM

- Arrange your furniture so that you have clear pathways within the room and in and out of the room.
- Avoid unnecessary clutter.
- Throw away old newspapers and magazines.
- Store footstools out of the way when not in use.
- Keep extension cords and wires against the wall, not under rugs.
- Discard frayed electrical cords.
- Periodically clean your chimney and fireplace.

FLOORS

- On wood floors, use a nonskid wax or nonslip finish.
- Keep tile floors dry and unwaxed.
- Remove small scatter rugs.
- Anchor all rugs and pieces of carpeting to the floor with adhesive material, carpet tacks, or nonskid mats.
- Flat rugs are safer than deep piled rugs.
- Promptly repair all cracks, holes, and unevenness in the floors.

STAIRS

- Install handrails or banisters on both sides of all stairways.
- Mark the top and bottom of each stairway and the edge of each step with brightly colored adhesive tape.

- Attach adhesive nonskid treads on indoor and outdoor stairs to prevent falls.
- Install light switches at the top and bottom of all stairways.

INDOOR LIGHTING

- The entire house should be brightly lit, especially in stairways.
- Overhead lighting is better than floor lamps, which only illuminate small areas.
- Nightlights in the bedroom and bathroom will help you find your way if you have to get up during the night.

OUTDOOR LIGHTING

- Install bright lights outside, especially near the front pathway and door.

INDOOR TEMPERATURE

- The nighttime temperature in your house should not go below 65 degrees Fahrenheit. Long-term exposure to a lower temperature can cause dizziness and falling.

For more home safety recommendations, write to:

Hartford House
% Hartford Insurance Group
Hartford Plaza
Hartford, CT 06115
203-547-5000

Request a free copy of "The Hartford House: How to Modify a Home to Accommodate the Needs of an Older Adult," which includes 120 tips, a product list, and ordering information.

AARP Fulfillment
601 E Street, N.W.
Washington, DC 20049
202-434-2277

Request a free copy of "The Doable, Renewable Home" for tips on making a home more accessible, and "The Perfect Fit," which suggests ways you can maintain your current living arrangement. You can also rent or buy the audio tape or video "Making Life a Little Easier: Self-Help Tools for the Home."

Publications Request
U.S. Consumer Product Safety Commission
Washington, DC 20207
800-638-2772

Send a postcard to request the free booklet "Safety for Older Consumers: Home Safety Checklist"

Center for Study of Responsive Law
P.O. Box 19367
Washington, DC 20036
202-387-8030

For $8, you can purchase *The Home Book: A Guide to Safety, Security and Savings in the Home.*

ACCIDENT-PROOF YOURSELF

If you are serious about improving the safety of your environment, don't stop at your home. You can make a number of personal changes to minimize your accident potential.

- Have regular check-ups. Your vision and hearing are especially important in preventing accidents.
- Exercise special caution when taking medications that impair your coordination or balance, or when drinking alcohol.
- Avoid getting up suddenly after eating, sitting, or lying down. You may experience dizziness.
- When walking on slippery, uneven, or unfamiliar ground, wear shoes with a low heel, good support, and a rubber sole, or use a cane, walking stick, or walker.
- Avoid carrying heavy packages. Additional weight can throw you off balance. Use a shopping cart for heavy loads. When you do carry packages, hold them in front of your chest with your arms wrapped around them; hanging bags off one shoulder or in one hand is more likely to cause you to tip over to one side.
- If your doctor gives you the go-ahead, start a regular exercise program. Physical activity increases your safety by improving your strength and flexibility.

You should have a list of emergency telephone numbers near every phone in your house so that you can quickly get the help you need if you do have an accident. Make a note of the following numbers:

- Ambulance.
- Taxi.
- Police department.
- Neighbor.
- Relative.
- Fire department.
- Physician.

A well-stocked first aid kit is also important. Your kit should include:

- Sterile cotton.
- Adhesive tape.
- Bandages.
- Gauze pads.
- Tweezers.
- Scissors.
- Matches.
- Aspirin.
- Antiseptic.
- Vaseline.
- Burn ointment.
- Safety pins.

These simple and inexpensive safety recommendations minimize your risk of injuring yourself at home. You now have one less reason to give up your own home or apartment.

Fireproofing Your Home

Many fire departments offer free at-home fire safety inspections. If you would like a fire fighter to inspect your home, call the public service office of your local fire department. The fire fighter will advise you about where to install smoke alarms, inspect your electrical outlets, and suggest escape routes.

Also, the following precautions will help protect your home against fires.

- Never smoke in bed.
- Do not cover your electric blanket, or tuck it in, while it is turned on.

- Do not fall asleep with a heating pad on.
- Check that all embers are cold before emptying ash trays into the garbage.
- Before you leave your home, check that the stove and all gas and electrical appliances are turned off.
- Promptly repair all frayed wires and loose connections.
- Do not use light bulbs with excessive wattage for the fixture. If you do not know the maximum wattage, use a 60-watt bulb.
- Keep flammable materials away from heaters.
- Install smoke alarms on every floor of your house, and change the batteries at least once a year.
- If you use a fireplace, clean your chimney at least once a year.
- Keep towels, pot holders, plastic utensils, and curtains away from oven burners.
- Periodically clean oven fan exhaust filters.
- Use a timer as a reminder to turn off the oven, or install an automatic cut-off valve.
- Avoid wearing clothes with loose hanging sleeves when cooking.
- Do not turn on your microwave unless there is food in it, and then only for the specified cooking time.
- Beware of kerosene heaters, which release dangerous fumes and can cause serious burns and fires if defective or misused.
- Do not lock your bedroom door when you go to sleep.

If you do have a fire, try not to panic. What you should do depends on the type of fire you have:

- Fire in an oven. Turn off the oven and keep the oven door closed.
- Fire in a microwave. Push the stop button and keep the microwave door closed.
- Grease fire in your oven or on stove top. Shut off the source of heat and smother the fire with baking soda. If possible, put a lid on a pan with burning grease. Do not pour water on the fire.
- Electrical fire. Use a fire extinguisher that is rated for electrical fires.

Only use a fire extinguisher on small fires. If the fire is large or out of control, leave your house as quickly as possible and call the fire department.

Smoking, alcohol, or sedatives are involved in 75 percent of all deaths at home due to fire. Exercise special care if you are at risk due to one or more of these factors.

IMPROVING YOUR HOME SECURITY

Your local office on aging and police department can help you make your home or apartment more secure. In most communities these organizations work together to publish educational materials about crime prevention and sponsor crime prevention projects.

Many police departments also offer free burglary audits. A police officer can come to your home to check on your home security. Some of the more common security recommendations are:

- Cut back bushes near doors and windows and tree limbs reaching toward second-floor windows.
- Install a sturdy dead-bolt lock and night chain.
- Install and use a peephole.
- Never leave your home or garage unlocked, even if you are at home or just step out briefly.
- When you are out of the house, lock your windows as well as your doors.
- Use timers to keep lights on inside and outside the house in the evening or if you are away.
- If you go on vacation:

  > Stop your mail and newspapers, or ask a reliable neighbor to pick up all deliveries.

  > Arrange for someone to maintain your yard or shovel the snow if you plan to be away for an extended time.

  > Turn your telephone bell down.

  > Hide your empty garbage cans.

  > Ask a neighbor to check on your house while you are away.

- Keep outside areas well-illuminated.
- Noise, such as a dog barking or a television playing, keeps burglars away.
- Keep your valuable personal property in a safe that weighs at least 250 pounds.
- Do not keep large amounts of cash in the house.
- Do not hide an extra set of keys to your house under your doormat, on the ledge above your door, in a planter, or in a mailbox.

- Do not put your name or address on your key ring. If you lose your house keys, promptly change your locks.

For more information about improving your personal security, contact:

AARP Fulfillment
601 E Street, N.W.
Washington, DC 20049

You can request the free publications "How to Protect Your Home," "How to Conduct a Security Survey," and "How to Protect Your Neighborhood."

IF YOU ARE A VICTIM

If you are the victim of a crime, your state crime victims board, or some similarly named organization, may be able to help you. These organizations generally reimburse crime victims for some or all of the following: certain types of personal property that are lost, stolen, damaged, or destroyed during a crime; medical expenses; lost earnings; burial expenses; counseling services; and transportation expenses for court appearances. Usually you must report the crime to the police within one week to qualify for assistance. A claim for reimbursement usually must be filed within one year of the crime.

To find out about programs in your community that assist crime victims and witnesses, call your local police department or district attorney's office, or contact:

National Organization for Victim Assistance (NOVA)
1757 Park Road, N.W.
Washington, DC 20010
202-232-6682

NOVA provides a range of services to victims of crime, including referrals to local victim assistance programs, direct counseling and assistance if no local program is available, and help establishing local victim assistance programs. Individuals who join NOVA for $30 a year receive a monthly newsletter and discounts on publications and the annual conference.

National Crime Prevention Council
1700 K Street, N.W.
Washington, DC 20006
202-466-6272

The National Crime Prevention Council refers victims of crime to local victims assistance organizations.

You stand a better chance of recovering property that is stolen from you if you take the following precautions:

- Engrave valuable personal property with your Social Security number.
- Photograph your valuable personal property.
- Keep a list of your valuable personal property with serial numbers in your safe deposit box.

MOBILITY CONCERNS

A house or apartment can be a virtual obstacle course if you have a physical disability. You may find that the doorways are too narrow for your wheelchair, or the steps are forbiddingly steep for your arthritic legs. Do not give up on your house or apartment. It is more adaptable than you may think.

MODIFYING YOUR HOME OR APARTMENT

Think of your home or apartment as a work in progress. The bedroom your son occupied while he lived at home is now a den. The playroom has become your study. You may now need to make some changes in your living quarters to accommodate new physical limitations.

Deferred Payment Loans

If you are a homeowner, a deferred payment loan may help you finance the renovation of your house. A deferred payment loan is a type of home equity conversion plan (see page 276). With almost any type of deferred payment loan, you do not have to repay the loan until you die (and then your estate must pay), move, or sell your home.

The following questions and answers will help you decide whether a deferred payment loan is for you, and help you obtain a loan.

- What can you do with a deferred payment loan? Almost every lender will permit you to use the deferred payment loan to make changes that are necessary to meet mobility limitations, such as widening doorways for a wheelchair, and to improve the security and energy efficiency of your home. You will probably not be permitted to use the deferred payment loan to improve the appearance of your home.

- Are you eligible for a deferred payment loan? You will probably have to prove financial need to qualify for a deferred payment loan. There may also be requirements related to age, the value of your home, the location of your home, and the amount of any outstanding mortgage.

• What is the cost of taking out a deferred payment loan? Probably nothing. Deferred payment loans are usually made without any loan fees or points.

• What type of interest would you have to pay on a deferred payment loan? Probably very low interest, or none at all.

• Who makes deferred payment loans? Local government agencies make most deferred payment loans. Private nonprofit community development and housing organizations also offer deferred payment loans.

• How do you apply for a deferred payment loan? To find out who makes deferred payment loans in your area, contact your area agency on aging (see Appendix 1), local community development agency, or state department on aging or housing. Ask for information about loans that you do not have to repay until you die or sell your home.

• What is the primary benefit of a deferred payment loan? You get an interest-free (or very low-interest) source of money to improve your home, and probably increase the value of your home.

• What is the primary problem with deferred payment loans? They may be difficult to obtain in your area.

PUBLIC GRANTS AND LOW-INTEREST LOANS

The federal Department of Housing and Urban Department (HUD) makes money available to older adults for the purpose of repairing or renovating their homes under two programs:

1. Community Development Block Grant (CDBG) program. Some local governments make this money available as grants to help residents fix up their homes.

2. Direct loan program. The federal government lends money to neighborhood development and employment agencies to be used for home improvements.

To get more information about these programs, contact the local HUD field office in your area. The address and number should be listed in the blue pages of your telephone directory.

If you are a veteran, contact the Veterans Administration to see if low-interest loans are available to help defray the cost of construction.

You will probably have to prepare a proposal to obtain public funding for home remodeling. If the agency to which you are applying does not have its own application, you should write a two- or three-page letter that includes the following information:

- An introduction stating the purpose of the letter and thanking the agency for its consideration.
- An explanation of why you need to modify your home.
- A description of the modifications you are proposing.
- An explanation of how the proposed modifications will solve your problem.
- A breakdown of the anticipated costs of the modifications.
- A brief summary of your financial status and inability to finance the modifications.

If you can, type the proposal. Also, attach any documents that support your application (such as a written estimate from a contractor and your most recent bank statements). These two steps may position you somewhat ahead of your competition.

Private Sources of Funding

A number of private organizations offer small amounts of money to help homeowners with disabilities modify their living accommodations. These organizations include:

- American Cancer Society.
- Muscular Dystrophy Association.
- Multiple Sclerosis Society.
- Cerebral Palsy Society.
- Knights of Columbus.
- Rotary, Lions, Shriners, or 4H Clubs.
- B'nai B'rith.

For more information on private sources of funding, contact:

Adaptive Environments Center
374 Congress
Boston, MA 02115
617-695-1225
Send $5 plus postage for the publication "Stalking the Elusive Buck."

TAX CONSEQUENCES OF HOME MODIFICATIONS

The costs of modifying, equipping, and refurnishing your home to accommodate your changing physical needs may be tax deductible under the medical expense deduction (see page 341). Itemize your expenses on Form 1040 Schedule A with your other medical expenses. To be thoroughly prepared for a possible audit, obtain the following:

- A written statement from your doctor certifying the reasonableness of the modifications.
- A written statement from a real estate agent certifying that the modifications do not increase the value of your property.
- An itemized bill from your contractor.

For more information about the deductibility of home repairs, call the Internal Revenue Services at 800-TAX-FORM (829-3676) and request IRS Treasury Publication Number 907.

REPAIRING YOUR HOME

Your home may no longer be safe because you have been unable to maintain it properly because of failing health or insufficient funds. Home maintenance and repair programs offer inexpensive home maintenance and repair services to older homeowners. You cannot use the service to make aesthetic changes or major improvements to your home.

Most home maintenance and repair programs are run by nonprofit organizations. The cost for joining the program is small, usually not more than $20 a year. This fee entitles you to the discounted services of contractors affiliated with the program, including one free annual visit, reduced rates on construction work, and emergency services (such as the repair of a burst pipe). Some organizations will provide the labor for free if you pay for the materials. You should contact your area agency on aging for more information on programs in your area.

The Neighborhood Reinvestment Corporation makes low-interest loans available to homeowners for home repairs. These federal funds are distributed through housing service offices located across the country. To find out the address and telephone number of the neighborhood housing service office in your area, write or call:

Neighborhood Reinvestment Corporation
1325 G Street, N.W.
Washington, DC 20005
202-376-2400

MODIFYING PUBLIC HOUSING

If you live in public housing and require some special modification due to a physical limitation, the housing authority is required to take "reasonable" steps to accommodate you so that you can remain in your apartment. For example, if you need a bench in the lobby or a ramp over some steps, the housing authority should make these modifications. A modification is "reasonable" if it does not cost a lot of money, does not harm the other tenants, and benefits you. Your right to "age in place" is protected by the Fair Housing Amendment Act, the Rehabilitation Act, and the Americans with Disabilities Act.

You should file all requests for reasonable accommodations with your local housing authority.

HEALTH CARE CONCERNS

For detailed information about obtaining and paying for a broad range of home care services, see Chapter 9.

BACK TO ANN

I answered Ann's question with an emphatic yes. There was a lot she could do to make living at home alone easier.

She could start by hiring a housekeeper to help with her housework. If money was a problem, she could look into increasing her monthly income by tapping into some of her home equity.

To find the funds to repair her roof, I suggested looking into the availability of a deferred payment loan, or contacting the regional office of the federal Department of Housing and Urban Development for information about a low-interest loan or grant.

Finally, to allay her concerns about having an accident at home, I had two recommendations. First, improve the safety of her home by making such simple and inexpensive changes as installing grab bars in the bathroom and removing all small throw rugs from the living room. Second, join a telephone reassurance program or postal alert program, or purchase a personal emergency response system.

By the end of our meeting, Ann was confident that she could continue her current living arrangement for many years to come.

11.

INVESTING FOR MAXIMUM BENEFIT

Fran and Mike are in their early 60s. Mike is an engineer and Fran is a psychologist. They both plan to retire within the next 10 years. Their two children, Max and Jake, are grown and financially independent.

Mike and Fran both have individual retirement accounts, which are invested in bank certificates of deposit and bonds. They also have about $200,000 in other savings. For the past 10 years, they have followed the advice of their financial planner, who recommended liquidating their investments so they would have ready access to cash should the need arise.

Now Fran and Mike are concerned. They see that they will not be able to live off their savings after they retire, as they had always hoped, even with only a modest 4 percent rate of inflation. In 15 years their $200,000 nest egg will only be able to purchase what $111,000 buys today.

They know that they have to move their money into alternative investments, but don't know where to begin. Neither is knowledgeable about financial matters. Mike barely glances at the business section on his way to the comics, and Fran thinks Ginnie Mae is the name of a country singer.

Most older adults want three things out of their investments:

- Enough income to cover their expenses after retirement.
- Ready access to their money in the event of an emergency.
- Security against loss of their savings.

If these three goals are the cornerstones of your investment philosophy, where do you go from here?

First, you must acquire a general understanding of investing. If your eyes glaze over at the mention of mutual funds and annuities, the first part of this chapter, on the basics of investing, is for you.

Armed with general information about investing, you can start to focus on the investments that make the most sense for you. What combination of investments best suits your age, financial situation, lifestyle, personality, and life experience? The section on selecting your investments will help you answer this important question. This part of the chapter includes a series of charts. Each chart explains a particular type of investment and analyzes the investment with a special focus on the needs and goals of the older adult.

Finally, if you have no interest in managing your own finances, and would like to enlist the services of a professional, the last section, dealing with financial planners, will help you find the best money consultant.

BASICS OF INVESTING

As the saying goes, you have to walk before you can run. So get out your walking shoes, because this section of the chapter is your introduction to the world of investing.

TWO TYPES OF INVESTMENTS

All investments can be categorized either as a type of loan or as a type of purchase. Loan and purchase investments are both discussed below. As a general matter, investments that are loans are usually safer than those that are purchases.

INVESTMENTS THAT ARE LOANS

All the investments in this category are loans of money that investors make to borrowers. The most common borrowers are banks, corporations, and the government. In return for receiving the loaned funds, the borrowers agree to

1. Pay the investors interest on the loan.
2. Repay the investors the full amount of the loan when the loan comes due (matures).

Investments that are loans are called fixed-income investments.

The most common example of a fixed-income investment is a savings account. When you invest money in a savings account, you lend your money to the bank. In return, the bank pays you interest and gives you back your money at the end of the loan (when you make a withdrawal). If you lend money to a bank for a fixed period of time, the loan is called a certificate of deposit (CD).

Other fixed-income investments include corporate bonds, which are loans to corporations, and municipal bonds, which are loans to state or local government agencies. You lend money to the federal government when you buy Treasury bills, notes, or bonds.

Fixed-income investments are generally quite secure. Unless the borrower goes broke, you can count on receiving interest for the term of the loan and recovering the full amount of your investment when the loan comes due. However, every fixed-income investment does not carry the same degree of security.

The degree of risk is directly related to the financial health of the borrower. A bond issued by the federal government, for example, is generally more secure than a bond issued by a corporation. Although the United States is up to its proverbial neck in debt, it is still the most creditworthy borrower around.

Investors who lend money to less financially secure borrowers are compensated with a higher interest rate. Their money grows faster, but they face greater risk of losing some or all of their investment.

INVESTMENTS THAT ARE PURCHASES

Some investments are not loans, but rather are purchases. Investors purchase part of a corporation or business with their money.

Stocks are the most common example of this type of investment. An investor who buys a share of stock actually buys part of the company that issues the stock. Other investments that are purchases include mutual funds, through which investors purchase parts of many different companies, and business partnerships, through which investors purchase parts of a business.

Investments that are purchases are called equity investments.

As a general matter, equity investments are riskier than fixed-income investments. With equity investments, the value of the investment rises and falls with the value of the purchased property. For example, the value of a company's stock rises when the profits of that company increase. But when a stock-issuing company is in financial trouble, the price of its shares usually tumbles.

As with fixed-income investments, different equity investments carry different degrees of risk. Stocks issued by well-established utility companies, for example, are almost risk-free, while stocks issued by new corporations are highly unstable. Also, like fixed-income investments, riskier equity investments generally pay a higher rate of interest.

THREE CHARACTERISTICS OF INVESTMENTS

Investments can be compared based on three fundamental characteristics: risk, return, and liquidity.

DEGREE OF RISK

The degree of risk is the chance that the investor will lose some or all of the investment. Investments have varying degrees of risk. Some investments are secure against loss; others are not.

RATE OF RETURN

People invest their money in the hope that it will increase in value. The rate at which an investment increases in value is called the rate of return.

Different investments offer different rates of return. The rate of return on a savings account is the interest the bank pays the depositor. With stocks, the rate of return includes increases in the value of the stock and dividends the company may pay to the investor. (Dividends are payments of profits some stock-issuing companies periodically make to shareholders.)

An investment that pays a high rate of return quickly increases in value. However, high return almost always means high risk. If you are enjoying rapid growth in your investment, odds are that you are not enjoying a high degree of security.

MEASURE OF LIQUIDITY

Liquid investments can be turned into cash quickly and easily.

The best example of a highly liquid investment is a savings account. You can easily turn a savings account into cash by filling out a withdrawal slip. A share of stock is somewhat less liquid. Although you can almost always sell a publicly traded stock through a broker, you may lose money on your investment if the stock market is in a slump. A share of a failing business is one of the least liquid investments of all. There is not much of a market for poorly performing businesses.

As a general matter, fixed-income investments are more liquid than equity investments (see page 305).

TYPES OF INVESTORS

Are you a gambler? Do you like to play the odds? Or are you most comfortable sticking your money in a sock and putting it under your mattress?

If you answered the first two questions in the affirmative, you are probably an aggressive investor. If not, you may be more accurately described as a conservative investor.

AGGRESSIVE INVESTORS

Aggressive investors are usually young or wealthy. They are drawn to equity investments because:

- They can afford to take risks with their money.
- They can afford to tie up their money for a long time.

CONSERVATIVE INVESTORS

Conservative investors are usually older and more concerned about their immediate financial future.

This class of investors generally favors fixed-income investments because:

- The investments are more secure.
- The interest provides them with a guaranteed source of income.
- They can easily turn their investment into cash.

Now that you have some general information about investors and investments, we are ready to move into specifics. Which investments meet your particular needs?

SELECTING YOUR INVESTMENTS

The matchmaker's credo is: There's someone for everyone. With the infinite variety of investments on the market today, chances are there's an investment out there that's right for you. Are you ready to look for it?

You have so many investment opportunities that it is easy to be overwhelmed. How do you begin to sort them out?

The charts in this section are designed to help you make sense of the multitude of investment options. The charts break each investment down into its basic features: the type of investment; how the investment is made; and the security, liquidity, and rate of return of the investment. Then the charts analyze each investment in terms of the older adult's key goals: earning enough *income* to cover post-retirement expenses, guaranteeing a ready source of *emergency* funds, and ensuring *security* against loss of savings.

SAVINGS ACCOUNTS

A savings account is a loan from a depositor to a bank, savings and loan, or credit union. In exchange for the loan, the borrower pays the depositor interest until the depositor withdraws the loan.

Savings accounts are the mother of all secure and liquid investments. However, this security and liquidity comes at a price. Savings accounts offer among the lowest rates of return of all investments.

Features of Savings Accounts

Nature of the investment	Savings accounts are fixed-income investments.
Making the investment	Investors should open savings accounts in institutions that are: 1. Insured. 2. Pay interest from day of deposit to day of withdrawal. 3. Compound interest daily. 4. Pay interest quarterly. 5. Offer the highest basic interest rate in the area.
Security	The federal government insures each depositor for up to $100,000.
Liquidity	Investors may withdraw money from their savings accounts at any time.
Rate of return	Interest rates on savings accounts reflect prevailing economic conditions. As a general rule, savings accounts have among the lowest rates of return of all fixed-income investments. The low rate of return is the price the investor pays for the security of the investment. Banks usually pay the lowest interest rates; credit unions and some savings and loans pay slightly higher rates.

Pros and Cons of Investing in Savings Accounts

	Pros	Cons
Income	Investor receives guaranteed income in the form of periodic interest payments.	Interest rate is among the lowest of all investments.

	Pros	Cons
Emergency	Funds can be withdrawn at any time.	
Security	Every account is insured by the federal government for up to $100,000.	

CERTIFICATES OF DEPOSIT

A depositor who opens a certificate of deposit agrees to lend a sum of money to a bank, savings and loan, or credit union for a period of several days, months, or years. During the term of the loan, the depositor collects interest from the borrower. At the end of the term, the depositor is free to withdraw the funds. Premature withdrawals are penalized.

CDs are as secure as savings accounts, but are slightly less liquid because the money cannot be withdrawn at the whim of the depositor. Since investors in CDs sacrifice some liquidity, they earn a slightly higher rate of interest than with savings accounts. However, the interest rate on CDs is still relatively low, and promises to stay low under the Clinton Administration. President Clinton has promised to keep short-term interest rates down. This means that money invested in CDs is unlikely to grow at a rate that keeps up with inflation.

When shopping around for a financial institution in which to open a CD, beware of advertised interest rates that are substantially higher than those at competing institutions. There is a good chance that the advertising institution has seen financial trouble.

Features of Certificates of Deposit

Nature of the investment	CDs are fixed-income investments.
Making the investment	Some institutions require a minimum amount to open a CD. CDs should be opened at institutions that pay compound interest and offer competitive rates. Rates of return vary widely among institutions. Brokered CDs from major brokerage firms, such as Dean Witter Reynolds, Merrill Lynch, and E. F. Hutton often pay higher interest rates.
Security	CDs are insured by the federal government for up to $100,000 per bank. Investors with more than $100,000 can open more than one CD account in different banks.

Liquidity	An investor who opens a CD agrees not to withdraw the principal of the CD (the money used to open the account) for the term of the loan. Withdrawals of principal before the end of the term are penalized. Interest earned on the CD can be withdrawn at any time.
Rate of return	Interest rates vary among institutions offering CDs. However, a few general rules govern CD interest rates: 1. The longer the term of the CD, the higher the rate of return. 2. Larger CDs pay higher interest rates. 3. CDs that pay compound interest have a higher rate of return than those that pay simple interest. 4. Short-term and variable CDs are recommended if interest rates are expected to rise.

Pros and Cons of Investing in Certificates of Deposit
(with terms of one year or less)

	Pros	Cons
Income	Investor can withdraw interest at any time.	Interest rates may be only slightly higher than rates for savings accounts.
Emergency	Interest and principal are always available.	Premature withdrawals of principal are penalized.
Security	Every account is insured by the federal government for up to $100,000 per bank.	

MONEY MARKET FUNDS

In a money market fund, a number of individuals pool their money to make large investments in government securities, bank certificates of deposit, corporate bonds, and other investments. By spreading the money of the fund investors among a number of different investments, money market funds minimize the risk of loss to each individual investor. If one investment goes bad, the fund is still protected. This diversification gives money market funds an extra degree of security.

Minimum withdrawal requirements make money market funds slightly less liquid than savings accounts, but this is offset by somewhat higher interest rates. Most money market funds pay about the same rate of return as bank certificates of deposit. The primary advantage of a money market account over a certificate of deposit is that, when interest rates go up, the higher rates are more quickly reflected in the growth rate of the money market account.

Features of Money Market Funds

Nature of the investment	Money market funds invest in fixed-income assets.
Making the investment	Banks, brokers, and independent companies offer money market funds. Some institutions charge a fee for deposits and withdrawals. Some funds are part of a family of funds, which permit investors to freely transfer their money among different types of investments to take advantage of changing economic conditions.
Security	As a general matter, money market funds are safe investments. Fund managers invest the money under their control in many different types of investments to minimize the risk of loss if any one investment fails. Bank money market funds are insured by the federal government.
Liquidity	Investors can withdraw cash directly from a money market fund, but there may be a minimum withdrawal amount (usually $250 or more).
Rate of return	Interest rates among money market funds vary to some extent among the institutions that offer the funds. Usually the interest rate paid on bank money market funds is slightly lower than that paid on funds managed by brokerage houses and independent companies. The rate of return on money market funds has traditionally been about twice that of savings accounts, but this changes with the economic times.

Pros and Cons of Investing in Money Market Funds

	Pros	Cons
Income	Investor receives interest payments. Interest rates are generally somewhat higher than rates for other equally secure investments.	

	Pros	Cons
Emergency	Funds can be withdrawn at any time.	May be minimum withdrawal requirements.
Security	Accounts are generally quite secure; less secure if invested in corporate bonds.	

STOCKS

Investors who purchase a share of stock actually purchase a small part of the company that issues the stock. For example, a holder of AT&T stock owns a very small part of AT&T. In return for investing in the company, the owner of a share of stock participates in the profits of the issuing company. The value of stock rises when corporate profits are up. Some stock-issuing companies distribute profits among their stockholders by paying dividends.

Experts predict that stocks will become an increasingly attractive investment during the Clinton Administration. President Clinton has indicated that he favors keeping the capital gains tax rate at 28 percent, while letting the top income tax rate go as high as 39 percent. Stocks that increase in value over time generate capital gains.

If you are thinking of entering the stock market, here are some tips for you:

➤ **TIP #1** *Research a stock's price/earnings ratio before you buy.*

The price/earnings ratio tells you whether the value of the stock justifies its cost. The price/earnings ratio is published in the *Value Line Investment Survey*, published once a week and available in most public libraries. If you would like to order the survey, the cost for a 10-week trial subscription is $55. An annual subscription costs $525. To subscribe, contact:

> **Value Line**
> 711 Third Avenue
> New York, NY 10017
> (800) 833-0046

To decide whether a stock's price/earnings ratio is favorable, use the following formula:

1. Write down the stock's high price/earnings ratios for each of the past 5 years. Add them together and divide by 5.

2. Write down the stock's low price/earnings ratios for each of the past 5 years. Add them together and divide by 5.

3. Add the totals from #1 and #2 together, and divide by 2. This number is the stock's average price/earnings ratio for the last 5 years.

4. Look up the stock's current price/earnings ratio in *Value Line*. Compare this number to the average price/earnings ratio from #3. Do not buy the stock if its current price/earnings ratio is higher than its average ratio.

➤ **TIP #2** *Buy stocks with a projected steady and predictable growth rate.*

Once again, you can refer to the *Value Line Investment Survey* for information about a stock's anticipated growth. The investment survey ranks over 1,700 stocks from 1 (best) through 5 (worst) in terms of projected performance over the next 12 months. Look for rankings of 1 or 2, and avoid rankings of 4 or 5.

➤ **TIP #3** *Only invest in risky stocks if you can afford to lose some or all of your investment, and the upside potential is sufficiently high to justify the risk.*

Value Line and other such reports provide the information you need to determine the upside/downside ratio for each stock. To determine the ratio of a prospective stock, use the following formula:

1. Determine the projected high price of the stock (say $50), and subtract the current price of the stock (say $20).

2. Take the current price of the stock ($20), and subtract the projected low price of the stock (say $15).

3. Divide the total from #1 ($30) by the total from #2 ($5) to determine the ratio (6 to 1 in the example).

You do not want to invest in a stock with a ratio of less than 3 to 1.

➤ **TIP #4** *Know when to sell.*

When you buy stock, you should have a strategy about when you plan to sell the stock. Set a time to reevaluate the stock, say after 5 years. If at that time the stock price is the same or less than what you paid, look at the status of the issuing company. Refer to the *Value Line Investment Survey* or similar report to find out if the company's debt accounts for more than one-third of its capitalization. If it does, sell the stock and take a loss. If after 5 years the stock is still strong, and you don't need the cash, hold on to your shares.

Features of Stocks

Nature of investment	Stocks are equity assets.
Making the investment	Most investors make stock purchases and sales through brokers, for which the brokers charge a fee. The fee for purchasing stocks from a broker is generally lower if the investor purchases shares of the stock in units of 100 or a multiple of 100 (a round lot). Investors who purchase just a few shares of the stock (an odd-lot trade) pay the highest sales commissions.
	Sales commission vary among brokerage houses. Full-service brokers charge high commissions, but they offer their customers investment advice. Discount brokers charge lower sales commissions (sometimes 50 percent less than full-service brokers), but do not offer any investment advice. Discount brokers only process purchase and sales requests. Investors must monitor the market themselves and rely on their own judgment.
Security	All stocks do not offer the same degree of security. Preferred stocks are favored by more conservative investors. Common stocks are favored by more aggressive investors. Holders of a company's preferred stocks are paid a fixed dividend before holders of the company's common stocks are paid anything. However, even preferred stock holders are not guaranteed a fixed return on their investment if the issuing company's profits are down. If the issuing company prospers, preferred stocks do not increase in value as fast as common stocks.
Liquidity	Stocks can usually be easily sold through brokers. Investors sell their shares of stock by turning over their stock certificates. Many investors ask their brokers to hold the stock certificates; other investors store the stock certificates in safe deposit boxes. Stock certificates must be safeguarded because they can be easily turned into cash.
	Investors who must immediately convert their stocks into cash risk losing money. The value of stocks goes up and down, depending on the performance of the issuing company and market conditions. Investors who have the most success in the stock market hold their shares

for long periods of time and can afford to wait until the ideal time to sell.

Rate of return   Rates of return on stock investments are influenced by a number of factors: the quality of the particular stock, the timing of the investor's purchase and sale of the stock, and the current economic climate.

Unlike many other investments, stocks do not earn interest. Rather, the rate of return on stocks varies according to the earnings of the issuing corporation. When the issuing corporation's profits are high, the stockholders may be paid a share of these profits in the form of a dividend. The higher the corporate profits, in general, the higher the stockholder's dividend.

Historically, dividends have provided investors with some of the best protection against inflation. Corporate profits and dividends often increase in inflationary times.

Pros and Cons of Investing in Stocks
(high-grade preferred stocks)

	Pros	Cons
Income	Investors receive dividends, which have historically provided some of the best inflation protection.	Dividends are not guaranteed. They depend on the profits of the issuing company.
Emergency	Shares can usually be sold anytime on the open market.	Value of stock may drop depending on the market generally, and on the financial health of the issuing company.
Security	Preferred stock dividends are paid before common stock dividends, so they offer a greater degree of security.	Preferred dividends will not be paid if the issuing company is failing.

BONDS

An investor who purchases a bond lends money to the issuer of the bond, which may be a corporation, a municipality, or the federal government. In return for the loan, the bond issuer agrees to pay the investor a fixed rate of interest for the term of the loan and repay the investor at a specified time in the future (called the maturity date). The investor selects the term of the bond.

As a general matter, bonds offer a stable source of income. The problem with bonds, however, is that the income they generate does not increase with inflation.

Features of Bonds

Nature of the investment	Bonds are fixed-income investments.
Making the investment	All bonds can be purchased through brokers. In addition, information about purchasing Treasury bonds from the federal government is available from Treasury Direct at the local branch of the Federal Reserve Bank.
	Bond prices can be confusing because they are quoted in percentages, not dollar amounts. However, it is easy to translate bond prices into dollar amounts. Simply multiply the quoted price by 10. A bond price of 94½ or 94.5 is a dollar price of $945. A bond price of 110 is a dollar price of $1,100.
Security	Bonds are considered a safe investment. Bondholders are guaranteed a fixed return on their investment over the life of the bond. The only threat to the security of the bond is the financial health of the bond issuer. Bonds issued by the federal government, such as U.S. Treasury bonds and U.S. savings bonds, offer the most security. Municipal bonds are somewhat less secure because municipalities have been known to postpone or cancel payments. Some municipalities are more financially secure than others. Municipalities are rated by two bond-rating services: Moody's Investors Service and Standard and Poor's Corporation. (Bond ratings can be found in most public libraries.) The rating for the safest municipal bonds is Aaa (Moody's) or AAA (Standard and Poor's). Municipal bonds that are privately insured are the most secure. The rate of return of insured municipal bonds is slightly lower than that for uninsured municipal bonds.
	Corporate bonds, like municipal bonds, have varying degrees of security. They are also rated for security by Moody's and Standard and Poor's. Low-risk corporate and municipal bonds are commonly called Triple-A bonds.

Liquidity	Investors can usually cash out their bonds before maturity, but sometimes at a cost. As interest rates rise, bond prices decline. (Conversely, bond prices rise when interest rates fall.) Bonds also drop in value during inflationary times, and when the bond issuer is in financial trouble. Bondholders who are forced to sell when bond prices are down lose money on their investment.
Rate of return	The rate of return depends on the security of the bond. Bonds issued or insured by the federal government are extremely secure, so they yield a relatively low rate of return. Among corporate bonds, those issued by financially strong companies pay a lower return than so-called junk bonds, which are issued by less stable corporations.

Pros and Cons of Investing in Bonds
(high-grade corporate bonds issued by utilities,
oil companies, and stable corporations)

	Pros	Cons
Income	Investors receive a fixed rate of interest. Rates for corporate bonds are generally higher than those for government bonds.	
Emergency	Bonds can usually be sold at any time.	Bonds might be sold at a loss if interest rates have increased since date of purchase, or if issuing entity is in financial trouble.
Security	Bonds issued by financially sound companies and government agencies are secure.	

ZERO COUPON BONDS

Investors purchase zero coupon bonds for a fraction of what the bonds are worth when they mature (the face value of the bond). The term of a zero coupon bond is usually between 5 and 30 years. When the bond matures, the issuer pays the bondholder the face value of the bond, plus all the interest earned over the term of the bond. Although the bondholder does not collect payments of interest during the life of the bond, the bondholder is taxed as if interest payments were made.

Zero coupon bonds are not highly liquid. The sale of a zero coupon bond before maturity often means a loss of part of the investments. Holders of zero coupons should hold on to their bonds until the bonds mature.

Features of Zero Coupon Bonds

Nature of investment	Zero coupon bonds are fixed-income investments.
Making the investment	Zero coupon bonds are issued by the U.S. Treasury, federal agencies, municipalities, and corporations. They can be purchased directly from the bond issuer or through a broker. Many brokerage firms offer packages of zero coupon bonds in investment trusts.
	The two most important considerations in shopping for a broker are fees and minimum investments. Most brokers charge a commission for purchasing and selling bonds. The amount of the commission varies from broker to broker. Some brokers refuse to sell small amounts of bonds and may require investors to purchase a minimum number of bonds. This can pose a problem to small investors.
Security	Zero coupon bonds are generally quite secure. Many are backed by the federal government, mortgages, or municipal bonds. Zero coupon bonds backed by U.S. Treasury securities are the most secure of all.
Liquidity	Investors should plan to hold their zero coupon bonds until maturity, if possible. The investor who sells zero coupon bonds before maturity may lose money, depending on what has happened to interest rates since the purchase date. If interest rates have risen, the investor will lose money on the sale of the bonds. If interest rates have fallen, though, the investor may gain money.
Rate of return	Zero coupon bonds have a high rate of return because interest earned on the bonds is reinvested over the life of the bond. That is, the interest is compounded.
	Assume, for example, an investor invests $10,000 in a zero coupon bond with a 20-year maturity date and a 10 percent interest rate. In 20 years, the investor's $10,000 would be worth about $70,000. The 10 percent rate of re-

turn would not vary over the life of the bond, and the interest earned on the investment would be compounded during the 20-year term.

Pros and Cons of Investing in Zero Coupon Bonds

	Pros	Cons
Income	The rate of return is high relative to other equally secure investments because the interest is compounded.	The bondholder cannot collect the interest until the bond matures, usually after 5 to 30 years.
Emergency	The bonds can almost always be sold.	Investors must usually pay a sales commission when selling their bonds. Also, bonds sold before maturity may have dropped in value if interest rates have risen during the term of the bond.
Security	The bonds are quite secure, especially when backed by the U.S. government.	

GOVERNMENT SECURITIES

U.S. Treasury bills, notes, bonds, and savings bonds are issued and insured by the U.S. government. Municipal bonds are issued by states and local government bodies.

Government securities have varying degrees of liquidity. Treasury bills (commonly called T-bills) usually mature in 3, 6, or 12 months. Treasury notes (commonly called T-notes) usually have maturities of 2 to 10 years. Treasury bonds (commonly called T-bonds) usually mature in 20 or 30 years. Although government securities can be sold before maturity, there may be some loss to the investor.

Special tax rules apply to different types of government bonds. Interest earned on U.S. government bills, notes, and bonds is free from state, but not federal, income tax. Interest earned on Series EE and HH U.S. savings bonds is not taxed (and cannot be collected) until the bonds are redeemed. Interest earned on municipal bonds is free from federal tax and state tax in the state in which the bonds are issued.

The security of an investment in government securities is reflected in relatively low interest rates. However, the favorable tax treatment of income generated by government securities makes them very attractive investments.

Municipal bonds promise to become even more attractive if tax rates go up. The yields on municipal bonds can continue to go down, and investors will still be getting a good buy on an after-tax basis. But if you are thinking of investing in municipal bonds, you will probably be better off getting into a municipal bond mutual fund (see page 328). Mutual funds have the bargaining power to get better bond prices than individual bond purchasers.

If you are considering investing in U.S. savings bonds, find out the guaranteed and current rates of interest. You can get this information by calling the U.S. Treasury savings bond information office at 304-480-6112 or the Federal Reserve Bank's savings bond information line (202-447-1775).

Once you have the savings bond rate information, compare the bond rates with the rates of other equally secure investments, such as bank savings accounts, certificates of deposit, and money market accounts. As long as you are not looking for growth investments, you may find savings bonds to be an attractive and secure investment.

If you already have savings bonds, here are some tips for you:

➤ **TIP #1** *Make sure you do not redeem your bonds just before they increase in value.*

Find out when your bonds will increase in value. (The date you purchased the bonds will determine the date of increase.) Bad timing in redeeming your bonds can cost you several months of interest.

➤ **TIP # 2** *If you have Series EE savings bonds, consider holding on to them even after they reach face value.*

Series EE bonds bought between November 1993 and April 1994 will reach face value in 18 years, but will continue earning interest for 30 years after the date of purchase. To update this information, call the savings bond information office at 202-447-1775. By holding on to your EE bonds past maturity, you will earn two to four times the face value of the bond while your investment continues growing tax-free.

➤ **TIP #3** *Get rid of E bonds that were purchased before May 1953.*

All E bonds purchased before May 1953 are no longer earning interest. Bonds that are less than 41 years old can be traded in for interest-earning HH bonds.

Before you invest in municipal bonds, there are also some things you should know. Investors view "munis" as an almost risk-free way of earning interest that is free from federal, and sometimes local, taxes. But in fact, municipal bonds are not risk-free.

Some municipal bonds are plagued by hidden risks. Concern about the unknowing purchase of high-risk municipal bonds by small investors has motivated federal regulators to consider tightening the regulation of municipal bond sales. Unless and until new regulations are implemented, protect yourself by following these guidelines:

1. Never buy unrated bonds. (Independent bond rating firms issue frequently updated reports that are available in most public libraries.)

2. To keep your risk to an absolute minimum, never buy a bond that has less than an AAA rating.

3. If you are willing to take some risk, do not buy any bonds that are not rated at least investment grade.

4. General obligation bonds are the most secure because they are backed by the taxing authority of the issuer. That means that even if the issuing state or municipality has to raise taxes to pay you, you will get paid.

5. Avoid revenue bonds that depend on an uncertain future source of revenue (such as a bridge that is not yet built or a housing complex that is not yet constructed).

6. Do not buy bonds that are described as inverse floaters and conduit bonds. These are especially risky.

7. Only purchase traditional municipal bonds that mature at a certain date in the future and pay a set rate of interest at regular intervals.

8. Beware of bonds that pay an unusually high rate of interest. They probably entail a high degree of risk.

For more information about government securities, write:

Consumer Information Center
P.O. Box 100
Pueblo, CO 81002

Request the free publication "Information About Marketable Treasury Securities" and send 50 cents for "The Savings Bonds Question and Answer Book."

Features of U.S. Treasury Bills, Notes, and Bonds

Nature of investment	Government bills, notes, and bonds are fixed-income investments.

Making the investment	The purchase of U.S. government securities can be made through banks, brokers, and the U.S. Treasury in Washington, D.C. Banks and brokers charge investors a small sales commission for each order. Investors can save the sales commission by purchasing government securities for no charge from a local branch of the Federal Reserve Bank or the U.S. Treasury in Washington, D.C. Mail order purchases are available. Contact your local branch of the Federal Reserve Bank for more information on purchasing Treasury securities.
Security	The federal government backs all of its securities. They are therefore extremely secure investments. Municipal bonds are only marginally less secure.
Liquidity	Government securities may be sold at any time without penalty. However, investors who need to sell their securities before maturity risk losing money if interest rates have climbed since the date of purchase. If interest rates have fallen, the investors will make a profit.
Rate of return	Government securities offer interest rates that are competitive with other very secure investments. Treasury securities are less attractive investments during inflationary times because they pay a fixed income that does not rise with inflation. Interest paid on government securities is free from state and local taxes, but not federal taxes.

Pros and Cons of Investing in Government Securities
(U.S. T-Bills, T-Notes, and T-Bonds)

	Pros	Cons
Income	Investors receive fixed semiannual interest payments, free of state and local tax.	Payments do not increase with inflation.
Emergency	Bonds can be sold anytime without penalty.	Investors may lose money if interest rates have risen since date of purchase.
Security	Bonds offer maximum security, since they are backed by the full faith and credit of the U.S. government.	

(Series EE U.S. Government Savings Bonds)

	Pros	Cons
Income	Investment grows tax-free.	Interest is not available until bonds are redeemed.
Emergency	Bonds can be sold anytime without penalty.	Investors may lose money if interest rates have risen since date of purchase.
Security	Bonds offer maximum security, since they are backed by the full faith and credit of the U.S. government.	

(Municipal bonds)

	Pros	Cons
Income	Fixed interest payments are free of federal tax and state tax in issuing state.	Bonds offer no inflation protection.
Emergency	Bonds can be sold anytime without penalty.	Investors may lose money if interest rates have risen since date of purchase.
Security	Bonds may be backed by highly rated municipalities or privately insured.	Bonds can be backed by low-rated municipalities or uninsured.

GINNIE MAES

Ginnie Maes are packages of home mortgages that are guaranteed by the federal government. The name Ginnie Mae comes from the initials of the Government National Mortgage Association, the federal agency that underwrites the mortgages.

Ginnie Maes offer investors a secure source of income in the form of monthly interest and principal payments. Their degree of security rivals that of other types of government securities (see page 324).

As with bonds, the value of Ginnie Mae shares drop if interest rates rise sharply. The value of Ginnie Mae shares may also drop if mortgage rates go down significantly. A drop in mortgage rates motivates homeowners to refinance their mortgages. When large numbers of homeowners refinance, some of the higher-rate mortgages in Ginnie Mae funds are replaced with lower-rate mortgages.

Ginnie Mae investors are compensated for taking this additional risk with about a 1 percentage point higher interest rate than regular government bond funds.

Features of Ginnie Maes

Nature of the investment	Ginnie Maes are fixed-income investments.
Making the investment	Investors can purchase Ginnie Maes from brokers and banks. Small investors who cannot afford the minimum investment required by some banks and brokers should purchase Ginnie Maes from brokerage houses that offer packages of Ginnie Maes in mutual funds.
Security	Since these investments are backed by the federal government, they are almost risk-free. However, the value of Ginnie Mae shares generally drops when interest rates rise, or when rates drop so substantially that many homeowners refinance their mortgages.
Liquidity	Investors who must sell Ginnie Maes in a rush risk losing money, depending on what has happened to interest rates since the investments were made. If interest rates have increased, the price of the Ginnie Maes will be down and the investor will lose money. If general interest rates are down, the price of the Ginnie Maes will be up (unless the rates have dropped so substantially that homeowners refinance their mortgages in large numbers). As a general rule, Ginnie Mae investors should plan to hold their shares for at least 3 to 5 years to maximize the benefits of this investment.
Rate of return	A characteristic of Ginnie Maes is that almost every month some percentage of the principal is returned to the investor. The amount of principal returned is related to current mortgage rates. That is, when rates are high, payments of principal are small; when rates are low, principal payments are larger. Ginnie Maes have traditionally paid about 1 percentage point more than government bond funds. The exact rate of interest depends on the current mortgage rates.

Pros and Cons of Investing in Ginnie Maes

	Pros	Cons
Income	Investors receive monthly payments of interest and some principal.	
Emergency	Shares can be sold at any time, but it is best to hold them at least 3 to 5 years.	Sale before maturity can result in loss if interest rates have risen since purchase.
Security	Investment is secure, backed by the full faith and credit of the U.S. government.	

ANNUITIES

An investor who purchases an annuity lends money to an insurance company. During the term of the annuity, the insurance company makes periodic payments to the investor. The payments represent a return of the investor's initial investment, plus interest. The part of the income that represents a return of principal is not taxable.

Two significant drawbacks to an annuity are loss of liquidity and no inflation protection. The loss of liquidity can be a problem if you need to make a sudden withdrawal of principal. The absence of inflation protection is a natural consequence of the flat income stream. Annuity income payments often fall increasingly short of expenses as inflation drives up the cost of living. Annuity holders also typically pay high management costs, sales charges, and administrative fees.

Tax-deferred variable annuities are covered in detail in Chapter 13. Keep the following points in mind if you go shopping for an annuity:

➤ TIP #1 *Compare the relative performances of a number of companies that offer annuities; the rates of return realized by different companies vary widely.*

➤ TIP #2 *Watch out for companies that have high sales costs, management fees, withdrawal penalties, and miscellanous charges.*

➤ TIP #3 *Be on the lookout for annuity sellers who neglect to advise you that the annuity you are considering has two rates of return: a higher rate that is guaranteed for only 1 or 2 years, and a much lower rate of return thereafter.*

➤ **TIP 4** *Try to find an annuity prospectus with an out clause that will let you transfer your money without penalty if you are not satisfied with the annuity's performance.*

➤ **TIP #5** *Do not buy an annuity from a company that has less than an A rating from* **Best's Insurance Reports.**

A higher rating is even better. Best rates insurance companies according to their financial strength. You can find a copy of Best's latest report in your local library.

➤ **TIP #6** *Variable annuities are monitored and ranked by Lipper Advisory Services.*

Ask your insurance agent how the company's annuities rated in Lipper's latest survey and request a copy of it.

For more information on annuities, write to:

> **Consumer Information Center**
> P.O. Box 100
> Pueblo, CO 81002
>
> Request the free publication "Building Your Future With Annuities: A Consumer's Guide."

Features of Annuities

Nature of the investment	Annuities are fixed-income assets.
Making the investment	An investor opens an annuity by depositing a sum of money with the insurance company and signing a contract with the insurer. When shopping for an annuity, investors should only consider insurance companies that:
	1. Have been in business for at least 100 years.
	2. Have over $2 billion in assets.
	3. Have a segregated trust account for their variable annuities with a major commercial bank.
	4. Charge little or no commission for the purchase of an annuity.
	5. Charge the lowest fee or penalty for cashing out the annuity before the end of its term or for switching investments.

6. Offer the best interest rates. Beware of companies that offer a high rate at the beginning of the term to attract investors, and then drop their rate substantially.

7. Have at least an A rating from A. M. Best Company for at least 10 years. A. M. Best Company, located in Oldwick, New Jersey, rates insurance companies for their financial security. The ratings are published in *Best's Insurance Reports,* which can be found at most public libraries.

8. Do not charge surrender penalties higher than 7 percent or for more than 7 years.

9. Charge annual fees closer to 1 percent than to 4 percent.

Security

Annuities are as secure as the insurance company that issues them. Annuities purchased from a financially sound insurance company have security comparable to money market funds and certificates of deposit. Consult *Best's Insurance Reports* for insurance company ratings.

Liquidity

Investors who need to make a lump-sum withdrawal from an annuity may have to pay the insurance company a surrender charge or penalty that typically starts at 7 percent and is reduced each year until it terminates in 7 to 10 years. Also, with certain annuities, if the money is withdrawn before the investor is age $59\frac{1}{2}$, the investor may have to pay a withdrawal penalty.

Rate of return

The rate of return on an annuity depends on the nature of the annuity. Some annuities are invested more aggressively than others. Annuities that are put into high-return investments, such as stocks, precious metals, or real estate, pay a higher rate of return and carry an increased risk of loss over annuities that are invested in certificates of deposit or Treasury bills. Beware of companies that offer exceptionally high rates; they are often financially unstable.

Interest earned on some annuities is not taxed until it is withdrawn. When the annuity holder starts receiving regular payments from the insurance company, only the interest portion of each payment is taxed. The rest of the payment is a return of the investor's initial investment, and is not taxed.

Pros and Cons of Investing in Annuities
(immediate fixed commercial annuities)

	Pros	Cons
Income	Investor receives periodic payments of interest and some principal.	Interest does not increase with inflation. Annuities sold by financially strapped companies offer highest rates of return.
Emergency		Withdrawals during term of annuity are heavily penalized.
Security	Annuities are secure if sold by a financially sound company and invested wisely.	Annuities are risky if sold by a financially unstable insurer and invested aggressively.

MUTUAL FUNDS

In a mutual fund, a number of individual investors pool their money to make large investments in stocks and bonds. Mutual fund investors can elect to receive periodic payments of income in the form of cash dividends or can reinvest their dividends.

Mutual funds that invest in short-term bonds are especially attractive to mature investors. Short-term bonds have a term of 1 to 3 years. Investors who are willing to tie up their money for this period of time earn about 1 to 1½ percent more than if they invested in a money market fund (see page 310). Although there is some risk that the value of the fund will drop if interest rates go up, investors in a short-term bond fund can quickly move their money out of low-interest bonds and into higher-interest bonds.

Some mutual funds invest in tax-free securities. Investors with taxable income between $36,900 and $89,150 (the 28 percent tax bracket, if married and filing jointly) or $22,100 and $53,500 (if single), should probably put at least some of their money in a tax-free fund. The rate of return of a tax-free fund may appear low compared to alternative investments, but may yield more money after taking into account the bite of federal, state, and local taxes.

As already mentioned, municipal bond mutual funds are especially attractive in light of the higher taxes promised by the Clinton Administration (see page 312). Some investment advisers recommend investing half your money in a single state municipal bond fund, and half in a national municipal fund. The state fund will be slightly riskier, but the income you earn will be exempt from federal, state, and local taxes. The national fund will be safer, but the income will be exempt only from federal taxes.

If you invest in a mutual fund, remember: The fund belongs to you. If you are not pleased with the investment decisions the manager of your fund is making, don't stew in silence:

- Call the fund's service number and ask to speak with the fund's manager. If the manager comes to the phone, state your complaint.

- If the manager does not come to the phone, or you are dissatisfied with the response you receive, ask to be connected with the chairman of the board. If you are nervous about asking to speak to the head honcho, just think about who pays the head honcho's salary. You do.

- If you remain dissatisfied, there is only one thing left to do. Pack up your toys and go home. In other words, sell your shares and exit the fund.

For more information about mutual funds, request a free copy of the 52-page booklet "Understanding Mutual Funds: A Guide for Investors Aged 50 and Over" from AARP by calling 800-424-2430, ext. 4729.

Features of Mutual Funds

Nature of the investment	Mutual funds pool investors' money in fixed income and equity assets.
Making the investment	Investors purchase shares in a mutual fund through a broker. Most brokers require a minimum initial fund investment. After the initial investment, smaller investments are generally accepted.
	Investors who do not have a lot of money to invest should look for brokers that require small minimum initial investments. Interested investors should carefully read the fund's prospectus, review the fund's performance history, become familiar with market trends, and study the nature of the fund's investments before making a commitment to a particular fund. Lipper's Analytical Services publishes a quarterly survey of mutual fund performances called the *Lipper Gauge*. This survey should be available in most public libraries. *Money* magazine also publishes surveys of mutual funds' performance.

When selecting a broker and a fund, inquire about fees. Funds that charge a sales commission are called load funds. Funds that do not charge a sales commission are called no-load funds. Most no-load funds perform about as well as load funds. Only a few exceptional load funds are worth the additional expense. In addition to sales commissions, management fees vary among companies.

Security

Within each fund, money managers seek to maximize the fund's security by investing in a number of different securities. The fund's money is spread among many different investments to reduce the damage done by the failure of any single investment. This strategy is called diversification.

There are basically three categories of mutual funds. The security of the fund varies according to the category.

1. Stock funds invest in stocks. Their security depends on the type of stocks the fund chooses for its investments.
   - Aggressive stock funds invest in fairly risky stocks that are predicted to increase greatly in value.
   - Growth stock funds invest in more conservative stocks that are also expected to grow significantly.
   - Growth and income stock funds invest in stocks that pay high dividends with the expectation of increasing in value.
2. Bond funds invest in one type of bond or in a variety of different bonds (high-grade corporate bonds, junk bonds, zero coupon bonds, government bonds). As with stock funds, the security of the bond funds depends on the security of the underlying bonds. Bonds issued by the government are more secure than low-grade corporate bonds. Unit investment trusts are bond funds that invest in a range of securities that all mature around the same date. The value of the fund fluctuates according to interest rates.
3. Stock and bond funds invest in a combination of stocks and bonds that promise a high income and some increase in value.

Liquidity | Investors can easily sell their shares in a mutual fund through their broker or by calling the fund directly. The value of each mutual fund is quoted in the financial section of many newspapers.

Rate of return | The rate of return depends on the riskiness of the investments and the skill of the fund managers. For example, among corporate bond funds, the funds that invest in financially unstable corporations that offer so-called junk bonds generally pay a higher rate of return than funds that invest in well-established corporations. Likewise, among stock mutual funds, aggressive funds usually pay higher returns than growth funds.

Pros and Cons of Investing in Mutual Funds

	Pros	Cons
Income	Mutual funds are a good source of income.	Depending on the nature of the fund's investments, income may not keep pace with inflation.
Emergency	Shares can be sold anytime without penalty.	With a bond fund, value may drop if interest rates have risen since date of purchase. With a stock fund, value may drop with the performance of the issuing entity.
Security	Mutual funds are low risk, if invested in highly rated government bonds or corporate stock.	Risk of loss can be substantial if fund invests in junk bonds or low-grade stocks.

Selecting a mutual fund from the more than 4,200 stock and bond funds on the market today can be extremely confusing. In an attempt to help investors, newspapers, magazines, and private financial services rate mutual funds on various criteria, including performance, cost, risk, and future potential. Unfortunately, there is no uniformity among the many rating services. This makes comparison difficult, if not impossible. Your best bet is to rely on the three most trusted rating services:

Lipper Analytical Services Corporation of New York City; Morningstar, Inc., of Chicago; and CDA Investment Technologies, Inc., of Rockville, Maryland.

FINANCIAL PLANNERS AND MONEY MANAGERS

Before you can embark on your new life as a retiree with a clear mind and a serene heart, you need to resolve one very important question: Is your nest egg invested as wisely as possible?

To find the answer, you may want to seek out the services of a money professional, such as a financial planner or money manager.

FINANCIAL PLANNERS

Some of the reasons people consult financial planners are:

- They want a second opinion on their planned investment strategy.
- They have some discretionary funds to invest, but have neither the time nor the interest to research investment opportunities.
- They want to know whether their existing investments still make sense in light of market conditions and their current life situation.
- They need assistance managing their debt.
- They want advice about lowering their tax bill.
- They are considering buying or selling life insurance.
- They operate a business or are thinking of starting one.
- They need to plan for the future needs of a disabled child.
- They have questions about investing their retirement savings.

Qualified financial planners have an expertise in investments, taxes, retirement plans, and insurance. They generally perform the following services:

- Review the client's financial status, including the client's income, expenses, savings, debt, family situation, and attitude toward investing and money management.
- Identify any problems with the client's financial picture.
- Suggest ways to address identified problems.
- Make referrals to other professionals, such as accountants and lawyers, when necessary.

If you are considering consulting a financial planner, you are probably interested in knowing what a consultation with a financial planner will cost.

Financial planners are usually compensated through fees, commissions, or a combination of fees and commissions.

• Fee arrangement. The financial planner charges you an hourly rate or a flat fee to review your financial status, discuss your future needs, and develop a financial plan. Clients of fee-only financial planners are usually well-to-do.
• Commissions. The financial planner meets and consults with you for no charge. If you agree to invest in insurance, annuities, mutual funds, or any number of other investments, the financial planner earns a commission. Clients of commission-only financial planners have discretionary funds to invest, but are not usually high rollers.
• Fees and commissions. The financial planner charges a fee for the consultation, but the fee is reduced by any commissions the planner earns for selling you investment products.

SAFEGUARDS WHEN CHOOSING A FINANCIAL PLANNER

Before you get started with a financial planner, request a written estimate of the planner's fee and the services that are included in the fee. If you are signing up with a fee-only planner, make sure you know what additional expenses you can expect: Will you be charged if you call with a 5-minute follow-up question? How much will you be charged for an update of your financial plan? If you will be paying an hourly rate instead of a flat fee, ask for an estimate of what you can expect as a final bill.

Take the recommendations of commission-only planners with a grain of salt. Remember, these planners get paid only when they succeed in selling you the investment products they represent. Only an extraordinarily honest financial planner would suggest you go elsewhere to purchase the investment product you really need, or recommend you to a product that pays a smaller commission than an alternative investment. To be safe, limit your dealings with commission-only planners to those who come highly recommended by friends and family.

When you are ready to select a financial planner, use this guide:

STEP-BY-STEP GUIDE TO SELECTING
A FINANCIAL PLANNER

You can get the names of financial planners from:

Institute of Certified Financial Planners
3443 South Galena, Suite 190
Denver, CO 80231
800-282-7526

(Within 7 to 10 days, you will receive in the mail a list of certified financial planners who practice in your area.)

You may also find names through:

- Personal recommendations.
- Community organizations (such as a senior center).

Check the planner's qualifications. Many financial planners have a string of letters following their name. Joe Accountant, CFP, ChFC, CPA. In most cases, these letters indicate that the planner participated in some training program and possibly passed an examination.

The titles tell you very little about the planner's level of competence. In fact, when it comes to evaluating a planner's qualifications, the consumer has very little to go on.

That said, here are what the letters mean:

CFP	Certified financial planner
CPA	Certified public accountant
ChFC	Chartered financial consultant
CLU	Chartered life underwriter
CFA	Chartered financial analyst
RIA	Registered investment adviser

The field of financial planning is virtually unregulated. Up to half of the nation's 200,000 planners have no credentials at all, regardless of the letters that follow their name.

- Is the financial planner registered with the federal Securities and Exchange Commission (SEC)? The SEC requires planners who provide investment advice to register as registered investment advisers, and disclose their background and fees. If a planner is not registered, find out why not.

- Check the planner's criminal and disciplinary history with the SEC and the state securities agency.

• Check with the Better Business Bureau to see if any grievances have been filed against the financial planner you plan to use.

• Find out if financial planning is the individual's full-time occupation. You only want to employ an individual who offers financial planning services as a primary career.

• Check the number of years the financial planner has been in business, and inquire about the planner's background. You do not want to hire an individual who decided to start a financial planning business only after his singing career went bust and he gambled away his trust fund.

Request a sample financial plan, and ask what investments have been recently recommended.
Look into the services each planner offers.

• Does the financial planner represent more than one or two investment products? The more products the planner sells, the more likely you are to find a product that really suits your needs.

• Make sure the financial planner plans to keep you advised about future developments that may affect your financial plan. A financial plan that helps you today may harm you tomorrow if the laws change. Your financial planner has a professional obligation to keep you apprised of relevant changes.

• Inquire whether you'll be working with more than one professional in the financial planner's office. If several individuals will be working on your plan, be sure you have the name of one contact person who will be responsible for coordinating your services.

• Ask the planner for about five client references and then call the references.

Know your rights.

• If, despite your best efforts to select a competent, ethical financial planner, you run into problems, contact one or both of the following organizations:

Office of Consumer Affairs
Securities and Exchange Commission
450 Fifth Street, N.W.
Washington, DC 20549
202-272-7440

Institute of Certified Financial Planners
3443 South Galena, Suite 190
Denver, CO 80231-5093
800-282-7526

Professional organizations that distribute lists of their members include the Institute of Certified Financial Planners (800-282-7526), American Institute of Certified Public Accountants' Personal Financial Planning Division (800-862-4272), International Association of Financial Planners (404-395-1605), National Association of Personal Financial Advisers (708-537-7722), fee only, and the LINC Society of CPA Financial Planners (615-782-4240), fee only.

One way to avoid the high fees of financial planners is to call 800 ASK-A-CPA (800-275-2271). For $3.95 a minute you can get financial advice from an accountant or certified financial planner over the telephone.

To receive the booklets entitled "Facts About Financial Planners" and "Money Matters" send 50 cents per booklet to the Consumer Information Center, P. O. Box 100, Pueblo, CO 81002.

Money Managers

Instead of giving you advice about how to invest your money, like financial planners, money managers actually invest your money for you. They create and oversee your own personal investment portfolio.

Until recently, when hiring a money manager you were well-advised to take the phrase *caveat emptor* (buyer beware) to heart. You could ask prospective money managers about their investment record, but you had no way of distinguishing fact from fiction. A money manager who boasted an impressive 25 percent average annual return for clients over the last 10 years could be spinning a yarn, and you wouldn't have a clue. The estimation of investment returns was completely unregulated.

This changed somewhat in 1993. Two professional investor associations, the Association for Investment Management and Research (AIMR) and the Investment Management Consultants Association (IMCA) issued standards governing the calculation of "average returns." Although compliance with the standards is voluntary, consumers have pressured money managers into complying. Money managers who refuse to calculate their average returns using the recommended standards are not patronized.

What happens if you entrust a money manager with your life savings and, after 5 years of following the manager's advice, you find yourself left with only half of your money? Is there anything you can do?

Probably yes. Start by consulting a securities law attorney. If you were steered into investments that were not well-suited for you, or your funds were otherwise mishandled, you may be eligible for damages in an arbitration action against the broker and the brokerage firm. If the panel of arbitrators finds fault, you will be awarded a sum of money to cover your losses. An arbitration award has the same effect as a judgment issued by a court of law.

If you are considering bringing legal action against a money manager, heed these two warnings:

1. Do not let the brokerage firm talk you into putting off legal action while the firm investigates the matter. You may lose the opportunity to recover your damages. The law limits the time within which you must make your claim.

2. Filing a claim against the firm or individual with a regulatory agency, such as the Securities and Exchange Commission or the National Association of Securities Dealers, and bringing a lawsuit are not mutually exclusive. Although the regulatory agency can discipline the investors, only a lawsuit will get you your money back.

BACK TO FRAN AND MIKE

Fran and Mike decide to move just over half of their nest egg out of certificates of deposit and into a mix of growth and income investments. By making this change, their investment earnings jump from 6 percent to 10 percent. Also, because they are investing a bit more aggressively, their income stands a better chance of keeping up with inflation.

Although selecting new investments entailed some loss of security and liquidity, Fran and Mike decided that they had to take some additional risk with their money if they hoped to have sufficient post-retirement income to maintain their standard of living.

12.
UNDERSTANDING TAX BENEFITS

Charlie's taxes were always very straightforward. He had no trouble preparing his own tax returns, and never sought the advice of a tax expert.

But 1994 was different. In that year Charlie had a heart attack, and his medical expenses skyrocketed. He also sold his home and moved into an apartment. Finally, in 1994 Charlie gave his daughter $20,000 to celebrate her college graduation.

Charlie wanted to know: Could he deduct any of his medical expenses? Was there any way he could minimize the capital gains tax that was due on the profit he realized on the sale of his home? What tax, if any, was due on the gift he made to his daughter?

Nobody likes to talk about taxes, with the possible exception of a very committed accountant (or, rather, an accountant who should be committed). Taxes are generally unpleasant business. But this chapter is about tax *benefits*. These are tax breaks offered to you by your government. If you can overcome your tax phobia, read on. You might save yourself some money.

This chapter will make learning about taxes fun—or at least somewhat less painful than root canal. Each section of the chapter is devoted to one of four categories of tax benefits that are of special interest to older Americans: income tax benefits, tax benefits on the purchase and sale of property, property tax benefits, and gift and estate tax benefits. For each type of tax benefit you will find background information, definitions of relevant terms, and, perhaps most important, tips for maximizing your tax savings.

The chapter concludes with suggestions for getting help preparing your tax return.

The Internal Revenue Service has prepared a seniors tax package. The package includes Form 1040A, which has lines for distributions from IRAs, pensions, and annuities, Social Security benefits, and estimated tax payments. It also includes Schedule 1, for reporting over $400 of interest or dividend income, and Schedule 3, for computing the credit for the elderly or disabled. To request the senior tax package, call the IRS at 800-TAX-FORM (829-3676) and also ask for Publication Number 1615. Large print versions of the package are available.

INCOME TAX BENEFITS

Perhaps no date evokes stronger negative feelings than April 15. The very thought of the IRS, income taxes, and Form 1040 sends shivers down the spine of even the heartiest of Americans.

About 1.5 million lucky countrymen and women do not have to file a tax return or pay income taxes. And about 660,000 of them are age 65 or older. Are you one of them?

To find out if you have to deal with the tax man (or woman) this year, follow these steps:

1. Add up your total gross income (including wages, salaries, taxable interest, dividends, capital gains, pensions, and annuities).

2. Compare your total income to the amounts on the list below:

Single and under age 65	$6,050
Single and age 65 or older	$6,950
Married, filing jointly, and both under age 65	$10,900
Married, filing jointly, and one under age 65	$11,600
Married, filing jointly, and both age 65 or older	$12,300
Married, filing separately, any age	$23,050

   (These numbers apply to tax year 1993.)

3. If your total income is below the listed amounts and you are not claimed as a dependent on someone else's tax return, you probably do not have to file a tax return unless one of the following exceptions applies:

   a. You sold stocks, bonds, or your home during the tax year.

   b. You received distributions from an IRA during the tax year.

   c. You are expecting a refund of taxes withheld by your employer.

   d. You are self-employed and your net earnings exceeded $400 during the tax year (for 1993).

   e. You are applying for earned income credit (EIC).

You are eligible for the EIC if your earnings were low enough (less than $23,050 for 1993, not counting Social Security and tax-exempt income), and a child or grandchild (under age 19, or a full-time student under age 24, or disabled) lived with you for more than 6 months out of the year. The amount of the credit can be as high as $1,434 for one child; $1,511 for two or more children. The credit reduces any tax you owe, or is sent to you in a check if you don't owe taxes. The schedule for computing the credit appears in your tax return. If you want the IRS to compute your EIC for you, enter "EIC" on the dotted line next to line 28c of your Form 1040A tax return or line 56 of Form 1040, attach Schedule EIC with page 1 completed, and send it in.

If the bad news is that you have to file a return and pay taxes, the good news might be that you qualify for some tax benefits that will ease your pain.

At a minimum, you will be entitled to a personal exemption and a standard deduction. As an older American, you will also probably be entitled to some additional tax credits, exemptions, and deductions that will reduce or eliminate your income tax debt.

INCOME TAX TERMS DEFINED AND ILLUSTRATED

• Adjusted gross income (AGI) is your total taxable income reduced by your business-related expenses, qualified contributions to retirement plans, alimony, and certain additional deductions.

• A deduction reduces the amount of income on which your tax is based.

For example, Jack has $10,000 of income. He is entitled to a $3,000 standard deduction. Jack pays taxes on $7,000 of income.

• Exempt income is income that is not taxed.

For example, Mary has $10,000 of income, of which $2,000 is interest on a tax-exempt retirement plan. Mary only pays taxes on $8,000 of income.

• A credit reduces the amount of tax the taxpayer would otherwise owe. A credit is more valuable than a deduction because a credit reduces, dollar for dollar, the tax you would otherwise have to pay.

For example, Sam owes the government $3,000 in taxes. But because Sam is entitled to a $1,000 credit, he only has to pay $2,000.

An example will pull all these terms together: Jacob has $20,000 gross income (not including exempt income). He has $10,000 in deductions, and a $2,000 credit. His taxable income is $10,000 ($20,000 gross income minus the $10,000 in deductions). He is taxed at a rate of 30 percent. The tax on his taxable income is $3,000 (30 percent of $10,000). When he subtracts the $2,000 tax credit from $3,000, his tax liability is reduced to $1,000.

EXTRA STANDARD DEDUCTION

You would think that taxable income is the income on which you have to pay tax, but that would be too simple. Every taxpayer's taxable income is reduced by the greater of the standard deductions or the taxpayer's itemized deductions. (Itemized deductions include such tax-deductible expenses as charitable contributions, union dues, work equipment, and some medical expenses, and are listed on Schedule A of Form 1040.)

Your taxable income may be reduced even further if you are age 65 or older at the end of the tax year, or blind. Elderly and blind taxpayers who check line 33(a) on their IRS Form 1040 tax return, and do not itemize their deductions, get an even larger standard deduction allowance than the run-of-the-mill taxpayer. The extra large standard deduction reduces taxable income even further, which in turn reduces tax liability. If you were 65 or older in 1993 and single, you got an additional $900 deduction allowance; $700 if married.

For more on the standard deduction, call the IRS at 800-TAX-FORM (829-3676) and request Publication Number 501, "Exemptions, Standard Deduction, and Filing Information."

MEDICAL EXPENSE DEDUCTION

This section of the chapter is dedicated to taxpayers with high medical and dental bills. If your medical costs are high, you may be able to turn your medical expenses into a tax benefit, in much the same way you would make lemonade out of lemons.

Depending on how much money you spend on medical care for yourself, your spouse, and your dependents, you may be able to reduce your taxable income with a medical expense deduction. (Dependency is defined on page 345. The same definition applies for purposes of the medical expense deduction, except the dependent's income is irrelevant.)

You are only entitled to a medical expense deduction if you spend more than 7.5 percent of your adjusted gross income on medical care. To determine whether a medical bill counts toward your medical expense deduction, ask yourself these questions:

- Does the good or service in question have a medical purpose?
- Would my doctor substantiate my medical need for the good or service in question?

If the answer to both questions is yes, you are virtually home free. Here is a partial list of medical expenses that are deductible (to the extent that they are not reimbursed by insurance):

- Fees of health care providers, including:

  Chiropractors.

  Dentists.

  Opticians.

  Optometrists.

  Licensed osteopaths.

  Physicians.

  Physiotherapists.

  Podiatrists.

  Nurses.

  Psychiatrists.

  Psychologists.

- Cost of equipment and supplies, including:

  Air conditioner where necessary to aid breathing.

  Contact lenses.

  Elastic hosiery.

  Eyeglasses.

  Health aids.

  Hearing devices.

  Orthopedic shoes (cost over regular shoes).

  Reclining chair prescribed by doctor.

  Special mattress for relief of arthritis.

  Wheelchair.

  Wig advised by doctor to enhance patient's mental well-being.

- Cost of dental services, including cleaning, extracting, filling, and straightening teeth.

- Cost of medical procedures, including:

  Hearing services.

  Navajo healing ceremonies ("sings").

  X-rays.

- Cost of prescription drugs (not over-the-counter medicines).

- Cost of laboratory examinations and tests.

- Cost of hospital services.

- Cost of traveling to and from a doctor's office.
- Cost of making structural changes to a residence, such as adding ramps and widening doorways to accommodate a wheelchair.
- Some costs of nursing home care, as explained more thoroughly below.

Unfortunately, if you were hoping to deduct the cost of the dance lessons that relieve your varicose veins, or the divorce that improved your mental health, you're out of luck. The IRS has ruled that these expenses do not qualify for the medical expense deduction.

To claim a medical expense deduction, you or your accountant must complete Schedule A of IRS Form 1040.

NURSING HOME EXPENSES

Special deduction rules apply to the costs of nursing home care. The deductibility of nursing home expenses depends on the kinds of services the taxpayer receives in the nursing home.

If the taxpayer is in the nursing home primarily to receive medical care, then all nursing home expenses are deductible, including the costs of lodging and meals and medical care. But if the taxpayer is in the home primarily to receive assistance with such activities as eating, dressing, walking, and bathing, then only expenses that are directly related to the provision of medical and nursing care are deductible. Lodging and meal expenses are not deductible.

You stand the best chance of convincing the IRS that nursing home payments are fully deductible if you submit a statement from the nursing home resident's doctor stating that the resident entered the nursing facility to receive treatment of a specific medical ailment, and that the resident has derived a direct therapeutic benefit from institutionalization.

POINTS TO CONSIDER ABOUT
THE MEDICAL EXPENSE DEDUCTION

- If your child is paying your medical expenses, your child may be able to use the medical expense deduction. Many older patients do not pay their own medical bills. Children often pay the medical expenses of parents who cannot afford the high cost of their own care. A child may be able to deduct medical expenses paid on behalf of a parent if the parent is a dependent of the child. (see page 345 for the definition of a dependent, but ignore the limit on the dependent's income.)

To claim the medical expense deduction, your child must pay your health care providers directly. That is, your child cannot give you money that you then use to pay your medical bills. Your child must pay your bills using checks that are payable to the doctor, nursing home, medical supplier, or whatever.

When your child claims you as a dependent, the medical expense deduction is computed by adding your medical expenses and your child's medical expenses. If the total exceeds 7.5 percent of your child's adjusted gross income, your child will qualify for a medical expense deduction.

• You and your family as a unit may be able to save money if you give money to your child, and then your child pays your medical bills. The medical expense deduction can sometimes be used to help a family preserve its savings when one family member faces a long-term chronic illness. The idea is for you to give a sum of money to your child, with the understanding that the money will be used to pay for your medical care in the future.

However, this planning strategy has a few potential problems. First and foremost, there is the concern that the money will not be available to you when you need it. Say your child is in a car accident, is sued, and loses the lawsuit, resulting in a lien being placed on all your child's accounts (including your money). Or what if your child predeceases you and leaves everything to a spouse (including your money)? Or suppose your child goes bankrupt, or gets divorced. These events, often beyond your child's control, put your money at risk. This is not to say you shouldn't make the gift anyway—just do it with your eyes open.

There are two other potential problems with this attempt at maximizing the medical expense deduction, both of which can probably be avoided with good timing. The dangers are that the government will view your gift to your child as a fraud since you expect the "gift" to be returned to you, and that the government will not agree that you are your child's dependent since you made a substantial gift to your child. To minimize these dangers, several years should pass between the date of the gift and the time your child starts to pay your medical bills.

• You may want to file separate tax returns if you are married, and only one of you has high medical expenses. Many married couples choose to file separate returns when one partner has high medical expenses because filing separately may enable them to deduct the ill partner's medical expenses. A couple filing jointly can only take a medical expense deduction if their total medical expenses exceed 7.5 percent of their joint adjusted gross income. When one partner's medical expenses exceed 7.5 percent of his or her own income, but do not exceed 7.5 percent of the couple's joint adjusted gross income, filing separately is the only way to claim the medical expense deduction.

For example, Eric's adjusted gross income is $50,000. Carol, his wife, also has $50,000 of adjusted gross income. Eric's medical expenses in 1994 were $5,100. Although Eric's medical expenses do not exceed 7.5 percent of $100,000 (the couple's joint adjusted gross income), they do exceed 7.5 percent of $50,000 (Eric's adjusted gross income). Eric should consider filing separately. He will have to look into whether the benefit of the medical expense deduction more than offsets the higher tax he will have to pay as a single filer, and other benefits he will sacrifice, such as the Elderly Tax Credit (see page 346).

•   You should try to bunch your medical expenses together. By accumulating your medical expenses in a single year, you increase the likelihood that your bills will exceed 7.5 percent of your annual adjusted gross income. There are basically two ways you can bunch your medical expenses. First, move up or postpone your purchase of any medical goods or services that are not time-sensitive. For example, wait until the first of the year to buy a new pair of orthopedic shoes. Or schedule your next dental appointment in 9 months instead of a year. Second, think twice before rushing to pay your medical bills. Paying a number of large bills in the same year could get you a medical expense deduction in that year.

•   You should try to reduce your adjusted gross income. Your medical expenses must exceed 7.5 percent of your adjusted gross income if you are to qualify for the medical expense deduction. If you can't increase your medical bills (and who'd want to?), your only other choice is to decrease your adjusted gross income. But how?

One option is to put your money into tax-exempt and tax-deferred investments. Although you may sacrifice the higher rate of interest taxable investments generally pay, the medical expense deduction will probably be worth it. You will have to speak with a tax specialist to know for sure.

For more on the medical expense deduction, call the IRS at 800-TAX-FORM (829-3676) and request Publication Number 502, "Medical and Dental Expenses."

DEPENDENCY DEDUCTION

Statistics show that more and more adult children are returning home. If your empty nest has been filled by someone you are helping to support (a dependent), you may be eligible for a dependency deduction. The dependent can be your child, grandchild, or parent.

To find out if you are eligible for this deduction, take the following test. You must answer yes to all five questions to qualify for the deduction:

1.   Is your dependent's income $2,350 or less (in 1993)? In counting your dependent's income, do not include welfare benefits and nontaxable Social Security benefits. Tip: To meet this requirement, the prospective dependent should consider investing in tax-free investments, such as municipal bonds. Although tax-free investments pay a lower rate of interest, the dependency deduction should compensate for the loss.

2.   Do you pay over one-half of your dependent's support? "Support" includes the costs of housing, food, utilities, clothing, medical care, transportation, laundry, and other necessities of life. Life insurance premiums and taxes are not considered support.

To find out if you meet this requirement, add up your dependent's total expenses. If the dependent is living with you rent-free, determine the fair market rent you could charge a tenant. Divide your monthly food bills by the number of people in your household to determine your dependent' share of the food expenses. Take a look at how much your dependent contributes to his or her own support each year. Is it less than half? If yes, you meet the support requirement, even if your dependent is putting all of his or her income into the bank while you pay the bills.

What if you have an agreement with other family members to work together to support someone, but none of you alone contributes more than 50 percent of that person's support? This is called a multiple support agreement. Any party to a multiple support agreement can claim the dependency deduction if that party provides over 10 percent of the individual's support. The parties to the agreement can alternate years in which they claim the deduction. In the years they do not claim the deduction, they must file IRS Form 2120 with their tax return.

3. Is your dependent a U.S. citizen or U.S. resident?

4. Is your dependent single, or, if married, does your dependent file a single tax return? A member of a couple that files jointly with a spouse can only qualify as a dependent if the joint filing is necessary to claim a refund of withheld taxes.

5. Is your dependent related to you, or a member of your household? A dependent who is a close relative (a child, sibling, parent, in-law, grandparent, blood uncle, aunt, niece, or nephew) does not have to live with you to qualify. However, more distant relatives (cousins, grandnieces, grandnephews, and step grandchildren) must live with you for more than half the year to qualify as your dependent.

In 1993, the amount of the dependency deduction if $2,350. For every dependent you help support, you can reduce your taxable income by $2,350.

For more on the dependency deduction, call the IRS at 800-TAX-FORM (829-3676) and request Publication Number 529, "Miscellaneous Deductions."

ELDERLY TAX CREDIT

You qualify for a special break on your taxes if you are at least age 65 or under 65 and retired on disability and receiving disability income, and your income is sufficiently low. Let's look at each of these requirements in greater detail.

AGE OR DISABILITY RETIREMENT

You can qualify for the Elderly Tax Credit either on the basis of age or disability. The age requirement is 65.

You meet the disability requirement if your doctor signs IRS Schedule R, Part II of Form 1040 (or Schedule 3, Part 2, of Form 1040A), confirming that a physical or mental impairment that is expected to last at least a year or result in your death renders you unable to do any substantial work. This is the same definition of disability that is discussed in depth in connection with the Social Security disability benefits program (see Chapter 7). You only have to submit Schedule R once if your doctor states that your condition is unlikely ever to improve.

INCOME

There are actually two income requirements for the credit. Your adjusted gross income cannot equal or exceed $17,500 for a single taxpayer, $25,000 if married and filing jointly with a spouse who also qualifies for the credit, or $20,000 if married and filing jointly with a spouse who does not qualify for the credit. Your nontaxable Social Security or pension income cannot equal or exceed $5,000 for a single taxpayer, $7,500 for a married taxpayer filing jointly with a spouse who also qualifies for the credit.

The amount of the Elderly Tax Credit is periodically adjusted for inflation. You can compute the amount of the credit yourself using Schedule R, or ask the IRS to compute your credit for you by writing "CFE" on the dotted line next to line 42 of Form 1040, or line 24b of Form 1040A, and attaching Schedule R to Form 1040 or Schedule 3 to Form 1040A. Fill in your name and age, and get your doctor's signature if you are claiming disability.

For more on the Elderly Tax Credit, call the IRS at 800-TAX-FORM (829-3676) and request Publication Number 524, "Credit for the Elderly or the Disabled."

TAXABILITY OF SOCIAL SECURITY BENEFITS

The tax on Social Security benefits has had a long and sordid history. Prior to 1984, Social Security benefits were not taxed. Then, in 1984, up to 50 percent of a taxpayer's Social Security benefits became taxable. Now, as of the 1994 tax year, up to 85 percent of a taxpayer's Social Security benefits may be subject to taxation.

About 5.5 million Social Security recipients are expected to be affected by this latest development. You are unlikely to be one of the 5.5 million affected recipients if your Social Security benefits were not taxed in tax years prior to 1994, unless your income has increased. However, if you have paid a tax on your Social Security benefits in the past, the amount of your taxable benefits may increase in 1994 and beyond.

The computation of the taxability of Social Security benefits is somewhat complex. If you're not prepared to tackle the task of assessing the taxability of your Social Security benefits yourself, you should enlist the services of a qualified tax preparer (see page 364). You may be liable to the IRS for quarterly estimated tax payments if your benefits are, in fact, taxable. A penalty may be assessed against you if you fail to make timely estimated tax payments. The government will not withhold the tax due on your Social Security benefits from your Social Security checks.

The discussion that follows will help you determine whether or not a portion of your Social Security benefits are taxable, but it stops short of actually computing the tax on your benefits. We happily leave this job to the experts.

To determine whether any of your Social Security benefits are taxable, add to your adjusted gross income your annual tax-exempt interest and one-half your annual Social Security benefit amount. The number you get is your provisional income.

Example: Joe is over age 70, married, and files a joint return with his wife. His adjusted gross income is $25,000, and he receives $8,000 a year from Social Security and $3,000 in tax-exempt interest. Jack's provisional income is $32,000 ($25,000 + $4,000 + $3,000).

Compare your provisional income to the applicable base amount using the following chart:

	If your provisional income exceeds *this* base amount	Up to this percentage of your benefits *may* be taxable
Individual	$25,000	50 percent
	$34,000	85 percent
Couple filing jointly	$32,000	50 percent
	$44,000	85 percent

Continuing the example: Joe's $32,000 of provisional income does not exceed the minimal base amount of $32,000 for a couple. Accordingly, none of Joe's Social Security benefits are taxable.

What happens if Joe starts a part-time job that pays $10,000 a year? His provisional income will increase from $32,000 to $42,000. His income will exceed the minimal base amount of $32,000. Up to 50 percent of Joe's Social Security benefits will become subject to taxation as a direct result of his work activity.

The lesson to learn from Joe's story is to exercise care if you plan on increasing your income. Additional income can push your income over the base amount, thereby exposing previously untaxed Social Security benefits to taxation.

ADDITIONAL TIPS FOR REDUCING YOUR TAXABLE SOCIAL SECURITY BENEFITS

If you want to reduce the amount of your Social Security benefits that are subject to tax—and who wouldn't?—consider the following suggestions.

• If you are married, you will keep the tax on your Social Security benefits down by filing a joint return. Couples who file separately, often to claim a medical expense deduction (see page 341), should make sure they would not save more money by filling jointly and possibly reducing or eliminating the tax on their Social Security benefits. An accountant can help you determine the best way to file.

• Select investments that will minimize the types of income that increase the percentage of taxable Social Security benefits. Tax-exempt bonds are one of the most popular investments for older adults. These bonds offer a secure source of income, and pay interest that is free from federal tax (see page 319). There is, however, a little appreciated downside to tax-exempt bonds: The income they earn can increase the tax due on the investor's Social Security benefits. Income from tax-exempt bonds is added to adjusted gross income in computing the percentage of taxable Social Security benefits.

An alternative investment that does not increase income for purposes of the Social Security benefits tax is Series EE U.S. savings bonds. However, with Series EE bonds you cannot collect the interest the bonds earn until you redeem them. As a result, this investment is not a good option for people who need all their investment income to live on.

For more information on the taxability of your Social Security benefits, call the Internal Revenue Service at 800-TAX-FORM (829-3676) and request Publication Number 915, "Social Security Benefits," and Publication Number 553, "Highlights of 1993 Tax Changes" which includes a worksheet to calculate how much of your benefit is taxable.

CHARITABLE DEDUCTIONS

When you give something of value to your favorite charity, you benefit in two ways: You feel good inside, and you may reduce your taxes.

There are a number of different ways to take advantage of the charitable deduction, besides making outright gifts of money to charity.

• Donate old clothing, furniture, and appliances. You will need to get a signed receipt from the charity itemizing the donated items in order to take the deduction.

• Volunteer your time and keep track of your expenses. Although you cannot deduct the reasonable cost of your labor, you can deduct any out-of-pocket expenses you incur in connection with your volunteer work. The most common deductible expenses are for transportation, phone calls, and uniforms.

• Contribute appreciated assets. If you give away stock or mutual fund shares that you have held for more than a year, and that have increased in value, you will not only get the charitable deduction for the current value of the asset, but you will also avoid paying a capital gains tax on the increased value. (If you donate property that you held for one year or less, your charitable deduction is limited to the purchase price of the asset.)

• Attend a fundraiser. Unfortunately, if you are fed or entertained at the fundraiser, the full price of your ticket will not be deductible. You must reduce the price by the value of the meal and entertainment.

INVESTMENT INCOME TAX BENEFITS

Certain types of investments offer attractive tax savings. A number of these investments are discussed below.

INVESTING IN RETIREMENT PLAN

IRAs, Keoghs, retirement annuities, and pensions (discussed in Chapter 13) are tax-deferred retirement plans. Much of the money you invest in these accounts, and the interest they earn, are not taxed until you withdraw the funds from the account. Tax-deductible contributions to these types of retirement plans will permit you to reduce your taxable income, accelerate the growth of your savings (since interest your money earns will not be taxed until it is withdrawn), and probably pay taxes at a lower rate when you withdraw the funds after retirement.

INVESTING IN HOME OWNERSHIP

If you have money invested in a home, you may be entitled to additional income tax deductions. Interest on a mortgage and property taxes are generally tax deductible.

BUYING MUNICIPAL BONDS

The federal government does not tax interest on municipal bonds. In addition, no state tax is due in the state in which the municipal bond is issued (see page 319).

BUYING U.S. GOVERNMENT SAVINGS BONDS

Interest you earn on certain U.S. Government savings bonds is not taxed until the bonds are redeemed (see page 319). For information on U.S. savings bonds, call the U.S. Treasury savings bond information service at 304-480-6112 or the Federal Reserve Bank at 202-447-1775.

MAKING INTEREST-FREE LOANS TO CHILDREN

There are a number of advantages to making interest-free loans to children, perhaps to be used to put a down payment on a home, to pay for graduate school, or to buy a new business. Here are some points you should know about interest-free loans:

• If the amount of the loan is under $10,000, the IRS will not treat you as receiving any interest on the loan (unless your child invests the borrowed money and earns income on the investment).

• If the amount of the loan is between $10,000 and $100,000, the IRS will not treat you as receiving any interest on the loan as long as your child does not have more than $1,000 of investment income. Your child can keep the investment income below $1,000 by investing in savings bonds, municipal bonds, and non-dividend-paying growth stocks.

• By making a loan, you save the taxes you would otherwise have to pay on your investment income.

• Even if the IRS treats you as receiving interest on the loan (if the loan is for $10,000 or more, or the loan is for up to $100,000 and your child has $1,000 or more of investment income), the imputed interest rate will probably be lower than the rate charged by commercial lenders.

If you do make a low-interest loan to a family member, put the loan agreement in writing. Even though it might feel odd to enter into a formal legal contract with your own flesh and blood, failure to do so could lead the IRS to find that the loan was really a gift. The loan agreement should spell out the interest rate, repayment schedule, penalties for default, and the nature of any collateral.

STATE TAX BENEFITS

Most states offer income tax benefits to their older residents. Many of the state benefits are similar to those offered by the federal government. For example, a number of states provide an additional personal exemption, standard deduction, or tax credit to state residents over age 65. In some states, older homeowners who do not file a tax return are eligible for a rebate.

TAX BENEFITS RELATED TO
PURCHASE AND SALE OF PROPERTY

This section covers tax benefits that may apply to you when you sell a home and buy another home, when you sell a home but do not buy another home, when you give away a home during your lifetime, or when you give away a home at your death.

Did you buy your house years ago for a fraction of what it is worth today? If you did, when you sell or give away your home you may face some imposing tax consequences. Read on to find out how you can take full advantage of tax benefits that hold down the taxes triggered by the transfer of a home (or any other property that has appreciated in value).

Before you get into the nitty gritty of these tax rules, you should familiarize yourself with some relevant tax terminology.

PURCHASE AND SALE TAX TERMS DEFINED

The following terms appear repeatedly throughout this discussion of taxes and the purchase and sale of property, so you should probably know what they mean.

• Appreciated property is property that has increased in value.

• Basis is the price you paid for your property (including the mortgage, if any), plus the costs of purchasing your home (including loan fees, attorney fees, escrow fees, appraisals, title insurance, transfer taxes, and engineer's report), plus the costs of increasing the value of your property (such as by adding a new room, finishing a basement, putting on a new roof, installing air conditioning, replacing the plumbing or wiring, or buying a new boiler). Home improvements that you use to take a medical expense deduction (see page 341) and home repair and maintenance expenses do not increase your basis.

• Capital gain is the difference between your basis and the sale price of your property, less the costs you incur selling the property, such as real estate commissions and advertising. In other words, it is your profit. For example, if you bought a home for $50,000, paid $1,000 in closing costs and $20,000 in home improvements, your basis in the home will be $71,000. You then sell that property for $150,000, after spending $5,000 on real estate commissions and advertising. Your capital gain will be $74,000 (the difference between $145,000 and $71,000).

• Capital gains tax is the tax that may be due when you sell property that has increased in value.

• Rollover refers to the use of the money you make on the sale of one home to buy another home; you roll over your profit from the sale.

• A window is a 2-year period of time you have to buy a new home with the profit you made on the sale of an old home. The 2-year period can precede the sale of your old home or follow it.

• Stepped-up basis is the increase in basis that results when property is transferred at the property owner's death.

SELLING YOUR HOME AND BUYING A NEW HOME

Are you ready for a change of scene? Would you like to know what it's like to live in the Midwest? The Northeast? The Deep South?

If you fulfill the following two requirements, you will not have to pay any capital gains tax when you sell your old home:

- You buy a new home within 2 years of selling your old home.
- The price of your new home is at least as much as the sale price of your old home.

As long as you roll over the profit from the sale into the purchase of a new home within the 2-year window, you do not have to pay any capital gains tax.

You can use this tax benefit any number of times during your lifetime.

SELLING YOUR HOME AND NOT BUYING A NEW HOME

What if you want to sell your house, but you do not want to buy a new house? Maybe you plan to rent an apartment, move in with a child, or enter a nursing home.

You may still be able to minimize your capital gains tax if, when you sell your home, you meet the following three requirements:

- You are age 55 or older.
- The property you sell is your principal residence.
- You owned and lived in the home for at least 3 out of the last 5 years.

Each of these requirements is examined in closer detail in the following three sections.

AGE REQUIREMENT

Your age when you transfer title to your home at the closing is what's relevant; not your age when you sign the sales contract, when you move out, or when the new homeowners move in. (See page 355 for the rules that apply when only one member of a couple is 55 or older.)

PRIMARY RESIDENCE REQUIREMENT

Your principal residence is the house, condominium, cooperative, mobile home, or houseboat you occupy more than 6 months a year. You can only have one principal residence.

DURATION REQUIREMENT

The 3 years of the duration requirement do not have to be consecutive. If you left your home temporarily for vacations or hospitalizations, you still pass the test.

In fact, if you left your home for an extended hospitalization or nursing home stay, you get a break on the duration requirement. As long as you lived in the home for at least 1 (not 3) out of the last 5 years, you qualify. For example, a massive heart attack in January 1992 keeps you in and out of nursing homes and hospitals. As long as you sell by January 1996, you will have met the requirement of occupying your home for 1 year (1991) out of the 5 years (January 1991 to January 1996) preceding the sale. Without the extension, you would have to sell by January 1994, 2 years after your institutionalization.

Another exception to the duration requirement applies to widows and widowers. A surviving spouse can use the $125,000 exclusion even if he or she did not live in the home for 3 of the last 5 years, as long as the deceased spouse lived in the house long enough. For example, you marry someone and move into the house your spouse owned and occupied for the last 15 years. Soon after the marriage your spouse meets an untimely death. You promptly sell the home. As long as you are age 55 or older, you can exclude $125,000 of your gain, even though you didn't occupy the home for 3 of the last 5 years.

The duration requirement can pose a big problem to homeowners who retire out-of-state, and then can't sell their former residence in the tight real estate market. Take, for example, Larry, a 67-year-old New York homeowner who retired and moved to Florida in January 1992. He put his house up for sale. By January 1994 he still hadn't sold his New York property. If Larry doesn't sell his house by January 1995, he may lose out on the one-time exclusion because he will not have lived in the house for at least 3 of the last 5 years.

Is there anything Larry can do? If worse comes to worst, he can ask the IRS for an extension of time. Some courts have ruled that the time a taxpayer spends waiting for a house to sell in a tight market should not count toward the duration requirement. This would mean that if Larry sells his home by January 1996, he would still meet the duration requirement (because the 5-year period would exclude 1992 through 1995). In the alternative, Larry could return to New York for at least 6 months a year until his house is sold (not a terrible alternative, speaking as a die-hard New Yorker myself).

If you meet the three criteria listed above, you are eligible for a one-time $125,000 capital gains exclusion. This exclusion is a once-in-a-lifetime opportunity to avoid paying any tax on the first $125,000 of capital gain you realize on the sale of your home (unless you used the exclusion before July 26, 1978, in which case it's a twice-in-a-lifetime opportunity).

The worksheet below will help you compute approximately how much of your profit will be taxed, if you qualify for the $125,000 exclusion (the precise amount of your taxable profit will be affected by certain additional expenses, such as capital improvements):

Capital Gains Tax Worksheet

	Price paid by purchaser (less your costs of advertising the property, real estate agent's commission, legal fees, and other costs of selling the property)	$ _____
	Price you paid for the home (your basis—see page 352)	− $ _____
LESS		
EQUALS	Capital gain	=
LESS	$125,000	− $ _____
EQUALS	Taxable capital gain	=

If you are married, keep the following rules in mind:

• If you own your home jointly with your spouse, and file a joint tax return, you can get the full $125,000 exclusion if either you or your spouse meets the three requirements of eligibility for the $125,000 exclusion.

• If you own your home jointly with your spouse, but file separate tax returns, you can only claim a $62,500 exclusion when you sell the home if you qualify for the exclusion.

• If you do not own your home jointly with your spouse, and only you meet the three requirements to qualify for the $125,000 exclusion, you can get the full exclusion.

• If your spouse used the $125,000 exclusion before, neither you nor your spouse can use the exclusion again, even if your spouse used the exclusion in a prior marriage and whether or not you own your home jointly.

Does this mean you're completely out of luck if your new husband used the exclusion a year ago to avoid paying tax on the $50,000 he made when he sold his bachelor pad, and now you want to sell the $200,000 house you bought for $35,000? Yes, unless your spouse used the exclusion within the last few years and acts quickly enough to revoke it.

• If you were married to someone who used the exclusion, you can never use the exclusion again, even if your spouse (or former spouse) used the exclusion in connection with the sale of individually owned property. If you remarry, your new spouse can never use the exclusion either.

Because the rules for the one-time use of the exclusion are so strict, one spouse must give written consent before the other spouse can use the $125,000 exclusion (even if the spouses do not own property together, do not live together, and do not file a joint tax return).

You or your accountant can claim the $125,000 exclusion by electing to avoid tax on IRS Form 2119, Sale or Exchange of Personal Residence, which must be filed with your tax return. For more information on the tax consequences of selling your home, call the Internal Revenue Service at 800-TAX-FORM (829-3676) and request Publication Number 523, "Selling Your Home."

GIVING AWAY YOUR HOME DURING YOUR LIFETIME

What if you decide you would rather give away your home than sell it? Perhaps you want to give your house to your daughter, who cannot afford the down payment on a home of her own.

When you make a gift of your home, you do not have to worry about capital gains taxes because you do not make any profit. But you should worry about what will happen down the road. What sort of capital gains tax will your child have to pay if and when she sells the property?

When you give away a home, you also give away your basis in the home. As already discussed, your basis is essentially what you paid for the house, plus some adjustments.

If you give your child a home that you purchased for $15,000, your child's basis in the house will be about $15,000. This means that when your child eventually sells the home 60 years after you bought it for, say, $315,000, her capital gain will be $300,000. The tax bite on this profit would really leave marks, unless your daughter rolled over the profit from the sale into a new home (see page 352). An additional concern is that the value of the gift from you to your daughter would be $315,000, not $15,000, which might have gift tax implications for you (see page 360).

GIVING AWAY YOUR HOME UPON YOUR DEATH

If you do not sell or give away your home during your lifetime, you will leave your property to your heirs at your death.

Unlike lifetime gifts, where the person who receives the property gets your basis in the property, when you pass along property at death the recipient gets a stepped-up basis (or stepped-down basis if the market goes down). The new basis equals the value of the property at the time of your death.

For example, Junior inherits a house that his father bought for $35,000. At the time of the father's death, the house is worth $100,000. Although the father's basis in the house was $35,000, Junior's basis in the inherited property is $100,000, the value of the property at the time of his father's death. If Junior sells the house for $135,000, he will have a capital gain of only $35,000.

The advantage of getting a stepped-up basis is that there is a lower capital gain when the house is sold.

POINTS TO CONSIDER ABOUT GIVING AWAY PROPERTY

• If you plan to give to your children property that has increased substantially in value, think about your children's future tax liability. The amount of tax your children will have to pay when they eventually sell the property you give them will depend on whether you make the gift during your lifetime or after your death. Gifts made at death receive more favorable income tax treatment when they are ultimately sold (although there is a chance that the savings may be offset by estate taxes, which are higher than income taxes.)

Your decision about how and when to make a gift should really depend only in part on tax considerations. There are many good reasons you may want to make a lifetime gift. For one, you cannot see your child enjoy a gift that you make after you die. Or your child may have an immediate need for the gift. Or perhaps your accountant has advised you to make the gift to reduce your taxable estate. Whatever the reasons, you may simply decide the heck with the tax consequences.

• You do not have to leave property to your children in your will to minimize your children's future taxes. Parents who want to leave their children property at death often do so in a last will and testament. However, this is not the only way to leave property to your children. Other ways of leaving property at death offer the same tax benefits.

Two means of passing property at death are life estates and trusts.

A *life estate* is a special form of property ownership. If you have a life estate in your house, you are the legal owner of the house for the rest of your life. You are responsible for paying the property taxes, you retain all property tax benefits, and you must consent to any sale of the house. You are the "life tenant."

When you die, the house automatically passes to whomever you named on the deed as the "future tenant." Future tenants get a stepped-up basis in property they inherit because the property is included in the life tenant's estate. The future tenant's basis is equal to the value of the property at the time of the life tenant's death. This step-up in basis means that the future tenant faces a smaller capital gains tax if and when the property is sold (or possibly no tax if the property is sold shortly after the life tenant's death).

Do not rush to set up a life estate if you might sell your home during your lifetime. You could lose the benefit of the full $125,000 exclusion. The creation of a life estate may also benefit in gift tax liability.

A *trust* is another form of property ownership. To create a trust, you and the person you appoint to manage the property in the trust (the "trustee") must sign a trust agreement. (Depending on the trust, you may be the trustee of your own trust.) The agreement gives the trustee instructions about how to manage the property in the trust. For example, if your house is in the trust, you can instruct your trustee to permit you to live in the house for the rest of your life.

The agreement also spells out who gets the trust property when you die or when the trust terminates. You can draft your trust agreement so that whoever inherits the trust property at your death gets a stepped-up basis. Including this provision will reduce the capital gains tax that may be due upon the future sale of the property (but may increase your estate taxes). There are many additional advantages to trusts, some of which include the avoidance of probate and ongoing property management in the event of incapacity.

To put your home into a trust, you must have a new deed drafted transferring the property out of your individual name and putting it into the name of the trust. You should consult an attorney for additional information about setting up a trust.

• You should consider putting appreciated property into the sole name of an ill spouse or parent. You can take advantage of a step-up in basis within your marriage. Many couples own their most valuable property jointly. When one member of the couple dies, the surviving spouse gets a stepped-up basis of *half* of the value of the property. For example, you and your husband purchased a house for $50,000 that is worth $200,000 when your husband dies. You inherit your husband's share of the house, and become the sole owner of the property. Your basis in the house is $25,000 (your half of the original purchase price) plus $100,000 (half of what the house is worth at your husband's death), for a total combined basis of $125,000. If you sold the house for $200,000, your taxable gain would be $75,000.

What would have happened if you knew that your husband's death was imminent, and you transferred your share of the house to him before he died? Then, when you inherited the house from your husband, your basis would have been $200,000. The entire basis in the property would have been stepped up to the market value at the time of your husband's death. If you subsequently sold the house for $200,000, you would have zero taxable gain.

The same planning technique works between child and parent. Here's how: A child who owns property that has appreciated in value gives the property to an ill parent. The parent dies and leaves the property to the child. The child inherits the property with a stepped-up basis that equals the market value of the property at the parent's death. The child sells the property, and pays no capital gains tax. Any state estate or inheritance tax (of up to 10 percent) is more than offset by the saved capital gains tax (of about 28 percent).

There is, however, one potential hitch. A gift recipient must survive at least one year to leave property with a step-up in basis back to the giver of the gift. For example, a 50-year-old son transfers his home to his mother, who is terminally ill with cancer. Six months after the transfer, the mother dies. The son inherits his home, but without any step-up in basis because the mother died within one year of the gift.

The way to avoid this limitation has probably already occurred to you: For a year after the gift is made, have the recipient of the gift leave the property to someone other than the gift giver (or the gift giver's spouse). Continuing the example above, if the mother had left the property to her 20-year-old grandson instead of her son in the year after the gift was made, the basis in the property would have been stepped up. The grandson could have then sold the property, realized no taxable gain, and given some money to his father a few years down the road.

PROPERTY TAX BENEFITS

Many states and localities give older homeowners a break on their property taxes. Which of the following benefits are available to you?

PROPERTY TAX DEDUCTION AND CREDIT

A property tax deduction reduces the assessed value of a taxpayer's home. This reduction results in lower property taxes. Higher taxes are due on homes that have a higher assessed value. In some states, this tax benefit is even available to renters who pay property taxes as part of their rent.

A property tax credit reduces the amount of tax that would otherwise be due on a taxpayer's home.

PROPERTY TAX DEFERRAL

Property tax deferral programs are a type of home equity conversion plan (see page 276). State and local governments with property tax deferral programs let resident taxpayers borrow money to pay their property taxes. Repayment is not required until the homeowner dies, moves, or sells the home.

Only about one-third of all states offer property tax deferral loans.[1] Even where

---

[1] Property tax deferral is available on a statewide basis in California, Colorado, Georgia, Illinois, Maine, Oregon, Texas, Utah, Washington, and Wisconsin. It is available as a local program in Connecticut, Florida, Iowa, Massachusetts, New Hampshire, and Virginia.

available, a minority of eligible taxpayers take advantage of tax deferral. In Oregon, the state where tax deferral is most popular, only 10 to 11 percent of eligible taxpayers use the program. If your state offers property tax deferral loans, and you would like more information, contact the receiver of property taxes, your state unit on aging (see Appendix 1), or your state department of taxation.

Participants in property tax deferral programs pay a moderate rate of interest compared to other lenders. The rate is set by law.

Property tax deferral loans are secured by a lien on your house. When you move or sell your home, you will have to repay the accumulated amount of unpaid property taxes, plus interest. If you die while still residing in the home, your estate will be responsible for repayment.

Most property tax deferral programs have the following eligibility restrictions:

1. You must be at least 65 years of age.
2. Your income must be below specified limits, which rarely disqualify middle-income taxpayers.
3. You must not have a large outstanding mortgage on your home.

GIFT AND ESTATE TAX BENEFITS

Whenever you make a gift, be it cash, a house, or some other type of property, you have to think about gift taxes—as if you didn't have enough to think about already, what with capital gains taxes and income taxes. If you find yourself wondering whether the gift is worth the bother, think of Homer's famous words: "A gift, though small, is precious."

Gift taxes and estate taxes are discussed together because the federal government instituted a unified gift and estate tax system in 1976. Under the unified system, all transfers of property are taxed the same. The government does not care if you give away property during your lifetime or at your death.

A taxpayer may transfer property (including cash) with a total value of up to $600,000 during life or at death free of federal estate and gift taxes. This is called the unified credit because every taxpayer gets a credit that wipes out the tax that would otherwise be due on transfers of up to $600,000. The unified credit is reduced by large taxable gifts the taxpayer makes during his or her lifetime. Whatever is left of the credit at the time of the taxpayer's death reduces the estate tax.

An example illustrates use of the unified credit: In the four years before her death, Mary, a widow, gave her grandson $100,000 each year for a total of $400,000. She reported each gift to the IRS on a gift tax return. When Mary died, she had $500,000 left in her estate. Since Mary transferred $400,000 during her lifetime, she only had $200,000 left to pass tax-free at her death. When she died, $300,000

($500,000 minus $200,000) of her estate was subject to estate tax starting at a rate of approximately 37 percent.

Three types of transfers do not reduce the unified credit:

1. Gifts worth up to $10,000 given to one person in one year. Married couples can give away a joint gift of $20,000 to a person each year tax-free, or $40,000 to a couple each year tax-free. Gifts within these exempt amounts do not even have to be reported on a gift tax return.
2. Transfers between spouses. Bequests to a surviving spouse do not use up the unified credit, unless the surviving spouse is not a U.S. citizen.
3. Property left to a tax-exempt charity.

The generous unified credit is always in danger of being reduced. Make sure you know the current exempt amount before you do any estate planning.

If your estate is clearly worth less than $600,000, and you didn't make any large gifts during your life, you don't have to worry about federal gift or estate taxes, but you may still have to worry about state taxes. The state where you live or own real estate may impose an estate tax on your estate at the time of your death.

Gift Tax Benefits

As already discussed, every taxpayer is permitted to make tax-free gifts of up to $10,000 to any number of individuals each year. Gifts within this amount do not have to be reported to the IRS on a gift tax return, and do not reduce the giver's $600,000 unified credit.

Every gift over $10,000 ($20,000 for a gift-giving couple) must be reported to the IRS on a gift tax return. This filing requirement applies even if no gift tax is due because the gift is within the unified credit. The gift tax return must be filed by April 15 of the year following the year of the gift. For example, a gift tax return for a February 1991 gift must be filed by April 15, 1992. The form for a gift tax return is IRS Form 709. The person who makes the gift is primarily responsible for paying any gift tax that may be due.

A gift is not taxable income to the recipient. However, the gift recipient must pay income tax on any interest or dividend income the gift earns.

Estate Tax Benefits

A federal estate tax return does not have to be filed if the decedent did not transfer, either during life or at death, property worth at least $600,000. Bequests left to a surviving spouse (unless not a U.S. citizen) are never taxed, regardless of their value.

Federal estate taxes are very steep. They start at 37 percent of the excess over $600,000, and top off at 50 percent for amounts over $2.5 million. (The cap is likely to be raised during the Clinton Administration, possibly to as high as 70 percent.)

To compute an estate tax, the total value of the estate is reduced by the following deductions:

- Funeral expenses.
- Expenses of administering the estate.
- Taxes owed by the decedent.
- Charitable pledges made by the decedent prior to death.
- Mortgages owed on property in the estate.
- Debts of the decedent.

The total estate, less the deductions and bequests to the surviving spouse, is called the taxable estate.

The tax due on the taxable estate must be paid 9 months after the date of death. The executor of the estate can request an extension of time to pay the estate tax.

Some states also collect estate taxes. In certain cases, the state's estate tax will reduce the federal estate tax.

Many lawyers, accountants, and financial planners make their living telling people how to save money on their estate taxes. The topic is far too complex to be dealt with adequately in this chapter. However, two estate planning tactics are especially beneficial to older adults.

CREDIT SHELTER TRUST

As already discussed, every individual is permitted to transfer up to $600,000 without paying any federal estate or gift taxes, either during life or at death. If you are married, and the total value of your estate exceeds $600,000, you should consider some type of estate tax planning.

You may be thinking: Why do I have to worry about estate taxes when I plan to leave everything to my spouse when I die? Transfers between spouses are never taxed.

If you leave everything outright to your spouse, you will succeed in putting off your estate tax problem, but not dealing with it. The estate tax problem will re-emerge upon the death of your spouse. If your surviving spouse's estate exceeds $600,000, there may be a huge tax bill to pay.

For example, imagine a couple with $800,000 in joint savings. When the husband dies, he leaves everything to his wife. No estate taxes are due. After 3 years, his wife dies. She still has $750,000 in her estate. Six hundred thousand dollars passes to her children without incurring estate tax, but the remaining $150,000 is taxed at a rate starting at 37 percent.

If the husband and the wife had both been able to use their $600,000 exemptions, they could have passed $1.2 million tax-free and the $150,000 bequest would not have been taxed. As it worked out, only the wife used her exemption. The husband's exemption was effectively wasted, resulting in a taxable estate.

So what's the solution for married taxpayers who want to leave their property to each other when they die, but also want to minimize their estate taxes? For many couples, the solution is a credit shelter trust (also called a marital life estate trust, an A-B trust, or a bypass trust). A credit shelter trust enables both members of a couple to use their $600,000 credit. Under the terms of a credit shelter trust, the surviving spouse has the right to receive the trust income, and has limited access to the principal. Whatever is left in the trust at the surviving spouse's death passes to the "remaindermen" (usually the children), without incurring estate tax.

A credit shelter trust will only work to shelter $1.2 million of a couple's savings from estate taxation if ownership of the property is split equally between husband and wife. Whatever property is jointly owned passes automatically to the survivor, and does not pass through the credit shelter trust.

If each member of the couple in the example put $400,000 in his or her sole name, and set up a unified shelter trust, the trust would work as follows: When the husband died, his $400,000 would pass into the trust. The surviving wife would have had the right to collect all the income the $400,000 generated.

The surviving spouse may also be permitted to use as much of the principal as she needs to maintain her standard of living (with the consent of any named co-trustees), and may be given the right to obtain annually the greater of 5 percent of the trust principal or $5,000, for any reason whatsoever. When the wife died, whatever property is left in the trust would pass free of estate taxes to the couple's children.

A trust of this type can be included in a will or a living trust. An attorney can provide you with additional information about the benefits and drawbacks of a credit shelter trust.

QUALIFIED PERSONAL RESIDENCE TRUST

Many people would not have a taxable estate but for their home. The value of a residence pushes the net worth of many taxpayers' estates above the $600,000 limit for tax-free bequests (see page 360).

What these homeowners need to do is get their house out of their estate, but not lose the right to live in their house. Impossible? Maybe not.

Consider the qualified personal residence trust (QPRT), also called a residential grantor retained income trust (GRIT). QPRTs have the following features:

- They preserve the homeowner's right to live in the house for a specified term of years. The term need not be of any minimum or maximum duration.
- During the term, the homeowner continues to enjoy all tax benefits related

to the home, including income tax deductions for property taxes and mortgage interest.

- At the end of the term, the home automatically passes to whoever is named in the trust.

- The homeowner saves taxes because the value of the home is discounted for tax purposes.

Although QPRTs don't entirely solve the problem of including a valuable home in a taxable estate, they do lessen the problem somewhat by reducing the taxable value of the home.

An example should help illustrate the use of a QPRT. A 55-year-old homeowner has a home worth $400,000. He wants to leave it to his daughter, but he wants to continue living in the home until he moves down to Florida in 15 years. He transfers his home into a QPRT, and retains the right to live in the house for the next 15 years. He names his daughter as the beneficiary of the trust.

At the end of 15 years, when the home passes to his daughter, it is worth $700,000. If the father gave the house outright to his daughter, either during his life or at death, a tax would have been due on the excess over $600,000. But with a QPRT, the homeowner is not treated as making a $700,000 gift. Rather, he is treated as making a gift worth only about $115,000 ($400,000 minus the value the IRS assigns to the homeowner's right to occupy the home for 15 years).

But if the homeowner had died within the 15-year term, the full value of the home would have been included in his estate.

The QPRT is a specialized type of trust that should be drawn up by an experienced attorney. The average cost of drafting such a trust is about $2,500.

HELP WITH YOUR TAX RETURN

At best, filing an annual tax return is a pain in the neck. At worst, it is a severe cervical myospasm.

To file, you need to know what forms to complete, how to fill them out, whether to file jointly or singly, and whether to itemize deductions. You also need to know what deductions, credits, and exemptions are available to you.

- Your local IRS office offers tax preparation assistance to taxpayers age 65 and older. IRS representatives are instructed to help taxpayers pay the lowest taxes possible. The telephone numbers of local IRS offices are listed in Appendix 12.

- Tele-Tax is a service run by the IRS that gives taxpayers prerecorded answers over the telephone to the most commonly-asked questions. Instructions for using Tele-Tax are reprinted in Appendix 13.

• Volunteer tax counselors are available to assist senior taxpayers with their tax returns. There are three volunteer tax programs. Two of these programs, Volunteer Income Tax Assistance and Tax Counseling for the Elderly, are run exclusively by the IRS. Volunteers in these programs are trained and tested by the IRS. To find out more about these programs, call the toll-free taxpayer assistance numbers listed in Appendix 12. The third program is jointly run by the IRS and the American Association of Retired Persons (AARP) between February 1 and April 15 of each tax year. To get more information about AARP's volunteer tax program, contact:

AARP/NRTA
Tax-Aide Program
601 E Street, N.W.
Washington, DC 20049
202-434-2277

• IRS publications may be useful. The IRS publishes a number of free booklets on a range of tax matters, including "Your Rights as a Taxpayer" (Publication Number 1), "Your Federal Income Tax" (Publication Number 17), "Tax Information for Older Americans" (Publication Number 554), and "Guide to Free Tax Services," which includes a list of all publications (Publication Number 910) by calling the IRS at 800-TAX-FORM (829-3676).

• Accountants, tax preparation services, and attorneys are always available to help you with your taxes for a fee.

BACK TO CHARLIE

Charlie was pleased to learn that at least some small good came out of the medical problems he had in 1992. He was eligible for a medical expense deduction. Because he did not have any private insurance to supplement his Medicare coverage, and had to pay a number of his medical bills out-of-pocket, his medical expenses exceeded 7.5 percent of his adjusted gross income.

Charlie was also cheered by the news that he qualified for the once-in-a-lifetime exclusion of $125,000 from the capital gains he realized upon the sale of his house since he met the age and residency requirements.

And finally, Charlie rejoiced upon learning that he would not have to pay any gift tax. Although the $20,000 gift exceeded his $10,000 annual gift tax exclusion, it was still well within the unified credit that applies to transfers of up to $600,000.

Good news all around for Charlie.

13.
ENJOYING THE BENEFITS OF RETIREMENT SAVINGS

At age 58, Sandy decided to stop working and move to Florida. Most of her savings were in two individual retirement accounts (IRAs) and a pension plan at work. Sandy needed a portion of these savings to buy a condominium in Florida and pay her moving expenses.

Sandy was confused about her rights to her pension savings, and was concerned that she would be penalized for withdrawing funds from her IRA. She was also petrified of the penalties and taxes she would have to pay.

Sandy need to know: What would be the consequences of tapping into her retirement savings to finance her move to Florida?

Like many Americans, you have probably invested some of your earnings in retirement savings. Also, like others, you may be wondering what to do now. When can you start withdrawing funds from your individual retirement account (IRA)? Are you ever required to withdraw your Keogh savings? What will happen to the pension plan you have with your employer when you stop working? What kinds of taxes are you going to have to pay when you begin to withdraw your retirement savings? Is there any way to avoid early withdrawal penalties and minimize your taxes? How safe are your retirement savings?

You need answers to all these questions, and more, if you are to enjoy the full benefits of saving for retirement.

You may also be wondering about the security of your retirement savings. A 1993 Gallup poll found that six in ten American adults fear that their retirement savings will not see them through the rest of their lives. Do you share their concern? If yes, you will be interested to read about the safety of your retirement plan.

This chapter will help you get the most out of your retirement savings by defining some relevant terms, briefly discussing IRAs, Keoghs, pension plans, 401(k)s, simplified employee pensions (SEPs), employee stock ownership plans (ESOPs), and retirement annuities, and then explaining the following benefits of each type of plan:

- Tax-deductible contributions.
- Tax-free growth.
- Penalty-free withdrawals.
- Post-retirement income.
- Lump-sum withdrawal.
- Tax treatment of lump-sum withdrawals.
- Income late in life (after age 70½).
- Vesting.
- Borrowing against retirement savings.
- Retirement savings for surviving spouses and other beneficiaries.

The section that closes this chapter includes a discussion of the safety of your retirement savings.

DEFINITIONS OF COMMONLY USED RETIREMENT PLANNING TERMS

To maximize the benefits of your retirement savings, you must understand the language of retirement planning.

• Annuity. An annuity is a method of collecting retirement savings. A retiree with an annuity collects retirement savings in a number of periodic payments spread out over a term of years. For example, when Jack retired he decided to collect his pension as a lifetime annuity. A lifetime annuity lasts for the lifetime of the retiree. Jack will receive a pension check each month for the rest of his life.

• Beneficiary. The beneficiary of a retirement account is the individual who inherits the money in the account when the worker dies. For example, Jane named her husband as the beneficiary of her IRA account. When Jane dies, her husband is entitled to any money left in her account.

• Defined benefit plan. With a defined benefit plan, the worker is guaranteed a specific benefit amount at retirement. The employer must then make sufficient contributions to the plan to fund that benefit amount.

• Defined contribution plan. With a defined contribution plan, the worker or the worker's employer must make monthly contributions to the pension account. The contribution is usually a percentage of the worker's salary. Some plans require the worker to make a contribution before the employer is required to make a matching contribution.

• Liquid. Investments are liquid when they can easily be converted to cash.

• Lump sum. A lump-sum withdrawal is a method of collecting retirement savings from a qualified retirement plan, such as a pension, 401(k), or Keogh. With a lump-sum payout, the retiree receives the retirement savings in a single payment.

• Rollover. A rollover is the movement of retirement savings from one retirement account to another. For example, Sam has $100,000 in his pension at work. He is planning on retiring, but does not need the money right away. Also, he doesn't want to have to pay taxes on his pension savings any sooner than necessary. He decides to roll over his pension funds into an IRA at his bank.

• Tax-deductible contributions. Workers who make tax-deductible contributions to their retirement accounts do not pay taxes on the money they invest in retirement savings. They only pay taxes on the money when they withdraw it later. Money used to make tax-deductible contributions is sometimes called pre-tax dollars. For example, Mary earned $50,000 in 1992. She invested $2,000 of her earnings in an IRA. Mary was taxed as if she earned only $48,000 in 1992. She is not taxed on the $2,000 until she withdraws it from her IRA account.

• Tax-free (or tax-deferred) growth. Retirement savings are said to grow tax-free because the worker does not pay taxes on interest the retirement savings earn until the interest is withdrawn from the account.

• Vested benefits. Employees who have a retirement plan with their employer are only entitled to receive vested retirement benefits. For example, Bob started working for a new employer in 1990. His pension plan provided that all his benefits would be vested after 5 years of employment. When Bob is fired in 1996, he is entitled to the full amount of money in his pension account.

SEVEN POPULAR RETIREMENT PLANS

INDIVIDUAL RETIREMENT ACCOUNT

If you earn money, either by working for someone else or for yourself, you can put money for retirement in an IRA. Some or all of your investment in an IRA may be tax-deductible, and your investment will grow tax-free. You will not have to pay taxes on your IRA savings until you withdraw the funds from your account.

KEOGH

A Keogh is a retirement plan for full- or part-time self-employed workers (workers who work for themselves.) Self-employed workers can contribute a portion of their pretax earnings to a Keogh account, where the money will not be taxed until withdrawn. A Keogh can be either a defined benefit plan or a defined contribution plan (see page 367). Most Keoghs are defined contribution plans because these are easier and cheaper to administer.

PENSION

Employers set up pension plans to help their employees save for retirement. Under most plans, employees age 21 and over can participate in the plan after one year of employment. There are two types of company pensions: defined benefit plans and defined contribution plans (see page 367). Defined benefit plans have been decreasing in popularity since the 1980s. More than 80 percent of all qualified private sector pension plans are now defined contribution plans. Many firms favor defined contribution plans because they are easier to administer, and many do not require employer contributions.

401(K) PLAN

A 401(k) plan is one of the most common types of defined contribution pension plans (see page 368). Most employees over age 21 can participate in a 401(k) after one year of employment. If you participate in a 401(k) plan, you can put part of your wages into the plan without first paying taxes on them. Your employer may or may not contribute money to your 401(k) account on your behalf. The 401(k) savings and interest are not taxed until they are withdrawn.

A 401(k) plan can be qualified or nonqualified. Participation in a nonqualified plan is risky for several reasons:

- Nonqualified plans are not actually funded. Although records are kept of plan contributions, no funds are actually set aside for the plan participants. Employers who run into financial problems can renege on the promised distributions.

- Distributions from nonqualified plans are taxed immediately. Techniques for deferring taxation of distributions from qualified plans are not available (see page 379).

- Participants in nonqualified plans who leave their company are required to take their plan savings with them. The result can be a hefty tax liability.

SIMPLIFIED EMPLOYEE PENSION

Many small employers use SEPs because they are an inexpensive way to offer their workers a retirement plan. With a SEP, the employer contributes money to the employee's existing retirement account (usually an IRA or retirement annuity). The worker pays no taxes on the contributions, or the interest the contributions earn, until the money is withdrawn. Self-employed workers can also contribute to a SEP.

EMPLOYEE STOCK OWNERSHIP PLAN

ESOPs are retirement plans that corporations set up and fund with their own stock. Employees who participate in an ESOP actually become part owners of the corporation that employs them; in fact, some employees who own stock in an ESOP have voting rights and can influence their company's policies.

VARIABLE ANNUITY

An annuity is a contract between an investor and an insurance company that provides for regular payments to be made to the investor over a period of time. Sales of variable annuities have skyrocketed in recent years for a couple of reasons. First, annuity contributions are not capped. Unlike annual IRA contributions, which have been capped at $2,000 since 1986, annuity investments are unlimited. Second, like a life insurance policy, an annuity guarantees the investor a death benefit at least equal to the amount of the original investment.

The biggest drawback to an annuity is management-related expenses. In addition to an annual administration fee of about $35, and sales charges, the typical annuity holder loses 2 percent of the investment to operating costs. Most annuities also carry a surrender charge to discourage holders from withdrawing their investment. The surrender penalty usually drops from 10 percent to zero over an average 6.5 year period.

Typically purchasers of variable annuities are between ages 45 and 60. Younger investors are frightened by the surrender penalty, and older investors like the security of a guaranteed death benefit.

BENEFITS OF RETIREMENT SAVINGS

While you were working, you may have contributed money to a retirement account. Some of these contributions may have been tax-deductible. Making tax-deductible contributions to your retirement savings reduced your taxable income.

Tax-deductible contributions to a retirement account are not taxed until the funds are withdrawn from the account. If you do not withdraw your tax-deductible contributions until after you stop working, when the loss of earned income will push you into a lower tax bracket, you will enjoy tax savings on this money.

Contributions to retirement savings are not always tax-deductible. When you make a non-deductible retirement plan contribution, you are taxed on the money before you invest it in retirement savings.

The difference between deductible and non-deductible contributions becomes significant when you start withdrawing your retirement savings. The portion of a withdrawal that represents a withdrawal of a tax-deductible contribution is taxed because this money was not taxed before; the portion that represents a withdrawal of a non-deductible contribution is not taxed.

The money you invest in retirement savings grows tax-free, whether it is tax-deductible or not. This means you are not taxed on the interest, dividends, or capital gains your retirement savings earn, as long as the savings remain in a retirement account. Non-tax-exempt investments outside retirement accounts generate taxable income.

As a general rule, you benefit by maximizing your retirement savings. The reason is simple. You invest your retirement savings in taxable investments that pay a higher rate of interest than non-taxable investments, and you don't pay any tax on your investment income.

One exception to this rule applies to short-term investments. You should not make a non-deductible contribution to a retirement account that also holds deductible contributions unless you plan to let your investment ride for awhile. If you do not leave your investment alone, and you withdraw funds from the account, part of the withdrawal will be taxed to reflect the fact that you have withdrawn some of your tax-deductible contributions. When you withdraw part of your tax-deductible contributions, you lose out on additional potential tax savings.

Retirement accounts come in a variety of shapes and sizes. If you were self-employed, you probably saved for retirement in a Keogh account. If you were a corporate executive, you are probably covered under a pension plan. If you worked for a number of different employers, you may have all your retirement savings in an IRA.

Each type of retirement account is governed by a different set of rules and regulations. Some retirement plans permit tax-deductible and non-deductible contributions; others only permit non-deductible contributions. Some retirement plans limit annual contributions; others don't. The discussion that follows briefly examines the contribution rules that govern IRAs, Keoghs, pensions, 401(k)s, SEPs, ESOPs, and variable annuities.

IRA

You are permitted to make a tax-deductible contribution of $2,000 a year to an IRA account (or your total earned income, if less). If you and your spouse both work, your total deductible contribution cannot exceed $4,000. Excess contributions, and those made after age 70½ are non-deductible.

If you or your spouse participates in a pension plan, some or all of your IRA contribution will be non-deductible if your income exceeds certain limits. The limits for 1994 are listed below.

Filing Status	Income	Deductibility of Contribution
Single	under $25,000 between $25,000 and $35,000 over $35,000	Fully deductible Partially deductible Not deductible
Married and filing jointly	under $40,000 between $40,000 and $50,000 over $50,000	Fully deductible Partially deductible Not deductible
Married and filing separately	under $10,000 $10,000 and above	Partially deductible Not deductible

If your income is too high for you to qualify for the full $2,000 IRA deduction, take a long hard look at your investments. Is there anything you can do to reduce your taxable investment income so that you drop below the IRA earnings limitations and become eligible for the full deduction?

For example, maybe you should consider moving your money out of taxable money market accounts and into such tax-free investments as bonds. Although such a move would entail the loss of investment income as you switch from a taxable investment to a non-taxable investment, this loss may be more than offset by the IRA deduction.

KEOGH

The maximum allowed contribution to a Keogh will depend on the type of Keogh plan selected. With a Keogh money purchase plan, the maximum allowed tax-deductible contribution in 1994 is 25 percent of earned income or $30,000, whichever is less. With a profit sharing Keogh, where contributions can fluctuate year to year, the maximum deductible contribution is capped at the lesser of 15 percent of earned income or $30,000. As of 1994 a change in the law caps the worker's maximum compensation at $150,000. Earnings in excess of $150,000 are not applied to the 15 percent limit. The effect of this cap on maximum earnings is to limit contributions to $22,500 (instead of $30,000). Non-deductible Keogh contributions are rarely permitted.

Unlike IRA investors, self-employed workers can continue to make tax-deductible Keogh contributions after age 70½ as long as they keep earning income from self-employment.

PENSION, 401(K), ESOP

An employee who contributes to a pension, 401(k), and/or ESOP retirement plan can elect to defer from taxation the percentage of compensation specified in the plan. For example, an employee who participates in a 6 percent plan can defer taxation of up to 6 percent of his annual compensation. Regardless of the terms of the plan, however, in 1994 the employee can never defer taxation of more than 15 percent of compensation or $9,240, whichever is less. Non-deductible contributions are almost always prohibited.

Some plans provide for matching employer contributions. These contributions are also limited.

SEP

In 1994, tax-deductible SEP contributions are limited to the lesser of 15 percent of the worker's compensation or $30,000. As of 1994 a change in the law caps the worker's maximum compensation at $150,000. Earnings in excess of $150,000 are not applied to the 15 percent limit. This, in effect, limits the maximum deductible contribution amount to $22,500 (down from $30,000 before 1994). Self-employed workers can contribute to a special type of SEP called a SAR-SEP, which is governed by the same rules as a profit-sharing Keogh (see above). Non-deductible SEP contributions are never permitted.

VARIABLE ANNUITY

All money you invest in a variable annuity has already been taxed. Tax-deductible contributions to a variable annuity are not permitted.

Variable annuity investments are not capped. Each year you are free to decide the amount of your investment.

BENEFITS OF RETIREMENT PLAN INVESTING

Your options with respect to the investment of your retirement savings depend on the nature of your retirement account.

IRA, SEP, AND KEOGH

IRAs, SEPs, and Keoghs give you the greatest investment flexibility. You can put your money in certificates of deposit, money market accounts, real estate investments, or any of the 4,000 mutual funds.

PENSION

If you participate in a pension plan through work, your investment opportunities will depend on whether you participate in a defined contribution or a defined benefit pension plan. Defined contributions plans give participants greater control over their investments than defined benefit plans. With a defined benefit plan, the employer decides how the funds are invested.

401(K)

Some 401(k) plans give the participant a choice among several investment options. Other plans reserve investment decisions for the employer. Employers traditionally invest 401(k) funds very conservatively because with aggressive investing they risk being sued if the investments go bad.

ESOP

Money invested in an ESOP is always invested in the employer's company stock. Participants are not permitted to select alternative investments.

VARIABLE ANNUITY

Most variable annuities have several investment choices. In fact, in recent years annuities have begun offering their investors more and more options in an effort to compete with IRAs and Keoghs. However, even an annuity that offers a generous selection of 15 investment opportunities falls short of the thousands of investments that are available to IRA and Keogh investors.

If you invested your annuity in one state, and subsequently retire to another state, you may be contacted by tax authorities from your former state of residence. A few high-income-tax states, such as New York and California, have been known to seek taxes from out-of-state retirees who are collecting annuity income that grew tax-free while invested in their former home state. Residents of a state like Florida, which has no income tax, have had to pay taxes on current income to their former state of residence.

Investors who control the investment of their retirement savings are well-advised to follow the general rules of thumb outlined below:

Rules of Thumb for Retirement Account Investing

Age of Investor	Investment Goal	Investment Strategy
25 to 50	Build capital	Invest in long-term instruments with growth potential, such as stocks, bonds, certificates of deposit, and Ginnie Maes.
50 to 59½ or retirement	Liquidate investments	Sell stocks and put proceeds in money funds; trade in bonds for one-year Treasury bills; convert long-term certificates of deposit that come due to short-term certificates.
59½ or retirement	Withdraw investments	Pace withdrawals so your savings last your lifetime.

Investors in their 50s and 60s are usually advised to keep their retirement savings accessible so they can raise cash quickly in the event of illness, disability, or other emergency. Between ages 50 and 59½ you may want to take advantage of upswings in the market and start selling off your stock portfolio when the selling is good. You can invest the proceeds from the sale of your stock shares in highly-liquid money market funds. When your long-term bonds and certificates of deposit come due, you can switch over to investments with terms of several months or one or two years.

Of course, such conservative investing has a downside. Your money may not keep up with inflation. Even with a modest annual inflation rate of only 4 percent, in 15 years $1,000 will buy what $555 buys today.

If you do not plan to retire for at least 3 years, some retirement planners recommend keeping at least 50 to 60 percent of your retirement savings in the stock market. Stocks have averaged a 12.85 percent return over the past 50 years, and may be your best bet for keeping pace with inflation.

BENEFIT OF PENALTY-FREE WITHDRAWALS

The government does not fool around when it comes to your retirement savings. Uncle Sam will give you a tax break on your retirement savings, but only if you are committed to using the savings to finance your retirement. Early withdrawals of retirement savings are heavily penalized.

With the limited exceptions discussed immediately below, you must pay a 10 percent penalty tax if you withdraw your retirement savings before age 59½. In real numbers this tax means that you will owe the IRS $7,000 if you withdraw $70,000 from your retirement savings to buy yourself a hot new sports car for your 50th birthday (10 percent of $70,000) plus income tax on the withdrawal. The early withdrawal penalty applies to withdrawals from an IRA, Keogh, pension, 401(k), SEP, ESOP, or variable annuity made before age 59½. (Most variable annuities carry an additional early withdrawal penalty called a surrender charge, which can also be as high as 10 percent.)

You avoid the early withdrawal penalty tax when you withdraw money from any type of retirement account before age 59½ if one of the following circumstances applies:

• You are disabled. The standard for disability is the same that applies under the Social Security program; see Chapter 7.

• You are instructed to make the withdrawal by a judge in a domestic relations order, such as a divorce decree.

• The withdrawals are made in "substantially equal payments." (Note that this exception does not apply to most employer pensions.) To take advantage of this exception, you must take at least one distribution a year from the retirement account, and the distributions must continue for at least 5 years or until you reach age 59½, whichever happens later. After the minimum payout period, you can discontinue the distributions.

The IRS has approved three methods for computing the amount of the substantially equal distributions. Each method is briefly summarized on the following page.

LIFE EXPECTANCY METHOD

This method offers the advantage of simplicity, but the disadvantage of smaller annual payments than the other two methods. The annual withdrawal is figured by dividing the balance in the retirement account by your life expectancy or by the joint life and survivor expectancy of you and your beneficiary (see life expectancy charts in Appendix 14). For example, if you are 50 in 1994 and your IRA account balance is $100,000 at the beginning of the year, you may take a penalty-free distribution of $3,496 in 1994 ($100,000 divided by 28.6 life expectancy). If you were using the joint and survivor expectancy of you and your beneficiary, and you were both 55 in 1994, the penalty-free distribution for 1994 would be $2,906 ($100,000 divided by 34.4).

AMORTIZATION METHOD

Under this method of computation, the annual penalty-free withdrawal will be larger than under the life expectancy method. The amortization method uses the same life expectancy tables, but then amortizes the balance in the retirement account like a mortgage based on an IRS-approved long-term interest rate. For example, assuming an interest rate of 8.6 percent, a 50-year-old with a $100,000 balance in his retirement account could withdraw $8,600 without penalty in the first year (as opposed to $3,496 under the life expectancy method).

ANNUITY FACTOR METHOD

This method of computation yields the largest penalty-free withdrawals. Unlike the first two methods, which rely on the IRS life expectancy tables, the annuity factor method uses insurance mortality tables, which project shorter life expectancies. The 50-year-old with the $100,000 account balance could withdraw $9,002 under this method (as opposed to $3,496 under the life expectancy method, or $8,600 under the amortization method).

Before you decide to start making substantially equal withdrawals from your retirement account, remember this: each withdrawal is not penalized, but it will be taxed as ordinary income (unless it is allocable to non-deductible contributions, as explained at page 371). Also, keep in mind that you will have to pay a 10 percent penalty tax for all payments received before age 59½ if you don't continue the payments for the minimum number of years.

EXCESS WITHDRAWAL PENALTY

Your freedom to draw on your retirement savings between ages 59½ and 70½ is checked by a tax on excess distributions. This 15 percent penalty tax is triggered by an IRA distribution of over $150,000. Thus, the penalty tax on a $200,000 IRA distribution would be $7,500 (15 percent times the $50,000 excess over $150,000).

When you are getting ready to retire, and are trying to decide what to do with your pension savings, keep this penalty tax in mind. If you think you might need to withdraw more than $150,000 from your retirement savings within three years of leaving your job, you probably shouldn't move your pension savings into an IRA. Even though moving your pension savings into an IRA would defer taxation of your retirement funds (see page 368), and would avoid the early withdrawal penalty if you are under age 59½, you might end up paying a 15 percent penalty tax if you have to withdraw over $150,000 from the IRA in a single year before you reach 70½. You might be better off taking your pension distribution, paying the 10 percent penalty tax (if you are under 59½), and using income averaging to reduce the tax on the distribution (see page 379).

BENEFIT OF RETIREMENT SAVINGS AFTER AGE 59½

When you reach age 59½ you can finally start enjoying your retirement savings without worrying about any early withdrawal penalty. This doesn't mean, however, that it makes good financial sense to start tapping your retirement savings sooner than necessary.

One good reason to resist the lure of your retirement savings is the uncertainty of the future. You do not want to outlive your retirement savings. Your retirement savings, once used, cannot easily be replaced.

Another reason to avoid the unnecessary depletion of your retirement savings gets back to the T word: taxes. As long as your retirement savings are in a retirement account, they enjoy tax-free growth. Take the money out of the retirement account, and you will start paying tax on its interest, dividends, and capital gains. You will also have to pay income tax on at least part of each withdrawal of retirement savings.

If your retirement account is funded exclusively with tax-deductible contributions, then each withdrawal will be fully taxed. If your account is funded by a mix of tax-deductible and non-deductible contributions, the taxable portion of each withdrawal will reflect the ratio of non-deductible contributions in the account. If you only funded your retirement account with non-deductible contributions (as with a variable annuity), you will only owe tax on the interest portion of each withdrawal.

This can get quite confusing. How are you supposed to know how much of each withdrawal is taxable?

According to the IRS, you are responsible for keeping track of your non-deductible contributions. If you have good records, you can use Form 8606 to figure the taxable and non-taxable portion of each distribution. If you don't have good records, you may be taxed on the same money twice.

If you need another reason to keep away from your retirement savings for as long as possible, think Social Security. The more income you have, the greater the likelihood that some percentage of your Social Security benefits will be taxed. Withdrawals of retirement savings can boost a retiree's income over the base amounts, and trigger a tax on Social Security benefits (see pages 342–350). If the withdrawal of retirement savings is inevitable, and your Social Security benefits are at risk, consider bunching your receipt of retirement income in alternating years. By keeping your income low one year, and letting it rise the next, you may be able to escape taxation of your Social Security benefits every other year.

Despite the many reasons for leaving your retirement savings alone, you may have an equally compelling reason for tapping into a retirement account: you need the money. You may need a chunk of cash to pay off some bills, relocate to a warmer climate, or start a business. Or you may need monthly income payments that will help you cover your monthly expenses.

LUMP-SUM WITHDRAWALS

There is a potentially devastating cost associated with a lump-sum withdrawal of retirement savings. Lump-sum distributions are taxed as ordinary income to you, and the tax can be prohibitively high.

That's the bad news. The good news is that you can reduce the tax due on a lump-sum distribution by using income averaging, capital gains tax treatment, or both. These methods of reducing your tax liability are examined below.

INCOME AVERAGING

With income averaging, the IRS treats the lump-sum distribution as if it is the only income you receive over a 5- or 10-year period. Of course this is a fiction since you actually receive the entire distribution in a single year (either in one sum or in installments), but the fiction keeps you out of the higher tax bracket that might otherwise apply in the year of the distribution. Income averaging reduces the rate at which your lump-sum distribution is taxed to the lowest tax rate available (currently 15 percent).

For example, Sue takes a $100,000 lump-sum distribution, and elects 5-year averaging. She divides the $100,000 by 5, and pays 5 times the tax due on $20,000 (using tax rates for a single person even if she's married) by April 15 of the year following the distribution. She does this calculation on IRS Form 4972. She only pays the tax once; not five times.

Ten-year averaging almost always yields better results than 5-year averaging with larger distributions (of $390,000 or more).

Not every investor qualifies for income averaging. For one thing, income averaging is not available for lump-sum withdrawals from an IRA account. Also, income averaging is only available to pension plan participants who have been in their plan for at least 5 years plus the year of the distribution. Finally, a lump-sum distribution can only be averaged if, at the time of distribution, the investor was at least 59½. Ten-year averaging (but not 5-year averaging) can be used by investors before age 59½ if they take the lump-sum pension on account of disability or termination of employment for any reason (firing, layoff, or retirement). Of course, most investors who take a lump-sum distribution before age 59½ will still have to pay the 10 percent early withdrawal penalty tax whether or not they qualify for income averaging (see page 376).

Income averaging is a once-in-a-lifetime proposition. You can only income average if you've never done it before (unless the first time you income averaged was before 1987). This restriction makes it important to plan ahead. If you have several pension plans, take all your lump-sum withdrawals in the same year so that you can use income averaging or save income averaging for your largest anticipated lump-sum withdrawal.

Is it too late to do anything if you took a lump-sum distribution two years ago, before you ever heard of income averaging? No. The law generally gives you until the later of three years after your return was filed, or two years after the tax was paid, to go back and income average.

CAPITAL GAINS TAX TREATMENT

You may be able to elect to have part of your non-IRA lump-sum distribution taxed at a maximum 20 percent capital gains tax. Only if you were covered by a pension plan before 1974 can you elect to have part of your lump-sum payment taxed at a maximum 20 percent tax rate.

Capital gains tax treatment and income averaging are not mutually exclusive. If you qualify, you can elect to use one or the other, or both. As a general rule, 5- or 10-year averaging on the entire distribution yields the lowest tax unless the portion of the distribution earned after 1974 exceeds about $110,500.

PERIODIC PAYMENTS

You may not need a lump-sum from your retirement savings. A periodic payout may better suit your needs.

If you participate in a company pension plan, you may be permitted to spread out your pension payments over your life expectancy (or the joint life expectancies of you and your spouse). The administrator of your plan can provide you with the details of your payout options.

If you opt for a periodic pension payout, you must also select a time period for the payout. Your choices usually include:

• A single life annuity, which pays benefits for your lifetime. The benefits start when you retire and end at your death. If you are married, your spouse must consent to your selection of this type of annuity by signing a waiver form. Your spouse will not be paid any benefits after your death. A single life annuity makes sense if your spouse is unlikely to need income from your pension (because your spouse is unlikely to survive you, or has another source of retirement income).

• A joint and survivor annuity, which pays benefits for your lifetime and the lifetime of your spouse. Since benefits are paid for two lifetimes instead of one, each payment is smaller than with a single life annuity. A joint and survivor annuity is good for couples when the nonworking spouse does not have a pension, or is likely to outlive the worker.

An alternative to a joint and survivor annuity is life insurance. By planning to provide for your surviving spouse with life insurance instead of pension income, you eliminate the risk that your spouse will predecease you and leave you with a lifetime of reduced pension benefit checks. You can use some of the increased pension benefit you will get by electing a single life annuity to pay the life insurance premium. Then, if your spouse predeceases you, you can let the policy lapse or name a new beneficiary.

• A term annuity, which pays benefits for a certain number of years (usually 5, 10, 15, or 20 years). The term of years cannot be longer than the life expectancies of you and your spouse. If you or your spouse dies before the end of the term, benefits will continue to be paid to the surviving spouse until the end of the term. You should only consider this option if you retire in ill health.

Since you will be stuck for life with whichever option you select, give the decision some serious thought.

Some of the reasons a pension plan participant might elect a periodic payout include:

• The participant doesn't want the responsibility of investing the retirement funds. By making only periodic withdrawals from the pension account, the participant leaves the job of managing the retirement savings with the pension plan administrator. The downside to leaving investment decisions to a plan administrator is that administrators tend to invest pension funds conservatively, which results in a low rate of return.

• The participant likes the security of a monthly income payment. The election of a pension plan payout guarantees the participant a monthly cash payment. The downside of a monthly income payment is that the payment may lose ground to inflation.

• The participant plans on outliving the applicable life expectancy. A participant who outlives life expectancy makes money on a pension plan payout that is based on life expectancy.

Pension plan participants are not the only investors who can draw on their retirement savings over a period of time. IRA investors can also make periodic withdrawals from their account.

An IRA investor who starts making periodic withdrawals of retirement savings must exercise great care so as not to deplete the IRA account too rapidly. The investor does not want to outlive the retirement savings. The life expectancy method of computation explained at page 377 helps to coordinate IRA withdrawals and the investor's life expectancy (or the joint life expectancies of the investor and spouse).

ROLLOVERS

A lump-sum distribution or periodic payout is for you if you plan on spending your retirement savings. But what if you just want to move your retirement savings from one account to another?

The movement of retirement savings is called a rollover. Some of the reasons people roll over their retirement savings from a pension or 401(k) into an IRA or Keogh (if self-employed) include the following:

• An investor who wants greater control over the investment of his or her retirement savings can roll over the pension or 401(k) savings into a self-directed IRA or Keogh, and decide which of the 4,000 mutual funds to invest in.

• An investor who questions the safety of an employer's pension fund can roll over the pension or 401(k) savings into an IRA or Keogh, and stop worrying about the loss of years of savings to mismanagement or company failure.

Some pension plans also permit rollovers to the pension plan of a new employer. Three important advantages to rolling over your pension funds are:

1. You do not have to pay taxes on your pension benefit until you withdraw it from the new retirement account.

2. You do not have to pay tax on interest you earned on your pension savings until you withdraw the interest from the new retirement account.

3. You do not have to pay a 10 percent penalty tax if you are under age 59½ at the time of the rollover.

If a rollover sounds right for you, here's what you have to do: Either instruct your employer to transfer your retirement savings directly into an IRA account that you have set up for the express purpose of receiving the funds (not an existing IRA), or tell your employer to send a check for the lump-sum distribution to you and then reinvest your retirement savings in a specially opened IRA account within 60 days.

Under a new law that took effect on January 1, 1993, the second route became considerably less attractive than the first route. The new legislation requires employers who make lump-sum distributions to their employees to withhold 20 percent of the employee's account for tax purposes. This means that if you ask your employer to send you a check for the lump-sum distribution, the check will be for only 80 percent of your pension savings.

You can, however, continue to enjoy tax-free growth of your entire pension, and get the withheld 20 percent returned to you, if you roll over the full amount of your retirement savings. This means reinvesting the check for 80 percent in a new IRA or Keogh, and also putting an amount equal to the withheld 20 percent in the new account. You may need to withdraw money from your savings account to replace the withheld 20 percent, but it will be worth your while. By rolling over the full amount of your pension, you get the withheld 20 percent returned to you when you file your tax return the following April, and you get the benefit of continued tax-free growth of your entire retirement account.

> **S**pecial rollover rules apply to IRAs. You can roll over your IRA funds either by instructing the financial institution that holds your IRA to transfer your savings directly to another IRA or Keogh (if self-employed) account in a different institution, or by requesting a check for the balance in your retirement account, and then depositing the check in the same or different IRA or Keogh account within 60 days of withdrawal. Neither method will result in the taxation of your IRA savings. However, you may have to pay some fees for leaving your old account, and starting up a new account.

The consequences of failing to reinvest the entire amount of your pension (the 80 percent distribution, plus an amount to make up for the withheld 20 percent) is even worse than you might think. Not only will you lose additional tax-free growth on 20 percent of your retirement savings, and not only will you have to pay income tax on the withheld 20 percent, you may also have to pay an early withdrawal penalty, depending on your age when you receive the distribution (see page 376).

Only by having your employer transfer your pension savings directly into another retirement account (and keeping your sweaty palms off the check!) can you avoid the 20 percent withholding tax. Simply open a new IRA or Keogh account, and instruct your former employer to transfer your retirement funds directly into the new account.

Do not have the funds transferred into an existing IRA. If you do, you will lose the ability to transfer the funds to a future employer's pension plan (should you go back to work) or Keogh (should you go to work for yourself). After 5 years in the new employer's plan or Keogh, you will qualify for income averaging when you finally withdraw the money. (See page 379 for more on income averaging.) This will save you money in taxes.

LEAVING PENSION SAVINGS WITH A FORMER EMPLOYER

If you don't need the money in your pension or 401(k) account right away, and you want to avoid paying taxes on your retirement savings for as long as possible, and you don't want to roll over your retirement savings into an IRA, you may be able to leave your retirement fund with your former employer even after you retire. Your employer may or may not agree to let you remain in the company plan.

There are advantages and disadvantages to remaining in a former employer's plan. First, the advantages. By leaving the money with your employer, you may be able to take out a loan against your retirement savings. This is not an option once your retirement savings are in an IRA. Also, you may be able to use income averaging to hold down your taxes when you eventually withdraw your savings. Income averaging is not available with IRA withdrawals (see page 380). Finally, your retirement savings will be protected from creditors in the event you have to file for personal bankruptcy. Money in IRAs is usually not protected from creditors.

The disadvantage to leaving retirement savings with an employer is loss of control. You gain control over the investment of your retirement funds when you roll them over into an IRA or Keogh.

BENEFIT OF RETIREMENT SAVINGS LATE IN LIFE (AFTER AGE 70½)

When you reach age 70½ you must start withdrawing your retirement savings from your IRA, Keogh, pension, 401(k), SEP, or ESOP (but not a variable annuity).

The withdrawals must begin by April 1 following the year of your 70½ birthday even if you are still working.

A hefty penalty tax is assessed against any taxpayer who fails to make the required minimum withdrawals of retirement savings after age 70½. The tax equals 50 percent of the amount that should have been withdrawn. Thus, a taxpayer who withdraws $10,000 instead of the required $20,000 would be liable for a $5,000 penalty tax (half the difference between $20,000 and $10,000). The required minimum withdrawal can be made in one payment, or monthly installments over the course of the year.

If you have more than one retirement account, you do not have to take the required minimum withdrawal from each account. You can take the full amount of the withdrawal out of one account, usually the account paying the lowest rate of interest.

AVOIDING MINIMUM REQUIRED WITHDRAWALS

The best way to maximize the period of time that your money grows tax-free in a retirement account is to minimize the size of your mandatory distributions after age 70½. What, if anything, can you do to influence the size of your mandatory distributions?

The amount of your mandatory distribution can be computed under one of two methods. The recalculation method recalculates the distribution year after year based on your revised life expectancy. The term-certain method uses a specified payout period that does not change over time. There is general consensus among estate planners that the term-certain method is the best method for prolonging the tax-deferred growth of retirement savings, and preserving your retirement savings for your heirs. (Life expectancy tables are reprinted in Appendix 14.)

Let's say a husband and wife have a joint life expectancy of 25 years. Under the recalculation method, when the husband reaches age 70½ the couple would have to withdraw 1/25 of their retirement account balance. The following year, when their recalculated life expectancy was just over 24 years, they would have to withdraw just over 1/24 of their retirement account balance. And so on.

The problem would arise when either the husband or the wife died. The survivor's minimum distributions would start to be based on the survivor's single life expectancy, not the couple's joint life expectancy. The change to the single life expectancy payout would increase the amount of each minimum distribution, increase the survivor's tax liability, and deplete the survivor's estate more rapidly.

Now consider the term-certain method. The same couple would lock into a 25-year payout based on their combined life expectancy when the husband turned 70½. When one member of the couple died, the payouts would continue unchanged. Upon the survivor's death, the money would be paid to the estate for the duration of the 25-year term, thus prolonging its tax-deferred growth.

Although you probably don't know it, you can elect either the term-certain or the recalculation method. If you don't make any election before April 1 of the year following the year in which you turn 70½, the IRS will elect the recalculation method for you. The IRS has not given taxpayers any guidance about how to choose one method over another, but written notification appears to work. Here's a prototype of the letter you want to send:

Sample Letter of Instruction

Date

Name of financial institution
Address
City, State, Zip

Re: Your account number
    Your Social Security number
    Your date of birth

Dear Sir/Madam:

This letter of instruction shall serve as formal notification that I elect the term-certain method of distribution with respect to the above-referenced account. The beneficiary of said account is [insert relationship and name of beneficiary].

Please send me confirmation of this election at your earliest convenience.

Sincerely,

Your signature
Your printed name

You should send a letter of instruction to each institution that holds any retirement money for you. Send the letter by certified mail with return receipt requested before April 1 following the year in which you turn 70½.

BENEFIT OF VESTING

Vesting is an important concept if your employer has contributed to your pension, 401(k), profit-sharing plan, or ESOP. Until you vest, you will not be legally entitled to all your retirement savings.

Money *you* contribute to your pension plan is immediately vested. You are usually allowed to withdraw these funds at any time, whether you are still working, or you quit, or you are fired.

But different rules apply to funds that your employer has contributed to your pension account. Your employer has selected the vesting rules that apply to your plan. Three of the more common types of vesting rules are:

• Cliff vesting. You are entitled to your benefit after 5 years of employment. If you stop working before 5 years, you are probably not entitled to any of the money your employer contributed to your pension account. However, in specific situations you can earn a benefit after less than 5 years of employment.

• Graded vesting. You are entitled to 20 percent of your benefit after 3 years of employment, then an additional 20 percent of your benefit each year until you become fully vested after 7 years.

• Vesting upon entry. After 3 years of employment, you are entitled to 100 percent of your pension benefits.

To figure out when you vest, you must know how your employer defines a year of employment or a year of service. Typically, a year of service is defined as a continuous 12-month period during which you worked at least 1,000 hours (about half-time).

Some plans use a different rule called the elapsed time rule. Under this rule, you receive credit only if you are employed on the first and last day of each plan year. However, if you stop working before the last day of the plan year because of a layoff, disability, or leave of absence, you are entitled to credit for an extra year.

A break in employment, such as for an illness or temporary leave, may interrupt a year of service, depending on the plan. Paid time off, for vacation, sick days, personal days, or disability leave, however, does not interrupt a year of service.

A different but related concern of pensioners is: When can you start collecting your (vested) retirement benefits? Once again, the answer depends on the details of your employer's plan. There are four times you may be permitted to start collecting your pension:

• Normal retirement. Most plans permit you to collect retirement benefits at the normal retirement age of 65. Some plans offer increased benefits if you continue to work after age 65.

• Early retirement. Many plans allow you to collect a reduced benefit if you stop working before age 65, usually at age 55, 60, or 62.

• Disability retirement. Some plans pay retirement benefits if you become unable to work due to an illness or disability.

• Termination of employment. Some plans will permit you to withdraw your pension funds when you terminate employment, regardless of your age.

For more information on pension entitlement rules, send $3.50 for the booklet entitled "Can You Count on Getting a Pension" to:

> **Pension Publications**
> 918 16th Street, N.W., Suite 704
> Washington, DC 20006

BENEFIT OF BORROWING
AGAINST RETIREMENT SAVINGS

Some plans permit employees to take out loans from their pension plan. If your plan permits loans, you need to find out: What interest rate does your employer charge? How does the rate compare to those of alternative lenders? Your plan administrator should be able to provide you with this information.

There are several benefits of borrowing against a pension account. First, you get to use your retirement savings without having to pay a tax or penalty on the distribution. Second, you can expect to pay a lower rate of interest than banks charge. Third, whatever rate of interest you pay, you pay the interest to yourself. Finally, taking out the loan is often as simple as making a bank withdrawal. Since you are essentially lending the money to yourself there are no credit checks or lengthy applications.

However, there are some restrictions:

• You can usually borrow up to half of your vested pension benefit (see page 387) or $50,000, whichever is less, unless your plan only permits loans of up to $10,000.

• You will probably have to repay the loan within 5 years, but you may be eligible for a back-to-back loan, or an extension on repayment if the purpose of the loan is to purchase a home.

Any outstanding balance on the loan you are unable to repay will be treated as a distribution. Income tax will be due on the distribution, as well as a 10 percent early withdrawal penalty tax if you are under 59½.

IRA investors are not permitted to borrow against their IRA savings.

BENEFIT OF
INHERITED RETIREMENT SAVINGS

The rules that apply to surviving beneficiaries of retirement plans vary considerably, depending on the nature of the plan. Each plan is discussed in a separate section below.

IRA BENEFICIARIES

The rules governing inherited IRA accounts are somewhat different for spousal and non-spousal beneficiaries. In the discussion that follows, you are assumed to be the IRA owner.

A surviving spousal beneficiary of an IRA has two options. The first option is to treat your IRA as his or her own. The election of this option will permit the spouse to contribute money to the IRA and roll over the IRA into another retirement account.

A spousal beneficiary who makes the IRA his or her own can continue to enjoy the tax-free growth of your IRA savings. The future of the spouse's IRA account will depend on your age at death.

If you died before age $70\frac{1}{2}$, your spouse can delay taking any distributions from the account until April 1 of the year after the year in which your spouse reaches $70\frac{1}{2}$. Distributions will then be based on the joint life and survivor's life expectancy of your spouse and your spouse's new beneficiary. If you died after age $70\frac{1}{2}$, your spouse can still usually take smaller distributions than if he or she elected the alternative option, discussed below. Distributions to the spousal beneficiary before the spouse reaches $59\frac{1}{2}$ are subject to the 10 percent penalty tax for early withdrawals.

The alternative option available to a surviving spousal beneficiary is to remain on your IRA account as a beneficiary. If this option is elected, the remaining payout period will depend on your age at death.

If you died before starting to collect mandatory distributions at age $70\frac{1}{2}$, your plan may give your spouse a choice between withdrawing the funds over your spouse's life expectancy or withdrawing the entire account balance by the end of the fifth year following your death. If you died after receiving a required minimum distribution at $70\frac{1}{2}$, your spouse must continue to receive distributions at least as rapidly as you were receiving them. Unlike distributions made to the spouse before age $59\frac{1}{2}$ under the first option, distributions made under the second option are not subject to the 10 percent penalty tax for early withdrawals.

A spouse who plans to use your IRA savings to fund his or her retirement after age $59\frac{1}{2}$ should exercise the first option, and move the IRA money in the spouse's own account within a year of your death. A spouse who is under age $59\frac{1}{2}$ and needs the IRA funds to live on is better off with the second option.

Under no circumstances should your surviving spouse move the funds from your IRA account into an existing IRA account. Your spouse must keep the inherited money separate to preserve the option of naming a new beneficiary (which could become important in prolonging the tax-free growth of your savings).

If your spouse does nothing (doesn't elect a distribution within 5 years of your death, or a periodic payout, or to treat the IRA as his or her own), the IRA will be paid out in periodic payments over the course of your spouse's life expectancy. The payout will start by December 31 of the year you would have turned 70½, or December 31 of the year following the year of your death.

A non-spousal beneficiary does not have the option of making your IRA his or her own. All of the other rules discussed in connection with spousal beneficiaries apply equally to non-spousal beneficiaries.

Pension, 401(k), and ESOP Plan Beneficiaries

Most company retirement plans pay benefits to the worker's surviving spouse. If you elect survivor's benefits, the payments you receive during your lifetime will be reduced. Your spousal beneficiary will usually be entitled to 50 percent of your benefit amount.

If you do not elect survivor's benefits, and are married, your spouse must sign a written waiver form. As a general matter, married couples are well-advised to elect survivor's benefits.

If you elect a joint and 50 percent survivor payout, and die before receiving any payments, your surviving spouse may have a couple of options, depending on the plan:

- The spouse can collect 50 percent of the benefit you would have received as soon as you would have received it (an option with a defined benefit or defined contribution pension, but probably not with a profit-sharing plan).

- The spouse can withdraw the balance of your account in a lump-sum payment, and either pay taxes on it or roll it over into an IRA (an option with a defined contribution pension or profit-sharing plan, IRA, Keogh, SEP, or ESOP).

The second option is best for a surviving spouse who does not immediately need the funds and wants to keep your retirement savings growing tax-free.

SAFETY OF RETIREMENT SAVINGS

Will your retirement savings be around when you need them? Good question.

SAFETY OF YOUR IRA

The Federal Deposit Insurance Corporation (FDIC) covers up to $100,000 of IRA deposits in each bank and savings and loan where you have an account. This $100,000 of coverage is in addition to the $100,000 of coverage per bank that protects your savings and checking accounts.

As of December 19, 1993, all your retirement savings in a single bank or savings and loan institution are applied toward the $100,000 coverage limit. This means that if you have one $75,000 IRA and a $50,000 IRA in the same bank, only $100,000 of your $125,000 investment will be covered. Prior to December 19, 1993, the full $125,000 would have been insured.

If you have substantial retirement savings, and are concerned about the $100,000 cap on your coverage, the best thing to do is to open a number of accounts in different banks. There is no limit on the number of accounts you can open to hold your retirement savings.

SAFETY OF YOUR KEOGH INVESTMENT

The FDIC insures retirement accounts in banks that are members of the FDIC. Prior to December 19, 1993, each Keogh retirement account was insured for up to $100,000. Under new regulations, however, the total extent of coverage is $100,000 per institution. A depositor who has $300,000 of retirement savings spread among four different accounts at a single bank is only insured up to $100,000. To ensure adequate coverage, never have more than $100,000 of total retirement savings in any one bank.

SAFETY OF YOUR PENSION

What you can do to maximize the security and growth of your pension savings depends on whether you participate in a defined contribution plan or a defined benefit plan.

DEFINED CONTRIBUTION PLANS

Defined contribution pension plans, including 401(k) plans (which are discussed on page 369), are not insured by the federal government. If the company holding your defined contribution plan goes bankrupt, your pension funds should be protected because the law requires the fund to be separately maintained in a trust account. You may, however, have to wait some time before you see any of your money.

Pension plans held at a bank are insured by the FDIC. Before December 19, 1993, every pensioner was insured for up to $100,000 if the bank holding the plan failed. As of December 1993, however, pensions deposited at weak banks will only be insured for up to $100,000 *per plan,* not per individual. This means that if a pension plan covering nine thousand people puts its multimillion-dollar pension plan into a financially unstable bank, and the bank fails, each pensioner would get $11.11 ($100,000 divided among nine thousand pensioners). Note that this change only applies to weak banks that are found to have inadequate amounts of capital.

The FDIC has issued a report finding about 20 percent of all banks to be weakly capitalized. The problem is that plan managers do not have any way to identify which are the weak banks. The best a pension plan manager can do is demand written assurance from the bank holding its funds that the bank qualifies for the more extensive insurance coverage, and will notify the manager of any change in its status. As a pensioner, all you can do is urge your plan administrator to obtain this written guarantee.

The biggest risk for pensioners in defined contribution plans is bad investments. You can decide how your pension funds are invested, and you should. To maximize the security and growth of your funds, keep the following words of advice in mind:

• Diversify, diversify, diversify. The law requires professional pension plan administrators to diversify their investments, and for good reason. You do not want to invest too much of your assets in one company's stock, because if the value of the stock drops, so will your income and principal.

You also do not want to invest too much in guaranteed investment contracts (GICs), which are sold by insurance companies. The issuing company could go bust, and you could find yourself at the mercy of the state's insurance guaranty fund. In addition, the fixed income you earn on the investment will likely lose ground to inflation.

• Read the small print. Compared to your plan's annual statement, the back of a cereal box makes for fascinating reading. Review the plan to see how much money you and your employer have contributed to your plan, and how your investments are growing.

• Take your company's temperature. Is it enjoying good financial health? If it looks like your company could be heading for bankruptcy or a takeover, consider taking out your pension savings in a lump-sum withdrawal or rolling it over into an IRA. Make sure you are aware of the tax consequences of any distribution!

DEFINED BENEFIT PLANS

The Pension Benefit Guaranty Corporation (PBGC) is the government agency that insures defined benefit pension plans. Unfortunately, the PBGC only insures part of each worker's pension.

For plans that terminate in 1993–1994, the maximum monthly PBGC guarantee is $2,556.82 a month for a 65-year-old retiree. This means that the PBGC will step in and pay every single 65-year-old participant in the terminated plan up to $2,556.82 a month if the terminated plan was not fully funded. (The guaranteed amount drops when the worker is married and the benefit will be paid for the joint life expectancy of the worker and spouse.) A 60-year old participant is only guaranteed $1,661.93 a month from the PBGC, and a 55-year-old worker only gets up to $1,150.57 a month. Early retirees are guaranteed a smaller maximum monthly benefit than normal age and late retirees because they stand to collect the PBGC payments over a longer period of time.

The PBGC appears to be on shaky financial ground itself, with a budget deficit in the billions of dollars.

If you have any questions about benefits guaranteed by the PBGC, contact:

> **Pension Benefit Guaranty Corporation**
> 2020 K Street, N.W.
> Washington, DC 20006
> 202-326-4000

The PBGC will send you a free publication entitled "Your Guaranteed Pension" on request.

Most defined benefit pensions are well-funded, and are earning competitive rates of interest in diversified investments (mostly stocks and bonds). However, if you are a pensioner with a defined benefit plan, you still face three risks.

First, your plan may be one of the underfunded plans. Employers in financial trouble often cut back on the annual contributions they make to their employees' pensions, or promise their workers higher pension benefits without increasing the amount of the contributions. If your company is facing bankruptcy, and your plan is not adequately funded, you may have a problem on your hands. Pension plan funding receives low priority when a company is on the brink of bankruptcy. According to PBGC estimates, some 5 million workers and retirees were covered by underfunded pension plans in 1992.

Second, your company may terminate your pension plan to get at "surplus" money. Some pension plans have more money than they need to pay off their pensioners. Companies in this position have the option of shutting down their plan, paying off their pensioners, and keeping whatever money is left over (less a tax of up to 50 percent on the recaptured funds). Sometimes a company exercising this option will purchase annuities from insurance companies to meet their outstanding obligations to their pensioners. According to federal estimates, the pensions of 3 to 4 million people have been transferred to insurance companies.

How secure are these pension annuities? In recent years the insurance industry has undergone a shakedown of sorts, with hundreds of insurers going bankrupt. An annuity issued by a financially unstable insurance company is not secure at all.

Pensions that are transferred to an insurance company lose the protection of the PBGC. In the event of the insurance company's bankruptcy, a state insurance guaranty association assumes the annuity obligations of the failed insurer. The only problem is that state insurance guaranty associations are not sufficiently well-funded to handle the large numbers of insurance company failures. According to federal estimates, more than one-sixth of all retirees are not adequately protected, even in states with well-funded insurance guaranty associations.

New regulations require employers to notify their pensioners if and when they intend to purchase annuities from an insurance company. Upon receipt of such a notice you should check out the financial health of the prospective insurance company. Go to your local library and look up the ratings the company was given by A. M. Best Company, Moody's Investors Service, and Standard and Poor's. If the ratings are less than A + + or A + from Best ("superior"), or AA from the others, file an objection with your employer. If your employer goes ahead with the purchase anyway, consider collecting your pension in a lump-sum payout if that option is available to you.

Third, your pension plan may fall victim to mismanagement and/or outright fraud. This risk is most substantial with small companies. Often the manager of a small company is also the pension plan administrator. These administrators have been known to "borrow" money from the pension plan to cover operating expenses when profits are down or simply exercise poor judgment when it comes to investing the pension funds. There is less opportunity for abuse of large corporate pension plans, which are overseen by professional corporate fiduciaries.

What, if anything, can you do to protect yourself from these many pitfalls?

• Learn as much as you can about how the money in your defined benefit plan is invested. Has the plan administrator diversified the funds to minimize your risk of loss?

• Request, read, and keep the 1- to 2-page summary annual report (SAR). The SAR will itemize the plan's administrative expenses and show the rate at which your savings are growing. Are sales commissions and management fees reasonable? Is your plan losing money when financial times are generally favorable? Has the plan loaned any money to company executives?

• Get a copy of the full annual report, called Form 5500, from your plan administrator or the Department of Labor. This report is especially important if you suspect mismanagement. Regardless of who sends you the report, you will have to pay copying costs. Since the document is lengthy and technical, you may want to ask a financial adviser or lawyer to review it for you.

• Seek legal assistance. If you think your plan administrator is violating the law, you may want to contact:

> **National Employment Lawyers Association (NELA)**
> 535 Pacific Avenue
> San Francisco, CA 94133
> 415-397-6335

Over 1200 lawyers who specialize in employment-related matters are members of NELA. You may also want to contact:

> **National Pension Assistance Project (NPAP)**
> 918 16th Street, N.W., Suite 704
> Washington, DC 20006
> 202-296-3776

NPAP, an arm of the Pension Rights Center, refers workers, retirees, and their families to lawyers who need representation in connection with pension disputes.

For detailed information about what you can do to make sure your pension savings are being managed and invested in accordance with federal law, send $8 for the booklet entitled "Protecting Your Pension Money" to:

> **Pension Publications**
> 918 16th Street, N.W., Suite 704
> Washington, DC 20006

Before pensioners were concerned about underfunding, termination, and embezzlement, their primary concern was inflation. The average 65-year-old retiree can expect to live at least 17 more years. If inflation runs at 5 percent a year, the pension in the 17th year will be worth less than half of what it was worth in the first year of retirement. Although public pensions (federal, state, and municipal) have some inflation protection, only about a third of all private corporate pensions have cost-of-living increases. The only way to get some inflation protection for your retirement savings is to collect your pension in a lump-sum payment and invest it in some type of income and growth fund.

ℹ️ *For more information*

Some good sources of information about your rights as a pensioner are available from:

Pension Rights Center
918 16th Street, N.W., Suite 704
Washington, DC 20006
202-296-3776

The Pension Rights Center publishes a booklet entitled "Where to Look for Help With a Pension Problem" in addition to a number of other informative publications. You can order the book for $8.50 from the center. You can also order "Your Pension Rights at Divorce" for $16.50. To receive a publication list, send a self-addressed stamped envelope to the center.

AARP Fulfillment
601 E Street., N.W.
Washington, DC 20049

For general information about your pension rights, request "A Guide to Understanding Your Pension Plan," "A Woman's Guide to Pension Rights," and "Women, Pensions, and Divorce."

Older Women's League
666 11th Street, N.W., Suite 700
Washington, DC 20001
202-783-6686

Send $2 for members, or $4 for nonmembers, for the tabloid "Women and Pensions."

Superintendent of Documents
U.S. Government Printing Office
Washington, DC 20402-9328
202-783-3238

Send a check for $1 for the booklet "Your Pension: Things You Should Know About Your Pension Plan," Document S/N 068-000-00003-3.

Publications Desk
Division of Public Affairs
PWBA-DPA-#N/5511
U.S. Department of Labor
Pension and Welfare Benefits Administration
200 Constitution Avenue, N.W., Room N-5511
Washington, DC 20210
202-219-8921

Request the free publications "What You Should Know About the Pension Law," "How to File a Claim for Your Benefits," and "How to Obtain Employee Benefit Documents from the Labor Department."

Internal Revenue Service
800-TAX-FORM (829-3676)

Request the free publications "Pension and Annuity Income" (Publication Number 575), "Looking Out for #2: A Married Couple's Guide to Understanding Your Benefit Choices at Retirement From a Defined Contribution Plan" (Publication Number 1565), "Looking Out for #2: A Married Couple's Guide to Understanding Your Benefit Choices at Retirement from a Defined Benefit Plan" (Publication Number 1566).

Consumer Information Center
P.O. Box 100
Pueblo, CO 81002
719-948-3334

Send a check for 50 cents payable to Superintendent of Documents, and request the publication "What You Should Know About the Pension Law," Document S/N 443X.

Pension and Welfare Benefits Administration
Division of Technical Assistance and Inquiries
U.S. Department of Labor
200 Constitution Avenue, N.W., Room N-5658
Washington, DC 20210
202-219-8776

A recorded message will direct your call to personnel who can answer your questions about your pension plan.

SAFETY OF YOUR 401(K) SAVINGS

Money in your 401(k) plan is safe even if your employer goes bankrupt. Some plans, however, give the employer sole responsibility for making investment decisions. This is most common with small employers. Participants in these types of funds face the risk that the employer will not make profitable investment decisions on their behalf.

SAFETY OF YOUR ESOP

What can you do if you fear a drop in the value of your company's stock? Many ESOP participants are unaware of an important provision in ESOP plans that allows employees age 55 and over, who have been in the plan for at least 10 years, to shift 25 percent of their ESOP savings out of company stock and into other investments. The employee can then move an additional 25 percent of ESOP funds out of company stock 5 years after the first transfer.

Where you can move your ESOP funds depends on your employer. Some companies permit their employees to invest in stock or bond funds; others let workers roll over their retirement savings into an IRA.

Diversifying ESOP savings is often a good idea, even for workers who do not see bad times ahead for their company's stock. For more information on ESOPs, contact:

> **National Center for Employee Stock Ownership**
> 2201 Broadway, Suite 807
> Oakland, CA 94612
> 510-272-9461

A variable annuity is only as sound as the insurance company that issues it. See page 409 for tips on investing with a financially sound insurance carrier.

For additional information on retirement plans, request the free publication "Receiving a Lump Sum Distribution" from:

> **AARP Investment Program/Scudder**
> Box 2540
> Boston, MA 02208
> 800-322-2282, ext. 4686

For more information on the tax consequences of withdrawing your retirement savings, request Publication Number 590 from the IRS at 800-TAX-FORM (829-3676).

BACK TO SANDY

After reviewing the rules that govern IRAs, Sandy decided not to touch those savings until she reached age 59½.

But, after speaking to the pension administrator at work, she decided to collect her pension savings in a single payment. The funds were available to her as of age 55, and she was able to lessen the tax bite by spreading out the tax due on the pension payout over several years.

Sandy used the large sum of cash she got from her pension to make a down payment on a luxurious condominium in Florida, where she enjoys entertaining her three children and six grandchildren.

14.

BENEFITING FROM LIFE INSURANCE

Stan had always maintained term life insurance. He knew that if anything happened to him while the insurance was in effect, his wife and two college-age children would be protected.

When Stan turned 50 years old, he started to rethink his life insurance plan. He realized that he was wasting his money on increasingly costly term life insurance premiums now that his family was almost grown.

He started wondering: Should he cancel his insurance entirely and invest the money he saved in premiums in the stock market? Or should he purchase some other type of life insurance?

Now that you have finished raising your family, paying off your mortgage, and financing your children's college education, you may think you are finished with life insurance. Not necessarily. You might still be able to benefit from life insurance.

Older adults can derive many benefits from life insurance: They can increase their post-retirement income, secure retirement savings, provide for a surviving spouse, finance nursing home care, and cover anticipated estate taxes. This chapter will help you see if you can still benefit from life insurance.

Before you can make an intelligent decision about purchasing or maintaining life insurance, you must understand life insurance terminology, recognize the differences among the various types of policies, and familiarize yourself with the relevant tax laws.

The background information in the first part of this chapter will equip you to tackle the second part of this chapter, which identifies a number of individual needs and discusses whether they can be met with life insurance. Finally, you will find important tips about shopping for life insurance in the third section of this chapter.

LIFE INSURANCE PRIMER

Two terms that are unavoidable when discussing life insurance are:

- Face value (or death benefit) is the amount of money the insurance company pays the beneficiary of a life insurance policy when the insured individual dies.

- Cash reserve (or cash value or cash fund) is the portion of the policyowner's premiums that are invested in savings with the insurance company; the sum of money the policyowner can collect from the insurance company when the policy is surrendered; the sum of money the policyowner can use to secure a loan from the insurance company.

VARIETIES OF LIFE INSURANCE POLICIES

What follows is a brief summary of the most common types of life insurance policies.

TERM INSURANCE

Term insurance is well-named because it provides coverage for a specified term of years. Most often, term insurance provides coverage for 1, 5, 10, or 20 years. Term insurance pays a specific death benefit if the insured dies before the end of the term. If the insured lives longer than the term, the insurance company does not pay any death benefit. Most term policies end when the insured reaches age 65 or 70.

There are different types of term insurance:

- Annual renewable term. The insured has the right to renew the policy at the end of each year for a higher premium without taking a new physical examination.

- Revertible annual term. The insured has the right to renew the policy at the end of each year, but can apply for a lower renewal rate by submitting medical evidence of good health.

- Convertible term. The insured can exchange the term policy for a different type of policy that provides more permanent insurance coverage without taking a new physical examination.

- Decreasing term. The insured can renew the term policy without paying an increased premium, but the face value of the policy gradually decreases to zero.

- Participating term. The policyholder collects dividends from the insurance company.

WHOLE LIFE INSURANCE

Whole life insurance policies provide the insured with a lifetime of coverage. These policies are more costly than term insurance because part of the policyowner's premium is put aside by the insurance company into a cash reserve. The value of the cash reserve is closely tied to the yield of bonds and mortgages.

Policyowners can use their cash reserve to secure a loan. If the loan is not repaid by the date of the insured's death, the death benefit is reduced by the amount of the loan. If the policyowner does not use the cash reserve to secure a loan, the cash reserve can be used in later years to pay the insurance premiums, or can be withdrawn when the policy is canceled. The premium for whole life insurance usually stays the same year after year.

There are different types of whole life policies:

- Limited payment. The policyowner pays premiums for a certain period of time, after which the policy is all paid up. The policy continues to provide a lifetime of coverage.
- Graded premium. The rate at which the policyowner builds cash reserves starts off low in the early years of coverage, but then increases after 10 years or so.

ADJUSTABLE LIFE INSURANCE

Adjustable life insurance is often called interest-sensitive whole life insurance because the rate of return varies according to market conditions, unlike whole life.

UNIVERSAL LIFE INSURANCE

Universal life insurance, like whole life insurance, is both an insurance policy and an investment vehicle for the policyowner. Each premium the policyowner pays is split between the cost of the insurance and the cash reserve.

The primary difference between whole and universal life insurance is flexibility. With universal life, the policyowner decides how much of each premium payment goes to purchase insurance and how much is invested in the savings plan. Typically, a young breadwinner policyholder uses most of each premium to buy a lot of insurance coverage with less going into the cash reserve. As the policyowner's needs for insurance coverage decrease over time, more of each premium payment is usually invested in savings in the cash reserve.

With universal life insurance, policyholders can change how much they pay in premiums (sometimes even skipping premium payments), how much they invest in savings, and the value of their death benefit. This feature is especially attractive to policyholders with irregular income. In a low-income month, the policyholder can make a small or no premium payment and put nothing into the cash reserve.

The downside of universal life is twofold. First, universal life generally guarantees a relatively low rate of interest. The return is linked to short-term cash yields. Many insurance companies guarantee their policyowners a certain rate of return for a period of time; others set their rate according to Treasury bills, money market funds, or some other investment.

A second drawback to universal life is the risk of loss of coverage. Because policyholders have the flexibility to decrease their premiums, they can neglect to pay the minimum necessary to continue the policy. Policyowners who pay too little in premiums lose their coverage and must prove they are insurable before they will be issued a new policy.

VARIABLE LIFE INSURANCE

The insurance company invests the policyowner's premiums in stock, bond, and money market funds selected by the policyowner. The amount of the death benefit and the value of the cash reserve reflect the performance of the selected investments. The cash reserve grows or shrinks with the performance of the investment. The death benefit increases when the fund performs well, but in no event does it fall below what it was worth when the policy was issued.

JOINT LIFE INSURANCE

Joint life insurance insures the lives of two people, but only pays a death benefit when the first insured dies. Joint life insurance is available in whole life, term, and mortgage policies. Mortgage policies are designed to pay off the balance of a mortgage when the insured dies.

SECOND-TO-DIE (OR SURVIVOR) LIFE INSURANCE

Second-to-die life insurance insures the lives of two people, but only pays a benefit at the time of the second death. The cost of this type of insurance is generally less than the cost of insuring either life separately. Some second-to-die policies offer the survivor the option of drawing an income from the policy's cash reserve after the first death.

COLLECT NOW, DIE LATER INSURANCE

Despite its ghoulish name, this new type of life insurance offers many benefits to older adults. Benefits can be paid under a collect now, die later policy *before* the insured dies. These prepaid death benefits (sometimes called accelerated or living benefits) are often used to pay the high cost of a policyowner's long-term medical care, such as care in a nursing home. Benefits paid before the insured's death reduce the amount of benefits that are paid when the insured dies. Some policies only make part of the death benefit available prior to the insured's death. Prudential, Aetna, Cigna, and Northwestern Mutual now all offer accelerated death benefits.

Insurance benefits paid prior to death, just like those paid after death, are not taxable to the beneficiary under the federal tax code and most state tax codes (which usually track federal law automatically). Living benefits may, however, affect a recipient's Medicaid eligibility. Although Medicaid has not yet required a recipient to access available living benefits, policies that the recipient converts to living benefits do become a countable source of income and resources for Medicaid purposes.

TAXES AND LIFE INSURANCE

You should know some important points about taxes and life insurance.

• As a holder of a universal life insurance policy, your cash reserves grow tax-deferred. A cash reserve is a savings account with the insurance company. If your insurance policy permits you to invest part of your premiums in a cash reserve, you will not be taxed on interest your cash reserve earns as long as your policy remains in effect. This tax break makes investing in life insurance more attractive. Insurance companies generally pay a relatively low rate of interest, but since the buildup of cash reserves is tax-deferred, you may be able to earn more than you could with other taxed investments.

Most financial planners and accountants agree that life insurance is an inferior investment unless you hold on to your policy for a long period of time. A cash-value policy only yields a competitive rate of return after about 20 years of tax-deferred growth.

• Usually little or no income tax is due when you withdraw cash reserves from your insurance policy. If you surrender your insurance policy and withdraw your cash reserve, you will only be taxed if the value of the cash reserve exceeds the value of the premiums you paid for the policy. To figure out the tax due on the withdrawal of your cash reserve, if any, follow the steps below:

STEP 1	Total premiums paid	$ _____
	LESS Total dividends received (if any)	− $ _____
	Subtotal	= $ _____
	LESS Loan from insurance company (if any)	− $ _____
	Total A	= $ _____

STEP 2   Cash reserve (Total B) $ _____

STEP 3   Compare Total A and Total B. If Total B
is larger than Total A, you will be taxed
on your withdrawal of the cash reserve.

• If you are a beneficiary of an individually owned life insurance policy, you are not taxed on benefits you collect when the insured dies. Only beneficiaries who collect the death benefit in several payments over time must pay income tax on part of each payment.

• Death benefits may be subject to estate taxation. Proceeds paid to a beneficiary upon the insured's death will be subject to estate taxation in the insured's estate if these three conditions exist:

- The insured owned the policy.
- The insured's estate is large enough.
- The insured left the estate to someone other than a surviving spouse.

The easiest way to avoid estate taxation of life insurance proceeds is to have someone other than the insured own the policy. That someone is usually a beneficiary of the policy or a trust.

If you have only one child, you might as well give the policy to that child outright. This will solve your estate tax problem: The policy will not be part of your estate, and will not be subject to estate taxes (but if the cash value of the policy exceeds $10,000, the gift may trigger a gift tax; see page 360).

If you have more than one child, however, and want to distribute the insurance proceeds equally, you may want to consider an irrevocable life insurance trust. The trust will accomplish the same goal of keeping the proceeds of the policy out of your taxable estate. You can continue to pay the premiums on the policy by making "gifts" to the trust, and the trustee of the life insurance trust must have the right to change beneficiaries and other "incidents of ownership" over the trust. An attorney who specializes in trusts and estates can draft an irrevocable life insurance trust for you.

Life insurance trusts are also a good idea for retirees who receive extensive term life insurance coverage from their employers. Since term coverage has no cash value, the transfer of the policy into the trust will not trigger any gift taxes (see page 360). Depending on the size of the death benefit, the estate tax savings may be significant.

USING LIFE INSURANCE TO PAY ESTATE TAXES

If, at the time of your death, your estate is valued at over $600,000, your beneficiaries' inheritance may be reduced by federal estate taxes. Federal estate taxes are among the steepest of all taxes. The rates start at 37 percent for estates between $600,001 and $750,000, and top off at 55 percent.

Many Americans do not think their net worth approaches the $600,000 mark, until they take a closer look at their assets. Add up the fair market value of your home, all your savings and investments, your valuable personal effects, and the face value of any life insurance policies you hold on your own life. Are you getting close to $600,000? Surprised?

If your net worth is in the $600,000 neighborhood, you may want to consider using life insurance to pay the estate taxes that may be due upon your death. The benefit of using life insurance for this purpose is that it leaves your estate intact for your beneficiaries. The insurance provides a quick source of liquid cash to pay the federal government its due.

Before you tell your insurance agent to sign you up, consider the following points:

• How do you feel about getting money back on your investment when you are not around to enjoy it? If you use your money to purchase life insurance, you will not benefit from this investment. Your heirs will. Is this what you want? Would you rather have and use the money yourself?

• Would you like to see your children enjoy a gift of money while you are alive, rather than leave them a larger inheritance when you die? Making a lifetime gift can be a source of great pleasure. The gift giver can see the recipient use the money to go to school, start a new business, or backpack across Europe.

• Would your money grow faster if it was invested in stocks and bonds, rather than insurance? This is hard to predict because the return on a life insurance policy will depend on how long you live. Imagine, for example, a 65-year-old husband and his 62-year-old wife who buy a $1 million policy. They must pay off the policy in 10 years. The first 9 years the premium is about $25,000 a year, the last year it is about $12,500. If both husband and wife die the first year, their heirs get an impressive 3,995 percent return. If the couple lives for 20 years, however, the return drops to 10.36 percent. If they live for 30 years, it is down to 7.72 percent. And remember, the return is tax-free.

• As a general rule, policyholders who live 20 years or more after purchasing insurance would have been better off in alternative investments. Of course, you have no way of knowing if you will die before your expected mortality. If you gamble on a premature death and are wrong, take comfort in knowing that insurance rarely provides a lower rate of return than tax-free bonds.

The National Insurance Consumer Organization will estimate the rate of return of an insurance policy for a $40 fee ($35 for each additional policy sent at the same time). To get an estimate send a copy of the financial portion of your policy, a check for payment, and a stamped, self-addressed envelope to the National Insurance Consumer Organization, P. O. Box 15492, Alexandria, VA 22309.

• Make sure you buy a policy from a top-rated company. You hope the company insuring your life will not have to come up with the money to pay your beneficiaries for many years. This is why you need a highly rated insurance company that will be around for several more decades, at least. Some of the most financially secure insurers that offer reasonably priced policies include State Farm Life, Guardian Life, Northwestern Mutual Life, Metropolitan, Prudential, John Hancock, New York Life, Massachusetts Mutual Life, Manulife Financial, and Principal Mutual Life. In no event should you purchase life insurance from a company that is rated less than A + + by A. M. Best Company. (You can get current Best ratings at your local public library.)

BENEFITING FROM LIFE INSURANCE

The left column of the chart below describes a number of common situations. If you find your situation described here, look in the right column for information about how you might be able to benefit from life insurance.

How Can Life Insurance Benefit You?

IF YOU:	THEN YOU:
• Are single, or married but not planning on leaving your estate to your spouse.	Should maintain enough life insurance to cover your anticipated estate taxes.
• Expect your estate to be worth $500,000 or more at the time of your death.	
• Are heavily invested in property or nonliquid investments, like stocks and bonds.	

Note: If your estate owes taxes, and there is not enough cash in your estate to pay the taxes, your executor will have to quickly sell property in your estate to raise the cash needed to pay the taxes. This can result in a loss to your estate if, for example, there is a glut in the real estate market or a slump in the stock market.

Your estate is sure to have enough ready cash to pay estate taxes if sufficient insurance benefits are payable at the time of your death. Any type of insurance on your life will serve this purpose.

IF YOU:	THEN YOU:
• Are married and plan to leave the bulk of your estate to your spouse.	Should consider purchasing a second-to-die policy, which pays a benefit upon the death of your surviving spouse.
• Expect your estate to be worth $500,000 or more at the time of your death.	
• Are heavily invested in property or nonliquid investments, like stocks and bonds.	

Note: If you predecease your spouse, and leave most of your estate to your spouse, no estate taxes will be due. However, when your spouse dies, a large estate tax may be due. Second-to-die policies are often used to pay the estate taxes that come due when a surviving spouse dies.

IF YOU:	THEN YOU:
• Already have term life insurance.	May want to convert some or all of your term policy to whole or universal life insurance, or purchase whole or universal life insurance.
• Are between 40 and 50 years of age.	
• Have some discretionary funds to invest.	

Note: Many investors are reluctant to put their money in life insurance because they see their savings reduced by sales commissions and operating costs. Also, insurance companies do not have a sterling investment performance history. However, assets in life insurance grow tax-deferred. Death benefits are exempt from income tax (and can also be exempt from estate tax with some planning; see page 404). The bottom line is that your post-tax return on money you have invested in securities earning 12 percent may be significantly less than the 8 percent or so you earn on a whole life insurance policy. Federal income tax, state taxes, and an estate tax as high as 55 percent can reduce your taxable investments by as much as one-third.

IF YOU:	*THEN YOU:*
• Own universal life insurance.	Should look into purchasing a collect now, die later rider for your universal policy.
• Do not own long-term care insurance (see Chapter 4).	
• Are not concerned about leaving a large death benefit to a spouse or children.	

Note: This rider enables you to tap into the death benefit of your policy during your lifetime. In the event you require costly long-term care in a nursing home, you can pay for the care with some or all of the death benefit from your policy. This may enable you to avoid the need for public medical assistance. The death benefit will be reduced by the amount you withdraw during your lifetime.

IF YOU:	*THEN YOU:*
• Want to increase your post-retirement income.	Can tap into the cash reserve of your whole or universal life policy.
• Are not concerned about leaving a large death benefit to a spouse or children.	

Note: There are three ways you can use your cash reserve to help cover your post-retirement expenses: (1) Take a loan from the insurance company and use the cash reserve to secure the loan. If you choose this option, you will probably pay a lower rate of interest than if you borrowed money from a bank or credit union. There is, however, a downside. Loans slow down the growth of your cash value. The insurance company will move an amount equal to the loan out of your selected investments and into a fixed-rate account that pays a lower rate of interest, about 4 percent. (2) You can withdraw your entire cash reserve by canceling your policy. You can elect to receive your savings either in a single lump-sum payment or in a number of payments spread out over time. The period of time can be the lifetime of you and your spouse. Some companies charge a fee for a periodic payout. If your insurer charges a fee, you may want to withdraw the cash reserve in a lump sum and purchase an annuity elsewhere. (3) You can withdraw part of your cash reserve. This is called a partial withdrawal. Many insurance companies charge $25 or 2 percent of the amount withdrawn as a fee. There is a tax advantage to a partial withdrawal over a full withdrawal. Withdrawals up to the value of the premiums you paid are tax-free because they are a return of your capital.

IF YOU:	*THEN YOU:*
• Are paying for whole or universal life insurance.	Can save money by reducing your insurance coverage.
• Are having trouble paying the premiums.	

Note: There are two ways you can reduce your insurance costs without sacrificing the coverage you need: (1) Convert an existing whole life policy into a reduced, paid-up insurance policy. You can stop paying premiums in exchange for a smaller death benefit and cash reserve. Just be sure to maintain enough coverage to pay the costs of settling your estate and providing for your spouse and children. (2) Elect an extended term option and stop paying your premiums. You will remain covered for a specified number of days, months, or years (determined by your age and the value of your cash reserve). At the end of the extended term, your coverage will terminate and the value of your cash reserves will be zero.

SHOPPING FOR INSURANCE

The first rule of buying insurance is to remember that the insurance agent's income is directly linked to your purchase. Insurance agents are highly motivated to make a sale, so be strong. Never buy a product you don't understand, and never buy a product you don't need. Try to meet with more than one agent before making any final decisions about a purchase.

Some additional tips for savvy life insurance shopping follow below.

CHECK THE INSURANCE COMPANY'S FINANCIAL SOUNDNESS

Avoid insurance companies that do not enjoy robust financial health. You and your family want your insurer to be around when you are ready to collect your benefits. You don't want to outlive your life insurance company.

One good way to evaluate an insurer's staying power is to review *Best's Guide to Life Insurance Companies* and *Best's Insurance Reports—Life and Health*. These publications, which profile the most prominent life insurance companies, can be found in most public libraries. They are published by A. M. Best Company, which is located in Oldwick, NJ 08858. Best, and other rating firms, evaluate the relative strength of competing insurance companies. The strongest companies have ratings that range from AAA or A + + + to A − or A3 (depending on the rating system).

LOOK FOR LOW-LOAD POLICIES

Low-load policies have much lower expenses and commission charges than typical insurance policies because they are sold directly to consumers by the insurance company. Only a handful of insurance companies sell low-load policies. Some insurance consultants and financial planners charge a flat fee of about $150 an hour, with no commissions, to help consumers select an appropriate low-load policy.

BE SUSPICIOUS

Consumers Union alerts life insurance consumers to the following common example's of misleading and deceptive sales techniques:

- Unrealistic growth projections.
- Use of dividends earned in the past to prove future earning potential.
- Altered computer printouts.
- Details buried in footnotes and small print.
- Unclear description of insurance features.

BACK TO STAN

Stan spoke with an insurance salesperson who recommended converting his term insurance policy to whole life insurance.

This strategy offered Stan two primary advantages over investing in the stock market. First, it enabled him to avoid paying taxes on the interest his insurance savings earned. This tax saving made the rate of return under the policy competitive with the return he hoped to realize with his stock investments. Second, it assured him of having enough cash in his estate to pay estate taxes. Since the bulk of his estate was tied up in property and stocks, he knew his executor would otherwise have trouble raising the cash to pay the estate taxes.

Although Stan was never a big fan of insurance salesmen, he felt confident that the agent he consulted had finally steered him right.

15.

BENEFITS OF ALTERNATIVE HOUSING ARRANGEMENTS

Ethel raised three children in a five-bedroom center hall colonial on Long Island. After her husband died, and her children moved out, she found that she was no longer enjoying her house. The monthly electric bills cost a fortune, there were always bothersome repairs to attend to, and all her friends in the neighborhood had relocated to Florida.

She decided she needed a change, but felt too young to move to a retirement community. She started wondering: What were her housing options? If she decided to keep the house, could she get some help with the expenses and chores? And was there anything she could do about her dismal social life?

People fit their house like they fit their clothes. The house that suits all your needs for 30 years can become a burden to you, in much the same way as your favorite wide-lapel burgundy dinner jacket with cravat can start collecting dust in the nether reaches of your bedroom closet. If you think you might be ready for a new living arrangement (and a new wardrobe?), this chapter is for you.

You will find an array of alternative housing arrangements once you start looking to change your living situation: You can live alone or with other people; prepare your own meals or eat communally; take care of your own household chores or leave them to others.

The first section of this chapter answers the same four questions with respect to six popular housing alternatives:

- What type of housing is it?
- Who would be interested in the housing?

- What does the housing offer its residents?
- How much does the housing cost?

Your own financial situation, medical condition, and personal preferences will determine which type of housing is right for you. The chart that appears in the second part of this chapter is designed to help you find the living arrangement that best fits your circumstances.

Finally, at the end of the chapter you will find some tips on shopping for an alternative housing arrangement.

ALTERNATIVE HOUSING OPTIONS

CONGREGATE HOUSING

WHAT IS CONGREGATE HOUSING?

Congregate housing, also known as sheltered housing or enriched housing, is any group living arrangement. Most congregate housing projects have between 30 and 300 units. Nonprofit organizations sponsor the majority of congregate housing, but some projects are publicly subsidized.

WHO WOULD BE INTERESTED IN CONGREGATE HOUSING?

Congregate housing is most suitable for older individuals who do not want the responsibility of owning their own home. Residents of congregate housing are usually able to care for their own basic personal needs, but may require assistance with some housekeeping chores, cooking, and shopping. Some people are attracted by the social aspect of congregate housing.

WHAT DOES CONGREGATE HOUSING OFFER ITS RESIDENTS?

Congregate housing provides residents with:

- A private living space and small kitchen.
- A common dining room that serves one or more daily meals.
- A variety of services, usually including some or all of the following:

  Social services.

  Housekeeping (such as cooking, cleaning, and shopping).

Transportation.

Some on-site health services.

Recreational activities.

Some personal care services.

WHAT DOES CONGREGATE HOUSING COST?

Rents vary tremendously from building to building. Sometimes a federal subsidy is available to help low-income residents pay their rent. Local housing authorities administer the subsidy programs.

CONTINUING CARE RETIREMENT COMMUNITY (CCRC)

WHAT IS A CONTINUING CARE RETIREMENT COMMUNITY?

A continuing care retirement community (CCRC), also known as a life care community, is a special type of congregate housing. CCRCs guarantee residents all the care and services they currently need, or may require in the future. Residential units as well as nursing facilities are usually located together on a CCRC campus. A CCRC can look like a city high-rise apartment, or garden apartments and cottages. Most CCRCs range in size from 100 to 500 living units.

WHO WOULD BE INTERESTED IN A CCRC?

CCRC applicants must usually:

- Meet certain health standards.
- Be able to get around, with or without the assistance of a cane or walker.
- Demonstrate sufficient financial resources to pay all anticipated expenses.
- Fall within a certain age range.

WHAT DOES A CCRC OFFER ITS RESIDENTS?

Not all CCRCs provide the same services to its residents. Any or all of the following services may be offered at a CCRC: meals, home maintenance, laundry, housekeeping, recreational activities, transportation, physician services, nursing services, dental and eye care, personal care services, companion services, drugs, and medical equipment. All CCRCs guarantee residents lifetime accommodations, some personal care and household services, and medical and nursing care.

WHAT DOES A CCRC COST?

CCRC residents are charged an entrance fee and monthly maintenance charges. Although the cost varies from community to community, depending on geographic location, type, size of unit, and services, the one-time entry fee can range from $25,000 to as high as $325,000. Monthly fees typically range from $600 to $3,500.

The cost of medical and nursing services may or may not be in addition to the entry fee and monthly fees. At an all-inclusive CCRC, long-term nursing care costs little or nothing extra. At a modified facility, long-term nursing care is provided at little or no additional cost for a limited period of time. At a fee-for-service CCRC, residents are charged for nursing services, as needed.

SHARED HOUSING

WHAT IS SHARED HOUSING?

In shared housing, also known as home matching, two or more unrelated individuals live together in a house or apartment. There are two popular models for shared housing. In one, the cohabitants are all of a certain age, usually 60 or older. In another, an elderly homeowner shares accommodations with a younger person who helps around the house and provides companionship and security.

WHO WOULD BE INTERESTED IN SHARED HOUSING?

Shared housing is most attractive to individuals who can live independently, but have trouble affording their own home, fear living at home alone, or simply prefer to live in the company of others.

WHAT DOES SHARED HOUSING OFFER ITS RESIDENTS?

Residents of shared housing usually have their own bedroom, but share the common areas of the house such as the kitchen, bathrooms, dining room, and living room. Residents also commonly share responsibility for running the house.

WHAT DOES SHARED HOUSING COST?

In a shared housing arrangement where all the residents are of approximately the same age, it is common to pool funds to maintain the house or apartment, and pay rent, utilities, and other household expenses. The average monthly rents in most of the 450 shared housing programs around the country are between $300 and $400. In some communities the local department of senior citizen affairs helps fund shared living arrangements so that the cost to each resident is based on ability to pay.

Where an older homeowner lives with a younger housemate who does chores and errands for the homeowner, the housemate rarely pays any money toward household expenses and may or may not pay rent.

BOARD AND CARE HOMES

WHAT IS A BOARD AND CARE HOME?

A board and care home, also known as adult care, sheltered care, and a residential care facility, is a group living arrangement where each resident is given a room, meals, supervision, and some services. Most board and care homes are privately operated. A minority of board and care homes are licensed by the local health department.

WHO WOULD BE INTERESTED IN A BOARD AND CARE HOME?

Board and care homes are most appropriate for moderately disabled individuals who can walk without difficulty, but cannot live entirely on their own. The average age of a board and care resident is between 60 and 75.

WHAT DOES A BOARD AND CARE HOME OFFER ITS RESIDENTS?

In most board and care homes, residents receive:

- At least three daily meals.
- Assistance with housekeeping chores.
- Personal care assistance.
- Social and recreational services.

WHAT DOES A BOARD AND CARE HOME COST?

The cost of board and care housing varies considerably from facility to facility, depending largely on location. Rents can range from $250 to $1,500 a month. In some homes, additional fees are charged for certain services. Residents receiving Supplemental Security Income (SSI) may be eligible for rental assistance in board and care housing, depending on the state. Financial assistance programs are administered through local offices of the department of social services or public welfare.

ACCESSORY APARTMENTS

WHAT IS AN ACCESSORY APARTMENT?

An accessory apartment is a complete and private second residence that is installed in a single family home.

WHO WOULD BE INTERESTED IN AN ACCESSORY APARTMENT?

Basically two groups of people are interested in accessory apartments. First, older homeowners who need additional income or help around the house may lease an accessory apartment to a friend, relative, or tenant either for rent or in exchange for help around the house. Second, younger homeowners may want an older relative to live nearby.

WHAT DOES AN ACCESSORY APARTMENT OFFER ITS RESIDENTS?

If you are an older homeowner renting out an accessory apartment, the primary benefit to you is an additional source of income.

If you are occupying an accessory apartment in a relative's home, you get the benefits of privacy and independent living, with the security of knowing that help is nearby.

Most accessory apartments, at a minimum, include a bedroom, living room, kitchen, and bathroom. They may or may not have a separate entrance.

WHAT DOES AN ACCESSORY APARTMENT COST?

As the occupant of an accessory apartment, you must pay any rent the homeowner charges. The fair rental value of an accessory apartment will depend on the size and location of the apartment.

If you are a homeowner thinking of building an accessory apartment in your house, the cost to you will depend on the design of your house and your plan for the apartment.

Accessory apartments may not be permitted under your local zoning laws, which will mean that you will have to request a zoning waiver. This will likely involve some additional expense.

ELDERLY COTTAGE HOUSING OPPORTUNITY

WHAT IS ECHO HOUSING?

Elderly Cottage Housing Opportunity (ECHO) units are temporary houses that are built on a family member's property, in clusters on property owned by a private investor or the local government, or on the grounds of a nursing home complex. ECHO housing units are premade at a factory and are easily built and removed.

WHO WOULD BE INTERESTED IN ECHO HOUSING?

ECHO housing is attractive to older adults who are interested in living independently, but do not want the expense or responsibility of maintaining a large home. Older adults who occupy ECHO housing on the grounds of a relative's house also have the benefit of ready access to assistance, should it be required.

WHAT DOES ECHO HOUSING OFFER ITS RESIDENTS?

ECHO housing units are extremely simple to maintain and are designed to be highly energy efficient. They do not have stairs and can be made wheelchair accessible. Most ECHO units are about 500 square feet, and come with a bedroom, bathroom, full kitchen, and living room.

ECHO housing enables older residents to stay in close contact with their family members who reside in the primary home.

WHAT DOES ECHO HOUSING COST?

ECHO units cost between $15,000 and $30,000 to construct. The cost of purchasing or renting an ECHO unit that has been built by a private investor will depend on housing costs in the area.

SELECTING ALTERNATIVE HOUSING

Now that you are familiar with some of your housing options, you can start to focus on what is right for you.

The chart that follows uses questions to help you identify your housing needs and preferences. Then, based on your answers, you can narrow in on your choice of alternative housing.

What Do You Want? Selecting an Alternative Housing Arrangement

If You Do, Pick: **If You Don't, Pick:**

Do you want your own bedroom?

All
Every alternative housing arrangement discussed in this section offers the option of a private bedroom.

Do you want meals prepared for you?

Congregate housing
Residents usually have a small kitchen to prepare light meals and snacks, but some or all meals are served in a communal dining room.

Shared housing
Residents share responsibility for meal preparation in the common kitchen.

Board and care homes
All meals are prepared by the operator of the home.

Accessory apartment
The apartment is equipped with a full kitchen.

CCRC
The facility provides three daily meals.

ECHO
The housing unit is equipped with a full kitchen.

Do you require assistance with your personal care, such as bathing, dressing, hair care, and shaving?

Congregate housing
Some facilities provide assistance with your personal care needs, but other homes expect residents to be able to live independently.

Shared housing
Residents must be able to care for their own personal needs, unless one resident is willing to assist another resident.

Board and care homes
About 80 percent of all homes provide some personal care services.

Accessory apartment
Residents must be able to care for their own personal needs, but the family member who owns the house in which the apartment is located may provide some assistance.

CCRC
A full range of personal care services are available.

ECHO
Residents must be able to care for their own personal needs, but the owner of the property on which the ECHO unit is located may provide some assistance.

If You Do, Pick: **If You Don't, Pick:**

Do you want on-site medical and nursing assistance?

CCRC
Every CCRC has a nursing facility either on campus or nearby. In addition, some CCRCs provide nurse's aides for home visits, on-site physicians, an outpatient clinic, and a pharmacy.

Congregate housing
Most congregate housing facilities do not provide extensive on-site health services. However, some facilities have on staff nutritionists and social workers to provide residents with health-related services.

Shared housing
No health services are provided, unless the resident arranges for home health care.

Board and care home
Some homes are under contract with an outside agency to provide residents with medical and nursing services. A minority of homes have nurses on staff. Some state-operated homes, usually those housing mentally disabled individuals, offer additional health-related services.

Accessory apartment
No health services are provided.

ECHO
No health services are provided.

Do you want social and recreational activities to be arranged for you?

Congregate housing
Most homes provide social activities.

Board and care home
Most homes organize social get-togethers and outings.

CCRC
Residents can enjoy a range of activities that may include arts and crafts, exercise classes, book clubs, slide shows, and singing groups.

Shared housing
Residents interact socially with each other.

Accessory apartment
Residents generally interact socially with the family member who owns the home in which the apartment is located.

ECHO
Residents whose ECHO unit is located on a family member's property may socialize with the family member. Residents living in an ECHO complex may have access to a clubhouse.

TIPS ON SHOPPING FOR A NEW HOUSING ARRANGEMENT

Once you have selected a type of housing that appeals to you, you must get down to the business of putting your new living arrangement in place.

Shopping for new quarters is serious business. You do not want to move into new accommodations unless and until you are absolutely sure they are right for you.

A little detective work can go a long way in making sure you know what you are getting yourself into:

- Make a surprise visit to the facility. Are the grounds well-kept? What are the residents doing? How do you feel about the way the staff relates to the residents?

- Talk to some residents. Are they satisfied with their living environment? What do they like most about the facility? What gripes do they have?

- Ask probing questions of the staff. Do you get complete answers? Do you sense a genuine interest in the well-being of the residents? Are they proud of the facility and the work that they do?

Once you have gathered all your information, you are ready to make an intelligent, well-reasoned, decision about your future living arrangements. But remember, rational thought only goes so far. Heed your intuition. Does it *feel* right? Even if everything looks good on paper, the change may not be right for you.

CONGREGATE HOUSING

One of the best sources for finding congregate housing is *The National Directory of Retirement Facilities*, published by Oryx Press. The directory lists congregate housing facilities alphabetically by state, city, or name. This publication should be available at your local public library.

Before you settle on a congregate housing facility, you should get answers to the following questions:

FINANCES

- What is the rent?
- What is and is not included in the monthly rent?
- Can you choose to pay only for the services you actually use?

MEALS

- How many meals are served each day, and when?
- Can you request a special diet?
- What kitchen facilities do you have in your room or apartment?
- Are meals delivered to your room, if necessary?

SERVICES

- What personal care services are available?
- What housekeeping services are available?
- What arrangements are made for social and recreational activities?
- What medical, nursing, therapy services, or health screening services are provided?

LIVING QUARTERS

- Can you bring your own furnishings?
- Are there restrictions on visitors or pets?
- Is there a telephone in your room?
- How often are the rooms cleaned?

STAFF

- Which of the following professionals are on staff?

        Social workers?
        Therapists?
        Psychologists?
        Nutritionists?
- Are the professional staff members licensed and certified?

CONTINUING CARE RETIREMENT COMMUNITY

CCRCs are located throughout the country. If you are interested in looking into a CCRC, and want to get the names and addresses of some facilities, contact:

American Association of Homes for the Aging Publications
901 E Street, N.W.
Washington, DC 20005
202-508-9442

Send $19.95 plus $5 shipping and handling for the latest edition of *The Consumers' Directory of Continuing Care Retirement Communities*, which describes more than 300 CCRCs across the country. You can also request the free publication "Non-profit Housing and Care Options for Older People."

The Oryx Press also publishes *The National Directory of Retirement Facilities*, which includes listings of CCRCs. You should be able to find the directory in your local public library.

When you sign a contract with a CCRC, you make a lifelong commitment. In return for a guarantee of housing and health care for the rest of your life, you must make a substantial financial investment in the facility.

Don't be hasty when you select a CCRC. Protect yourself by inquiring into the following matters:

- The security of your financial investment.
- The terms of your contract with the CCRC.
- The quality of care and services provided by the CCRC.

Each of these matters is explored in greater depth below.

SECURITY OF YOUR FINANCIAL INVESTMENT

The primary benefit of a CCRC is the peace of mind you get from knowing that your housing and health care are taken care of for the rest of your life. A CCRC that is not financially sound will not be able to deliver on this promise to you. If your CCRC goes bankrupt, you will probably lose a substantial amount of money, and may be left without a place to live.

Between the mid-1970s and mid-1980s, about forty CCRC facilities went belly-up. For most of the residents of these facilities, the failures meant the loss of a lifetime of savings.

In 1985 CCRCs started to regulate themselves under the American Association of Homes for the Aging (AAHA). The AAHA established the Continuing Care Accreditation Commission to accredit CCRCs. Only a minority of CCRCs are accredited, in part because the process is still relatively new. CCRCs are now also publicly regulated in some thirty-five states.

Despite the added public and private oversight of CCRCs, there are still risks associated with investing in this type of housing. To protect the security of your financial investment in a CCRC, you should take the following precautions:

• At the time of admission, only pay the one-time entrance fee. Do *not* agree to either of the following financial arrangements (both of which are now quite rare):

> • Pay in full. At the time of admission, you must pay a lump-sum amount to cover all future expenses.
>
> • Turn over assets. At the time of admission, you must sign over all your financial assets to the CCRC.

• Find out if the CCRC uses entrance fees paid by incoming residents to cover the facility's daily operating expenses. CCRCs that cannot cover their day-to-day expenses with the monthly fees paid by residents are often in financial trouble. Your entrance fee should be held in a separate reserve fund.

• Make sure your entrance fee will be held in an interest-bearing account with a licensed escrow agent, and will not be available to the CCRC's creditors for at least 90 days. During the 90-day period (the minimum probationary period), you should have the right to terminate the contract and receive a full refund (less the cost of any care you already received).

• Inquire about potential changes in your monthly fees. Find out under what circumstances the CCRC can increase your rates. A CCRC that ties increases to an objective indicator, such as the Consumer Price Index, is safest. The frequency of increases should be limited to one a year, with a minimum advance notice of 30 days. If you are priced out of a facility because you cannot afford an increase, you may not be entitled to a refund of your large entrance fee. Some CCRCs have a financial assistance program for residents who become unable to afford increases in the monthly fee.

• Find out who owns the CCRC. A CCRC that is affiliated with a well-established organization, such as a religious organization, is usually more secure than a CCRC owned by an individual. However, just because a CCRC advertises that it is "sponsored" by a nonprofit group or church does not mean that the sponsoring organization has any financial responsibility for the CCRC. Find out who has the legal obligation to provide continuing care to the CCRC residents. Also, learn as much as possible about the identity, experience, and credentials of the officers, directors, and managers of the facility.

• Find out whether the facility is a party to any current or previous judicial or administrative proceedings.

• If the facility is under construction, find out whether a reputable firm has prepared a marketing and feasibility study.

• Stay away from facilities that have a policy of nonrefundable entrance fees. Ideally, the fee should be fully refunded if you move out, or die, within one month of admission. At a minimum, the CCRC should have a formula for computing a *pro rata* refund based on your length of occupancy. The formula should apply regardless of whether you terminate the contract and whether your unit is reoccupied by a new resident.[1]

• Check if any complaints against the facility have been filed with the Better Business Bureau or the Department of Consumer Affairs.

• A waiting list deposit should always be fully refundable and held by a licensed escrow agent in an interest-bearing account.

• Nonrefundable application fees should not exceed $200.

• Make sure that a team of specialists will evaluate your need to move into a nursing facility, and that you will have the right to file an appeal with an independent review panel if you disagree with the determination.

• Ask the facility for information on past complaints. How many have there been? How have they been resolved? Is there a formal procedure for addressing complaints? Is there a policy forbidding retaliatory conduct against complaining residents? Are these procedures and policies incorporated in the contract?

PAYING FOR CCRC

There are three basic payment models for CCRC facilities:

• Entrance fee plus monthly fees. With this arrangement, the resident usually signs a long-term lease. The entrance fee should be at least partially refundable (although CCRCs that offer 100 percent refundability usually charge higher monthly fees). The monthly fees generally increase periodically to keep pace with inflation or if the resident requires higher levels of medical or nursing care.

• Pay as you go. With this arrangement, the resident enters into a straightforward rental agreement with the CCRC and pays for services as needed. The benefit is no entrance fee; the downside is a heightened risk of monthly fee increases.

• Condominiums or cooperatives. With this arrangement, the resident purchases an ownership interest in the CCRC. The price you pay includes a package of services. These arrangements are still quite new, so they should be approached with caution.

A portion of the entrance fee and monthly fees may be tax deductible as medical expenses (see page 341). To claim the deduction you will need a breakdown of what proportion of the fees is a prepayment of future medical expenses.

---

[1] A popular formula for a *pro rata* refund of the entrance fee offers a declining refund schedule amortized at 1 percent or 2 percent per month. A 2 percent decline each month means that your entitlement to a refund ends after 4 years and 2 months. The best formula multiplies the entrance fee by a fraction, whose numerator is your life expectancy at the time the contract is terminated and whose denominator is your life expectancy at the time of admission.

CCRC CONTRACTS

You will probably not find a CCRC contract that has every provision you want. However, you can use the guidelines below as a basis for comparing different facilities. When you are ready to sign, you should have an experienced lawyer review the contract.

Finances

- Is the entrance fee refundable if you move out within a month?
- Is your estate entitled to a portion of the fee if you die within a month of moving in?
- Is an itemized list of additional expenses that are not covered by the entrance or monthly fee available for review?
- What procedures apply if you are unable to pay your monthly fee? Is financial assistance available?
- Does the facility accept Medicare? What about Medicaid? Are different services provided to Medicare and Medicaid recipient residents?
- What insurance coverage is available, and at what cost (e.g., group insurance programs, long-term care coverage)?
- Is there a lifetime right to renew (termination only for "just cause")?

Services

- How many meals are provided, what allowances are made for special dietary needs, what is the extent of meal selection?
- What is the availability and cost of personal and housekeeping assistance?
- Where is the closest nursing facility? What does it cost? Is Medicare or Medicaid reimbursement available? What if a bed is not available?
- How is a personal physician selected? What home care services are available? What are the qualifications and schedules of staff doctors, nurses, and therapists?
- What is the cost and availability of funeral services?
- What is the cost and availability of social activities?
- What counseling services are offered? What is the cost?
- What transportation services are offered? What is the cost?
- What services are the sole responsibility of the resident?
- What are the qualifications of resident health care personnel? How are they trained and supervised?

Housing

- What is the average apartment size?
- What is the availability and cost of home maintenance?
- What housekeeping services are provided?
- What furnishings are provided?
- What policies govern temporary absences (e.g., vacations, hospitalizations, family visits)?
- Under what circumstances can a resident be involuntarily discharged?
- Are there any guest or pet restrictions?
- Is there wall-to-wall carpeting, Venetian blinds, telephone, cable?
- Who determines the need for a transfer to assisted living? What are the resident's appeal rights?
- Is there a residents' council? Do residents serve on the board of directors?

In addition to the contract, there are some additional papers you will want a lawyer to review. The facility should provide you with the following materials at least 2 weeks before you are scheduled to sign a resident contract or pay a waiting list deposit:

- Balance sheets and earnings statements for the past 5 years.
- An actuarial study with a 10-year demographic projection of the resident population and service costs, and a calculation of the provider's actuarial assets and liabilities calculated over the expected lifetime of residents.
- A projection of the sources and use of funds for the next 5 years.
- Documentation of health care services use (especially differences between actual use and actuarial projections).
- Identification of any assets pledged as collateral.
- Disclosure of any late payments on mortgage loans or other long-term financing.
- Documentation of the facility's record of fee increases over the last 5 years, and projected increases for the coming 5 years.
- The most recent detailed financial audit of the facility, including a statement of all reserve funds. Make sure the audit was conducted by a reputable certified public accounting firm.

QUALITY OF CARE AND SERVICES

Some CCRCs are accredited. A CCRC that is accredited has been found by the Continuing Care Accreditation Commission (CCAC) to meet certain national standards for quality care. Most accredited CCRCs proudly display a CCAC seal of accreditation on their doors and on promotional materials. To find out if a particular CCRC is accredited, call the administrative office of the facility, or get a free listing of accredited facilities from:

> **Continuing Care Accreditation Commission**
> 901 E Street, N.W., Suite 500
> Washington, DC 20004
> 202-783-7286

Many quality CCRCs have not yet been reviewed for accreditation because the CCAC was only recently established. For this reason, you should not reject a CCRC out of hand simply because it is not accredited. You should, however, ask the administrator of the unaccredited CCRC when the facility anticipates becoming accredited.

If you encounter a problem at an accredited facility, contact the CCAC. Your complaint will be investigated.

ℹ️ *For more information*

> **American Association of Homes for the Aging**
> 901 E Street N.W., Suite 500
> Washington, DC 20004
> 202-508-9442

> To find out more about shopping for a CCRC, you can order "The Continuing Care Retirement Community: A Guidebook for Consumers" for $5.

> **National Consumers League**
> 815 15th Street, N.W., Suite 928
> Washington, DC 20005
> 202-639-8140

> For information about selecting a CCRC, you can purchase "A Consumer Guide to Life-Care Communities" for $4.

SHARED HOUSING

You can find a shared housing arrangement in several ways, each of which is examined on the following pages.

• Informally. You and one or more acquaintances can rent a home or apartment together in a location where the zoning rules permit shared housing.

• Word of mouth. Most group houses are owned by nonprofit organizations. Residents usually hear about these homes through religious and community affiliations.

• Through a match-up program. Match-up programs are designed to bring compatible housemates together. You can find matching services in the real estate section of the yellow pages of your telephone book. The matching service you select should require references, personally interview clients, and be available to resolve future conflicts among matched roommates.

• Through an organization that leases or buys buildings specifically designed for shared housing arrangements. Sometimes the organization that sponsors shared housing facilities also provides supportive services, such as assistance with cleaning, shopping, and cooking. Your local area agency on aging (call 800-677-1116) can provide you with the names of these organizations.

• Through the local department of senior citizen affairs or office of aging. In some communities these organizations provide funding and staff to arrange shared housing facilities, screen applicants, and provide such support services as homemakers and social workers.

If you are thinking about entering a shared housing arrangement, get to know your future housemates ahead of time. You want to know if a prospective housemate likes beer and rowdy card games (especially if you prefer tea and a good book) *before* you unpack your bags.

Some of the important matters to discuss ahead of time include:

FINANCES

• What expenses will you share?
• How will you divide up the following expenses:

> Food?
> Utilities?
> Rent?
> Employees' salaries?

LIVING ARRANGEMENTS

• What are desirable daytime and nighttime temperatures?
• Are there any restrictions on guests or pets?
• Will meals be prepared and eaten together?

- How will housekeeping chores be divided?
- Are there any restrictions on tobacco or alcohol use?

Some parties to a shared housing arrangement agree to a trial live-in arrangement before they make a long-term commitment.

A shared housing arrangement may affect your eligibility for public benefits, such as Supplemental Security Income and food stamps. Once you start sharing your household expenses with others, you may be treated as having additional income. A representative at the department of social services or public welfare will be able to answer your questions.

ℹ️ *For more information*

If you would like to know more about shared housing, contact the National Shared Housing Resource Center, a nonprofit organization in Burlington, Vermont (802-862-2727) that advocates group housing. You can also write to:

AARP Fulfillment
601 E Street, N.W.
Washington, DC 20049
Request the free publication "Consumer's Guide to Homesharing."

BOARD AND CARE HOMES

There are essentially four sources of names and addresses of board and care homes:

- The state long-term care ombudsman. (Ombudsmen monitor the quality of long-term care facilities in the state.)
- The agency that licenses board and care homes in your state.
- The state unit on aging (see Appendix 1).
- Social services organizations.

The quality of board and care homes varies tremendously from location to location. Protect yourself by making an unannounced visit to the home. Speak to the residents, look at their rooms, examine the building and grounds, and ask a lot of questions. Some suggested questions follow.

LICENSING

- What are the state licensing requirements? (You can get this information from the department of health, mental health, or public welfare, or the state long-term care ombudsman's office. Licensing requirements can be minimal, such as requiring fire alarms and sprinklers, or extensive, such as requiring certain services or staff personnel.)
- Do the licensing requirements apply to the board and care home you are considering? (Some states only license homes that exceed a certain size, or meet some other criteria.)
- If the licensing requirements apply to the board and care home you are considering, is your prospective home licensed? (The license, if any, is usually posted on the outside door or at the administrative office of the home. Although a license assures you that, at the time of inspection, the home met certain standards, a licensed home is not necessarily the highest quality home. Similarly, an unlicensed home may be perfectly adequate. The two ways you can best protect yourself are to check out the facility yourself and make inquiries with the state long-term care ombudsman. Ombudsmen receive and investigate complaints against long-term care facilities.)

    Is the license up-to-date?
    Has the home ever lost its license?

FINANCES

- What is the monthly charge?
- What services are included in the monthly fee?
- What additional charges can you expect?
- Do you have the option of paying for only services you actually use?
- Are you required to continue paying the monthly costs while you are hospitalized?
- Must you turn over your monthly income to the home in exchange for a spending allowance?
- Are you permitted to manage your own funds, or to authorize a trusted friend or family member to manage your funds, or must you let the home manage your assets?
- Can you review the home's financial records?
- How long has the home been operating?

LEASE

- What is the term of the lease? (A month-to-month lease gives you maximum flexibility to leave the facility on short notice, but does not protect you against eviction. A longer lease of 6 months or 1 year provides more protection, but can be a problem if you want to move out early and will cost your estate money if you pass away during the lease term.)

- Does the lease spell out every fee, every service, and the cost of every service?

SERVICES

- Does the home provide you with the personal care and housekeeping services you require?
- Are there additional fees for the services you need?
- How often are the housekeeping services provided?
- What social and recreational activities, if any, are provided?
- What happens if you require additional services in the future? Will the home make the necessary arrangements, or ask you to leave?
- If you must leave the home, are you given help finding new quarters?

MEALS

- When are the meals served? Are snacks available between meals?
- Are special diets available?
- Do you have any access to a kitchen?
- Can you keep food in your room?

LIVING SPACE

- Are the bedrooms already furnished?
- Are private bedrooms available?
- How many residents share a bathroom?
- Are there restrictions on guests and pets?
- Are there restrictions on telephone use?
- Can bedroom doors be locked?
- How long is a bedroom held for a resident who enters a hospital or nursing facility?

SAFETY

- Does the home have the following precautions against fire?

     Sprinkler system?
     Smoke detectors?

Fire extinguishers?

Fire alarms that ring at the fire station?

Fire drills?

Trained personnel?

- Has the home taken the following steps to prevent and respond to accidents?

  Installed grab bars in the bathroom?

  Installed handrails on all stairways?

  Secured rugs to the floor?

  Staff trained in first aid?

- Are competent personnel on duty through the night?

- Is there a 24-hour emergency call service?

When speaking to other residents, find out if they are satisfied with the services, if they are treated well by the staff, and what they like and dislike most about the facility.

ℹ️ *For more information*

AARP Fulfillment
601 E Street, N.W.
Washington, DC 20049
202-434-2277

Request a copy of the free publication "A Home Away From Home: A Consumer's Guide to Board and Care Homes."

ACCESSORY APARTMENTS AND ECHO UNITS

If you would like additional information about ECHO housing and accessory apartments, write to:

AARP Fulfillment
601 E Street, N.W.
Washington, DC 20049
202-434-2277

Request the free publications "ECHO Housing: A Review of Zoning Issues," "ECHO Housing: Recommended Construction and Installation Standards,"

"ECHO Housing: Restrictions on Manufactured Housing," and "A Consumer's Guide to Accessory Apartments."

Coastal Colony Corporation
Box 452-A, R.D. 4
Manheim, PA 17545
717-665-6761

For information on building ECHO housing in the Northeast.

BACK TO ETHEL

Ethel decided to look into shared housing. She told the director of her local senior center that she was looking for three healthy adults, preferably nonsmoking females, to share her house with her. The director of the senior center put a notice on the bulletin board with Ethel's name and number.

Within 2 weeks, Ethel had the names of five interested applicants. She arranged a dinner meeting at her house. At the meeting, all the potential housemates shared their hopes and concerns about living together.

Two of the applicants eventually moved into Ethel's house. Ethel and her two new housemates established a budget that included the costs of utilities, communal food, the telephone, property taxes, and household maintenance and repairs. Each month they contribute money to a kitty, which they draw on during the month.

Every night a different housemate is the designated cook. On Tuesday afternoons they take the bus together to the senior center. On Thursday nights they rent videos. And on the first Saturday of each month they go into New York City to see a play.

APPENDICES

APPENDIX 1

State Units on Aging

Alabama

Commission on Aging
770 Washington Avenue, Suite 470
Montgomery, AL 36130
205-242-5743

Alaska

Older Alaskan Commission
Department of Administration
Pouch C-Mail Station 0209
Juneau, AK 99811-0209
907-465-3250

Arizona

Aging and Adult Administration
Department of Economic Security
1789 West Jefferson Street
Phoenix, AZ 85007
602-542-4446

Arkansas

Division of Aging and Adult Services
Arkansas Department of Human
  Services
1417 Donaghey Plaza South
Seventh and Main Streets
Little Rock, AR 72203
501-682-2441

California

Department of Aging
1600 K Street
Sacramento, CA 95814
916-322-3887

Colorado

Aging and Adult Services
Department of Social Services
1575 Sherman Street, 4th Floor
Denver, CO 80203-1714
303-866-3851

Connecticut

Department on Aging
175 Main Street
Hartford, CT 06106
203-566-7772

Delaware

Division on Aging
Department of Health and Social
  Services

1901 North DuPont Highway, 2nd
  Floor Annex
Administration Building
New Castle, DE 19720
302-577-4791

District of Columbia

Office on Aging
1424 K Street, N.W., 2nd Floor
Washington, DC 20005
202-724-5626

Florida

Program Office of Aging and Adult
  Services
Department of Health and
  Rehabilitative Services
1317 Winewood Boulevard
Tallahassee, FL 32301
904-922-5297

Georgia

Office of Aging
Department of Human Resources
878 Peachtree Street, N.E., Room 632
Atlanta, GA 30309
404-894-5333

Guam

Division of Senior Citizens
Department of Public Health and
  Social Services
Government of Guam
P.O. Box 2816
Agana, Guam 96910

Hawaii

Executive Office on Aging
Office of the Governor
335 Merchant Street, Room 241
Honolulu, HI 96813
808-586-0100

Idaho

Office on Aging
Statehouse, Room 108
Boise, ID 83720
208-334-3833

Illinois

Department on Aging
421 East Capitol Avenue
Springfield, IL 62701
217-785-3356

Indiana

Division of Aging Services
Department of Human Services
402 West Washington Street
P.O. Box 7083
Indianapolis, IN 46207-7083
317-232-7020

Iowa

Department of Elder Affairs
Jewett Building, Suite 236
914 Grand Avenue
Des Moines, IA 50319
515-281-5187

Kansas

Department on Aging
Docking State Office Building
915 S.W. Harrison, 122-S
Topeka, KS 66612-1500
913-296-4986

Kentucky

Division of Aging Services
Cabinet for Human Resources
CHR Building, 6th West
275 East Main Street

Frankfort, KY 40621
502-564-6930

Louisiana

Office of Elderly Affairs
4550 North Boulevard
P.O. Box 80374
Baton Rouge, LA 70898
504-925-1700

Maine

Bureau of Maine's Elderly
Department of Human Services
State House, Station 11
Augusta, ME 04333
207-624-5335

Maryland

Office on Aging
State Office Building
301 West Preston Street, Room 1004
Baltimore, MD 21201
410-225-1100

Massachusetts

Executive Office of Elder Affairs
1 Ashburton Place, 5th Floor
Boston, MA 02108
617-727-7750

Michigan

Office of Services to the Aging
611 West Ottawa Street
P.O. Box 30026
Lansing, MI 48909
517-373-8230

Minnesota

Board on Aging
Human Service Building

444 Lafayette Road, 4th Floor
St. Paul, MN 55155-3843
612-296-2770

Mississippi

Division of Aging and Adult Services
455 North Lamar Street
Jackson, MS 39202
601-359-6770

Missouri

Division on Aging
Department of Social Services
P.O. Box 1337
615 Howerton Court
Jefferson City, MO 65102
314-751-3082

Montana

Governor's Office on Aging
State Capitol Building, Room 219
Helena, MT 59620
406-444-3111

Nebraska

Department on Aging
P.O. Box 95044
301 Centennial Mall, South
Lincoln, NE 68509
402-471-2306

Nevada

Division for Aging Services
Department of Human Resources
340 North 11th Street, Suite 114
Las Vegas, NV 89101
702-486-3545

New Hampshire

Division of Elderly and Adult Services
State Office Park South

115 Pleasant Street
Annex Building 1
Concord, NH 03301
603-271-4680

New Jersey

Division on Aging
Department of Community Affairs
CN807
South Broad and Front Streets
Trenton, NJ 08625-0807
609-984-3951

New Mexico

State Agency on Aging
224 East Palace Avenue, 4th Floor
La Villa Rivera Building
Santa Fe, NM 87501
505-827-7640

New York

Office for the Aging
New York State Plaza
Agency Building 2
Albany, NY 12223
518-474-5731

North Carolina

Division of Aging
693 Palmer Drive
Caller Box 29531
Raleigh, NC 27626
919-733-3983

North Dakota

Aging Services
Department of Human Services
State Capitol Building
Bismarck, ND 58505
701-224-2577

Northern Mariana Islands

Office of Aging
Department of Community and
  Cultural Affairs
Civic Center, Susupe
Saipan, Northern Mariana Islands
  96950
9411 or 9732

Ohio

Department of Aging
50 West Broad Street, 9th Floor
Columbus, OH 43266-0501
614-466-1221

Oklahoma

Aging Services Division
Department of Human Services
312 Northeast 28th Street
Oklahoma City, OK 73125
405-521-2327

Oregon

Department of Human Resources
Senior Services Division
500 Summer Street, N.E., 2nd Floor
Salem, OR 97310
503-378-4728

Pennsylvania

Department of Aging
231 State Street
Harrisburg, PA 17101-1195
717-783-1550

Puerto Rico

Gericulture Commission
Department of Social Services
Apartado 11398

Santurce, PR 00910
809-722-2429

Rhode Island

Department of Elderly Affairs
160 Pine Street
Providence, RI 02903
401-277-2858

(American) Samoa

Territorial Administration on Aging
Office of the Governor
Pago Pago, American Samoa 96799
011-684-633-1252

South Carolina

Commission on Aging
400 Arbor Lake Drive, Suite B-500
Columbia, SC 29223
803-735-0210

South Dakota

Office of Adult Services and Aging
700 Governors Drive
Pierre, SD 57501
605-773-3656

Tennessee

Commission on Aging
706 Church Street, Suite 201
Nashville, TN 37243-0860
615-741-2056

Texas

Department on Aging
P.O. Box 12786 Capitol Station
1949 IH 35, South
Austin, TX 78711
512-444-2727

Trust Territory of the Pacific

Office of Elderly Programs
Community Development Division
Government of TTPI
Saipan, Mariana Islands 96950
9335 or 9336

Utah

Division of Aging and Adult Services
Department of Social Services
120 North—200 West, Box 45500
Salt Lake City, UT 84103
801-538-3910

Vermont

Office on Aging
103 South Main Street
Waterbury, VT 05671
802-241-2400

Virginia

Department for the Aging
700 Centre, 10th Floor
700 East Franklin Street
Richmond, VA 23219-2327
804-225-2271

Virgin Islands

Department of Human Services
19 Estate Diamond
Fredericksted

St. Croix, VI 00840
809-774-0930

Washington

Aging and Adult Services
Administration
Department of Social and Health
Services
P.O. Box 45050
Olympia, WA 98504-5050
206-586-3768

West Virginia

Commission on Aging
Holly Grove—State Capitol
1900 Kanawha Boulevard East
Charleston, WV 25305
304-558-3317

Wisconsin

Bureau of Aging
Division of Community Services
1 West Wilson Street, Room 480
Madison, WI 53707
608-266-2536

Wyoming

Commission on Aging
2300 Capitol Avenue
Hathaway Building, Room 139
Cheyenne, WY 82002-0710
307-777-7986

APPENDIX 2

Medicare Intermediaries

Note: The toll-free or 800 numbers listed on the following pages can be used only in the states or service areas indicated. Also listed are the local commercial numbers for some carriers.

Alabama

Medicare/Blue Cross-Blue Shield of
  Alabama
P.O. Box C-140
Birmingham, AL 35283
1-800-292-8855
205-988-2244

Alaska

Medicare/Aetna Life & Casualty
200 S.W. Market Street, P.O. Box 1998
Portland, OR 97207-1998
1-800-547-6333
503-222-6831 (customer service site
  actually in Oregon)

Arizona

Medicare/Aetna Life & Casualty
P.O. Box 37200
Phoenix, AZ 85069
1-800-352-0411
602-861-1968

Arkansas

Medicare/Arkansas Blue Cross and
  Blue Shield
A Mutual Insurance Company
P.O. Box 1418
Little Rock, AR 72203
1-800-482-5525
501-378-2320

California

*Counties of Los Angeles, Orange, San
  Diego, Ventura, Imperial, San Luis
  Obispo, Santa Barbara:*
Medicare/Transamerica Occidental
  Life Insurance Company
Box 50061
Upland, CA 91785-0061
1-800-252-9020

213-748-2311
Rest of state:
Medicare Claims Dept.
Blue Shield of California
Chico, CA 95976
(In area codes 209, 408, 425, 707, 916)
1-800-952-8627
916-743-1583
(In the following area codes, other
  than Los Angeles, Orange, San
  Diego, Ventura, Imperial, San Luis
  Obispo, and Santa Barbara counties:
  213, 619, 714, 805, 818)
1-800-848-7713
714-824-0900

Colorado

Medicare/Blue Shield of Colorado
700 Broadway
Denver, CO 80273
1-800-332-6681
303-831-2661

Connecticut

Medicare/The Travelers Ins. Co.
538 Preston Avenue
P.O. Box 9000
Meriden, CT 06454-9000
1-800-982-6819
(In Hartford) 203-728-6783
(In the Meriden area) 203-237-8592

Delaware

Medicare/Pennsylvania Blue Shield
P.O. Box 890200
Camp Hill, PA 17089-0200
1-800-851-3535

District of Columbia

Medicare/Pennsylvania Blue Shield
P.O. Box 890100
Camp Hill, PA 17089-0100
1-800-233-1124

Florida

Medicare/Blue Shield of Florida, Inc.
P.O. Box 2525
Jacksonville, FL 32231
1-800-333-7586
904-355-3680

Georgia

Medicare/Aetna Life & Casualty
P.O. Box 3018
Savannah, GA 31402-3018
1-800-727-0827
912-927-0934

Hawaii

Medicare/Aetna Life & Casualty
P.O. Box 3947
Honolulu, HA 96812
1-800-272-5242
808-524-1240

Idaho

EQUICOR, Inc.
P.O. Box 8048
Boise, ID 83707
1-800-632-6574
208-342-7763

Illinois

Medicare Claims
Blue Cross & Blue Shield of Illinois
P.O. Box 4422
Marion, IL 62959
1-800-642-6930
312-938-8000

Indiana

Medicare Part B
Associated Ins. Companies, Inc.
P.O. Box 7073

Indianapolis, IN 46207
1-800-622-4792
317-842-4151

Iowa

Medicare/Blue Shield of Iowa
636 Grand
Des Moines, IA 50309
1-800-532-1285
515-245-4785

Kansas

Counties of Johnson, Wyandotte:
Medicare/Blue Shield of Kansas City
P.O. Box 169
Kansas City, MO 64141
1-800-892-5900
816-561-0900
Rest of state:
Medicare/Blue Shield of Kansas
P.O. Box 239
Topeka, KS 66601
1-800-432-3531
913-232-3773

Kentucky

Medicare-Part B
Blue Cross & Blue Shield of Kentucky
100 East Vine Street
Lexington, KY 40507
1-800-432-9255
606-233-1441

Louisiana

Blue Cross & Blue Shield of Louisiana
    Medicare Administration
P.O. Box 95024
Baton Rouge, LA 70895-9024
1-800-462-9666
(In New Orleans) 504-529-1494
(In Baton Rouge) 504-272-1242

Maine

Medicare/Blue Shield of
    Massachusetts/Tri-State
P.O. Box 1010
Biddeford, ME 04005
1-800-492-0919

Maryland

Counties of Montgomery, Prince Georges:
Medicare/Pennsylvania Blue Shield
P.O. Box 890100
Camp Hill, PA 17089-0100
1-800-233-1124
Rest of state:
Maryland Blue Shield, Inc.
700 E. Joppa Road
Towson, MD 21204
1-800-492-4795
301-561-4160

Massachusetts

Medicare/Blue Shield of
    Massachusetts, Inc.
1022 Hingham Street
Rockland, MA 02371
1-800-882-1228
617-956-3994

Michigan

Medicare Part B
Michigan Blue Cross & Blue Shield
P.O. Box 2201
Detroit, MI 48231-2201
(In area code 313) 1-800-482-4045
(In area code 517) 1-800-322-0607
(In area code 616) 1-800-442-8020
(In area code 906) 1-800-562-7802
(In Detroit) 313-225-8200

Minnesota

*Counties of Anoka, Dakota, Filmore,
    Goodhue, Hennepin, Houston,*
*Olmstead, Ramsey, Wabasha,
    Washington, Winona:*
Medicare/The Travelers Ins. Co.
8120 Penn Avenue South
Bloomington, MN 55431
1-800-352-2762
612-884-7171
Rest of state:
Medicare
Blue Shield of Minnesota
P.O. Box 64357
St. Paul, MN 55164
1-800-392-0343
612-456-5070

Mississippi

Medicare/The Travelers Ins. Co.
P.O. Box 22545
Jackson, MS 39225-2545
1-800-682-5417
601-956-0372

Missouri

*Counties of Andrew, Atchison, Bates,
    Benton, Buchanan, Caldwell, Carroll,
    Cass, Clay, Clinton, Daviess, DeKalb,
    Gentry, Grundy, Harrison, Henry,
    Holt, Jackson, Johnson, Lafayette,
    Livingston, Mercer, Nodaway, Pettis,
    Platte, Ray, St. Clair, Saline, Vernon,
    Worth:*
Medicare/Blue Shield of Kansas City
P.O. Box 169
Kansas City, MO 64141
1-800-892-5900
816-561-0900
Rest of state:
Medicare
General American Life Insurance Co.
P.O. Box 505
St. Louis, MO 63166

1-800-392-3070
314-843-8880

Montana

Medicare/Blue Shield of Montana, Inc.
2501 Beltview
P.O. Box 4310
Helena, MT 59604
1-800-332-6146
406-444-8350

Nebraska

Medicare Part B
Blue Cross/Blue Shield of Nebraska
P.O. Box 3106
Omaha, NE 68103-0106
1-800-633-1113
913-232-3773 (customer service site in Kansas)

Nevada

Medicare/Aetna Life and Casualty
P.O. Box 37230
Phoenix, AZ 85069
1-800-528-0311
602-861-1968

New Hampshire

Medicare
Blue Shield of Massachusetts/Tri-State
P.O. Box 1010
Biddeford, ME 04005
1-800-447-1142
207-282-5991

New Jersey

Medicare/Pennsylvania Blue Shield
P.O. Box 400010
Harrisburg, PA 17140-0010
1-800-462-9360

New Mexico

Medicare/Aetna Life and Casualty
P.O. Box 25500
Oklahoma City, OK 73125-0500
1-800-423-2925
(In Albuquerque) 505-843-7771

New York

Counties of Bronx, Kings, New York, Richmond:
Medicare/Empire Blue Cross & Blue Shield
P.O. Box 100
Yorktown Heights, NY 10598
Counties of Columbia, Delaware, Dutchess, Greene, Nassau, Orange, Putnam, Rockland, Suffolk, Sullivan, Ulster, Westchester:
Medicare/Empire Blue Cross & Blue Shield
P.O. Box 100
Yorktown Heights, NY 10598
1-800-442-8430
County of Queens:
Medicare/Group Health, Inc.
P.O. Box 1608, Ansonia Station
New York, NY 10023
212-721-1770
Rest of State:
Medicare
Blue Shield of Western New York
P.O. Box 5600
Binghamton, NY 13902-0600
607-772-6906
1-800-252-6550

North Carolina

EQUICOR, Inc.
P.O. Box 671
Nashville, TN 37202
1-800-672-3071
919-665-0348

North Dakota

Medicare/Blue Shield of North Dakota
4510 13th Avenue, S.W.
Fargo, ND 58121-0001
1-800-247-2267
701-282-1100

Ohio

Medicare/Nationwide Mutual Ins. Co.
P.O. Box 57
Columbus, OH 43216
1-800-282-0530
614-249-7157

Oklahoma

Medicare/Aetna Life and Casualty
701 N.W. 63rd Street, Suite 100
Oklahoma City, OK 73116-7693
1-800-522-9079
405-848-7711

Oregon

Medicare/Aetna Life and Casualty
200 S.W. Market Street
P.O. Box 1997
Portland, OR 97207-1997
1-800-452-0125
503-222-6831

Pennsylvania

Medicare/Pennsylvania Blue Shield
Box 890065
Camp Hill, PA 17089-0065
1-800-382-1274

Rhode Island

Medicare/Blue Shield of Rhode Island
44 Westminster Mall
Providence, RI 02901

1-800-662-5170
401-861-2273

South Carolina

Medicare Part B
Blue Cross & Blue Shield of South
   Carolina
Fontaine Road Business Center
300 Arbor Lake Drive, Suite 1300
Columbia, SC 29223
1-800-922-2340
803-754-0639

South Dakota

Medicare Part B
Blue Shield of North Dakota
4510 13th Avenue, Southwest
Fargo, ND 58121-0001
1-800-437-4762
701-282-1100

Tennessee

EQUICOR, Inc.
P.O. Box 1465
Nashville, TN 37202
1-800-342-8900
615-244-5650

Texas

Medicare
Blue Cross & Blue Shield of Texas, Inc.
P.O. Box 660031
Dallas, TX 75266-0031
1-800-442-2620

Utah

Medicare/Blue Shield of Utah
P.O. Box 30269
Salt Lake City, UT 84130-0269

1-800-426-3477
801-481-6196

Vermont

Medicare
Blue Shield of Massachusetts/Tri-State
P.O. Box 1010
Biddeford, ME 04005
1-800-447-1142
207-282-5991

Virginia

*Counties of Arlington, Fairfax; Cities of
Alexandria, Falls Church, Fairfax:*
Medicare/Pennsylvania Blue Shield
P.O. Box 890100
Camp Hill, PA 17089-018
1-800-233-1124
Rest of state:
Medicare/The Travelers Inc. Co.
P.O. Box 26463
Richmond, VA 23261
1-800-552-3423
804-254-4130

Washington

Medicare/Washington Physicians'
Service
Mail to your local Medical Service
Bureau.
If you do not know which bureau
handles your claim, mail to:
Medicare Washington Physicians'
Service
4th and Battery Bldg., 6th Floor
2401 4th Avenue
Seattle, WA 98121
(In King County) 1-800-422-4087
206-464-3711
(In Spokane) 1-800-572-5256
509-536-4550

(In Kitsap) 1-800-552-7114
206-377-5576
(In Pierce) 206-597-6530
(In Thurston) 206-352-2269
Others: Collect if out of call area

West Virginia

Medicare/Nationwide Mutual
Insurance Co.
P.O. Box 57
Columbus, OH 43216
1-800-848-0106
614-249-7157

Wisconsin

Medicare/WPS
Box 1787
Madison, WI 53701
1-800-362-7221
(In Madison) 608-221-3330
(In Milwaukee) 414-931-1071

Wyoming

EQUICOR, Inc.
P.O. Box 628
102 Indian Hills Shopping Center
Cheyenne, WY 82003
1-800-442-2371
307-632-9381

American Samoa

Medicare/Hawaii Medical Services
Assn.
P.O. Box 860
Honolulu, HI 96808
808-944-2247

Guam

Medicare/Aetna Life and Casualty
P.O. Box 3927
Honolulu, HI 96812
808-524-1240

Northern Mariana Islands

Medicare/Aetna Life & Casualty
P.O. Box 3947
Honolulu, HI 96812
808-524-1240

Puerto Rico

Medicare/Seguros De Servicio De
  Salud De Puerto Rico
Call Box 71391

San Juan, PR 00936
800-462-7385
809-749-4900

Virgin Islands

Medicare/Seguros De Servicio De
  Salud De Puerto Rico
Call Box 71391
San Juan, PR 00936
(In St. Croix) 809-778-2665
(In St. Thomas) 809-774-3898

APPENDIX 3

Medicare Carriers

Carriers can answer questions about medical insurance Part B

Note — **The toll-free or 800 numbers listed below can be used only in the states where the carriers are located.**

Also listed are the local commercial numbers for the carriers. Out-of-state callers must use the commercial numbers.

— These carrier toll-free numbers are for beneficiaries to use and should not be used by doctors and suppliers.

— Many carriers have installed an automated telephone answering system. If you have a touch-tone telephone, you can follow the system instructions to find out about your latest claims and get other information. If you do not have a touch-tone telephone, stay on the line and someone will help you.

Alabama

Medicare/Blue Cross-Blue Shield of
  Alabama
P.O. Box 830-140
Birmingham, AL 35283-0140
800-292-8855
205-988-2244

Alaska

Medicare/Aetna Life and Casualty
200 Southwest Market Street
P.O. Box 1997

Portland, OR 97207-1997
800-452-0125 (customer service site
  actually in Oregon)
503-222-6831 (customer service site
  actually in Oregon)

Arizona

Medicare/Aetna Life and Casualty
P.O. Box 37200
Phoenix, AZ 85069
800-352-0411
602-861-1968

Arkansas

Medicare/Arkansas Blue Cross and
  Blue Shield
A Mutual Insurance Company
P.O. Box 1418
Little Rock, AR 72203-1418
800-482-5525
501-378-2320

California

*Counties of Los Angeles, Orange, San
  Diego, Ventura, Imperial, San Luis
  Obispo, Santa Barbara:*
Medicare/Transamerica Occidental
  Life Insurance Company
Box 5061
Upland, CA 91785-5061
800-675-2266
213-748-2311
Rest of state:
Medicare Claims Department
Blue Shield of California
Chico, CA 95976
(In area codes 209, 408, 415, 707, 916)
800-952-8627
916-743-1583
(In the following area codes—other
  than Los Angeles, Orange, San
  Diego, Ventura, Imperial, San Luis
  Obispo, and Santa Barbara
  counties—213, 619, 714, 805, 818)
800-848-7713
714-796-9393

Colorado

Medicare/Blue Cross and Blue Shield
  of Colorado
Coordination of Benefits:
P.O. Box 173550
Denver, CO 80217
Correspondence/Appeals:
P.O. Box 173500

Denver, CO 80217
(Metro Denver) 303-831-2661
(In Colorado, outside of metro area)
  800-332-6681

Connecticut

Medicare/The Travelers Companies
538 Preston Avenue
P.O. Box 9000
Meriden, CT 06454-9000
800-982-6819
(In Hartford) 203-728-6783
(In the Meriden area) 203-237-8592

Delaware

Medicare/Pennsylvania Blue Shield
P.O. Box 890200
Camp Hill, PA 17089-0200
800-851-3535

District of Columbia

Medicare/Pennsylvania Blue Shield
P.O. Box 890100
Camp Hill, PA 17089-0100
800-233-1124

Florida

Medicare/Blue Shield of Florida, Inc.
P.O. Box 2525
Jacksonville, FL 32231
For fast service on simple inquiries
  including requests for copies of
  "Explanation of Your Medicare Part
  B Benefits" notices, requests for
  MEDPAR directories, brief claims
  inquiries (status or verification of
  receipt), and address changes:
800-666-7586
904-355-8899
For all your other Medicare needs:
800-333-7586
904-355-3680

Georgia

Medicare/Aetna Life and Casualty
P.O. Box 3018
Savannah, GA 31402-3018
800-727-0827
912-920-2412

Guam

Medicare/Aetna Life and Casualty
P.O. Box 3947
Honolulu, HI 96812
808-524-1240

Hawaii

Medicare/Aetna Life and Casualty
P.O. Box 3947
Honolulu, HI 96812
800-272-5242
808-524-1240

Idaho

CIGNA
3150 North Lakeharbor Lane, Suite 254
P.O. Box 8048
Boise, ID 83707-6219
800-627-2782
208-342-7763

Illinois

Medicare Claims/Blue Cross and Blue
  Shield of Illinois
P.O. Box 4422
Marion, IL 62959
800-642-6930
312-938-8000

Indiana

Medicare Part B/AdminaStar Federal
P.O. Box 7073
Indianapolis, IN 46207

800-622-4792
317-842-4151

Iowa

Medicare/IASD Health Services Inc.
  (d/b/a Blue Cross and Blue Shield of
  Iowa)
636 Grand
Des Moines, IA 50309
800-532-1285
515-245-4785

Kansas

Counties of Johnson, Wyandotte:
Medicare/Blue Shield of Kansas City
P.O. Box 419840
Kansas City, MO 64141-6840
800-892-5900
816-561-0900
Rest of state:
Medicare/Blue Cross and Blue Shield
  of Kansas
P.O. Box 239
Topeka, KS 66601
800-432-3531
913-232-3773

Kentucky

Medicare-Part B/Blue Cross and Blue
  Shield of Kentucky
100 East Vine Street
Lexington, KY 40507
800-999-7608
606-233-1441

Louisiana

Arkansas Blue Cross and Blue Shield
Medicare Administration
P.O. Box 83830
Baton Rouge, LA 70884-3830
800-462-9666

(In New Orleans) 504-529-1494
(In Baton Rouge) 504-927-3490

Maine

Medicare B
C and S Administrative Services
P.O. Box 9790
Portland, ME 04104-5090
800-492-0919
207-828-4300

Maryland

Counties of Montgomery, Prince Georges:
Medicare/Pennsylvania Blue Shield
P.O. Box 890100
Camp Hill, PA 17089-0100
800-233-1124
Rest of state:
Maryland Blue Shield, Inc.
1946 Greenspring Drive
Timonium, MD 21093
800-492-4795
410-561-4160

Massachusetts

Medicare C and S Administrative
  Services
1022 Hingham Street
Rockland, MA 02371
800-882-1228
617-956-3994

Michigan

Medicare Part B
Michigan Blue Cross and Blue Shield
P.O. Box 2201
Detroit, MI 48231-2201
(In area code 313) 800-482-4045
(In area code 517) 800-322-0607
(In area code 616) 800-442-8020

(In area code 906) 800-562-7802
(In Detroit) 313-225-8200

Minnesota

Counties of Anoka, Dakota, Fillmore,
  Goodhue, Hennepin, Houston,
  Olmstead, Ramsey, Wabasha,
  Washington, Winona:
Medicare/The Travelers Insurance
  Company
8120 Penn Avenue South
Bloomington, MN 55431
800-352-2762
612-884-7171
Rest of state:
Medicare/Blue Shield of Minnesota
P.O. Box 64357
St. Paul, MN 55164
800-392-0343
612-456-5070

Mississippi

Medicare/The Travelers Insurance
  Company
P.O. Box 22545
Jackson, MS 39225-2545
(In Mississippi) 800-682-5417
(Outside Mississippi) 800-227-2349
601-956-0372

Missouri

Counties of Andrew, Atchison, Bates,
  Benton, Buchanan, Caldwell, Carroll,
  Cass, Clay, Clinton, Daviess, DeKalb,
  Gentry, Grundy, Harrison, Henry,
  Holt, Jackson, Johnson, Lafayette,
  Livingston, Mercer, Nodaway, Pettis,
  Platte, Ray, St. Clair, Saline, Vernon,
  Worth:
Medicare/Blue Shield of Kansas City
P.O. Box 419840

Kansas City, MO 64141-6840
800-892-5900
816-561-0900
Rest of state:
Medicare
General American Life Insurance
  Company
P.O. Box 505
St. Louis, MO 63166
800-392-3070
314-843-8880

Montana

Medicare/Blue Cross and Blue Shield
  of Montana
2501 Beltview
P.O. Box 4310
Helena, MT 59604
800-332-6146
406-444-8350

Nebraska

The carrier for Nebraska is Blue Shield
  of Kansas.
Claims, however, should be sent to:
Medicare Part B
Blue Cross/Blue Shield of Nebraska
P.O. Box 3106
Omaha, NE 68103-0106
800-633-1113
913-232-3773 (customer service site in
  Kansas)

Nevada

Medicare/Aetna Life and Casualty
P.O. Box 37230
Phoenix, AZ 85069
800-528-0311
602-861-1968

New Hampshire

Medicare B
C and S Administrative Services
P.O. Box 9790
Portland, ME 04104-5090
800-447-1142
207-828-4300

New Jersey

Medicare/Pennsylvania Blue Shield
P.O. Box 400010
Harrisburg, PA 17140-0010
800-462-9306
717-975-7333

New Mexico

Medicare/Aetna Life and Casualty
P.O. Box 25500
Oklahoma City, OK 73125-0500
800-423-2925
(In Albuquerque) 505-843-7771

New York

Counties of Bronx, Kings, New York,
  Richmond:
Medicare B/Empire Blue Cross and
  Blue Shield
P.O. Box 2280
Peekskill, NY 10566
516-244-5100
Counties of Columbia, Delaware,
  Dutchess, Greene, Nassau, Orange,
  Putnam, Rockland, Suffolk, Sullivan,
  Ulster, Westchester:
Medicare B/Empire Blue Cross and
  Blue Shield
P.O. Box 2280
Peekskill, NY 10566
800-442-8430
516-244-5100

County of Queens:
Medicare/Group Health, Inc.
P.O. Box 1608, Ansonia Station
New York, NY 10023
212-721-1770
Rest of state:
Blue Shield of Western New York
Upstate Medicare Division—Part B
7–9 Court Street
Binghamton, NY 13901-3197
607-772-6906
800-252-6550

North Carolina

Connecticut General Life Insurance
  Company
P.O. Box 671
Nashville, TN 37202
800-672-3071
919-665-0348

North Dakota

Medicare/Blue Shield of North Dakota
4510 13th Avenue, Southwest
Fargo, ND 58121-0001
800-247-2267
701-282-0691

Northern Mariana Islands

Medicare/Aetna Life and Casualty
P.O. Box 3947
Honolulu, HI 96812
808-524-1240

Ohio

Medicare/Nationwide Mutual
  Insurance Company
P.O. Box 57
Columbus, OH 43216
800-282-0530
614-249-7157

Oklahoma

Medicare/Aetna Life and Casualty
701 Northwest 63rd Street
Oklahoma City, OK 73116-7693
800-522-9079
405-848-7711

Oregon

Medicare/Aetna Life and Casualty
200 Southwest Market Street
P.O. Box 1997
Portland, OR 97207-1997
800-452-0125
503-222-6831

Pennsylvania

Medicare/Pennsylvania Blue Shield
P.O. Box 890065
Camp Hill, PA 17089-0065
800-382-1274
717-763-3601

Puerto Rico

Medicare/Seguros De Servicio De
  Salud De Puerto Rico
Call Box 71391
San Juan, PR 00936
(In Puerto Rico) 800-462-7015
(In U.S. Virgin Islands) 800-474-7448
(In Puerto Rico metro area) 809-749-
  4900

Rhode Island

Medicare/Blue Cross and Blue Shield
  of Rhode Island
444 Westminster Street
Providence, RI 02903-3279
800-662-5170
401-861-2273

(American) Samoa

Medicare/Hawaii Medical Services
  Association
P.O. Box 860
Honolulu, HI 96808
808-944-2247

South Carolina

Medicare Part B
Blue Cross and Blue Shield of South
  Carolina
Fontaine Road Business Center
300 Arbor Lake Drive, Suite 1300
Columbia, SC 29223
800-868-2522

South Dakota

Medicare Part B/Blue Shield of North
  Dakota
4510 13th Avenue, S.W.
Fargo, ND 58121-0001
800-437-4762
701-282-0691

Tennessee

Connecticut General Life Insurance
  Company
P.O. Box 1465
Nashville, TN 37202
800-342-8900
615-244-5650

Texas

Medicare/Blue Cross and Blue Shield
  of Texas, Inc.
P.O. Box 660031
Dallas, TX 75266-0031
800-442-2620
214-235-3433

Utah

Medicare/Blue Shield of Utah
P.O. Box 30269
Salt Lake City, Utah 84130-0269
800-426-3477
801-481-6196

Vermont

Medicare B
C and S Administrative Services
P.O. Box 9790
Portland, ME 04104-5090
800-447-1142
207-828-4300

Virginia

Counties of Arlington, Fairfax
Cities of Alexandria, Falls Church,
  Fairfax:
Medicare/Pennsylvania Blue Shield
P.O. Box 890100
Camp Hill, PA 17089-0100
800-233-1124
717-763-3601
Rest of state:
Medicare/The Travelers Insurance
  Company
P.O. Box 26463
Richmond, VA 23261
800-552-3423
804-330-4786

Virgin Islands

Medicare/Seguros De Servicio De
  Salud De Puerto Rico
Call Box 71391
San Juan, PR 00936
(In U.S. Virgin Islands) 800-474-7448

Washington

Medicare
Washington State Medicare Part B

P.O. Box 91070
Seattle, WA 98111-9170
(In Seattle) 800-422-4087
  206-464-3711
(In Spokane) 800-572-5256
  509-536-4550
(In Tacoma) 206-597-6530

West Virginia

Medicare/Nationwide Mutual
  Insurance Company
P.O. Box 57
Columbus, OH 43216
800-848-0106
614-249-7157

Wisconsin

Medicare/WPS
Box 1787
Madison, WI 53701
800-362-7221
(In Madison) 608-221-3330
(In Milwaukee) 414-931-1071

Wyoming

Blue Cross/Blue Shield of Wyoming
P.O. Box 628
Cheyenne, WY 82003
800-442-2371
307-632-9381

APPENDIX 4

Medicare Peer Review Organizations (PROs)

PROs can answer questions about hospital and skilled nursing facility coverage.

Alabama

Alabama Quality Assurance
  Foundation, Inc.
Suite 600
600 Beacon Parkway West
Birmingham, AL 35209-3154
800-288-4992

Alaska

Professional Review Organization for
  Washington
(PRO for Alaska)
10700 Meridian Avenue, North, Suite
  100
Seattle, WA 98133-9008
800-445-6941
(In Anchorage) 562-2252

Arizona

Health Services Advisory Group, Inc.
P.O. Box 16731
Phoenix, AZ 85011-6731
800-626-1577
(In Arizona) 800-359-9909
or 800-223-6693

Arkansas

Arkansas Foundation for Medical
  Care, Inc.
P.O. Box 2424
809 Garrison Avenue
Fort Smith, AR 72902
800-824-7586
(In Arkansas) 800-272-5528

California

California Medical Review, Inc.
60 Spear Street, Suite 500
San Francisco, CA 94105
800-841-1602 (in-state only)
415-882-5800*

Colorado

Colorado Foundation for Medical Care
260 South Parker Road
P.O. Box 17300
Denver, CO 80217-0300
800-727-7086 (in-state only)
803-695-3333*

Connecticut

Connecticut Peer Review Organization,
   Inc.
100 Roscommon Drive, Suite 200
Middletown, CT 06457
800-553-7590 (in-state only)
203-632-2008*

Delaware

West Virginia Medical Institute, Inc.
(PRO for Delaware)
3001 Chesterfield Place
Charleston, WV 25304
800-642-8686 ext. 266
(In Wilmington) 655-3077

District of Columbia

Delmarva Foundation for Medical
   Care, Inc.
(PRO for D.C.)
9240 Centreville Road
Easton, MD 21601

800-645-0011
(In Maryland) 800-492-5811

Florida

Blue Cross and Blue Shield of Florida,
   Inc.
PRO Review
P.O. Box 45267
Jacksonville, FL 32232-5267
800-964-5785 (in-state only)
904-791-8262

Georgia

Georgia Medical Care Foundation
57 Executive Park South, Suite 200
Atlanta, Ga 30329
800-282-2614 (in-state only)
404-982-0411

Guam

(See Hawaii)

Hawaii

Hawaii Medical Service Association
(PRO for American Samoa, Guam, and
   Hawaii)
818 Keeaumoku Street
P.O. Box 860
Honolulu, HI 96808-0860
808-944-3586*

Idaho

Professional Review Organization for
   Washington
(PRO for Idaho)
10700 Meridian Avenue, North, Suite
   100
Seattle, WA 98133-9008

---

* PRO will accept collect calls from out of state on this number.

800-445-6941
208-343-4617* (local Boise and collect)

Illinois

Crescent Counties Foundation for
  Medical Care
280 Shuman Boulevard, Suite 240
Naperville, IL 60563
800-647-8089

Indiana

Indiana Medical Review Organization
2901 Ohio Boulevard
P.O. Box 3713
Terre Haute, IN 47803
800-288-1499

Iowa

Iowa Foundation for Medical Care
6000 Westown Parkway, Suite 350E
West Des Moines, IA 50266-7771
800-752-7014 (in-state only)
515-223-2900

Kansas

Kansas Foundation for Medical Care,
  Inc.
2947 Southwest Wanamaker Drive
Topeka, KS 66614
800-432-0407 (in-state only)
913-273-2552

Kentucky

Kentucky Medical Review
  Organization
10503 Timberwood Circle, Suite 200
P.O. Box 23540

Louisville, KY 40223
800-288-1499

Louisiana

Louisiana Health Care Review, Inc.
8591 United Plaza Boulevard, Suite 270
Baton Rouge, LA 70809
800-433-4958 (in-state only)
504-926-6353

Maine

Health Care Review, Inc.
(PRO for Maine)
Henry C. Hall Building
345 Blackstone Boulevard
Providence, RI 02906
800-541-9888 or 800-528-0700 (both
  numbers in Maine only)
207-945-0244*

Maryland

Delmarva Foundation for Medical
  Care, Inc.
(PRO for Maryland)
9240 Centreville Road
Easton, MD 21601
800-645-0011
(in Maryland) 800-492-5811

Massachusetts

Massachusetts Peer Review
  Organization, Inc.
300 Bearhill Road
Waltham, MA 02154
800-252-5533 (in-state only)
617-890-0011*

---

* PRO will accept collect calls from out of state on this number.

Michigan

Michigan Peer Review Organization
40600 Ann Arbor Road, Suite 200
Plymouth, MI 48170
800-365-5899

Minnesota

Foundation for Health Care Evaluation
2901 Metro Drive, Suite 400
Bloomington, MN 55425
800-444-3423

Mississippi

Mississippi Foundation for Medical
    Care, Inc.
P.O. Box 4665
735 Riverside Drive
Jackson, MS 39296-4665
800-844-0600 (in-state only)
601-948-8894

Missouri

Missouri Patient Care Review
    Foundation
505 Hobbs Road, Suite 100
Jefferson City, MO 65109
800-347-1016

Montana

Montana-Wyoming Foundation for
    Medical Care
400 North Park, 2nd Floor
Helena, MT 59601
800-332-3411 (in-state only)
406-443-4020*

Nebraska

Sunderbruch Corporation—NE
1221 N Street, Suite 800

Lincoln, NE 69508
800-752-0548

Nevada

Nevada Peer Review
675 East 2100 South, Suite 270
Salt Lake City, UT 84106-1864
800-558-0829 (in Nevada only)
(In Reno) 702-826-1996)
702-385-9933*

New Hampshire

New Hampshire Foundation for
    Medical Care
5 Old Rollinsford Road, Suite 302
Dover, NH 03820
800-582-7174 (in-state only)
603-749-1641*

New Jersey

Peer Review Organization of New
    Jersey, Inc.
Central Division
Hill Court, Building J
East Brunswick, NJ 08816
800-624-4557 (in-state only)
201-238-5570*

New Mexico

New Mexico Medical Review
    Association
707 Broadway N.E., Suite 200
P.O. Box 27449
Albuquerque, NM 87125-7449
800-432-6824 (in-state only)
505-842-6236
(In Albuquerque) 842-6236

---

* PRO will accept collect calls from out of state on this number.

New York

Island Peer Review Organization, Inc.
1979 Marcus Avenue, 1st Floor
Lake Success, NY 11042
800-331-7767
516-326-7767*

North Carolina

Medical Review of North Carolina
P.O. Box 37309
1011 Schaub Drive, Suite 200
Raleigh, NC 27627
800-682-2650 (in-state only)
919-851-2955

North Dakota

North Dakota Health Care Review,
Inc.
900 North Broadway, Suite 301
Minot, ND 58701
800-472-2902 (in-state only)
701-852-4231*

Ohio

Peer Review Systems, Inc.
3700 Corporate Drive, Suite 250
Columbus, OH 43231-7990
800-233-7337

Oklahoma

Oklahoma Foundation for Peer
Review, Inc.
Paragon Building, Suite 400
5801 Broadway Extension
Oklahoma City, OK 73118-7489
800-522-3414 (in-state only)
405-840-2891

Oregon

Oregon Medical Professional Review
Organization
1220 Southwest Morrison, Suite 200
Portland, OR 97205
800-344-4354 (in-state only)
503-279-0100*

Pennsylvania

Keystone Peer Review Organization,
Inc.
777 East Park Drive
P.O. Box 8310
Harrisburg, PA 17105-8310
800-322-1914 (in-state only)
717-564-8288

Puerto Rico

Puerto Rico Foundation for Medical
Care
Suite 605 Mercantile Plaza
Hato Rey, PR 00918
809-753-6705* or 809-753-6708*

Rhode Island

Health Care Review, Inc.
Henry C. Hall Building
345 Blackstone Boulevard
Providence, RI 02906
800-221-1691 (New England-wide)
(In Rhode Island) 800-662-5028
401-331-6661*

(American) Samoa

(See Hawaii)

---

* PRO will accept collect calls from out of state on this number.

South Carolina

Carolina Medical Review
101 Executive Center Drive, Suite 123
Columbia, SC 29210
800-922-3089 (in-state only)
803-731-8225

South Dakota

South Dakota Foundation for Medical
  Care
1323 South Minnesota Avenue
Sioux Falls, SD 57105
800-658-2285

Tennessee

Mid-South Foundation for Medical
  Care
6401 Poplar Avenue, Suite 400
Memphis, TN 38119
800-873-2273

Texas

Texas Medical Foundation
Barton Oaks Plaza 2, Suite 200
901 Mopac Expressway South
Austin, TX 78746
800-777-8315 (in-state only)
512-329-6610

Utah

Utah Peer Review Organization
675 East 2100 South, Suite 270
Salt Lake City, UT 84106-1864
800-274-2290

Vermont

New Hampshire Foundation for
  Medical Care

(PRO for Vermont)
15 Rollinsford Road, Suite 302
Dover, NH 03820
800-639-8427 (in Vermont only)
802-655-6302*

Virginia

Medical Society of Virginia Review
  Organization
1606 Santa Rosa Road, Suite 235
P.O. Box K 70
Richmond, VA 23288
800-545-3814 (D.C., Maryland, and
  Virginia)
804-289-5320
(In Richmond) 289-5397

Virgin Islands

Virgin Islands Medical Institute, Inc.
IAD Estate Diamond Ruby
P.O. Box 1566
Christiansted
St. Croix, VI 00821-1566
809-778-6470*

Washington

Professional Review Organization for
  Washington
10700 Meridian Avenue, North, Suite
  100
Seattle, WA 98133-9008
800-445-6941
(In Seattle) 368-8272

West Virginia

West Virginia Medical Institute, Inc.
3001 Chesterfield Place
Charleston, WV 25304

---

* PRO will accept collect calls from out of state on this number.

800-642-8686, ext. 266
(In Charlestown) 346-9864

Wisconsin

Wisconsin Peer Review Organization
2909 Landmark Place
Madison, WI 53713
800-362-2320 (in-state only)
608-274-1940

Wyoming

Montana-Wyoming Foundation for
  Medical Care
400 North Park, 2nd Floor
Helena, MT 59601
800-826-8978 (in Wyoming only)
406-443-4020*

RETIREMENT RIGHTS

APPENDIX 5

Request for Reconsideration of Medicare Part A Decision

DEPARTMENT OF HEALTH AND HUMAN SERVICES
HEALTH CARE FINANCING ADMINISTRATION

Form Approved
OMB No 0938 0045

REQUEST FOR RECONSIDERATION OF PART A HEALTH INSURANCE BENEFITS

INSTRUCTIONS *Please type or print firmly* Leave the block empty if you cannot answer it Take or mail the WHOLE form to your Social Security office which will be glad to help you Please read the statement on the reverse side of page 2

1 BENEFICIARY S NAME	2 HEALTH INSURANCE CLAIM NUMBER

3 REPRESENTATIVE S NAME IF APPLICABLE
☐ RELATIVE ☐ ATTORNEY ☐ OTHER PERSON ☐ PROVIDER FILING

4. PLEASE ATTACH A COPY OF THE NOTICE(S) YOU RECEIVED ABOUT YOUR CLAIM TO THIS FORM.

5 THIS CLAIM IS FOR
☐ INPATIENT HOSPITAL ☐ SKILLED NURSING FACILITY (SNF) ☐ HEALTH MAINTENANCE ORGANIZATION (HMO)
☐ EMERGENCY HOSPITAL ☐ HOME HEALTH AGENCY (HHA)

6 NAME AND ADDRESS OF PROVIDER (Hospital SNF HHA HMO)	CITY AND STATE	PROVIDER NUMBER

7 NAME OF INTERMEDIARY	CITY AND STATE	INTERMEDIARY NUMBER

8 DATE OF ADMISSON OR START OF SERVICES	9 DATE(S) OF THE NOTICE(S) YOU RECEIVED

10 I DO NOT AGREE WITH THE DETERMINATION ON MY CLAIM PLEASE RECONSIDER MY CLAIM BECAUSE

11 YOU MUST OBTAIN ANY EVIDENCE (For example a letter from a doctor) YOU WISH TO SUBMIT

☐ I HAVE ATTACHED THE FOLLOWING EVIDENCE

☐ I WILL SEND THIS EVIDENCE WITHIN 10 DAYS

☐ I HAVE NO ADDITIONAL EVIDENCE OR OTHER INFORMATION TO SUBMIT WITH MY CLAIM

12 IS THIS REQUEST FILED WITHIN 60 DAYS OF THE DATE OF YOUR NOTICE?
☐ YES ☐ NO
IF YOU CHECKED NO ATTACH AN EXPLANATION OF THE REASON FOR THE DELAY TO THIS FORM

13 ONLY ONE SIGNATURE IS NEEDED THIS FORM IS SIGNED BY
☐ BENEFICIARY ☐ REPRESENTATIVE ☐ PROVIDER REP

SIGN HERE ▶

14 STREET ADDRESS

CITY STATE ZIP CODE

TELEPHONE	DATE

15 If this request is signed by mark (X) TWO WITNESSES who know the person requesting reconsideration must sign in the space provided on the reverse side of this page of the form

DO NOT FILL IN BELOW THIS LINE—FOR SOCIAL SECURITY USE—THANK YOU

16 ROUTING
☐ INTERMEDIARY
☐ HCFA RO MEDICARE
☐ BSS ODR

18 SSA OR INTERMEDIARY DATE STAMP

17 ADDITIONAL INFORMATION

FORM HCFA-2649 (8 /91)
DESTROY PRIOR EDITIONS

INTERMEDIARY FILE

APPENDIX 6

Request for Review of Medicare Part B Decision

DEPARTMENT OF HEALTH AND HUMAN SERVICES
HEALTH CARE FINANCING ADMINISTRATION

Form Approved
OMB No. 0938-0033

REQUEST FOR REVIEW OF PART B MEDICARE CLAIM
Medical Insurance Benefits - Social Security Act

NOTICE—Anyone who misrepresents or falsifies essential information requested by this form may upon conviction be subject to fine and imprisonment under Federal Law.

1 Carrier's Name and Address

2 Name of Patient

3 Health Insurance Claim Number

4 I do not agree with the determination you made on my claim as described on my Explanation of Medicare Benefits dated:

5 MY REASONS ARE: (Attach a copy of the Explanation of Medicare Benefits, or describe the service, date of service, and physician's name—NOTE.—If the date on the Notice of Benefits mentioned in item 3 is more than six months ago, include your reason for not making this request earlier.)

6 Describe Illness or Injury:

7 ☐ I have additional evidence to submit. (Attach such evidence to this form.)

☐ I do not have additional evidence.

COMPLETE ALL OF THE INFORMATION REQUESTED. SIGN AND RETURN THE FIRST COPY AND ANY ATTACHMENTS TO THE CARRIER NAMED ABOVE. IF YOU NEED HELP, TAKE THIS AND YOUR NOTICE FROM THE CARRIER TO A SOCIAL SECURITY OFFICE, OR TO THE CARRIER. KEEP THE DUPLICATE COPY OF THIS FORM FOR YOUR RECORDS.

8 SIGNATURE OF **EITHER** THE CLAIMENT **OR** HIS REPRESENTATIVE

Representative	Claimant
Address	Address
City, State, and ZIP Code	City, State, and ZIP Code
Telephone Number	Date	Telephone Number	Date

Form HCFA-1964 (8-85)   (over)

APPENDIX 7

Request for Earnings and Benefit Estimate Statement

SOCIAL SECURITY ADMINISTRATION

Form Approved
OMB No. 0960-0466

SP

Request for Earnings and Benefit Estimate Statement

To receive a free statement of your earnings covered by Social Security and your estimated future benefits, all you need to do is fill out this form. Please print or type your answers. When you have completed the form, fold it and mail it to us.

1. Name shown on your Social Security card:

First Name

Middle Initial

Last Name Only

2. Your Social Security number as shown on your card:

☐☐☐ - ☐☐ - ☐☐☐☐

3. Your date of birth

Month   Day   Year

4. Other Social Security numbers you have used:

☐☐☐ - ☐☐ - ☐☐☐☐
☐☐☐ - ☐☐ - ☐☐☐☐

5. Your sex: ☐ Male   ☐ Female

6. Other names you have used
(*including a maiden name*):

7. Show your actual earnings for last year and your estimated earnings for this year. Include only wages and/or net self-employment income covered by Social Security.

A. Last year's actual earnings: (*Dollars Only*)

$ ☐☐☐ , ☐☐☐ . 0 0

B. This year's estimated earnings: (*Dollars Only*)

$ ☐☐☐ , ☐☐☐ . 0 0

8. Show the age at which you plan to retire:

☐☐ (*Show only one age*)

9. Below, show the average yearly amount you think you will earn between now and when you plan to retire. We will add your estimate of future earnings to those earnings already on our records to give you the best possible estimate.

Enter a yearly average, not your total future lifetime earnings. Only show earnings covered by Social Security. Do not add cost-of-living, performance or scheduled pay increases or bonuses. The reason for this is that we estimate retirement benefits in today's dollars, but adjust them to account for average wage growth in the national economy.

However, if you expect to earn significantly more or less in the future due to promotions, job changes, part-time work, or an absence from the work force, enter the amount in today's dollars that most closely reflects your future average yearly earnings.

Most people should enter the same amount they are earning now (the amount in 7B).
Future average yearly earnings: (*Dollars Only*)

$ ☐☐☐ , ☐☐☐ . 0 0

10. Address where you want us to send the statement.

Name

Street Address (Include Apt. No., P.O. Box, or Rural Route)

City   State   Zip Code

11. ☐ Please check this box if you want to get your statement in Spanish instead of English.

I am asking for information about my own Social Security record or the record of a person I am authorized to represent. I understand that if I deliberately request information under false pretenses I may be guilty of a federal crime and could be fined and/or imprisoned. I authorize you to use a contractor to send the statement of earnings and benefit estimates to the person named in item 10.

▼

Please sign your name (Do not print)

Signature

(Area Code) Daytime Telephone No.   Date

Form SSA-7004-SM (2-93) Destroy Prior Editions

APPENDIX 8

Request for Correction of Earnings Record

DEPARTMENT OF HEALTH AND HUMAN SERVICES
Social Security Administration

Form Approved
OMB No. 0960-0029

REQUEST FOR CORRECTION OF EARNINGS RECORD

Paperwork/Privacy Act Notice: The information requested on this form is authorized by section 205(c)(4) and (5) of the Social Security Act. This information is collected to resolve any discrepancy on your earnings record. The information you provide will be used to correct your earnings record where any discrepancy exists. Your response to this request is voluntary; however, failure to provide all or part of the requested information may affect your future eligibility for benefits and the amounts of benefits to which you may become entitled. Information furnished on this form may be disclosed by the Social Security Administration to another person or governmental agency only with respect to Social Security programs to comply with Federal laws requiring the exchange of information between the Social Security Administration and another agency.

I have examined your statement (or record) of my Social Security earnings and it is not correct. I am providing the following information and accompanying evidence so that you can correct my record.

1. Print your name *(First Name, Middle Initial, Last Name)*

2. Enter your date of birth *(Month, Day, Year)*

3. Print your name as shown on your Social Security number card

4. Print any other name used in your work (If you have used no other name enter "None.")

5. (a) Enter your Social Security number

_ _ _ /_ _ /_ _ _ _

5. (b) Enter any other Social Security number(s) used by you or your employer to report your wages or self-employment. If none, check "None."
(1) ☐ None
(2) _ _ _ /_ _ /_ _ _ _
(3) _ _ _ /_ _ /_ _ _ _

6. **IF NECESSARY, SSA MAY DISCLOSE MY NAME TO MY EMPLOYERS:** ➤ ☐ YES ☐ NO
(Without permission to use your name, SSA cannot make a thorough investigation)

➤ If you disagree with wages reported to your earnings record, complete Item 7.
➤ If you disagree with self-employment income recorded on your earnings record, go to Item 8.

7. **Print** below in date order your employment **only** for year(s) (or months) you believe our records are not correct. If you need more space, attach a separate sheet. Please make only one entry per calendar period employed. Show quarterly wage periods and amounts for years prior to 1978; annual amounts, 1978 on.

1–Year(s) (or months) of employment 2–Type of employment (e.g., agricultural)	Employer's business name, address, and phone number *(include number, city, state, and Zip Code)*	My correct Social Security (FICA) wages were:	My evidence of my correct earnings (enclosed)
(a) 1. 2.			—W2 or W-2C —Other (Specify)
(b) 1. 2.			—W2 or W-2C —Other (Specify)
(c) 1. 2.			—W2 or W-2C —Other (Specify)

➤ If you do not have evidence of these earnings, you must explain why you are unable to submit such evidence in the remarks section of Item 10.
➤ If you do not have self-employment income that is incorrect go on to Item 10 for any remarks, and then complete Item 11.

8. Print below in date order your self-employment earnings **only** for years you believe our records are not correct. Please make only entry per year.

Trade or business name and business address	Year(s) of self-employment	My correct self-employment earnings were:
(a)		$
(b)		$

FORM **SSA-7008** (5-88)

(over)

RETIREMENT RIGHTS

9. Regarding your earnings from self-employment:
   a. Did you file an income tax return reporting your self-employment income? ➤

   ☐ YES
   (If "YES," go on to Item 9b.)

   ☐ NO
   (If "NO," explain why in Item 10.)

   b. Do you have a copy of your income tax return and evidence of filing, such as a cancelled check? ➤

   ☐ YES
   (If "YES," please enclose copies.)

   ☐ NO
   (If "NO," go on to item 9c.)

   c. Have you asked the Internal Revenue Service to furnish you copies from their records? ➤

   ☐ YES
   (But none available.)

   ☐ NO
   (If "NO," please do so if your return was filed less than 6 years ago.)

   d. If you are unable to submit a copy of your self-employment tax return, please explain in the remarks section (Item 10).

10. Remarks—You may use this space for any explanations. (If you need more space, please attach a separate sheet.)

We may also use the information you give us when we match records by computer. Matching programs compare our records with those of other Federal, State, or local government agencies. Many agencies may use matching programs to find or prove that a person qualifies for benefits paid by the Federal government. The law allows us to do this even if you do not agree to it. These and other reasons why information about you may be used or given out are explained in the Federal Register. If you want to learn more about this, contact any Social Security Office.

TIME IT TAKES TO COMPLETE THIS FORM

We estimate that it will take you about 10 minutes to complete this form. This includes the time it will take you to read the instructions, gather the necessary facts and fill out the form. If you have comments or suggestions on how long it takes to complete this form or on any other aspect of this form, write to the Social Security Administration, ATTN: Reports Clearance Officer, 1-A-21 Operations Bldg., Baltimore, MD 21235, and to the Office of Management and Budget, Paperwork Reduction Project (0960-0029), Washington, D.C. 20503. Do not send completed forms or information concerning your claim to these offices.

11. I affirm that all the information I have given in this document is true to the best of my knowledge. I understand that if I knowingly and willfully make a false statement, or request or receive a Social Security record under false pretenses, I may be guilty of a Federal crime and could be fined as much as $5,000 and/or imprisoned for up to 5 years.

Signature of person making statement (First Name, Middle Initial, Last Name)

Mailing Address (Number & Street, Apt. No., P.O. Box, Rural Route)

City	State	Zip Code

Date	Telephone Number (Include Area Code):
	1. Work ( ) 2. Home ( )

When you have filled out this form mail it in an envelope addressed to:

Social Security Administration
300 N. Greene Street
Baltimore, Maryland 21201

APPENDIX 9

Request for Reconsideration

DEPARTMENT OF HEALTH AND HUMAN SERVICES
SOCIAL SECURITY ADMINISTRATION

TOE 710

REQUEST FOR RECONSIDERATION

(Do not wirte in this space)

The information on this form is authorized by regulation (20 CFR 404.907 – 404.921 and 416.1407 – 416.1421). While your responses to these questions is voluntary, the Social Security Administration cannot reconsider the decision on this claim unless the information is furnished.

NAME OF CLAIMANT	NAME OF WAGE EARNER OR SELF-EMPLOYED PERSON *(If different from claimant.)*
SOCIAL SECURITY CLAIM NUMBER	SUPPLEMENTAL SECURITY INCOME (SSI) CLAIM NUMBER
SPOUSE'S NAME *(Complete ONLY in SSI cases)*	SPOUSE'S SOCIAL SECURITY NUMBER *(Complete ONLY in SSI cases)*

CLAIM FOR *(Specify type. e.g., retirement, disability, hospital insurance. SSI, etc.)*

I do not agree with the determination made on the above claim and request reconsideration. My reasons are:

SUPPLEMENTAL SECURITY INCOME RECONSIDERATION ONLY *(See reverse of claimant's copy)*

"I want to appeal your decision about my claim for supplemental security income, SSI. I've read the back of this form about the three ways to appeal. I've checked the box below."

☐ Case Review   ☐ Informal Conference   ☐ Formal Conference

EITHER THE CLAIMANT OR REPRESENTATIVE SHOULD SIGN – ENTER ADDRESSES FOR BOTH

SIGNATURE OR NAME OF CLAIMANT'S REPRESENTATIVE	CLAIMANT SIGNATURE
☐ NON-ATTORNEY ☐ ATTORNEY	
STREET ADDRESS	STREET ADDRESS

CITY	STATE	ZIP CODE	CITY	STATE	ZIP CODE
TELEPHONE NUMBER *(Include area code)* (— — —)		DATE	TELEPHONE NUMBER *(Include area code)* (— — —)		DATE

TO BE COMPLETED BY SOCIAL SECURITY ADMINISTRATION

See reverse of claim folder copy for list of initial determinations

1. HAS INITIAL DETERMINATION BEEN MADE?	☐ YES ☐ NO	2. CLAIMANT INSISTS ON FILING	☐ YES ☐ NO
3. IS THIS REQUEST FILED TIMELY? *(If "NO", attach claimant's explanation for delay and attach only pertinent letter, material, or information in social security office.)*			☐ YES ☐ NO

RETIREMENT AND SURVIVORS RECONSIDERATIONS ONLY (CHECK ONE) REFER TO (GN 03102.125)	SOCIAL SECURITY OFFICE ADDRESS
☐ NO FURTHER DEVELOPMENT REQUIRED (GN 03102.125)	
☐ REQUIRED DEVELOPMENT ATTACHED	
☐ REQUIRED DEVELOPMENT PENDING, WILL FORWARD OR ADVISE STATUS WITHIN 30 DAYS	

ROUTING INSTRUCTIONS (CHECK ONE) ▶	☐ DISABILITY DETERMINATION SERVICES *(ROUTE WITH DISABILITY FOLDER)*	☐ ODO, BALTIMORE	☐ PROGRAM SERVICE CENTER
	☐ INTPSC, BALTIMORE	☐ DISTRICT OFFICE RECONSIDERATION	☐ OCRO BALTIMORE

NOTE: TAKE OR MAIL COMPLETED COPIES TO YOUR SOCIAL SECURITY OFFICE

FORM **SSA-561-U2** (9-85)   **CLAIMS FOLDER**

RETIREMENT RIGHTS

APPENDIX 10

Request for Administrative Hearing

DEPARTMENT OF HEALTH AND HUMAN SERVICES
SOCIAL SECURITY ADMINISTRATION
OFFICE OF HEARINGS AND APPEALS

Form Approved
OMB No. 0960-0269

REQUEST FOR HEARING BY ADMINISTRATIVE LAW JUDGE [Take or mail original and all copies to your local Social Security Office]	**PRIVACY ACT NOTICE** **ON REVERSE SIDE OF FORM.**

1. CLAIMANT	2. WAGE EARNER, IF DIFFERENT	3. SOC. SEC. CLAIM NUMBER	SPOUSE's CLAIM NUMBER

5. I REQUEST A HEARING BEFORE AN ADMINISTRATIVE LAW JUDGE. I disagree with the determination made on my claim because:

You have a right to be represented at the hearing. If you are not represented but would like to be, your Social Security Office will give you a list of legal referral and service organizations. (If you are represented, complete form SSA-1696.)

An Administrative Law Judge of the Office of Hearings and Appeals will be appointed to conduct the hearing or other proceedings in your case. You will receive notice of the time and place of a hearing at least 20 days before the day set for a hearing.

6. Check one of these blocks.	7. Check one of the blocks:
☐ I have no additional evidence to submit.	☐ I wish to appear at a hearing.
☐ I have additional evidence to submit. (Please submit it to the Social Security Office within 10 days.)	☐ I do not wish to appear and I request that a decision be made based on the evidence in my case (Complete Waiver Form HA-4608)

[You should complete No. 8 and your representative (if any) should complete No. 9. If you are represented and your representative is not available to complete this form, you should also print his or her name, address, etc. in No. 9.]

8. (CLAIMANT'S SIGNATURE)	9. (REPRESENTATIVE'S SIGNATURE/NAME)
ADDRESS	(ADDRESS) ☐ ATTORNEY; ☐ NON ATTORNEY
CITY STATE ZIP CODE	CITY STATE ZIP CODE
DATE AREA CODE AND TELEPHONE NUMBER	DATE AREA CODE AND TELEPHONE NUMBER

TO BE COMPLETED BY SOCIAL SECURITY ADMINISTRATION—ACKNOWLEDGMENT OF REQUEST FOR HEARING

10.
Request for Hearing RECEIVED for the Social Security Administration on _____ by: _____

(TITLE)	ADDRESS	Servicing FO Code PC Code

11. ☐ Request timely filed	Request not timely filed–Attach (1) claimant's explanation for delay, (2) any ☐ pertinent letter, material, or information in the Social/Security Office.

12. Claimant not represented – ☐ list of legal referral and service organizations provided	13. Interpreter needed – ☐ enter language (including sign language): _____

14. Check one: ☐ Initial Entitlement Case ☐ Disability Cessation Case ☐ Other Postentitlement Case	15. Check claim type(s):
	☐ RSI only .... (RSI)
16. HO COPY SENT TO: _____ HO on _____ ☐ CF Attached: ☐ Title II; ☐ Title XVI; or ☐ Title II CF held in FO to establish CAPS ORBIT; or ☐ CF requested: ☐ Title II; ☐ Title XVI (Copy of teletype or phone report attached).	☐ Disability—worker or child only .... (DIWC) ☐ Disability—Widow(er) only .... (DIWW) ☐ SSI Aged only .... (SSIA) ☐ SSI Blind only .... (SSIB) ☐ Disability only .... (SSID) ☐ SSI Aged/Title II .... (SSAC) ☐ SSI Blind/Title II .... (SSBC)
17. CF COPY SENT TO: _____ HO on _____ ☐ CF attached: ☐ Title II; ☐ Title XVI ☐ Other attached _____	☐ SSI Disability/Title II .... (SSDC) ☐ HI Entitlement .... (HIE) ☐ Other—Specify: (_____)

FORM **HA-501-U5** (5-88)
Issue old stock

CLAIMS FOLDER

APPENDIX 11

Request for Appeals Council Review

DEPARTMENT OF HEALTH AND HUMAN SERVICES
SOCIAL SECURITY ADMINISTRATION/OFFICE OF HEARINGS AND APPEALS

Form Approved
OMB No. 0960-0277

REQUEST FOR REVIEW OF HEARING DECISION/ORDER
(Take or mail original and all copies to your local Social Security office)

See Privacy Act
Notice on Reverse

| CLAIMANT | (Check ONE) |
| | Initial Entitlement ☐   Termination or other Postentitlement Action ☐ |

WAGE EARNER (Leave blank if same as above)

Type Claim (Check ONE)

SOCIAL SECURITY NUMBER

Retirement or Survivors . . . . Only	☐ (RSI)
Disability, Worker or Child . . . . Only	☐ (DIWC)
Disability, Widow or Widower . . . . Only	☐ (DIWW)
Health Insurance, Part A . . . . Only	☐ (HIA)
SSI, Aged . . . . . . Only ☐ (SSIA) With Title II Claim	☐ (SSAC)
SSI, Blind . . . . . . Only ☐ (SSIB) With Title II Claim	☐ (SSBC)
SSI, Disability . . . Only ☐ (SSID) With Title II Claim	☐ (SSDC)

SPOUSE'S NAME AND SOCIAL SECURITY NUMBER
(Complete ONLY in Supplemental Security Income Case)

| NAME | SSN | Other (Specify) |

I disagree with the action taken on the above claim and request review of such action by the Appeals Council of the Office of Hearings and Appeals. My reasons for disagreement are:

ADDITIONAL EVIDENCE

Any additional evidence which you wish to submit must be either attached to this form or forwarded within 15 days to the Appeals Council at the address shown below. It is important that you write your Social Security number on any letter or material you send us. Where the evidence is not submitted within 15 days of this date, or within any extension of time granted by the Appeals Council, the Council will proceed to take its action based on the evidence of record.

Knowing that anyone making a false statement or representation of a material fact for use in determining the right to payment under the Social Security Act commits a crime punishable under Federal law, I certify that the above statements are true.

Signed by: (Either the claimant or representatives should sign—Enter addresses for both)

SIGNATURE OR NAME OF CLAIMANT'S REPRESENTATIVE ☐ ATTORNEY ☐ NON-ATTORNEY	CLAIMANT SIGNATURE
STREET ADDRESS	STREET ADDRESS
CITY, STATE, AND ZIP CODE	CITY, STATE, AND ZIP CODE
AREA CODE AND TELEPHONE NUMBER	DATE	AREA CODE AND TELEPHONE NUMBER

Claimant should not fill in below this line

TO BE COMPLETED BY SOCIAL SECURITY ADMINISTRATION

Is this request filed timely? ☐ Yes ☐ No   If "NO" is checked: (1) attach claimant's explanation for delay; (2) attach any pertinent letter, material or information in Social Security Office.

ACKNOWLEDGEMENT OF RECEIPT OF REQUEST FOR REVIEW OF HEARING DECISION/ORDER

This request for Review of Hearing Decision/Order was filed on _____ at _____
The APPEALS COUNCIL will notify you of its action on your request.

For the Social Security Administration:

| SIGNATURE BY: |
| TITLE |
| STREET ADDRESS |
| CITY |
| STATE | ZIP CODE |
| SERVICING SOCIAL SECURITY OFFICE CODE |

APPEALS COUNCIL
OFFICE OF HEARINGS AND APPEALS, SSA
5107 Leesburg Pike
Falls Church, VA 22041-3255

Form HA-520-U5 (5-93)
Destroy old stock

CLAIMS FOLDER

APPENDIX 12

IRS Information Offices and Telephone Numbers

WHERE DO I CALL TO GET ANSWERS TO MY FEDERAL TAX QUESTIONS?

CHOOSING THE RIGHT NUMBER

Use only the number listed below for your area. Use a local city number only if it is not a long distance call for you. **Please do not dial "1-800" when using a local city number.** However, when dialing from an area that does not have a local number, be sure to dial "1-800" before calling the toll-free number.

BEFORE YOU CALL

Remember that good communication is a two-way process. You can help the IRS provide accurate, complete answers to your tax questions by having the following information available:

1. The tax form, schedule, or notice to which your question relates.
2. The facts about your particular situation (the answer to the same question often varies from one taxpayer to another because of differences in their age, income, whether they can be claimed as a dependent, etc.).
3. The name of any IRS publication or other source of information that you used to look for the answer.

Alabama
1-800-829-1040

Alaska
Anchorage, 561-7484
Elsewhere, 1-800-829-1040

Arizona
Phoenix, 640-3900
Elsewhere, 1-800-829-1040

Arkansas
1-800-829-1040

California
Oakland, 839-1040
Elsewhere, 1-800-829-1040

Colorado
Denver, 825-7041
Elsewhere, 1-800-829-1040

Connecticut
1-800-829-1040

Delaware
1-800-829-1040

District of Columbia
1-800-829-1040

Florida
Jacksonville, 354-1760
Elsewhere 1-800-829-1040

Georgia
Atlanta, 522-0050
Elsewhere 1-800-829-1040

Hawaii
Oahu, 541-1040
Elsewhere 1-800-829-1040

Idaho
1-800-829-1040

Illinois
Chicago, 435-1040
  In area code 708, 1-312-435-1040
Elsewhere, 1-800-829-1040

Indiana
Indianapolis, 226-5477
Elsewhere, 1-800-829-1040

Iowa
Des Moines, 283-0523
Elsewhere, 1-800-829-1040

Kansas
1-800-829-1040

Kentucky
1-800-829-1040

Louisiana
1-800-829-1040

Maine
1-800-829-1040

Maryland
Baltimore, 962-2590
Elsewhere, 1-800-829-1040

Massachusetts
Boston, 536-1040
Elsewhere, 1-800-829-1040

Michigan
Detroit, 237-0800
Elsewhere, 1-800-829-1040

Minnesota
Minneapolis, 644-7515
St. Paul, 644-7515
Elsewhere, 1-800-829-1040

Mississippi
1-800-829-1040

Missouri
St. Louis, 342-1040
Elsewhere, 1-800-829-1040

Montana
1-800-829-1040

Nebraska
Omaha, 422-1500
Elsewhere, 1-800-829-1040

Nevada
1-800-829-1040

New Hampshire
1-800-829-1040

New Jersey
1-800-829-1040

New Mexico
1-800-829-1040

New York
Bronx, 488-9150
Brooklyn, 488-9150
Buffalo, 685-5432
Manhattan, 732-0100
Nassau, 222-1131
Queens, 488-9150
Staten Island, 488-9150
Suffolk, 724-5000
Elsewhere, 1-800-829-1040

North Carolina
1-800-829-1040

North Dakota
1-800-829-1040

Ohio
Cincinnati, 621-6281
Cleveland, 522-3000
Elsewhere, 1-800-829-1040

Oklahoma
1-800-829-1040

Oregon
Portland, 221-3960
Elsewhere, 1-800-829-1040

Pennsylvania
Philadelphia, 574-9900
Pittsburgh, 281-0112
Elsewhere, 1-800-829-1040

Puerto Rico
San Juan Metro Area, 766-5040
Elsewhere, 1-800-829-1040

Rhode Island
1-800-829-1040

South Carolina
1-800-829-1040

South Dakota
1-800-829-1040

Tennessee
Nashville, 259-4601
Elsewhere, 1-800-829-1040

Texas
Dallas, 742-2440
Houston, 541-0440
Elsewhere, 1-800-829-1040

Utah
1-800-829-1040

Vermont
1-800-829-1040

Virginia
Richmond, 649-2361
Elsewhere, 1-800-829-1040

Washington
Seattle, 442-1040
Elsewhere, 1-800-829-1040

West Virginia
1-800-829-1040

Wisconsin
Milwaukee, 271-3780
Elsewhere, 1-800-829-1040

Wyoming
1-800-829-1040

Phone Help for Hearing-Impaired People With TDD Equipment

All areas in U.S., including Alaska, Hawaii, Virgin Islands, and Puerto Rico: 1-800-829-4059

Hours of Operation for the Hearing-Impaired:

8 A.M. to 6:30 P.M. EST
(January 1–April 4)

9 A.M. to 7:30 P.M. EDT
(April 5–April 15)

9 A.M. to 5:30 P.M. EDT
(April 16–October 31)

8 A.M. to 4:30 P.M. EST
(November 1–December 31)

APPENDIX 13

Tele-Tax Topic Numbers and Subjects

WHAT IS TELE-TAX?

Tele-Tax is prerecorded tax information about approximately 140 topics that answer many federal tax questions. You can listen to up to three topics on each call you make.

CHOOSING THE RIGHT NUMBER

Use only the number listed below for your area. Use a local city number only if it is not a long distance call for you. Do not dial "1-800" when using a local city number. However, when dialing from an area that does not have a local number, be sure to dial "1-800" before calling the toll-free number.

Alabama
1-800-829-4477

Alaska
1-800-829-4477

Arizona
Phoenix, 640-3933
Elsewhere, 1-800-829-4477

Arkansas
1-800-829-4477

California
Counties of: Alpine, Amador,
   Butte, Calaveras, Colusa,
   Contra Costa, Del Norte,
   El Dorado, Glenn, Humboldt,
   Lake, Lassen, Marin,
   Mendocino, Modoc, Napa,
   Nevada, Placer, Plumas,
   Sacramento, San Joaquin,
   Shasta, Sierra, Siskiyou,
   Solano, Sonoma, Sutter,
   Tehama, Trinity, Yolo, and Yuba,
      1-800-829-4032
Oakland, 839-4245
Elsewhere, 1-800-829-4477

Colorado
Denver, 592-1118
Elsewhere, 1-800-829-4477

Connecticut
1-800-829-4477

Delaware
1-800-829-4477

District of Columbia
628-2929

Florida
1-800-829-4477

Georgia
Atlanta, 331-6572
Elsewhere, 1-800-829-4477

Hawaii
1-800-829-4477

Idaho
1-800-829-4477

Illinois
Chicago, 886-9614
In area code 708, 1-312-886-9614
Springfield, 789-0489
Elsewhere, 1-800-829-4477

Indiana
Indianapolis, 631-1010
Elsewhere, 1-800-829-4477

Iowa
Des Moines, 284-7454
Elsewhere, 1-800-829-4477

Kansas
1-800-829-4477

Kentucky
1-800-829-4477

Louisiana
1-800-829-4477

Maine
1-800-829-4477

Maryland
Baltimore, 244-7306
Elsewhere, 1-800-829-4477

Massachusetts
Boston, 536-0709
Elsewhere, 1-800-829-4477

Michigan
Detroit, 961-4282
Elsewhere, 1-800-829-4477

Minnesota
St. Paul, 644-7748
Elsewhere, 1-800-829-4477

Mississippi
1-800-829-4477

Missouri
St. Louis, 241-4700
Elsewhere, 1-800-829-4477

Montana
1-800-829-4477

Nebraska
Omaha, 221-3324
Elsewhere, 1-800-829-4477

Nevada
1-800-829-4477

New Hampshire
1-800-829-4477

New Jersey
1-800-829-4477

New Mexico
1-800-829-4477

New York
Bronx, 488-8432
Brooklyn, 488-8432
Buffalo, 685-5533
Manhattan, 406-4080
Queens, 488-8432
Staten Island, 488-8432
Elsewhere, 1-800-829-4477

North Carolina
1-800-829-4477

North Dakota
1-800-829-4477

Ohio
Cincinnati, 421-0329
Cleveland, 522-3037
Elsewhere, 1-800-829-4477

Oklahoma
1-800-829-4477

Oregon
Portland, 294-5363
Elsewhere, 1-800-829-4477

Pennsylvania
Philadelphia, 627-1040
Pittsburgh, 261-1040
Elsewhere, 1-800-829-4477

Puerto Rico
1-800-829-4477

Rhode Island
1-800-829-4477

South Carolina
1-800-829-4477

South Dakota
1-800-829-4477

Tennessee
Nashville, 781-5040
Elsewhere, 1-800-829-4477

Texas
Dallas, 767-1792
Houston, 541-3400
Elsewhere, 1-800-829-4477

Utah
1-800-829-4477

Vermont
1-800-829-4477

Virginia
Richmond, 783-1569
Elsewhere, 1-800-829-4477

Washington
Seattle, 343-7221
Elsewhere, 1-800-829-4477

West Virginia
1-800-829-4477

Wisconsin
Milwaukee, 273-8100
Elsewhere, 1-800-829-4477

Wyoming
1-800-829-4477

RECORDED TAX INFORMATION

Select by number from the list below the topic you want to hear. Then call the appropriate phone number listed above. Have paper and a pencil handy to take notes.

Tele-Tax Topics

Topic No.	Subject
	IRS Help Available
101	IRS services—Volunteer tax assistance, toll-free telephone, walk-in assistance, and outreach programs
102	Tax assistance for individuals with disabilities and the hearing impaired
103	Small Business Tax Education Program (STEP)—Tax help for small businesses
104	Problem Resolution Program—Help for problem situations
105	Public libraries—Tax information tapes and reproducible tax forms
911	Hardship assistance applications
	IRS Procedures
151	Your appeal rights
152	Refunds—How long they should take
153	What to do if you haven't filed your tax return (Nonfilers)
154	Form W-2—What to do if not received
155	Forms and Publications—How to order
156	Copy of your tax return—How to get one
157	Change of address—How to notify the IRS

Topic No.	Subject
	Collection
201	The collection process
202	What to do if you can't pay your tax
203	Failure to pay child support and other federal obligations
204	Offers in compromise
	Alternative Filing Methods
251	1040PC tax return
252	Electronic filing
253	Substitute tax forms
254	How to choose a tax preparer
	General Information
301	When, where, and how to file
302	Highlights of 1993 tax changes
303	Checklist of common errors when preparing your tax return
304	Extensions of time to file your tax return
305	Recordkeeping
306	Penalty for underpayment of estimated tax
307	Backup withholding
308	Amended returns
309	Tax fraud—How to report
310	Tax-exempt status for organizations
311	How to apply for exempt status
312	Power of attorney information
999	Local information

Topic numbers are effective January 1, 1994.

Topic No.	Subject	Topic No.	Subject
903	Federal employment taxes in Puerto Rico	953	Forms and publications—How to order
904	Tax assistance for Puerto Rico residents	954	Highlights of 1993 tax changes
		955	Who must file?
	Other Tele-Tax Topics in Spanish	956	Which form to use?
951	IRS services—Volunteer tax assistance, toll-free telephone, walk-in assistance, and outreach programs	957	What is your filing status?
		958	Social security and equivalent railroad retirement benefits
		959	Earned income credit (EIC)
952	Refunds—How long they should take	960	Advance earned income credit
		961	Alien tax clearance

APPENDIX 14

Life Expectancy Tables

Table I
Single Life Expectancy[1]

Age	Divisor	Age	Divisor
35	47.3	50	33.1
36	46.4	51	32.2
37	45.4	52	31.3
38	44.4	53	30.4
39	43.5	54	29.5
40	42.5	55	28.6
41	41.5	56	27.7
42	40.6	57	26.8
43	39.6	58	25.9
44	38.7	59	25.0
45	37.7	60	24.2
46	36.8	61	23.3
47	35.9	62	22.5
48	34.9	63	21.6
49	34.0	64	20.8

[1] Table I does not provide for IRA owners younger than 35 years of age.

Single Life Expectancy (*continued*)

Age	Divisor	Age	Divisor
65	20.0	88	5.7
66	19.2	89	5.3
67	18.4	90	5.0
68	17.6	91	4.7
69	16.8	92	4.4
70	16.0	93	4.1
71	15.3	94	3.9
72	14.6	95	3.7
73	13.9	96	3.4
74	13.2	97	3.2
75	12.5	98	3.0
76	11.9	99	2.8
77	11.2	100	2.7
78	10.6	101	2.5
79	10.0	102	2.3
80	9.5	103	2.1
81	8.9	104	1.9
82	8.4	105	1.8
83	7.9	106	1.6
84	7.4	107	1.4
85	6.9	108	1.3
86	6.5	109	1.1
87	6.1	110	1.0

Table II
Joint Life and Last Survivor Expectancy[2]

Ages	35	36	37	38	39	40	41	42	43	44
35	54.0	53.5	53.0	52.6	52.2	51.8	51.4	51.1	50.8	50.5
36	53.5	53.0	52.5	52.0	51.6	51.2	50.8	50.4	50.1	49.8
37	53.0	52.5	52.0	51.5	51.0	50.6	50.2	49.8	49.5	49.1
38	52.6	52.0	51.5	51.0	50.5	50.0	49.6	49.2	48.8	48.5
39	52.2	51.6	51.0	50.5	50.0	49.5	49.1	48.6	48.2	47.8
40	51.8	51.2	50.6	50.0	49.5	49.0	48.5	48.1	47.6	47.2
41	51.4	50.8	50.2	49.6	49.1	48.5	48.0	47.5	47.1	46.7
42	51.1	50.4	49.8	49.2	48.6	48.1	47.5	47.0	46.6	46.1
43	50.8	50.1	49.5	48.8	48.2	47.6	47.1	46.6	46.0	45.6
44	50.5	49.8	49.1	48.5	47.8	47.2	46.7	46.1	45.6	45.1
45	50.2	49.5	48.8	48.1	47.5	46.9	46.3	45.7	45.1	44.6
46	50.0	49.2	48.5	47.8	47.2	46.5	45.9	45.3	44.7	44.1
47	49.7	49.0	48.3	47.5	46.8	46.2	45.5	44.9	44.3	43.7
48	49.5	48.8	48.0	47.3	46.6	45.9	45.2	44.5	43.9	43.3
49	49.3	48.5	47.8	47.0	46.3	45.6	44.9	44.2	43.6	42.9
50	49.2	48.4	47.6	46.8	46.0	45.3	44.6	43.9	43.2	42.6
51	49.0	48.2	47.4	46.6	45.8	45.1	44.3	43.6	42.9	42.2
52	48.8	48.0	47.2	46.4	45.6	44.8	44.1	43.3	42.6	41.9
53	48.7	47.9	47.0	46.2	45.4	44.6	43.9	43.1	42.4	41.7
54	48.6	47.7	46.9	46.0	45.2	44.4	43.6	42.9	42.1	41.4
55	48.5	47.6	46.7	45.9	45.1	44.2	43.4	42.7	41.9	41.2
56	48.3	47.5	46.6	45.8	44.9	44.1	43.3	42.5	41.7	40.9
57	48.3	47.4	46.5	45.6	44.8	43.9	43.1	42.3	41.5	40.7
58	48.2	47.3	46.4	45.5	44.7	43.8	43.0	42.1	41.3	40.5
59	48.1	47.2	46.3	45.4	44.5	43.7	42.8	42.0	41.2	40.4
60	48.0	47.1	46.2	45.3	44.4	43.6	42.7	41.9	41.0	40.2
61	47.9	47.0	46.1	45.2	44.3	43.5	42.6	41.7	40.9	40.0
62	47.9	47.0	46.0	45.1	44.2	43.4	42.5	41.6	40.8	39.9
63	47.8	46.9	46.0	45.1	44.2	43.3	42.4	41.5	40.6	39.8
64	47.8	46.8	45.9	45.0	44.1	43.2	42.3	41.4	40.5	39.7
65	47.7	46.8	45.9	44.9	44.0	43.1	42.2	41.3	40.4	39.6
66	47.7	46.7	45.8	44.9	44.0	43.1	42.2	41.3	40.4	39.5
67	47.6	46.7	45.8	44.8	43.9	43.0	42.1	41.2	40.3	39.4
68	47.6	46.7	45.7	44.8	43.9	42.9	42.0	41.1	40.2	39.3
69	47.6	46.6	45.7	44.8	43.8	42.9	42.0	41.1	40.2	39.3
70	47.5	46.6	45.7	44.7	43.8	42.9	41.9	41.0	40.1	39.2
71	47.5	46.6	45.6	44.7	43.8	42.8	41.9	41.0	40.1	39.1
72	47.5	46.6	45.6	44.7	43.7	42.8	41.9	40.9	40.0	39.1
73	47.5	46.5	45.6	44.6	43.7	42.8	41.8	40.9	40.0	39.0
74	47.5	46.5	45.6	44.6	43.7	42.7	41.8	40.9	39.9	39.0
75	47.4	46.5	45.5	44.6	43.6	42.7	41.8	40.8	39.9	39.0
76	47.4	46.5	45.5	44.6	43.6	42.7	41.7	40.8	39.9	38.9
77	47.4	46.5	45.5	44.6	43.6	42.7	41.7	40.8	39.8	38.9
78	47.4	46.4	45.5	44.5	43.6	42.6	41.7	40.7	39.8	38.9
79	47.4	46.4	45.5	44.5	43.6	42.6	41.7	40.7	39.8	38.9
80	47.4	46.4	45.5	44.5	43.6	42.6	41.7	40.7	39.8	38.8
81	47.4	46.4	45.5	44.5	43.5	42.6	41.6	40.7	39.8	38.8
82	47.4	46.4	45.4	44.5	43.5	42.6	41.6	40.7	39.7	38.8
83	47.4	46.4	45.4	44.5	43.5	42.6	41.6	40.7	39.7	38.8
84	47.4	46.4	45.4	44.5	43.5	42.6	41.6	40.7	39.7	38.8
85	47.4	46.4	45.4	44.5	43.5	42.6	41.6	40.7	39.7	38.8
86	47.3	46.4	45.4	44.5	43.5	42.5	41.6	40.6	39.7	38.8
87	47.3	46.4	45.4	44.5	43.5	42.5	41.6	40.6	39.7	38.7
88	47.3	46.4	45.4	44.5	43.5	42.5	41.6	40.6	39.7	38.7
89	47.3	46.4	45.4	44.4	43.5	42.5	41.6	40.6	39.7	38.7
90	47.3	46.4	45.4	44.4	43.5	42.5	41.6	40.6	39.7	38.7
91	47.3	46.4	45.4	44.4	43.5	42.5	41.6	40.6	39.7	38.7
92	47.3	46.4	45.4	44.4	43.5	42.5	41.6	40.6	39.7	38.7

[2] Table II does not provide for IRA owners or survivors younger than 35 years of age.

Joint Life and Last Survivor Expectancy (*continued*)

Ages	45	46	47	48	49	50	51	52	53	54
45	44.1	43.6	43.2	42.7	42.3	42.0	41.6	41.3	41.0	40.7
46	43.6	43.1	42.6	42.2	41.8	41.4	41.0	40.6	40.3	40.0
47	43.2	42.6	42.1	41.7	41.2	40.8	40.4	40.0	39.7	39.3
48	42.7	42.2	41.7	41.2	40.7	40.2	39.8	39.4	39.0	38.7
49	42.3	41.8	41.2	40.7	40.2	39.7	39.3	38.8	38.4	38.1
50	42.0	41.4	40.8	40.2	39.7	39.2	38.7	38.3	37.9	37.5
51	41.6	41.0	40.4	39.8	39.3	38.7	38.2	37.8	37.3	36.9
52	41.3	40.6	40.0	39.4	38.8	38.3	37.8	37.3	36.8	36.4
53	41.0	40.3	39.7	39.0	38.4	37.9	37.3	36.8	36.3	35.8
54	40.7	40.0	39.3	38.7	38.1	37.5	36.9	36.4	35.8	35.3
55	40.4	39.7	39.0	38.4	37.7	37.1	36.5	35.9	35.4	34.9
56	40.2	39.5	38.7	38.1	37.4	36.8	36.1	35.6	35.0	34.4
57	40.0	39.2	38.5	37.8	37.1	36.4	35.8	35.2	34.6	34.0
58	39.7	39.0	38.2	37.5	36.8	36.1	35.5	34.8	34.2	33.6
59	39.6	38.8	38.0	37.3	36.6	35.9	35.2	34.5	33.9	33.3
60	39.4	38.6	37.8	37.1	36.3	35.6	34.9	34.2	33.6	32.9
61	39.2	38.4	37.6	36.9	36.1	35.4	34.6	33.9	33.3	32.6
62	39.1	38.3	37.5	36.7	35.9	35.1	34.4	33.7	33.0	32.3
63	38.9	38.1	37.3	36.5	35.7	34.9	34.2	33.5	32.7	32.0
64	38.8	38.0	37.2	36.3	35.5	34.8	34.0	33.2	32.5	31.8
65	38.7	37.9	37.0	36.2	35.4	34.6	33.8	33.0	32.3	31.6
66	38.6	37.8	36.9	36.1	35.2	34.4	33.6	32.9	32.1	31.4
67	38.5	37.7	36.8	36.0	35.1	34.3	33.5	32.7	31.9	31.2
68	38.4	37.6	36.7	35.8	35.0	34.2	33.4	32.5	31.8	31.0
69	38.4	37.5	36.6	35.7	34.9	34.1	33.2	32.4	31.6	30.8
70	38.3	37.4	36.5	35.7	34.8	34.0	33.1	32.3	31.5	30.7
71	38.2	37.3	36.5	35.6	34.7	33.9	33.0	32.2	31.4	30.5
72	38.2	37.3	36.4	35.5	34.6	33.8	32.9	32.1	31.2	30.4
73	38.1	37.2	36.3	35.4	34.6	33.7	32.8	32.0	31.1	30.3
74	38.1	37.2	36.3	35.4	34.5	33.6	32.8	31.9	31.1	30.2
75	38.1	37.1	36.2	35.3	34.5	33.6	32.7	31.8	31.0	30.1
76	38.0	37.1	36.2	35.3	34.4	33.5	32.6	31.8	30.9	30.1
77	38.0	37.1	36.2	35.3	34.4	33.5	32.6	31.7	30.8	30.0
78	38.0	37.0	36.1	35.2	34.3	33.4	32.5	31.7	30.8	29.9
79	37.9	37.0	36.1	35.2	34.3	33.4	32.5	31.6	30.7	29.9
80	37.9	37.0	36.1	35.2	34.2	33.4	32.5	31.6	30.7	29.8
81	37.9	37.0	36.0	35.1	34.2	33.3	32.4	31.5	30.7	29.8
82	37.9	36.9	36.0	35.1	34.2	33.3	32.4	31.5	30.6	29.7
83	37.9	36.9	36.0	35.1	34.2	33.3	32.4	31.5	30.6	29.7
84	37.8	36.9	36.0	35.1	34.2	33.2	32.3	31.4	30.6	29.7
85	37.8	36.9	36.0	35.1	34.1	33.2	32.3	31.4	30.5	29.6
86	37.8	36.9	36.0	35.0	34.1	33.2	32.3	31.4	30.5	29.6
87	37.8	36.9	35.9	35.0	34.1	33.2	32.3	31.4	30.5	29.6
88	37.8	36.9	35.9	35.0	34.1	33.2	32.3	31.4	30.5	29.6
89	37.8	36.9	35.9	35.0	34.1	33.2	32.3	31.4	30.5	29.6
90	37.8	36.9	35.9	35.0	34.1	33.2	32.3	31.3	30.5	29.6
91	37.8	36.8	35.9	35.0	34.1	33.2	32.2	31.3	30.4	29.5
92	37.8	36.8	35.9	35.0	34.1	33.2	32.2	31.3	30.4	29.5

Joint Life and Last Survivor Expectancy (continued)

Ages	55	56	57	58	59	60	61	62	63	64	65	66	67	68	69	70	71	72	73	74
55	34.4	33.9	33.5	33.1	32.7	32.3	32.0	31.7	31.4	31.1										
56	33.9	33.4	33.0	32.5	32.1	31.7	31.4	31.0	30.7	30.4										
57	33.5	33.0	32.5	32.0	31.6	31.2	30.8	30.4	30.1	29.8										
58	33.1	32.5	32.0	31.5	31.1	30.6	30.2	29.9	29.5	29.2										
59	32.7	32.1	31.6	31.1	30.6	30.1	29.7	29.3	28.9	28.6										
60	32.3	31.7	31.2	30.6	30.1	29.7	29.2	28.8	28.4	28.0										
61	32.0	31.4	30.8	30.2	29.7	29.2	28.7	28.3	27.8	27.4										
62	31.7	31.0	30.4	29.9	29.3	28.8	28.3	27.8	27.3	26.9										
63	31.4	30.7	30.1	29.5	28.9	28.4	27.8	27.3	26.9	26.4										
64	31.1	30.4	29.8	29.2	28.6	28.0	27.4	26.9	26.4	25.9										
65	30.9	30.2	29.5	28.9	28.2	27.6	27.1	26.5	26.0	25.5	25.0	24.6	24.2	23.8	23.4	23.1	22.8	22.5	22.2	22.0
66	30.6	29.9	29.2	28.6	27.9	27.3	26.7	26.1	25.6	25.1	24.6	24.1	23.7	23.3	22.9	22.5	22.2	21.9	21.6	21.4
67	30.4	29.7	29.0	28.3	27.6	27.0	26.4	25.8	25.2	24.7	24.2	23.7	23.2	22.8	22.4	22.0	21.7	21.3	2.10	20.8
68	30.2	29.5	28.8	28.1	27.4	26.7	26.1	25.5	24.9	24.3	23.8	23.3	22.8	22.3	21.9	21.5	21.2	20.8	20.5	20.2
69	30.1	29.3	28.6	27.8	27.1	26.5	25.8	25.2	24.6	24.0	23.4	22.9	22.4	21.9	21.5	21.1	20.7	20.3	20.0	19.6
70	29.9	29.1	28.4	27.6	26.9	26.2	25.6	24.9	24.3	23.7	23.1	22.5	22.0	21.5	21.1	20.6	20.2	19.8	19.4	19.1
71	29.7	29.0	28.2	27.5	26.7	26.0	25.3	24.7	24.0	23.4	22.8	22.2	21.7	21.2	20.7	20.2	19.8	19.4	19.0	18.6
72	29.6	28.8	28.1	27.3	26.5	25.8	25.1	24.4	23.8	23.1	22.5	21.9	21.3	20.8	20.3	19.8	19.4	18.9	18.5	18.2
73	29.5	28.7	27.9	27.1	26.4	25.6	24.9	24.2	23.5	22.9	22.2	21.6	21.0	20.5	20.0	19.4	19.0	18.5	18.1	17.7
74	29.4	28.6	27.8	27.0	26.2	25.5	24.7	24.0	23.3	22.7	22.0	21.4	20.8	20.2	19.6	19.1	18.6	18.2	17.7	17.3
75	29.3	28.5	27.7	26.9	26.1	25.3	24.6	23.8	23.1	22.4	21.8	21.1	20.5	19.9	19.3	18.8	18.3	17.8	17.3	16.9
76	29.2	28.4	27.6	26.8	26.0	25.2	24.4	23.7	23.0	22.3	21.6	20.9	20.3	19.7	19.1	18.5	18.0	17.5	17.0	16.5
77	29.1	28.3	27.5	26.7	25.9	25.1	24.3	23.6	22.8	22.1	21.4	20.7	20.1	19.4	18.8	18.3	17.7	17.2	16.7	16.2
78	29.1	28.2	27.4	26.6	25.8	25.0	24.2	23.4	22.7	21.9	21.2	20.5	19.9	19.2	18.6	18.0	17.5	16.9	16.4	15.9
79	29.0	28.2	27.3	26.5	25.7	24.9	24.1	23.3	22.6	21.8	21.1	20.4	19.7	19.0	18.4	17.8	17.2	16.7	16.1	15.6
80	29.0	28.1	27.3	26.4	25.6	24.8	24.0	23.2	22.4	21.7	21.0	20.2	19.5	18.9	18.2	17.6	17.0	16.4	15.9	15.4
81	28.9	28.1	27.2	26.4	25.5	24.7	23.9	23.1	22.3	21.6	20.8	20.1	19.4	18.7	18.1	17.4	16.8	16.2	15.7	15.1
82	28.9	28.0	27.2	26.3	25.5	24.6	23.8	23.0	22.3	21.5	20.7	20.0	19.3	18.6	17.9	17.3	16.6	16.0	15.5	14.9
83	28.8	28.0	27.1	26.3	25.4	24.6	23.8	23.0	22.2	21.4	20.6	19.9	19.2	18.5	17.8	17.1	16.5	15.9	15.3	14.7
84	28.8	27.9	27.1	26.2	25.4	24.5	23.7	22.9	22.1	21.3	20.5	19.8	19.1	18.4	17.7	17.0	16.3	15.7	15.1	14.5
85	28.8	27.9	27.0	26.2	25.3	24.5	23.7	22.8	22.0	21.3	20.5	19.7	19.0	18.3	17.6	16.9	16.2	15.6	15.0	14.4
86	28.7	27.9	27.0	26.1	25.3	24.5	23.6	22.8	22.0	21.2	20.4	19.6	18.9	18.2	17.5	16.8	16.1	15.5	14.8	14.2
87	28.7	27.8	27.0	26.1	25.3	24.4	23.6	22.8	21.9	21.1	20.4	19.6	18.8	18.1	17.4	16.7	16.0	15.4	14.7	14.1
88	28.7	27.8	27.0	26.1	25.2	24.4	23.5	22.7	21.9	21.1	20.3	19.5	18.8	18.0	17.3	16.6	15.9	15.3	14.6	14.0
89	28.7	27.8	26.9	26.1	25.2	24.4	23.5	22.7	21.9	21.1	20.3	19.5	18.7	18.0	17.2	16.5	15.8	15.2	14.5	13.9
90	28.7	27.8	26.9	26.1	25.2	24.3	23.5	22.7	21.8	21.0	20.2	19.4	18.7	17.9	17.2	16.5	15.8	15.1	14.5	13.8
91	28.7	27.8	26.9	26.0	25.2	24.3	23.5	22.6	21.8	21.0	20.2	19.4	18.6	17.9	17.1	16.4	15.7	15.0	14.4	13.7
92	28.6	27.8	26.9	26.0	25.2	24.3	23.5	22.6	21.8	21.0	20.2	19.4	18.6	17.8	17.1	16.4	15.7	15.0	14.3	13.7
93	28.6	27.8	26.9	26.0	25.1	24.3	23.4	22.6	21.8	20.9	20.1	19.3	18.6	17.8	17.1	16.3	15.6	14.9	14.3	13.6
94	28.6	27.7	26.9	26.0	25.1	24.3	23.4	22.6	21.7	20.9	20.1	19.3	18.5	17.8	17.0	16.3	15.6	14.9	14.2	13.6
95	28.6	27.7	26.9	26.0	25.1	24.3	23.4	22.6	21.7	20.9	20.1	19.3	18.5	17.8	17.0	16.3	15.6	14.9	14.2	13.5
96	28.6	27.7	26.9	26.0	25.1	24.2	23.4	22.5	21.7	20.9	20.1	19.3	18.5	17.7	17.0	16.2	15.5	14.8	14.2	13.5
97	28.6	27.7	26.8	26.0	25.1	24.2	23.4	22.5	21.7	20.9	20.1	19.3	18.5	17.7	16.9	16.2	15.5	14.8	14.1	13.5
98	28.6	27.7	26.8	26.0	25.1	24.2	23.4	22.5	21.7	20.9	20.1	19.3	18.5	17.7	16.9	16.2	15.5	14.8	14.1	13.4
99	28.6	27.7	26.8	26.0	25.1	24.2	23.4	22.5	21.7	20.9	20.0	19.2	18.5	17.7	16.9	16.2	15.5	14.7	14.1	13.4
100	28.6	27.7	26.8	26.0	25.1	24.2	23.4	22.5	21.7	20.8	20.0	19.2	18.4	17.7	16.9	16.2	15.4	14.7	14.0	13.4
101	28.6	27.7	26.8	25.9	25.1	24.2	23.4	22.5	21.7	20.8	20.0	19.2	18.4	17.7	16.9	16.1	15.4	14.7	14.0	13.3
102	28.6	27.7	26.8	25.9	25.1	24.2	23.3	22.5	21.7	20.8	20.0	19.2	18.4	17.6	16.9	16.1	15.4	14.7	14.0	13.3
103	28.6	27.7	26.8	25.9	25.1	24.2	23.3	22.5	21.7	20.8	20.0	19.2	18.4	17.6	16.9	16.1	15.4	14.7	14.0	13.3
104	28.6	27.7	26.8	25.9	25.1	24.2	23.3	22.5	21.6	20.8	20.0	19.2	18.4	17.6	16.9	16.1	15.4	14.7	14.0	13.3
105	28.6	27.7	26.8	25.9	25.1	24.2	23.3	22.5	21.6	20.8	20.0	19.2	18.4	17.6	16.8	16.1	15.4	14.6	13.9	13.3
106	28.6	27.7	26.8	25.9	25.1	24.2	23.3	22.5	21.6	20.8	20.0	19.2	18.4	17.6	16.8	16.1	15.3	14.6	13.9	13.3
107	28.6	27.7	26.8	25.9	25.1	24.2	23.3	22.5	21.6	20.8	20.0	19.2	18.4	17.6	16.8	16.1	15.3	14.6	13.9	13.2
108	28.6	27.7	26.8	25.9	25.1	24.2	23.3	22.5	21.6	20.8	20.0	19.2	18.4	17.6	16.8	16.1	15.3	14.6	13.9	13.2
109	28.6	27.7	26.8	25.9	25.1	24.2	23.3	22.5	21.6	20.8	20.0	19.2	18.4	17.6	16.8	16.1	15.3	14.6	13.9	13.2
110	28.6	27.7	26.8	25.9	25.1	24.2	23.3	22.5	21.6	20.8	20.0	19.2	18.4	17.6	16.8	16.1	15.3	14.6	13.9	13.2
111	28.6	27.7	26.8	25.9	25.0	24.2	23.3	22.5	21.6	20.8	20.0	19.2	18.4	17.6	16.8	16.0	15.3	14.6	13.9	13.2
112	28.6	27.7	26.8	25.9	25.0	24.2	23.3	22.5	21.6	20.8	20.0	19.2	18.4	17.6	16.8	16.0	15.3	14.6	13.9	13.2
113	28.6	27.7	26.8	25.9	25.0	24.2	23.3	22.5	21.6	20.8	20.0	19.2	18.4	17.6	16.8	16.0	15.3	14.6	13.9	13.2
114	28.6	27.7	26.8	25.9	25.0	24.2	23.3	22.5	21.6	20.8	20.0	19.2	18.4	17.6	16.8	16.0	15.3	14.6	13.9	13.2
115	28.6	27.7	26.8	25.9	25.0	24.2	23.3	22.5	21.6	20.8	20.0	19.2	18.4	17.6	16.8	16.0	15.3	14.6	13.9	13.2

Joint Life and Last Survivor Expectancy (continued)

Ages	75	76	77	78	79	80	81	82	83	84	85	86	87	88	89	90	91	92	93	94
75	16.5	16.1	15.8	15.4	15.1	14.9	14.6	14.4	14.2	14.0										
76	16.1	15.7	15.4	15.0	14.7	14.4	14.1	13.9	13.7	13.5										
77	15.8	15.4	15.0	14.6	14.3	14.0	13.7	13.4	13.2	13.0										
78	15.4	15.0	14.6	14.2	13.9	13.5	13.2	13.0	12.7	12.5										
79	15.1	14.7	14.3	13.9	13.5	13.2	12.8	12.5	12.3	12.0										
80	14.9	14.4	14.0	13.5	13.2	12.8	12.5	12.2	11.9	11.6										
81	14.6	14.1	13.7	13.2	12.8	12.5	12.1	11.8	11.5	11.2										
82	14.4	13.9	13.4	13.0	12.5	12.2	11.8	11.5	11.1	10.9										
83	14.2	13.7	13.2	12.7	12.3	11.9	11.5	11.1	10.8	10.5										
84	14.0	13.5	13.0	12.5	12.0	11.6	11.2	10.9	10.5	10.2										
85	13.8	13.3	12.8	12.3	11.8	11.4	11.0	10.6	10.2	9.9	9.6	9.3	9.1	8.9	8.7	8.5	8.3	8.2	8.0	7.9
86	13.7	13.1	12.6	12.1	11.6	11.2	10.8	10.4	10.0	9.7	9.3	9.1	8.8	8.6	8.3	8.2	8.0	7.8	7.7	7.6
87	13.5	13.0	12.4	11.9	11.4	11.0	10.6	10.1	9.8	9.4	9.1	8.8	8.5	8.3	8.1	7.9	7.7	7.5	7.4	7.2
88	13.4	12.8	12.3	11.8	11.3	10.8	10.4	10.0	9.6	9.2	8.9	8.6	8.3	8.0	7.8	7.6	7.4	7.2	7.1	6.9
89	13.3	12.7	12.2	11.6	11.1	10.7	10.2	9.8	9.4	9.0	8.7	8.3	8.1	7.8	7.5	7.3	7.1	6.9	6.8	6.6
90	13.2	12.6	12.1	11.5	11.0	10.5	10.1	9.6	9.2	8.8	8.5	8.2	7.9	7.6	7.3	7.1	6.9	6.7	6.5	6.4
91	13.1	12.5	12.0	11.4	10.9	10.4	9.9	9.5	9.1	8.7	8.3	8.0	7.7	7.4	7.1	6.9	6.7	6.5	6.3	6.2
92	13.1	12.5	11.9	11.3	10.8	10.3	9.8	9.4	8.9	8.5	8.2	7.8	7.5	7.2	6.9	6.7	6.5	6.3	6.1	5.9
93	13.0	12.4	11.8	11.3	10.7	10.2	9.7	9.3	8.8	8.4	8.0	7.7	7.4	7.1	6.8	6.5	6.3	6.1	5.9	5.8
94	12.9	12.3	11.7	11.2	10.6	10.1	9.6	9.2	8.7	8.3	7.9	7.6	7.2	6.9	6.6	6.4	6.2	5.9	5.8	5.6
95	12.9	12.3	11.7	11.1	10.6	10.1	9.6	9.1	8.6	8.2	7.8	7.5	7.1	6.8	6.5	6.3	6.0	5.8	5.6	5.4
96	12.9	12.2	11.6	11.1	10.5	10.0	9.5	9.0	8.5	8.1	7.7	7.3	7.0	6.7	6.4	6.1	5.9	5.7	5.5	5.3
97	12.8	12.2	11.6	11.0	10.5	9.9	9.4	8.9	8.5	8.0	7.6	7.3	6.9	6.6	6.3	6.0	5.8	5.5	5.3	5.1
98	12.8	12.2	11.5	11.0	10.4	9.9	9.4	8.9	8.4	8.0	7.6	7.2	6.8	6.5	6.2	5.9	5.6	5.4	5.2	5.0
99	12.7	12.1	11.5	10.9	10.4	9.8	9.3	8.8	8.3	7.9	7.5	7.1	6.7	6.4	6.1	5.8	5.5	5.3	5.1	4.9
100	12.7	12.1	11.5	10.9	10.3	9.8	9.2	8.7	8.3	7.8	7.4	7.0	6.6	6.3	6.0	5.7	5.4	5.2	5.0	4.8
101	12.7	12.1	11.4	10.8	10.3	9.7	9.2	8.7	8.2	7.8	7.3	6.9	6.6	6.2	5.9	5.6	5.3	5.1	4.9	4.7
102	12.7	12.0	11.4	10.8	10.2	9.7	9.2	8.7	8.2	7.7	7.3	6.9	6.5	6.2	5.8	5.5	5.3	5.0	4.8	4.6
103	12.6	12.0	11.4	10.8	10.2	9.7	9.1	8.6	8.1	7.7	7.2	6.8	6.4	6.1	5.8	5.5	5.2	4.9	4.7	4.5
104	12.6	12.0	11.4	10.8	10.2	9.6	9.1	8.6	8.1	7.6	7.2	6.8	6.4	6.0	5.7	5.4	5.1	4.8	4.6	4.4
105	12.6	12.0	11.3	10.7	10.2	9.6	9.1	8.5	8.0	7.6	7.1	6.7	6.3	6.0	5.6	5.3	5.0	4.8	4.5	4.3
106	12.6	11.9	11.3	10.7	10.1	9.6	9.0	8.5	8.0	7.5	7.1	6.7	6.3	5.9	5.6	5.3	5.0	4.7	4.5	4.2
107	12.6	11.9	11.3	10.7	10.1	9.6	9.0	8.5	8.0	7.5	7.1	6.6	6.2	5.9	5.5	5.2	4.9	4.6	4.4	4.2
108	12.6	11.9	11.3	10.7	10.1	9.5	9.0	8.5	8.0	7.5	7.0	6.6	6.2	5.8	5.5	5.2	4.9	4.6	4.3	4.1
109	12.6	11.9	11.3	10.7	10.1	9.5	9.0	8.4	7.9	7.5	7.0	6.6	6.2	5.8	5.5	5.1	4.8	4.5	4.3	4.1
110	12.6	11.9	11.3	10.7	10.1	9.5	9.0	8.4	7.9	7.4	7.0	6.6	6.2	5.8	5.4	5.1	4.8	4.5	4.3	4.0
111	12.5	11.9	11.3	10.7	10.1	9.5	8.9	8.4	7.9	7.4	7.0	6.5	6.1	5.7	5.4	5.1	4.8	4.5	4.2	4.0
112	12.5	11.9	11.3	10.6	10.1	9.5	8.9	8.4	7.9	7.4	7.0	6.5	6.1	5.7	5.4	5.0	4.7	4.4	4.2	3.9
113	12.5	11.9	11.2	10.6	10.0	9.5	8.9	8.4	7.9	7.4	6.9	6.5	6.1	5.7	5.4	5.0	4.7	4.4	4.2	3.9
114	12.5	11.9	11.2	10.6	10.0	9.5	8.9	8.4	7.9	7.4	6.9	6.5	6.1	5.7	5.3	5.0	4.7	4.4	4.1	3.9
115	12.5	11.9	11.2	10.6	10.0	9.5	8.9	8.4	7.9	7.4	6.9	6.5	6.1	5.7	5.3	5.0	4.7	4.4	4.1	3.9

Table III
Determining Applicable Divisor for MDIB[3]
(minimum distribution incidental benefit)

Age	Applicable Divisor	Age	Applicable Divisor
70	26.2	93	8.8
71	25.3	94	8.3
72	24.4	95	7.8
73	23.5	96	7.3
74	22.7	97	6.9
75	21.8	98	6.5
76	20.9	99	6.1
77	20.1	100	5.7
78	19.2	101	5.3
79	18.4	102	5.0
80	17.6	103	4.7
81	16.8	104	4.4
82	16.0	105	4.1
83	15.3	106	3.8
84	14.5	107	3.6
85	13.8	108	3.3
86	13.1	109	3.1
87	12.4	110	2.8
88	11.8	111	2.6
89	11.1	112	2.4
90	10.5	113	2.2
91	9.9	114	2.0
92	9.4	115 and older	1.8

APPENDIX 15

Legal Assistance for Older Americans

Legal Services Programs

Legal services and legal aid offices, which provide legal assistance to low-income Americans, are located throughout the country. In 1993 in most areas of the country,

---

[3] Use this table if your beneficiary is someone other than your spouse.

you are only eligible for free legal help if your income is around $8,500 or less a year for an individual, or $11,500 for a couple.

To find the name and address of an office near you, look in the business section of the white pages of your telephone book under Legal Assistance or Legal Services. The offices listed below are some of the programs that specialize in the needs of the older adult.

Legal Counsel for the Elderly
601 E Street, N.W., Building A, 4th Floor
Washington, DC 20049

Legal Counsel for the Elderly (LCE) is the legal arm of the American Association of Retired Persons (AARP). LCE provides free legal advice to individuals age 60 and over. LCE also operates a number of hotlines that provide free legal information to residents in the states listed below who are age 60 or older. Callers with problems that cannot be resolved over the phone are referred to free legal services (if low-income) or a panel of private attorneys who charge reduced fees (which are capped at $60 an hour).

Arizona (except Tucson)	800-231-5441
Tucson resident only	602-623-5137
District of Columbia	202-234-0970
Florida (except Dade County)	800-252-5997
Dade County only	305-576-5997
Maine (except Augusta)	800-750-5353
Augusta only	207-623-1797
Michigan (except Lansing)	800-347-5297
Lansing only	517-372-5959
New Mexico (except Albuquerque)	800-876-6657
Albuquerque only	505-842-6252
Ohio (except Hamilton County)	800-488-6070
Hamilton County only	513-621-8721
Pennsylvania (except Allegheny County)	800-261-5297
Allegheny County only	412-261-5297
Texas (except Austin)	800-622-2520
Austin only	800-477-3950

Legal Assistance to the Elderly
1453 Mission Street
San Francisco, CA 94103
415-861-4444

Legal Assistance to the Elderly provides free legal services to San Francisco residents 60 years old and older.

Legal Services for the Elderly
130 West 42nd Street, 17th Floor
New York, New York 10036
212-391-0120

Legal Services for the Elderly (LSE) is a small office with attorneys specializing in Social Security, Medicaid, pensions, and age discrimination. In addition to representing a small number of clients, LSE provides assistance and training to neighborhood legal services offices in the New York City area.

National Senior Citizens Law Center
1815 H Street, N.W., Suite 700
Washington, DC 20006
202-887-5280
and
1052 West 6th Street, 7th Floor
Los Angeles, CA 90017
213-482-3550

The National Senior Citizens Law Center does not do any direct client representation, but is available to make referrals to legal services offices and private attorneys who specialize in the needs of older individuals.

Legal Aid Foundation of Los Angeles
1636 West 8th Street, Suite 313
Los Angeles, CA 90017
213-389-3581

Staff of the Legal Aid Foundation of Los Angeles Employment Law Office have expertise in the employment problems of older workers and retirees, including pensions.

National Veterans Legal Services Project, Inc.
2001 S Street, N.W., Suite 610
Washington, DC 20009
202-265-8305

The National Veterans Legal Services Project provides assistance over the telephone, by written correspondence, and in person to low-income clients in a range of matters affecting veterans and older Americans in general.

Lawyer Referral Programs

Professional Organizations for Lawyers

Most lawyers belong to one or more professional organizations called bar associations. Bar associations are organized on the federal level (The American Bar Association), the state level (the New York State Bar Association, for example), and the local level (the Association of the Bar of the City of New York, for example). The majority of bar associations have lawyer referral programs. To find a lawyer referral program near you, look up Lawyer Referral Services or Lawyer Referral and Information Services in the white business pages of your telephone directory.

You can also purchase the "Directory of Lawyer Referral Services" for $5 from the American Bar Association, Publications, 750 North Lake Shore Drive, Chicago, IL 60611.

National Academy of Elder Law Attorneys, Inc.
655 North Alvernon Way, Suite 108
Tucson, AZ 85711
602-881-4005

The National Academy of Elder Law Attorneys (NAELA) is a membership organization for attorneys across the country who specialize in the legal needs of the older individual. NAELA publishes *The Experience Registry*, a directory of over 400 elder law attorneys with their areas of expertise. The registry is available from NAELA for $25.

National Employment Lawyers Association
National Office
535 Pacific Avenue
San Francisco, CA 94133
415-397-6335

The National Employment Lawyers Association is a professional organization for lawyers who specialize in employment-related cases.

National Organization of Social Security Claimants' Representatives
6 Prospect Street
Midland, NJ 07432
800-431-2804

The National Organization of Social Security Claimants' Representatives (NOSSCR) is a professional association of lawyers who represent individuals seeking Social Security retirement, disability, or survivor's benefits. NOSSCR refers callers to lawyers in their area.

Lawyer Referral Services

National Pension Assistance Project
918 16th Street, N.W., Suite 704
Washington, DC 20006
202-296-3776

The Pension Rights Center's National Pension Assistance Project is a national lawyer referral service that provides the names of lawyers who practice in the area of pensions. The service operates between 9 A.M. and 2 P.M. Eastern Standard Time on Tuesdays and Thursdays.

INDEX